THE SPACE OF OPINION

The Space of Opinion

MEDIA INTELLECTUALS AND THE PUBLIC SPHERE

Ronald N. Jacobs

Eleanor Townsley

OXFORD
UNIVERSITY PRESS

OXFORD
UNIVERSITY PRESS

Oxford University Press, Inc., publishes works that further
Oxford University's objective of excellence
in research, scholarship, and education.

Oxford New York
Auckland   Cape Town   Dar es Salaam   Hong Kong   Karachi
Kuala Lumpur   Madrid   Melbourne   Mexico City   Nairobi
New Delhi   Shanghai   Taipei   Toronto

With offices in
Argentina   Austria   Brazil   Chile   Czech Republic   France   Greece
Guatemala   Hungary   Italy   Japan   Poland   Portugal   Singapore
South Korea   Switzerland   Thailand   Turkey   Ukraine   Vietnam

Copyright © 2011 by Oxford University Press

Published by Oxford University Press, Inc.
198 Madison Avenue, New York, New York 10016

www.oup.com

Oxford is a registered trademark of Oxford University Press

Library of Congress Cataloging-in-Publication Data
A CIP record is available from the Library of Congress

ISBN 9780199797929
ISBN 9780199797936

1 3 5 7 9 8 6 4 2

Printed in the United States of America
on acid-free paper

Contents

Acknowledgments

THIS BOOK HAS benefited enormously from conversations with friends and colleagues over the last several years. Jeff Alexander, Peter Beilharz, Phil Smith, Neil McLaughlin, Sarah Sobieraj, Jenny Strommer-Galley and Ken Tucker provided helpful comments on various parts of the manuscript. Three anonymous reviewers offered exceptionally detailed and insightful comments. Their generosity made the book much stronger, and we owe them a special debt of gratitude.

Conversations with a broader group of colleagues have also shaped our thinking about media and deliberation. We are particularly grateful to Gianpaolo Baiocchi, Paul Lichterman, Nina Eliasoph, Ron Eyerman, Fuyuki Kurasawa, Paul Jones, Richard Lachmann, Beth Popp-Berman, Aaron Major, Roberto Velez, Mabel Berezin, Francesca Polletta, Steve Seidman and Brad West. The book has also benefited from ongoing exchanges with graduate students in cultural sociology at the University at Albany: Brian McKernan, Christina Wu, Anne Lin, Nickie Wild, Ian Sheinheit, Matthias Revers, Anibal Gauna-Peralta, Lina Rincon, Laura Milanes, and Yuching Cheng.

The book would not have been completed without research support from the National Endowment for the Humanities, the Marion and Jasper Whiting Foundation, the Culture Center at Flinders University, the Yale Culture Workshop, and Mount Holyoke College. We thank them for their support. We also wish to thank Megan Murphy, Laura Milanes, and Dan Santore for their assistance in data collection.

Special thanks also go to James Cook, our editor at Oxford. James offered enthusiastic support for the project, procured superb reviewers for the manuscript, and expertly shepherded the manuscript from inception to completion.

Finally, we thank our children Sophia and Vivian for their patience and their opinions.

Ron Jacobs and Eleanor Townsley
South Hadley Summer 2011

THE SPACE OF OPINION

1 Media Commentary and the Space of Opinion

ON JULY 6, 2003, the *New York Times* published an op-ed by Joseph Wilson, titled "What I Didn't Find in Africa." In that column—slightly longer than the typical op-ed piece, at 1,441 words—Wilson charged President Bush and his administration with manipulating intelligence about Saddam Hussein's weapons program in order to justify going to war with Iraq. After asserting this charge, Wilson was careful to lay out his expert credentials. He was a career foreign service officer and ambassador, the last American diplomat to meet with Saddam Hussein, and the person who had been asked by Vice President Cheney's office to explore a possible sale of uranium yellowcake from Niger to Iraq. Wilson described his visit to Niger in some detail, recounted conversations with embassy staff there who reported that the Niger-Iraq link had been debunked several times in reports to Washington, detailed why it would be so difficult and improbable for Niger to transfer uranium to Iraq, and described the briefings he had made to that effect to the CIA and the State Department. Wilson concluded:

> The question now is how that answer was or was not used by our political leadership. If my information was deemed inaccurate, I understand (though I would be very interested to know why). If, however, the information was ignored because it did not fit certain preconceptions about Iraq, then a legitimate argument can be made that we went to war under false pretenses. (It's worth remembering that in his March "Meet the Press" appearance, Mr. Cheney said that Saddam Hussein was

"trying once again to produce nuclear weapons.") At a minimum, Congress, which authorized the use of military force at the president's behest, should want to know if the assertions about Iraq were warranted. (*New York Times*, July 6, 2003, p. A9)

Wilson's op-ed piece in the *New York Times* created a furor that continues to resonate. Wilson was attacked as a liar and a political partisan in editorials in the *Wall Street Journal* and *Weekly Standard*, on a variety of television talk shows aired on Fox News, in countless blogs, and in numerous *Washington Post* columns by Robert Novak—who also, infamously, disclosed the identity of Wilson's wife, who worked for the CIA. Wilson was defended in frequent editorials in the *Nation*, in *New York Times* columns by Frank Rich and Paul Krugman, on a number of episodes of MSNBC's *Hardball with Chris Matthews* and *Countdown with Keith Olbermann*, in countless blogs, and by Wilson himself, who contributed additional op-ed pieces to the major newspapers and appeared regularly on almost all of television's political talk shows. In fact, the Wilson affair was debated by newspaper columnists and guest columnists at every major U.S. newspaper, by senior editors and contributing editors writing analytical pieces for the elite news magazines, by television talk show hosts and their guests, and by a raft of bloggers, radio talk show hosts, and political newsletters. In the process, these overlapping spaces of opinion provided a focal point for debates about the Iraq war, the Bush administration, and the role of journalism in a democratic society.

Despite their importance, however, there has been comparatively little systematic attention paid to these spaces of media opinion or to the role of media commentary in contemporary civil society.[1] With few exceptions, the scholarly research literature tends to be broadly critical of opinion and the rise of organized punditry during the twentieth century, without ever providing a close empirical analysis of it. Our book hopes to fill this important gap in research about media, politics, and society. We take mass-mediated opinion and commentary to be a central feature of U.S. democracy, and instead of evaluating "what is the balance of fact and opinion in the news?" as policy analysts or media watchdogs might, we ask the empirical questions: What is the sociological nature of the contemporary social space of opinion? What are its cultural and institutional structures, and how have they developed historically? What kinds of people speak in this space? What styles of writing and speech do they use? What types of authority and expertise do they mobilize in their commentaries? What kinds of deliberation do they make possible? And what impact do their commentaries have on larger spaces of public debate?

Focusing research attention on media opinion and commentary is important because it has a powerful impact on political elites and policy makers. Beginning in the 1930s with Walter Lippmann, the articles written by the syndicated columnists of the elite newspapers were read as a proxy for public opinion and were studied carefully by American presidents and their advisers. Beginning in the 1950s with NBC's *Meet the Press*, elected politicians also began to submit themselves to extended questioning by the hosts of television talk shows in a format where their statements were also subject to panels of journalists, political insiders, and experts. In both of these ways, media commentaries regularly find their way into the arguments being made by political principals, in a manner that is far more direct than for any other part of the press.

Examples of this kind of influence abound. In the late 1950s, John Kennedy relied heavily on Joseph Alsop's columns in the *New York Herald Tribune* to craft his critical position against President Eisenhower's defense policies (Preble 2003). During the 1990s, the argument that Bill Clinton had some kind of connection to Vince Foster's suicide was pushed repeatedly by *New York Times* columnist William Safire and picked up by many Republican politicians and other conservative commentators. In 2007, a series of television appearances and guest columns about Iraq written by Michael O'Hanlon and Kenneth Pollack set off a furious public debate about whether the "surge" of troops in Iraq was working. O'Hanlon and Pollack were both think tank intellectuals at the Brookings Institution at the time, and their arguments ignited a cascade of subsidiary debates: about the media's coverage of the surge, about the willingness of Bush critics to change their minds, and about how honest O'Hanlon and Pollack were in their self-representations as one-time critics of the war. More generally, it is quite clear that the politics of the war in Iraq were deeply shaped by arguments made in spaces of media opinion.

To be sure, other parts of the media space also have the capacity to change the agenda of elite political discussion in a powerful and direct way. Correspondents' work and that of investigative journalists are good examples. But in an era of declining revenues, most news organizations have reduced both the number of correspondents they employ and the number of investigative pieces they publish (Pew Research Center 2004–2010). At the same time, news organizations have actually increased the amount of opinion and commentary they publish (Diamond 1993; Pew Research Center 2004–2010). And while correspondents and investigative journalists tend to come exclusively from the world of journalism, our research shows that media commentary is open to a greater diversity of voices from a range of institutional settings, including universities and colleges, advocacy groups, think tanks, law firms, publishing, and a variety of political consultancies and polling organizations. In short, the space of media commentary calls out for closer empirical scrutiny since it is an influential and (potentially) diverse space of argument, with a clear and direct presence in political debates that, if anything, is increasing in significance.

Formulated in the theoretical terms of this book, our argument is that media opinion and commentaries are important because of the power they have to shape the world of collective representation and opinion formation in real civil societies. To be sure, these spaces of media opinion are limited, fragmentary, exclusionary, contradictory, and filled with artifice. In other words, spaces of opinion typically fail to satisfy minimum standards of reason or rational deliberation. Opinion columns and television talk show programs provide distortion as often as they provide clarity, and self-serving performances are at least as common as careful deliberations. Yet despite these kinds of limitations, as Jeffrey

Alexander has so forcefully argued, a sociology of civil society must do more than assess how well the real world measures up against a set of abstract moral principles. On the ground, the "normative stipulations of civil society turn out to be the language of the streets, the television, novels, polls, parties, politics, office, and scandal" (Alexander 2006: 551). The task for the sociologist is to understand this "rich and textured language" in all its complexities, contradictions, and institutional settings. While it would be nice if public debate emerged from the ground up, emanating from the bowling leagues to the halls of power, this turns out to be a rare occurrence. More typically, public debate is organized through media, and public opinion is articulated in conversations among journalists, politicians, experts, and insiders, all of whom are jockeying to represent the public interest, to extend a particular vision of the social good, and to bend the levers of power and public policy in a way that is consistent with the vision they have identified.[2]

In the chapters that follow, we develop a more detailed set of arguments about the history, cultural logic, deliberative possibilities, and composition of the contemporary U.S. space of opinion. We describe processes of centralization in the space of opinion that have occurred in lockstep with a growing diversity of voices and formats. We describe debates that are dominated by political partisanship, and others that are committed to an attitude of analytical disinterest. We find Manichaean expressions of moral certitude, as well as complex discourses of uncertainty and unintended consequences. And we identify different sources of format innovation, exploring how newer opinion formats display commitments to a vision of public deliberation that are quite different than what we see in traditional formats. In the end, we argue that coming to grips with the space of opinion requires more than an automatic denunciation of those opinion formats that deviate too far from the normative ideals of democratic theory. Instead, we suggest a more cultural model of media and deliberation, in which the possibilities and limitations of any particular opinion format are considered in the context of the full range of voices and rhetorics that populate the space of opinion as a whole.

News Media and Opinion in the Public Sphere Tradition

To speak of public debate in the democratic tradition is to speak of the *public sphere*— that part of civil society where private individuals gather as a public to discuss matters of common concern. As Habermas (1989) and others have documented, the emergence of the public sphere was one of the key events in the development of modern democracies, since public discussions produced an emboldened collective sense of a public opinion. Modern politics came to be defined not only by the demand that representatives of the state take careful stock of public opinion when formulating public policies but also by the demand that representatives of the state enter into discussions with representatives of the public to justify their policies in the public sphere. In the process, the principle of rational deliberation was institutionalized, based on the understanding that the publicity of reason—of logic and the force of the better argument—was more important than the status of the speaker in deciding debates. From the perspective of classical normative theories of the public sphere, then, deliberate, thoughtful contention is understood to be a democratic mode of deliberation that produces rational public opinion to which democratic governments can then be held accountable.

A corollary of this understanding is the idea that the news media are important because they provide the institutional framework for democratic public communication. And it is true that mass media have long played a central role in making democratic deliberation possible. From the beginnings of the public sphere in the seventeenth century, print technology transformed the practice of petitioning by enabling voluntary associations to circumvent elites and bring their issues directly to the public in the form of broadsides, pamphlets, and newspapers (Zaret 1998). By the beginning of the eighteenth century, the technology of print had become central to the public life of the English pub and coffeehouse. Coffeehouse discussions were disseminated through periodicals and journals, which typically produced letters of response that were discussed in turn and then published in the journals the following week (Habermas 1989: 42). This recursive relationship—from the mediated spaces of newspapers to the public spaces and associations that constitute civil society and then back to news media in the form of "public opinion"—defined the agenda-setting power of news media in eighteenth-century English public life and continues, in broad strokes, to describe how we understand public opinion formation in contemporary public spheres.[3]

Analytically speaking, the classical account of the public sphere argues that the media are important because they provide a space in which citizens can *make arguments* from a position of *relative autonomy* from political and economic power. That is, media provide a space of deliberation in which citizens use their rational capacities to (a) make arguments about matters of common concern, (b) make those arguments in public, (c) support their arguments with good reasons, and (d) defend their arguments against criticisms and alternative positions. It is best if those who enter the public sphere to speak are able to do so as individuals rather than as a mouthpiece for a particular group, and it is preferable if they justify their arguments on behalf of the general good, rather than partisan interest (Alexander 2006; Seligman 1992). Finally, it is understood that the media support democratic deliberation to the extent that they provide neutral and fair conditions for publicizing the widest possible range of opinions.

Objective News and Neutral Media

What kind of media practices support this understanding of democratic deliberation? For American journalists and their publics, the dominant answer for most of the twentieth century has been that media support democracy by providing objective information so citizens and elites can make informed decisions about how to act. Consider the following arguments about the importance of objective, factual news media.

> A fundamental task of the Twentieth Century [is] the insurance to a free people of such a supply of news that a free government can be successfully administered . . . the reliability of the news is the premise on which democracy proceeds. (Walter Lippmann and Charles Merz, *The New Republic*, 1920, pp. 3–4)
>
> "We now see that it is immensely important that the press shall give us the facts straight; and not merely the facts relating to department stores and other large business concerns, but the entire mass of facts about the world in which we live. (Frederick Lewis Allen, *Atlantic Monthly*, January 1922, p. 44)"

This idea was most clearly developed in the Hutchins Commission's 1947 report, *A Free and Responsible Press*, which assumed, as Baker argues (2002:155), "that what a properly functioning democracy needs most from the media is 'information.'" This view continues to be widely expressed, not only by early media critics like Lippmann and Allen but also in an enormous array of scholarship, in the mission statements of media outlets and professional associations, by media watchdogs and other media critics, and in widely held public attitudes. Indeed, normative ideas about a neutral and objective media have become so embedded as cultural "common sense" that it is very difficult to think beyond their limits.

Consider, for example, the preeminent source in contemporary applied media research—the annual reports on the State of the News Media produced by the Project for Excellence in Journalism. Required reading for any serious analysis of media and democracy, the State of the News Media reports address "basic questions in six areas: the trends in content, audience, economics, ownership, newsroom investment and public attitudes."[4] In fact, the reports not only describe the economic and institutional conditions of the various sectors of the news media in superb detail but also assess news content for scope, quality, and objectivity. Thus they investigate the range of topics covered by news media, they assess the diversity and transparency of sources used by journalists in reporting the news, and historically, they enumerate the ratio of facts to opinion in news articles.[5]

The premise of this massive data collection effort is much the same as those of contemporary media watchdogs and older critics like Lippmann and Merz, namely, that good fact-based reporting is the sine qua non of what journalists do since it is central to how a democracy functions. Contemporary media critics like Accuracy in Media (AIM), Fairness & Accuracy in Reporting (FAIR), and Media Matters for America (MMA) are also concerned with how the news media in their reporting affect democracy, and therefore they focus on balance and accuracy in the news. And recent scholarship on media criticism points to the importance of the "'pajamahadeen' bloggers who targeted CBS, CNN, and the Associated Press during 2004 and 2005" in Internet campaigns that effectively challenged the mainstream media's claims of fairness and accuracy in reporting (Hayes 2008: 3, 35–52). To be sure, this is important research. At the same time, however, we want to point out what is omitted from the research agenda. Nowhere do the State of the News

Media reports describe or assess the quality of opinion per se, nor do they chart the changing conditions and nature of media opinion over time. Rather, there is an unstated assumption that the increasing presence of opinion—referred to as "lighter fare" and criticized as "entertainment"—is a threat to serious, objective journalism and, by extension, a threat to civil society as a whole.

A half century of academic media research, however, challenges this common sense in several ways. Despite their obvious sympathy with the normative aspirations of professional journalism, most sociological researchers draw a complex picture of the news media as far more than a neutral vehicle to convey objective information to individual citizens (Schudson 2003: 2–4; Zelizer 2004: 45–80). Research on newsroom routines (Tuchman 1972, 1973; Fishman 1980), news production (Jacobs 1996; Klinenberg 2005; Cottle 2003), and hybrid news practices such as "infotainment" (Delli Carpini and Williams 2001; Jacobs 2005, 2011; Baum 2003; Glynn 2000) overwhelmingly documents how news media operate as sites of creative intellectual practice.

Given the scholarly emphasis on the constructed nature of journalistic objectivity, what accounts for the continued emphasis on fact-based reporting that we see in media criticism and applied media research? As we argue throughout this book, a preoccupation with neutrality, objectivity, and fairness is a marked feature of modern professional journalism (Schudson 1978). When journalists began to define standards for their nascent profession in the early years of the twentieth century, they developed a definition of objectivity rooted in a strict separation of fact from opinion (Chalaby 1998: 136–137). Opinion was to be segregated on the editorial page of the newspaper—the province of editors—while the rest of the paper would be devoted to objective reporting understood as a realistic account of the previous day's events (Schudson 1978: 179–181). Narrowly conceived as the product of objective methods, then, this understanding of objectivity came to be conflated with the larger idea of critical rationality, and purveyors of objective fact began to define themselves as distinct from (and often superior to) those who were interested in value-laden, politicized matters of opinion.

With the exception of certain versions of liberal theory, however, most theories of democracy do not share this mid-twentieth-century American view, which identifies the media's function as no more than a conduit of neutral information. In fact, as Hallin (1994: 172) suggests, the number of *journalists* who share this view of media and democracy has probably been in a steady decline since the 1970s. We take up this issue in greater detail in chapter 3, where we discuss different theories about media, deliberation, and opinion formation. For now, it suffices to point out that most democratic theories are generally in agreement with two arguments that Benjamin Page (1996: 123–125) makes about mediated deliberation in complex democracies. First, for mediated deliberation to be successful, it does not have to be perfectly balanced, neutral, or free of bias. And second, a full understanding of mediated deliberation requires a consideration of a larger range of communications media, which extends beyond the objective journalism that one can find in the front section of the quality press.

On these two points, media scholars and democratic theorists are in relative agreement. Media provide not only the facts but also the formats, norms, and rhetorics that citizens employ to develop their opinions and enter wider public discussion (Alexander 2006; Jamieson and Cappella 2008; Thompson 1995). For the most part, these media narratives and rhetorics are produced not by ordinary citizens, but rather by *professional communicators* like politicians, journalists, experts, and other high-status intellectuals who use the news media as a staging ground to gather and debate the issues of the day (Page 1996: 5–6). Studying who these communicators are and what cultural practices they use in their debates is just as important as identifying the range of relevant facts that news media do or do not provide.

Since the institutionalization of the opinion column in the 1920s and 1930s, there has been a dramatic expansion in news commentary and opinion in the United States, an expansion that accelerated particularly rapidly after the 1970s. This growth has also been marked by an increasing variety of opinion formats. Thus, the signed opinion column is different from the unsigned editorial. The syndicated columnist has a different position than the guest columnist. Television commentaries differ from newspaper commentaries, and within television, there are distinctions between cable, network, and public television shows, and there are distinctions between interview, panel, and commentary formats.

None of these differences are captured well by the "fact versus opinion" distinction that underlies so much traditional media criticism, but they are precisely the kinds of differences we aim to explore in this book. What is needed, we argue, is a close examination of the different styles of opinion and news commentary, the different types of people who produce opinion and commentary, and the different relationships that opinion and commentary maintain with the worlds of fact and rational argument. This is particularly important in the current media environment, where many of the spaces of television commentary have begun to rely on more entertaining formats and more dramatic styles of performance (Jones 2004; Delli Carpini and Williams 2001; Hallin 1994: 178–179).

Television, Commentary, and Neutral Media

Another problem with a research agenda that privileges fact-based reporting over other forms of news and commentary is that it tends to misperceive objective journalism as the only effective form of news work, and in so doing, it misses the empirical diversity of news styles. In England, such an oversight would miss the important history of the popular press and the way the meaning of the "quality press" was so closely related to its opposition to the tabloid papers (see Chalaby 1998, esp. pp. 168–172). In the United States, the meaning of the quality press is perhaps best understood in relation to television programming.

A key character in the U.S. story is Edward R. Murrow, who rose to prominence as a war correspondent for CBS Radio, and then developed and hosted the most important television news and public affairs program of the 1950s, *See It Now* (Doherty 2003). Murrow was immortalized as an icon of journalistic integrity and bravery after he criticized Senator Joseph McCarthy on his show in 1954. Notwithstanding its importance, however, *See It Now* was canceled in 1958, because the show was by far the most expensive news program on the air and also because television executives discovered they could make a lot more money broadcasting sitcoms, game shows, and westerns (Barnouw 1990; Jacobs 2003). Frustrated by these developments in television, Murrow lashed out in a 1958 speech in which he bemoaned the media industry's increasing emphasis on commercialism and entertainment, its insulation from the realities of the world, and its lack of respect for the intelligence of its viewers (Boddy 1990: 207). Murrow's speech not only was widely praised at the time but also has been reprinted in a variety of media and invoked by media critics ever since.

And yet, if we treat Murrow's charges uncritically, we fail to see the contradictions, the variations, and the different commitments to autonomy that characterized his own television program, as well as the successive genres of television commentary that his program helped to establish. After all, while Murrow's background as a war correspondent was deeply rooted in the world of objective reporting, his television program represented a significant departure from that kind of journalism. Indeed, what was distinctive and important about *See It Now* was the role that Murrow played as a public critic who insisted on his autonomy from corporate owners and from the powerful politicians who appeared on his program. Furthermore, while Murrow's program was serious, it was not "objective journalism." And many segments of the show combined these categories in complicated ways. For example, an episode that simulated a bomb attack on New York City was serious but certainly not objective. A profile of Danny Kaye was objective but hardly serious (at least in the usual understanding of the term). The point is that "serious," "entertaining," "fact-based," and "commentary-based" styles of journalism are analytically distinct forms that are increasingly being combined in new ways as creative personnel strive to develop new (and often hybrid) forms of media programming.[6]

It is the relationship between these forms and the way they shape public opinion and public agendas that our research examines. We know that the contemporary media environment is defined by variation, contradiction, and competing logics of entertainment, commerce, and autonomy, and we suspect that these vary in important ways. Some formats are likely to be more entertaining than others. Some formats are more likely than others to be committed to preserving the distinction between fact-based reporting and commentary. Our goal is to describe and analyze these patterns systematically, rather than to decide in advance which formats are democratic and which are counterdemocratic.

As we document in chapter 2, the growth of television commentary in the 1970s and 1980s took place alongside a similar expansion of the opinion pages in newspapers. This has all been magnified with the explosive growth of the Internet blogosphere during the first decade of the twenty-first century. In the process, media commentators have become more diverse. Once exclusively drawn from the ranks of journalism, now media commentary is produced by a variety of individuals from a wide range of social backgrounds (Rosenfeld 2000). Today, the space of opinion attracts academics, think tankers, political insiders, pollsters, social movement activists, and a range of others who want to contribute to public opinion regarding matters of common concern. Together, these various actors and the mediated spaces they speak within form a complex geography of speakers, occupations, institutions, rhetorical styles, claims to authority, and definitions of autonomy that we identify as the space of opinion.

When we focus on this space of opinion, we find that it is characterized by an incredible diversity of formats linked together in a nested series of multimedia conversations and citational references. So, for example, the venerable Sunday morning political talk show *ABC News This Week* regularly incorporates references to the late-night talk shows into its format as part of the weekly roundtable discussion among experts and pundits. Cable and radio talk show personalities have as much visibility in the space of opinion as elite columnists and staid network correspondents. Some of the most serious political commentary and media criticism take place on cable's Comedy Central, on programs such as *The Daily Show with Jon Stewart* and *The Colbert Report*. And the arguments being made in all of these spaces receive extensive commentary and circulation on political blogs, both large and small. In other words, it is not only private citizens who are compiling media and using them to have conversations. These acts of compiling, circulating, and metacommentary are the bread and butter of media intellectuals and central elements in the process of public opinion formation as it occurs in the contemporary space of U.S. opinion.

The Space of Opinion

A major goal of our book is to identify the space of opinion as an intelligible analytical object. By this we mean that the social relationships, actors, institutions, and cultural traditions that constitute the space of opinion, when taken all together, evince a distinct cultural logic and share a distinct social history. In the next chapter, we chart this history for the United States in the twentieth century. Before doing so, however, we need to distinguish the space of opinion from several related concepts.

First, although the space of opinion is clearly part of civil society and the public sphere, it is not identical with them. Civil society refers to the entire universe of relationships, institutions, and practices in which citizens engage with each other about matters of common concern. Thus civil society includes a range of voluntary associations and communicative institutions, and it encompasses informal interaction between citizens at their churches, gyms, and schools, as well as organized protest by social movements to alter or reform laws (Cohen and Arato 1992: 23; Jacobs 2003). The public sphere, by contrast, does not refer to all of the relationships in civil society but only to the part that is concerned primarily with communication and debate. The public sphere thus includes the informal conversations of face-to-face publics and also, importantly, local, national, and transnational communication media, including news, entertainment, opinion, and social networking media. Within these terms, we delineate the space of opinion as an especially influential part of the elite political public sphere; that is, it is that part of the public communicative infrastructure in which the elites of our huge, complex societies debate serious matters of common concern. In this connection, it is obvious why the space of opinion has long been connected to objective news traditions, because those offering commentary and opinion rely heavily upon the news to inform their arguments about the affairs of the day.

Second, while the space of opinion is connected to institutions of political and economic power, it is not reducible to them. As a part of the development of the journalistic field in the 1920s and 1930s, professional opinion authors struggled to develop an authority to speak that was separate from both the owners of the news media that published their opinion and the elite sources who provided them with information (Gordon 1994; Schudson 1978). As we saw in the case of Edward R. Murrow, a commitment to autonomy also characterized television commentary as represented by *See It Now* in the 1950s, and a commitment to autonomy has also migrated to Internet-based news and opinion formats in the last two decades, a fact to which the plethora of Internet-based news critics cited here attests. In short, the development of news commentary and opinion remains deeply connected to the intellectual tradition of autonomous professional journalism as it has developed in the Anglo-American world (Bendix 1980; Keane 1991). This does not mean, however, that the space of opinion is identical with fact-based reporting in the journalistic field.

This is an important distinction: while the space of opinion historically overlaps the journalistic and political fields, it is not synonymous with them. More precisely, we might say that the space of opinion is located at the overlapping intersection of several institutional orders, or cultural fields, such as the journalistic field from which it was born, as well as the media field more generally, including entertainment media. The space of opinion also intersects the political field of democratic institutions and office-holders and the nascent fieldlike space of think tanks, lobbies, and advocacy groups. The space of opinion also shares communicative connections with the academic field and other cultural fields, including trade publishing, small literary magazines, commercial and independent film, comedy, and so forth. Indeed, the "softer" sections of the newspaper—arts, sports, lifestyle, society, and so forth—all have their own columnists, who are connected to the political columnists at the same time that they are connected to the cultural fields about which they are providing commentary (Diamond 1993). Although it is centrally concerned with serious matters of politics and journalism, then, and although it orients primarily to the political and journalistic fields, we would observe that the space of opinion is a space through which virtually all matters of common social concern pass—or at least in a democracy, the space of opinion is the space through which all matters potentially pass or should pass. In one way, then, the space of opinion might be understood as the "democratic attention space" of the society at large, as it reflects, analyzes, and parses the events of the day; it is a central site of the communicative process in which public opinion is formed and a critical element of the communicative network that comprises the public sphere. We return to this argument in chapter 3.

We believe this analytical construction is useful because it defines the space of opinion as a relatively autonomous and influential part of the political public sphere, located at the chaotic intersection of multiple institutional orders. But this construction should not be taken as a definitive description of our object. Questions about the precise relationship between the space of opinion and the political or journalistic fields are historical and empirical ones that we seek to answer through a close analysis of the contemporary U.S. space of opinion.

The Project

To describe and analyze the contemporary space of U.S. media opinion, we have collected large samples of news commentary and opinion from the *New York Times* and *USA Today* and television transcripts from the *NewsHour, Face the Nation, Crossfire,* and *Hannity & Colmes* from 1993 to 1994 and 2001 to 2002, the first two years of the last two U.S. presidential administrations (*n* = 1,819). The choice of the *New York Times* was an obvious one, since it is widely regarded as the national paper of record. *USA Today* is the most widely circulated newspaper in the United States and the flagship brand of the Gannett group—the largest newspaper conglomerate in the country. The four television shows were chosen to represent the range of political talk shows on Sunday morning and daily television across network, public, and cable television.

We self-consciously chose to focus on mainstream newspapers and television rather than alternative media or new and emerging media for several reasons. First, these are the most influential parts of the space of opinion, in the sense that they are the places where representatives of the state come to justify their policies to representatives of the public. Newspaper and television commentaries also have a larger agenda-setting effect on public debates than other sources of opinion and commentary. In fact, the issues that are taken up and the arguments that are made in elite newspaper op-eds and on the major television talk shows are the object of intense discussion in other media spaces, as well as in other public and private spaces throughout civil society. Even in alternative media and Internet blogs, what gets written and said in mainstream media is the object of close focus and frequent commentary (Jacobs 2000). Rather than declining in significance in the face of the rise of new media, then, the elite spaces we study appear to be increasingly central to the large and densely networked public sphere we inhabit. If we are right, then it is crucially important to understand the dynamics of these elite spaces—to understand who speaks and under what conditions they speak.

Our research design has several other connected goals. First, we collected large representative samples so we can compare the first years of Republican and Democratic presidencies, since prior research has led us to suspect a relationship between the party of the administration and the occupational composition of the field of media intellectuals (Townsley 2000). Second, we sampled from two-year periods during each presidency to capture the second year of each new administration, by which time the honeymoon period with the media has ended (although see Clayman et al. 2007). Third, a historical comparison provides analytical heft as well as nuance to the design. Choosing two twenty-four-month periods helps us avoid event specificity, that is, a situation where a single event dominates the analysis, most obviously the events of September 11, 2001. At the same time, however, the sample is large enough to support more in-depth analysis of important cases, such as the Enron scandal (chapter 7) and the War on Terror (chapter 8). Fourth, the design is modular and can be expanded in the future. Another wave of data can be collected to track changes over time and/or additional publications can be incorporated to assess whether our findings hold in other formats. Fifth, the research is designed to enable us to link a traditional sociological analysis of institutions and actors with an interpretive, cultural analysis of opinionated speech. There are about 10,000 pages of text data in the newspaper sample and about the same again for the television sample. This allows us to make close readings of strategically selected textual material to supplement our content analyses. On the one hand, the narrative and rhetorical analyses of texts are an attempt to provide depth that anchors the more systematic analysis of the larger patterns in the space of opinion. On the other hand, our analysis of the morphology of the space of opinion provides a crucial context for the detailed cultural analysis of complex texts. Sixth, we have collected biographical data on all the authors of opinion in our sample. This means we can connect specific argument styles to specific types of authors and also examine the distribution of authors and argument types across different types of formats. The result is a close empirical mapping of the space of opinion and elite media commentary that provides not only an analysis of the media intellectuals who populate this space but also a thick description of its institutional and cultural organization.

This mapping traces change and continuity amid a massive expansion of the space of opinion. It tells a complex story of changing institutional intersections between journalism, politics, the academy, and the new sector of think tanks, policy institutes, and other nonprofit institutions, and it also reveals a proliferation of genres and forms of opinion. Thus it is not only that the people who speak within the space of opinion have become more diverse over time (chapters 4 and 5) but also that the formats of opinion—claims to authority, styles of speech, and modes of addressing publics—have all become more varied (chapters 5, 6, and 7). Notwithstanding these changes, however, we also find underlying historical continuities in the space of opinion. Older, more traditional formats continue to define the high-status, autonomous forms of opinion and news commentary, effectively anchoring the opinion space in the traditions of professional journalism. What these changes tell us about the nature of public communication in the contemporary U.S. democracy is the central focus of this book.

2 A History of Opinion in the U.S. Media

FOR THOMAS FRIEDMAN, 2002 was a busy year. In February, PBS's *Lehrer NewsHour* began a new feature called "Tom's Journal," a series of conversations with Friedman. In April, Friedman agreed to host a series of documentaries about current events, which would be televised quarterly on the newly formed Discovery Times Channel.[1] Also in April, Friedman received the 2002 Pulitzer Prize for Commentary, for a series of columns he had written for the *New York Times* about the terrorist threat. Friedman collected these columns and published them again in September 2002, this time as the best-selling book *Longitudes and Attitudes: Exploring the World after September 11*. In addition, as he did most years, Friedman traveled extensively, giving lectures and interviews throughout the world. And he continued to write his twice-weekly column for the op-ed page of the *New York Times*, a column that was syndicated to more than a hundred newspapers worldwide.

With his ubiquitous commentary, Friedman was traveling a well-marked path, covered first by Walter Lippmann but followed by other influential pundits such as David Broder, George Will, Charles Krauthammer, Clarence Page, and Paul Gigot. What all these individuals shared, in addition to their Pulitzer Prizes, was a vast web of multimedia influence, in which they played a key role in shaping debate about important matters of the day. For all, their influential status had its origin in the columns they wrote for elite newspapers. But their influence as opinion makers extended to radio, television, magazines, universities, think tanks, and often even to their private discussions with political leaders. Indeed, to the extent that the American media have been able to operate as a political public sphere, demanding that representatives of the state explain their positions and engage in a public debate about the best way to satisfy the public good, it has done so through a route that goes directly through the columnists and other media opinion leaders.

In today's news media environment, the space of opinion is increasing in both size and importance. Newspapers have expanded their op-ed pages and added interactive Internet features that allow their readers to circulate, discuss, and comment on the columns appearing in the paper. Political talk radio fills the airwaves, while cable television news channels continue to add new political talk programs, particularly during the prime-time hours. The Internet blogosphere is expanding at an exponential rate, too, providing yet another space for the leading commentators to interpret the meaning of the day's events and, occasionally, providing a new mechanism for aspiring critics to build an audience and become political insiders.[2] And all of these spaces of opinion are interconnected through forms of multimedia synergy that operate at different levels of scale and with different degrees of conscious coordination. These forces have combined to produce what Eric Alterman (1999: 4) calls a "punditocracy," which he describes as "a tiny group of highly visible political pontificators who make their living offering 'insider political opinions and forecasts' in the elite national media."

How did this special class of media pundits develop? From which part of the journalistic field did they emerge? How did they come to occupy such a central position within an industry that tends to judge itself according the ideals of unbiased, fact-based reporting? These are the questions we address in this chapter. We focus on two key developments in this history. First, and probably most important to the story, is the rise of the newspaper columnist. Aided by the unusual career of Walter Lippmann, by the 1930s, the newspaper columnist was already among the most influential and prestigious voices in the national public conversation The second key development was the rise of television in the 1950s and the corresponding development of political talk shows that have become an increasingly visible presence on the airwaves.

This history has shaped a contemporary media environment for opinion and commentary that is defined by the pull of contradictory forces. On the one hand, largely because of television, the media space has become more political, more dominated by political voices and others from the political field, and therefore more constricted. On the other hand, because of the continuing presence of print journalism, as well as the rise of new communication technologies and innovative new formats, there has been a significant expansion in the space of media opinion, an open commitment to the principle of diversity, and a clearer route for voices outside the fields of journalism and politics to participate in public discussion and commentary.

In addition to these contradictory forces, our historical analysis explores two different kinds of public roles that media intellectuals have tended to play. In the first role, the media intellectual is a participant in dialogue with other political elites. In this role, what matters is the direct conversation between politicians, experts, and journalists, and the discussions are treated as if they stand in for public opinion. Indeed, as Herbst (1998) has argued, this conflation of media conversation and public opinion is typical of the views of many journalists and policy experts. But this is not the only public role that media intellectuals occupy. The second role is as a participant in a more general process of mass political communication, in which the op-ed column and the television talk show serve as agenda-setting objects of commentary and discussion among smaller politically engaged publics. In this role, the media intellectual addresses a citizen audience as a way of clarifying issues and suggesting analytical frameworks that can be taken up in discussions about matters of common concern. As we document later in the chapter, this second role has been reinvigorated in recent years through a number of cultural and technological developments, including the expansion of the op-ed page, the development of new programming strategies on radio and television, and the rise of the Internet and other technologies of digital connectivity. This tension in orientation between political insiders and general citizens—as well as the circumstances that allow the two roles to be more complementary—is a concern that reappears throughout the book.

A historical perspective also makes it easier to identify what is truly new in the contemporary organization of opinion in the U.S. media and to distinguish it from developments that appear more consistent with long-term trends. Indeed, many of the key elements of the contemporary opinion space emerged decades earlier than common wisdom might suggest. From the beginning, U.S. news media were involved in the production and circulation of opinion, just like the newspapers of Europe. To be sure, the development of the journalistic norm of objectivity transformed newspaper formats in the Anglo-American press culture of the late nineteenth century (Chalaby 1998; Schudson 1978). But rather than eliminating opinion, objective journalism had a key role in the rise of a new class of opinion specialists, the columnists. By the 1930s, columnists were engaging in many of the same practices that they do today: providing the reading public with an interpretive framework for understanding the events of the day; writing on behalf of the public interest, while advocating specific policy positions in the space of opinion; and moving back and forth between the worlds of politics and journalism.

The ability of opinion specialists to participate in multiple media formats shows a similar historical continuity. Elite news magazines like the *Atlantic* and *McClure's* played an important role in the circulation of opinion and commentary from the late nineteenth century and provided a place for columnists, intellectuals, and politicians to trade their competing analyses of public policy. Television entered the realm of political analysis and commentary as early as 1947, and by the 1960s, its programs were already a regular part of the opinion circuit for print columnists, academics, and politicians. While the move toward multimedia synergy would increasingly come to define the space of media commentary in the beginning of the twenty-first century, this was a process that had begun nearly a century earlier.

To be sure, important changes have taken place in the world of media opinion, and it would be a mistake to paint a picture of absolute historical stasis. As the quantity of media has exploded, so, too, has the quantity of opinion and commentary. Television has brought about an increased focus on the actions of politicians and political parties (though this was a process that was initially set in motion with the rise of *The New Republic* in the 1930s and 1940s). Books have become less important in the world of media commentary. And while political endorsements have been a regular feature of the opinion pages since the early twentieth century, the proportion of media commentary that is explicitly linked to a political party affiliation does seem to have increased since the 1980s (though it probably still does not reach the levels of the mid-nineteenth century). Still, it would be a mistake to overstate the changes in media opinion or to claim that the rise of opinion is killing objective journalism. From the earliest moments of U.S. press history, there has been a complicated and interdependent relationship between opinion and objectivity. Our aim in this chapter is to trace this history, providing a broader context for the work of today's op-ed writers, magazine columnists, bloggers, and television pundits.

The Early History: Partisan Opinion and American Media

The most influential social history of American newspapers is probably Michael Schudson's (1978) *Discovering the News*. In that book, Schudson asks how an information-based, impartial, and "objective" form of news came to dominate American journalism in the early decades of the twentieth century. Driving this new image of what journalism should look like was the idea that facts and values should be separate and that it was facts that were more necessary for the cultivation of an informed citizenry. "This question assumes special interest," Schudson claims, "when one learns that, before the 1830s, objectivity was not an issue. American newspapers were expected to present a partisan viewpoint, not a neutral one" (1978: 4). In other words, the American press was initially created as a space of and for opinion.

Starr's (2004) *The Creation of the Media* describes eighteenth-century New England newspapers as more fully politicized and more committed to dissent than were comparable papers in England or Europe. Part of this distinctiveness was due to the rapid growth of commerce in New England, New York, and Pennsylvania, which helped to introduce competition into the media marketplace. Newspaper competition served to reinforce the value of the news-reading public and encouraged readers to think of themselves as part of an impersonal mass public that had an important role to play in political affairs (Starr 2004: 56; see also Schudson 1998: 40; Warner 1992). Competition also introduced more political content into the news environment, because a city's second paper tended to rely more on political controversy and provocation in its quest for readers (Starr 2004: 57–59; see also Benson 2005).

More important than competitive market dynamics, however, was the influence that the revolutionary movement had on American newspapers. As resistance to the British grew, American newspapers reported the activities of protesters and provided a forum for discussing the meaning of the opposition. Indeed, by reporting on news and opinion from other colonies, colonial newspapers helped to expand the public and to create a sense of common purpose and common identity (see Starr 2004: 66–68). Even more significantly than was the case in England or Europe, the press in America came to be seen as the central location where political debate and commentary could be found:

> Like the English and French Revolutions, the American Revolution generated an eruption of public debate in print; the difference was the outcome. The pre-Revolutionary crisis in America established the press as the central venue of discussion independent of government, and the conflict and its immediate aftermath consolidated the status and the rights of the press and the priority of open debate as a means of conducting politics in the new republic. None of the European dynastic states had previously experienced a comparable transformation, and notwithstanding the French Revolution, neither France nor the other principal nations of Europe would see such changes on a sustainable basis until well into the nineteenth century. (Starr 2004: 70–71)

The commitment to dissent continued to play a central role in the American press in the aftermath of the Revolution. An opposition press emerged as early as the 1790s, criticizing the Federalist administrations of Washington and Adams and advocating in favor of the new Democratic-Republican Party of Jefferson and Madison (Starr 2004: 77–78). Attempts by the state to use the Sedition Act to tame this emerging tradition of dissent not only failed to achieve its goal but also actually emboldened and strengthened the partisan advocacy of the opposition press.[3] By 1830, Starr (2004: 85) concludes, "partisan newspapers became the focal point of sustained party activity." Most newspapers spoke with a single editorial voice, and their readers expected to receive a clearly partisan viewpoint (Schudson 1998: 116).[4]

By the middle of the nineteenth century, most newspapers were in the business of producing political opinion in support of a particular party. As Schudson (1978: 47–49; 1998: 144–155) has argued, this shift in journalistic practice was part of a larger transformation in American politics, in which party loyalty came to occupy a central role in American public life. With the rise of the party machines and the development of the professional politician, there were more opportunities available to people who wanted to get involved in politics as a vocation. Writing for a newspaper was a way to get into politics, and it was common for newspaper editors to be appointed to high-level government positions when their political party was in power.[5]

Both in form and in content, then, American newspapers in the 1860s were probably more political and partisan than at any other point in their history. Indeed, many newspaper publishers were intimately involved in politics during this period. For example, Henry Raymond, who established the *New York Times* in 1851, gave the keynote speech at the Republican Party's national convention in 1856 and was elected to Congress in 1862 (Walker 1982: 213). Joseph Medill, who took over the struggling *Chicago Tribune* in

1855 and transformed it into a paper with a daily circulation of more than 100,000 by the time of his death in 1899, was also one of the founders of the Republican Party and served as mayor of Chicago from 1871 to 1873. In fact, only 5 percent of newspapers were registered as neutral or independent in 1850 (Alexander 1988: 136–137).

The politicization and partisanship of the newspaper in the 1860s is perhaps best illustrated by the figure of Horace Greeley and his *New York Tribune*. When Greeley founded the paper in 1841, he claimed that he wanted to develop a new style of "principled partisan politics" that avoided the disempowering stances of "servile partisanship" and "gagged neutrality" that seemed to have been established as the two available options for journalists (Schudson 1978: 22). Greeley was an active partisan supporter of his own political positions and, indeed, of his own political career. Upon its founding in 1841, the *New York Tribune* quickly became the leading Whig paper in New York. The paper shifted alliances after the 1854 founding of the Republican Party, which Greeley himself helped to establish. The *Tribune* was perhaps the loudest voice of the abolitionist movement, with a circulation of nearly 300,000 at the time of the Civil War. Adopting a radical position on abolition, Greeley was highly critical of Lincoln's strategy of moderation and became disaffected with the Republican Party during Reconstruction. In 1872, he left the Republican Party to help create the Liberal Republican Party, which nominated him to run for president in the 1872 election.

As a newspaper, the *New York Tribune* emphasized political reporting and opinion and avoided the emphasis on police reports, scandals, and personalities that was more characteristic of the *New York Sun* and other sensationalist papers of the time. The *Tribune* was involved in many important innovations in newspaper content, such as the invention of the syndicated column and the modern editorial page.[6] The significance of these innovations would not immediately be realized, though, because the distinction between fact and opinion had not yet become an important principle in organizing journalistic practice (Schudson 1978: 64–68). Indeed, while Greeley may have avoided sensationalism, he never hesitated to express a passionately partisan position throughout his newspaper, whether that position be against slavery and the Confederacy or in favor of westward expansion and the creation of a transcontinental railroad (Alterman 1999: 25; Serrin and Serrin 2002: 374–376). In fact, Alterman (1999: 26) argues that the vision of objective journalism was first articulated by a former managing editor of the *New York Tribune*, Henry Raymond, who established the *New York Times* as a newspaper that was to be the opposite of the *Tribune*'s passionate partisanship.[7]

Objectivity, Journalism, and the Rise of the Columnist

The modern press system began to develop after the 1870s, bringing the idea that objective reporting was the highest aspiration toward which the modern newspaper should strive. Indeed, the last decade of the nineteenth and the first decade of the twentieth century saw a competition between two visions of journalism (see Schudson 1978:

88–120). On one side were newspapers such as Joseph Pulitzer's *New York World*, which sought to entertain readers with good stories; on the other side were newspapers like the *New York Times*, which tried to inform readers with a sober recounting of the previous day's most significant events. While the more entertaining newspapers may have entered the contest with more resources and more readers, it did not take long for the informational, fact-based newspapers to win the moral battle and establish themselves as the dominant form of American journalism.

The new professional ideals of journalism did not initially challenge the model of journalism-as-entertainment, nor did they always necessitate a rigid separation of fact and value (Schudson 1978: 77–81). By the late 1890s, however, newspapers such as the *New York Times* and the *New York Sun* had launched an attack on the "yellow journalism" of the *New York World*, forcing journalists to make a choice: between fact and value and between information and entertainment (see Schudson 1978: 112–114; Alterman 1999: 26–28). Most journalists (as well as most elite readers) preferred to align themselves with the informational model of the newspaper. By the time Adolph Ochs placed the new motto of "All the News That's Fit to Print" on the masthead of his *New York Times* in 1897, there were already clear signs that the goals of detachment and impartiality would become the dominant ideals of American journalists (Campbell 2006; Schudson 1978).

The rise of fact-based reporting was intimately connected to the rise of modern opinion formats. On the one hand, there was the belief that democratic citizens required facts to make decisions and guide actions. On the other hand, however, it became increasingly apparent that readers required a guide to determine which facts were important, which facts could be trusted, and which public policies the facts supported.

There were a number of historical developments that highlighted the need for analysis and commentary to parse the facts for readers. During the First World War, for example, Woodrow Wilson employed many journalists to work in the Committee on Public Information, where they produced thousands of press releases and film shorts in support of the American war effort (Schudson 1978: 141–143). By the 1920s, public relations professionals had perfected their craft, helping business and government place convenient "facts" in the hands of reporters, often organizing these facts into typed copy that was supplied directly to reporters (Schudson 1978: 135–140). The 1920s and 1930s also saw advertisers and market researchers develop more rigorous and scientific methods for learning about the media audience, which allowed them to adjust their messages in a way that would make positive responses much more likely (Mayhew 1997: 189–208). Political consultants adopted these methods, quickly coming to rely on opinion polling and pre-tested, focus-grouped messages to tailor the political issues their clients would emphasize in a way that would achieve the maximum desired effects (Mayhew 1997: 209–217). Taken together, these developments led many to question whether it was possible to create a disinterested and impartial report of the facts.

Newspapers responded to the epistemological challenges of public relations and propaganda with a number of new journalistic devices. The practice of using bylines to identify the author of a news story increased dramatically in the 1920s and 1930s (Schudson 1978: 145), which lessened the reliance on anonymous sources and created accountability by linking particular authors to particular arguments. The weekend news summary was established during the 1930s to make connections between different events of the week and provide some interpretation of the significance of these events (Schudson 1978: 145–146). Finally, this period saw the rise of the syndicated political columnist who provided independent analysis, commentary, and an evaluation of the day's events. By the 1920s, the columnist had come to occupy a central position in the American newspaper.

Walter Lippmann and the First Golden Age of the Columnist

While political columnists made occasional appearances in American newspapers toward the end of the nineteenth century, it was not until about 1920 that the syndicated political column became a regular feature of the newspaper.[8] The earliest syndicated political columnists are without question among the most influential figures in the history of American journalism, testifying to how important this innovation was. One of the first syndicated political columnists was David Lawrence, who began writing a column for the *New York Evening Post* in 1915; Lawrence went on to create two weekly newsmagazines, *United States News* and *World Report*, which he merged in 1948 to create *U.S. News and World Report* (Riley 1998: 80–81). During his peak period of influence in the 1950s, Lawrence's column appeared in more than 350 newspapers (Riley 1998: 81). Other early political columnists included Raymond Clapper, Arthur Brisbane, Frank Kent, Heywood Broun, Dorothy Thompson, John Knight, Joseph Alsop, and perhaps the most important of them all, Walter Lippmann (Gordon 1994; Riley 1998: 81–90).

Lippmann is generally regarded as the most important political columnist in the history of American journalism. After graduating from Harvard, Lippmann went to work for Lincoln Steffens, a journalist in the muckraking tradition who was a reporter and editor at the *New York Evening Post*, the *Commercial Advertiser*, and *McClure's*. In 1914, Lippmann became one of the founding editors of *The New Republic*, which he left in 1920 to begin writing editorials for *Vanity Fair*. In 1922, he began writing a column for the *New York World*, and in 1924, he became the director of that newspaper's editorial page. The *World* was the first newspaper to establish the op-ed page and was the center of punditry during the 1920s (Alterman 1999: 34).[9] In 1931, Lippmann moved to the *New York Herald-Tribune*, where he would spend the next thirty-one years writing his syndicated column "Today and Tomorrow," which won Pulitzer Prizes in 1958 and 1962 (Riley 1998: 84). He moved his column to the *Washington Post* in 1963, the same year he began writing a biweekly column for *Newsweek* magazine. At its peak, Lippmann's syndicated column was distributed to 275 different newspapers (Riley 1998: 84). In addition, Lippmann was the first columnist to make the transition to television; CBS Television broadcast seven hour-length programs, "Conversations with Walter Lippmann," which aired between 1960 and 1965 and won Lippmann a Peabody Award in 1962 (Weeks 1965; Steel 1999: 517).

In addition to his impressive body of journalistic work, there are two other aspects of Lippmann's career that established the idealized image toward which columnists have aspired ever since. The first of these was Lippmann's ability to move back and forth between the journalistic field and the political field. In 1917, Lippmann became a formal adviser to Newton Baker, President Wilson's secretary of war, where he helped to write Wilson's "Fourteen Points" speech outlining a plan for world peace (Steel 1999: 107–110). Lippmann would spend the next fifty years offering formal and informal advice to presidents and other policy makers, often using his columns as a public extension of his role as foreign policy adviser.

Lippmann's most important contribution, though, was to articulate an intellectual rationale for why columnists were necessary in a modern democratic society. In *Public Opinion* (1922) and *The Phantom Public* (1925), Lippmann argued that most individuals had neither the time nor the analytical skills to develop a sufficiently detailed and nuanced understanding of the world around them. This problem was magnified, Lippmann argued, by the dominant practices of news reporting, which tended to compress the complexity of the day's events into oversimplified news leads that reinforced the simplistic stereotypes and emotional prejudices of its audience. But even if journalism *was* able to provide detailed and nuanced information about all aspects of society, Lippmann had serious reservations about a democratic ideal that required "omnicompetent citizens" who not only were experts about all public matters of the day but also were experts about all public matters that might arise in the future (Lippmann [1925] 2000: 12–29). As Lippmann wrote in *The Phantom Public*, the problem with this model of civic education was that

> It has not taught the child how to act as a member of the public. It has merely given him a hasty, incomplete taste of what he might have to know if he meddled in everything. The result is a bewildered public and a mass of insufficiently trained officials. . . . Our civic education does not even begin to tell the voter how he can reduce the maze of public affairs to some intelligible form. ([1925] 2000: 138–139)

What was needed, Lippmann felt, was a space for expert analysts who could help point citizens to a deeper understanding of what was really important. At the same time, these experts should be able to speak as proxies for the masses in a way that gave the public a voice in the political conversation. In other words, columnists were to speak in two different voices: as teachers to the lay public and as policy advocates who speak to elites in the space of opinion on behalf of the public interest.[10] In a speech he gave on his seventieth birthday to the National Press Club, Lippmann described this work as follows:

> If the country is to be governed with the consent of the governed, then the governed must arrive at opinions about what their governors want them to consent to.

How do they do this? They do it by hearing on the radio and reading in the news-papers what the corps of correspondents tell them is going on in Washington, and in the country at large, and in the world. Here, we correspondents perform an essential service. In some field of interest, we make it our business to find out what is going on under the surface and beyond the horizon, to infer, to deduce, to ima-gine, and to guess what is going on inside, what this meant yesterday, and what it could mean tomorrow. (Lippmann, in Rossiter and Lare 1963: 533–534)

For Lippmann, this work of peering beneath the surface could not take place in everyday journalism, because the press in its normal operation could only record what had been recorded for it by the working of social and political institutions (Lippmann [1922] 2007: 111–113). This type of recording was certainly helpful for the reader of the paper because it helped to identify the principal characters in a given policy debate, as well as the core elements of their competing proposals. In other words, as Lippmann wrote in *Public Opinion*, the press made it easier for members of the public to give a hearing to the public authorities but left the reader "virtually defenseless against a false premise that none of the debaters has challenged, or a neglected aspect that none of them has brought into the argument" (Lippmann [1922] 2007: 74). For this kind of help, the reader needed the insight and the analysis of a third party who had the time to study the issues, who was in direct contact with the leaders and the inner circle who were making the decisions, and who was not himself actually involved in the decision making. This person was the columnist. In Lippmann's view, then, the columnist should provide more than mere opinion; he should provide *analysis*, and he should ground his analysis in expertise and other legitimate claims to authority.

In his own columns, Lippmann tended to rely on three types of analysis, each of which included a specific type of authority claim. It is worth describing these in some detail because they form three of the most important ideal types from which columnists have drawn ever since. They also inform some of the initial categories that we develop in the empirical analyses in subsequent chapters.

The Columnist as a Policy Adviser

In the most typical format, Lippmann would adopt the subject position of the policy adviser to promote or criticize a specific policy recommendation that had been proposed. Lippmann did this famously in a series of columns he wrote in 1947 for the *New York Herald Tribune*. In them, he attacked the Truman Doctrine of Soviet containment and argued instead for a diplomatic initiative to establish a settlement with the Soviet Union, which, he argued, would increase the likelihood of a withdrawal of the Red Army from Eastern Europe (Lippmann 1947). In a series of fourteen columns, Lippmann offered a point-by-point rejection of the main assumptions of the Truman Doctrine, which had just recently been outlined by George Kennan in an anonymous article published in

Foreign Affairs. Lippmann argued that the Truman Doctrine (a) overemphasized the importance of Marxist ideology on Soviet foreign policy, (b) relied on a strategy of containment that would leave the U.S. military badly overextended, and (c) reinforced Soviet security fears by refusing to engage in serious diplomacy with them (Steel 1999: 443–445). Writing in his November 4 column of that year, Lippmann suggested that the Soviets already knew that they had lost the Cold War; U.S. policy, correspondingly, should be to "push toward a settlement which permits the recovery of Europe and of the world, and to relax the tension, to subdue the anxiety, and to end the panic" (quoted in Steel 1999: 447).

Another example of Lippmann writing as a policy adviser comes from a series of columns published in May 1932 for the *New York Herald Tribune*.[11] These columns concerned three competing bills for economic relief that were being debated in Congress.[12] In the first column, Lippmann addressed the general question of public works, summarizing the two competing positions while criticizing both for being unnecessarily dogmatic in their views. Lippmann argued that the "orthodox school" of noninvolvement had far more theoretical and empirical support but that it ignored the practical necessity of continuing to explore ways that new investment could be stimulated in a productive way. One of the most interesting features of these columns is that Lippmann explicitly criticized the editorial position of his own paper, the *New York Herald-Tribune*, which was against any program of government intervention. He argued that this position was cynical and confused; while any program of government intervention carries risk, he contended, "the risk of not doing anything, of sitting and letting the vicious spiral of deflation spin, are very great" (Lippmann, in Nevins 1932: 86). Having rejected the doctrine of nonintervention, Lippmann then reframed the issue around two central questions: (1) should the government limit itself to supporting self-liquidating projects, which would not compete with private enterprise? And (2) should government programs be limited to public enterprises, or should they include private companies as well? (see Nevins 1932: 82). Ultimately, Lippmann argued in favor of government investment in self-liquidating public projects, emphasizing the role that a public works program would have on stimulating investor confidence (as opposed to the direct employment benefits of such programs).

These types of columns offer superb practical examples of Lippmann's theory about the kinds of public interventions that columnists should make. The columnist should address a key issue of the day. He should identify the most important point of difference in the competing approaches. And he should do all of this in a way that is guided by reasoned analysis rather than political interest. In performing this service, moreover, the columnist helps to educate readers by providing a map of the political debate, including a small number of key signposts that readers can use to navigate the complexity of the debate. At the same time, however, the columnist is fully aware that the audience includes all the major political actors involved in the debate, and in this context, Lippmann hoped to influence the political debate and the decision making that surrounded the issue. He did this by drawing on a variety of authority claims and different forms of expertise, including historical knowledge, empirical facts, academic theories, and an insider's knowledge of the political process. All of these expert claims were united by the pragmatic insistence that experts need to provide answers and solutions to pressing public problems.

The Columnist as Teacher

The second type of analysis we can find in Lippmann's columns shows him in the role of a teacher who provides the social and historical context necessary for readers to understand the significance of a particular issue or recent event. This concern with helping the reader understand the complexity of current events and public policy was similar to the motivation in his "policy advice" columns, except here there was less of a concern to speak to political actors or to provide specific policy recommendations.[13] We can find an example of this kind of analysis in a series of columns Lippmann wrote during the 1932 Democratic Convention, in which he compared the strategic situation facing the Democrats to the 1896 and 1916 presidential candidacies of Bryan and Wilson (see Nevins 1932: 298–314). We also find frequent examples of Lippmann explaining to his readers the function played by specific political institutions in columns such as "The Ideal of Representative Government" (May 17, 1932), "The Function of the Supreme Court" (January 25, 1936), "The President" (April 19, 1941), "The President and the People" (January 29, 1942), "The Election Explained" (November 3, 1952), and "The American Idea" (February 22, 1954).[14]

Lippmann also used many of his columns to explain to his readers the meaning of specific political situations elsewhere in the world, particularly as they concerned the Cold War and international economic processes. In a 1931 column he wrote about British politics, for example, Lippmann provided his readers with a history lesson on the structural transformation of the global economy and its consequences for Britain (see Nevins 1932: 215–220). After explaining the economic forces that caused a collapse in the British currency, Lippmann went on to identify important political and human sources of England's dilemma. While economic theories would have called for a reduction in wages as a solution to the currency crisis, he argued, in practical terms this was not a politically viable solution. This, too, was a common feature of Lippmann's columns: that academic theory frequently needed to be reinterpreted and readjusted to fit practical political realities. By providing readers with a lesson in history, sociology, and political economy then, Lippmann's goal was to help them understand how difficult it was for political actors to solve the problems created by global economic crisis. Readers could then use the lessons learned from the column to interpret the political attempts to solve the American economic crisis and perhaps have a more "realistic" expectation about the difficulties that politicians faced in trying to respond simultaneously to political and economic challenges.

The Column as Political Portrait

The third type of Lippmann column was the political portrait. Lippmann wrote these columns when a political leader died or during any other moment when a portrait of an individual could serve usefully as a meditation on the nature of political leadership. Included among his portraits were columns about Mahatma Gandhi, Amelia Earhart, Winston Churchill, Queen Elizabeth II, John D. Rockefeller, John Foster Dulles, Al Smith, Charles DeGaulle, and Franklin Delano Roosevelt. More often than not, Lippmann had a personal relationship with the person he wrote about, and in all instances, the portrait was written to bring into bold relief a particular aspect of authentic, effective political leadership.

We can see in these political portraits the merging of columnist, political insider, and public philosopher. To be sure, Lippmann used rhetorical forms that suggested how his insider status gave him a special understanding of political leadership. This was a defining feature of all the major columnists during the Cold War period. But Lippmann's political portraits were more than just a display of his social contacts. Lippmann had a fully developed theory of political leadership, which he had already described in books such as *A Preface to Politics* (1913), *A Preface to Morals* (1929), and *The Public Philosophy* (1955). His columns provided an opportunity to make this philosophy visible to a broad, general public. In this theory, leaders were not mere servants of the people, nor were they followers of public opinion. Rather, the political leader needed to anticipate social problems and social desires. Surrounding himself with experts, the effective political leader could animate the public and help to express their wants and needs in ways that would result in some measure of control over their collective future (see Schlesinger 1959, esp. pp. 193–197). The political portraits that Lippmann offered in his columns were designed to emphasize these aspects of political leadership.

Insider or Citizen? The Tension between Access and Detachment in the Age of the Columnist

In the example that Lippmann provided, the effective columnist spoke with two different voices, which were not always easy to reconcile. On one side was the voice of the policy adviser, who spoke to an imagined audience of political insiders to make an intervention into an ongoing policy debate. The voice of the policy adviser, which depended largely on access and social connections, was often at odds with the journalistic ideal of autonomy, particularly for columnists who did not share Lippmann's intellectual reputation. On the other side was the voice of the teacher, who spoke to an imagined audience of citizens to help them appreciate the underlying context or the complexity surrounding a particular issue. The voice of the teacher depended largely on a commitment to detachment and was more easily aligned with the cultural project of autonomy. Among the two voices, it was the voice of the policy adviser that appeared more frequently, and upon which the political influence of the columnist largely depended. But it was the voice of the teacher—or, at the very least, the stance of detachment that typically accompanied this voice—that was more responsible for the columnist's professional and civic legitimation.

For Lippmann, balancing the competing demands of access and detachment required a hybrid cultural practice, somewhere between the academic scholar and the expert adviser. As a columnist, Lippmann strove to be more detached and autonomous than a political adviser, but not as detached as the academic scholar.[15] While not a scientist himself, Lippmann saw himself as a public advocate for *science* as the route to social improvement, and he viewed his columns as a place where he could translate and reformulate scientific principles in ways that would make them more practical and useful in light of political realities (Schlesinger 1959: 196). In other words, the intellectual practice of the columnist involved translating scientific expertise into a public vocabulary, while trying to persuade those same scientists to make sure that their work was engaged enough with the world to allow this sort of translation (Lippmann [1922] 2007: 111–113). Whether he was arguing for or against a particular public policy, providing public instruction about the meaning of a particular event or proposal, or offering up a political portrait, Lippmann's columns were always motivated by the desire to capture uncertainty and complexity in the world, as well as the "indispensability of the long view" (Schlesinger 1959: 224). It was this intellectual practice that made his columns so prestigious.

If Lippmann had a clear strategy for combining these two voices into a single intellectual project, many other columnists found the voice of the insider to be easier and more enticing than the role of the teacher. This preference for the insider's voice was seen clearly in the work of many of Lippmann's contemporaries, men such as James Reston (*New York Times*), Joseph Alsop (*New York Herald Tribune*), and Arthur Krock (*New York Times*). For these columnists, much of what they wrote depended almost wholly on their access and their social connections. In many ways, these insider columns more closely resembled the typical journalistic practices of Washington correspondents. Instead of providing theory, analysis, or historical context, what they typically provided was a report about what officials were thinking behind the scenes. The following, from Arthur Krock's "In the Nation" column, is a good example of the access-driven political column:

> A series of questions addressed to Vice President Barkley by this correspondent and his answers thereto appear to establish the fact that never before in American history has a President taken the pains that Mr. Truman has to see to it that the first citizen in the line of Presidential succession was made currently familiar and in detail with all administrative and policy problems. This must be the direct consequence of the situation the President found himself in when Franklin D. Roosevelt died suddenly. . . . Mr. Truman has often told of the towering mass of

documents he had to go through at the beginning of his Presidency to get even a perspective of matters he had to decide. (*New York Times*, March 2, 1950)

By moving closer to the standard practices of political reporting, the insider columnists did not become more objective or more autonomous. If anything, by relying too heavily on their access to important political leaders, these columnists forfeited most of their independence and offered little more than an index of the range of views that were circulating in official government debates about a given issue (see Bennett 1990). As Alterman (1999: 55) has argued, in a blistering attack on these insider columnists, "the post-Lippmann generation merely reinforced the borders set by others, all the while attempting to inject some drama and status into what otherwise would have been considered the most insignificant minutiae of insider politics."

Fortunately, the structural conditions that allowed a Walter Lippmann to exist were present for other columnists, provided they could establish a media practice that was not singularly defined by access and by the voice of the insider. Indeed, the practices of more analytical, detached, and critical opinion were supported in a variety of additional media spaces outside the mainstream newspapers and their Washington correspondents. Raymond Aron (1959) commented on this fact in an essay about Walter Lippmann, arguing that the defining feature of the American columnist was that he was published in many different papers, in a way that freed him from editorial control and increased his autonomy. This distinctive development allowed the American columnist to brand himself through the cross-promotion of his distinctive voice across a range of different media sites. The French commentator, employed by a single paper that had exclusive rights to his articles, was not able to write everything he thought about a particular subject in that paper, and he was forced to keep silent on a whole host of topics where he was certain that he would be in conflict with the paper's editorial position. In contrast, the American columnist was in a much stronger position relative to his editors and could write whatever he liked about whatever topic he chose.

There were two keys to the columnist's autonomy. First, as we have suggested, he needed to avoid a slavish devotion to the insider's voice and to maintain some level of independence from his insider sources. And second, he needed to develop his arguments and commentaries in a variety of media formats. For Lippmann and his more intellectual colleagues, this often involved developing their arguments in books and political magazines and then incorporating these arguments into their regular newspaper columns. It is to the history of this secondary market for opinion that we now turn.

News Magazines and the Secondary Market for Opinion

The long-form journalism of magazines such as the *Atlantic Monthly*, *McClure's*, the *Nation*, and *The New Republic* supported the dominant spaces of opinion that were established in the major metropolitan newspapers during the first half of the twentieth century. Combining in-depth analysis with social and cultural criticism, these types of magazines served as a home base and a launching pad for many of the most influential syndicated columnists of the time. They also provided a virtual meeting place where journalists, writers, artists, academics, and politicians could define and debate American public life.

The elite magazines are an important part of the history of opinion and analysis in American journalism, and a part of the history that is most often left out. As early as the 1860s, these magazines were developing as a conscious response to the mass-circulation newspapers, which many intellectuals saw as a threat to civilized and enlightened public discourse. When E. L. Godkin left the *New York Times* to establish the *Nation* in 1865, he announced that his magazine would discuss politics, economics, and culture "with greater accuracy and moderation than are now to be found in the daily press" (quoted in Emery, Emery, and Roberts 2000: 151). Several years earlier, in 1857, such intellectual luminaries as Ralph Waldo Emerson, Henry Wadsworth Longfellow, Oliver Wendell Holmes, and James Russell Lowell had gathered together to create a "journal of literature, politics, science, and the arts" whose goal was to help define a distinctively American voice and an American ethos. Their magazine, the *Atlantic Monthly*, published its first issue in 1857. During the next seventy years, the *Atlantic Monthly* would help to launch the careers of such distinctively American writers as Mark Twain and Henry James; it would also publish important and influential essays by Woodrow Wilson, Theodore Roosevelt, W. E. B. DuBois, Felix Frankfurter, John Muir, and other opinion makers. For both of these magazines, the stated goal was to produce independent critical analysis that was motivated by the public interest, rather than by political partisanship.

By the end of the 1890s, magazines had become a prime outlet for journalists in the muckraking tradition, who used these forums to write much longer, in-depth versions of the crusading, investigative social issues articles they were writing in many metropolitan papers. So, for example, Jacob Riis published dozens of articles about life in the slums in such magazines as *Atlantic Monthly*, *Scribner's Magazine*, and the *Century*. Lincoln Steffens, a reporter for the *New York Evening Post* and a mentor to Walter Lippmann, wrote a series of articles on corruption in city government for *McClure's* magazine. *Cosmopolitan*, *Everybody's*, *Collier's*, *Hampton's*, and *American Magazine* also provided outlets for journalists in the muckraking tradition, and in the process, most of them developed readerships well in excess of 100,000 (Emery, Emery, and Roberts 2000: 223–226).

McClure's magazine was the leading media outlet for the muckrakers during the period of their greatest influence and visibility, and it provides a good example of the possibilities and challenges that faced these kinds of magazines. Founded in 1893, *McClure's* emphasized serialized articles of American history and biography in its early years, using this format to build a circulation of nearly 400,000 by 1900 (Wilson 1970: 101). To give an example of this early content, almost 10 percent of all the articles published during the first decade of *McClure's* focused on Civil War heroes, including thirty articles on Lincoln and twenty-six on Grant (Wilson 1970: 109–110). By 1902, however, the writers and editors of the magazine were becoming increasingly preoccupied with the social consequences of industrialism. This led to a marked shift in the magazine's content, if not in its form. Now, instead of profiling great political and military heroes, the magazine profiled industrial robber barons, as well as the physical and social hardships suffered by factory workers. Politically oriented fiction rounded out the portrait of the industrial trusts and their victims. All of this culminated in Ida Tarbell's nineteen-part series on the Standard Oil trust, which was published between 1902 and 1904. Profiles of other trusts were to follow, as were a series of articles on corruption in the nation's cities.

By 1910, *McClure's* had fallen on hard times, as had the muckraking tradition it helped to found.[16] In the process, though, *McClure's* had helped to establish the idea that information-based, objective, straight reporting was not necessarily the best way to align journalism with the public interest. At the same time, the fate of *McClure's* testifies to the inherent difficulties in creating a sophisticated, literate magazine that resisted advertiser pressures and frequently attacked corporate interests. Many of these magazines ultimately succumbed to advertiser pressures, while those magazines that resisted such pressures found themselves losing both readers and contributing writers to the wealthier, advertising-supported magazines. As for *McClure's*, it resisted these pressures to the bitter end when, facing mounting debts, it was forcibly sold to its creditors, who turned it into a women's magazine.[17]

With the decline of the muckraking tradition during the second decade of the twentieth century, the new model for the opinion magazine came increasingly from *The New Republic*, which announced its arrival in 1914 as "an experiment . . . an attempt to find a national audience for a journal of interpretation and opinion." Initially established by Herbert Croly, a friend of Theodore Roosevelt and a supporter of the Progressive movement of the time, *The New Republic* enjoyed the security of significant financial subsidies from Dorothy Straight, an heiress from the Whitney family who subsidized the magazine for its first forty years at an average cost of about $100,000 per year (Steel 1999: 59–62).

With the magazine's financial security established, Croly was able to assemble an ambitious and talented editorial staff, which included Walter Lippmann as well as other writers drawn largely from the worlds of journalism and academia. From the world of journalism, Croly recruited Francis Hackett from the *Chicago Evening Post* and Walter Weyl, a labor economist who had written articles and books on socialism, capitalism, and the trade union movement. From academia, Croly recruited Phillip Littell and Felix Frankfurter from Harvard, as well as Alvin Johnson, an economist from Cornell, and George Soule, an economist who worked as director of the National Bureau of Economic Research.

The New Republic was different from its predecessors in form and content. The most important difference was the much heavier emphasis placed on the analysis of U.S. public policy. Each issue would begin with three or four short, unsigned editorials, primarily focusing on U.S. domestic and foreign policy. These would be followed by five or six signed articles, written by contributors as well as by editors. Most of these articles also concerned public policy analysis and commentary, with occasional articles on new developments in the world of culture. These articles would be followed by two or three letters to the editor, commenting on articles published in previous issues of the magazine. Finally, there would be a number of book reviews, equally divided between reviews of fiction and nonfiction.

This emphasis on analysis and political commentary differed from previous magazines, which had focused more on literature and social commentary and far less on an analysis of the issues of the moment. A typical issue of the *Atlantic Monthly*, for example, included only one or two articles devoted to the analysis of politics and public policy; the other contributions, which made up about three-quarters of the issue, were devoted to poetry, serialized fiction, history and biography, personal memoir, and social or cultural criticism. This emphasis was consistent with the magazine's more intellectual and cultural mission of defining a distinctive American voice. *McClure's* initial mission, which was to write in-depth articles that analyzed and reconstructed the events of the day (Wilson 1970: 81), quickly yielded to a narrower focus on political corruption and economic monopoly. *McClure's* also drew on distinctive literary conventions that focused on local stories and individual conflicts, both of which were intended to dramatize larger social issues with the hope of shocking public opinion into collective action (Wilson 1970: 190–200). Neither magazine adopted the voice of the policy adviser, which would become the dominant voice of the columnist and prove so successful at drawing political actors into the public discussion.

As compared with the other magazines of the day, the dominant voice of *The New Republic* was that of the policy adviser. *The New Republic* was written by political insiders who were confident that their readers included the most powerful political figures in the nation. Indeed, Roosevelt's presidential campaign was organized around the rhetoric of a "new nationalism," a phrase he drew directly from Herbert Croly's 1909 book, *The Promise of American Life* (Seideman 1986: 3–4). Walter Lippmann, who was also an editor of the magazine, was an adviser and a speechwriter for Woodrow Wilson, as we already observed, and for most of his career the most well-connected journalist in the nation (Seideman 1986: 43). Most other contributing writers had equally impressive social and political networks.

In this context, *The New Republic* never had to worry about being part of the public conversation; if anything, its main challenge in its early years was how to participate in these conversations without appearing beholden to those liberal politicians who formed the magazine's "inner circle" of readers.[18] These concerns lessened somewhat with the end of liberal political hegemony and the election of Harding as president in 1920. While *The New Republic* continued to actively endorse candidates—La Follette in 1924 and Al Smith in 1928—the editors increasingly saw their campaign endorsements as an "exercise in agitation" (Seideman 1986: 71–72). In fact, endorsements were almost always qualified, and they usually included as much criticism as praise.

By the time Dorothy Straight sold the magazine in 1953, *The New Republic* had established a new model for magazines that distinguished them from the mainstream press while guaranteeing them political influence that greatly exceeded their actual circulation. Editors of *The New Republic* saw themselves as providing a definite alternative to the kind of political journalism typically found in the mainstream press. This distinction had come out most clearly and famously in a forty-two-page article, "A Test of the News" (1920). In this work, Lippmann and Merz examined three years of *New York Times* coverage of the Bolshevik revolution. They found repeated mistakes, fabrications of events that never happened, and continual reports about the putative impending collapse of the Soviet Union. Far from being fact based, Lippmann and Merz concluded that press coverage of foreign affairs was "dominated by the hopes of the men who composed the news organization" (quoted in Steel 1999: 172).

To counteract this style of wishful reporting, writers for *The New Republic* tried to organize their commentaries around the general principle of *critique*, which the editors of the magazine felt was a more effective way to get to the truth of the matter. They also distrusted the style of mainstream reporting that gave undue attention to political leaders, believing instead that policies were more important than personalities and that the best way to understand a particular issue was to critically explore the general principles and ideas that informed specific policies. Ultimately, the editors of the magazine desired to publish articles that were opinionated without being partisan, disinterested without being disengaged, concerned with political ideas without being ideological, and engaged with politics without becoming a party organ. Or as Lippmann remarked during the fiftieth anniversary celebration for the magazine:

> The point of all this is that the paper was meant to be what it is now—the organ of no party, of no faction, of no sect, and of no cause, concerned not with liberalism and progressivism and conservatism as ideologies, but with all of them. (Lippmann 1964: 14)

This new format had a powerful and lasting effect on the nation's elite magazines. *The Nation*, which had become a journal for conservative literature professors (Douglas 1964), changed its format in 1918 to more closely mirror *The New Republic* format and even contemplated a merger with *The New Republic* in 1949 (Navasky 1990). *Vanity Fair*, *Atlantic Monthly*, and the rest of the "serious" magazines gradually increased their emphasis on the analysis of public policy and on a critical discussion of politics and the dominant events of the day. And conservatives, who felt that *The New Republic* had always been the official intellectual outlet for liberal politics, scrambled to create their own movement magazine, with William F. Buckley Jr. eventually establishing *National Review* in 1955.

Thus, by the 1950s, most of the features of media commentary in the space of opinion that we can see today had been established. The major newspapers had their syndicated political columnists, with the more ambitious among them trying to emulate Lippmann and the rest offering insider columns that chronicled backroom deals and political intrigue. Politicians read these columns with great interest, with full knowledge that their constituents defined the political agenda according to the topics covered and the arguments made in these columns. Alongside the public discussions that were carried on in and through the newspaper columns was a more extended discussion taking place in the elite magazines, which increasingly organized themselves around commentary informed by the goal of outlining general principles for specific political-intellectual movements: "centrist" liberals in *The New Republic*, anti–Cold War leftists in the *Nation*, and conservatives in the *National Review*. The magazines did an effective job of creating a stable space of commentary that included columnists, journalists, academics, politicians, and representatives from civil society organizations. In fact, many newspapers would attempt to emulate this more expansive view of the opinion space, as an expanded op-ed page increasingly became the norm during the 1970s.

Newspapers, the Op-Ed Page, and the Expansion of the Space of Opinion

The space of opinion in newspapers expanded and diversified significantly during the 1970s and 1980s. The key event in this expansion was the reemergence of the op-ed page, which was established in the *New York Times* in September 1970 and quickly copied by newspapers throughout the nation. Claiming the space that used to be occupied by obituaries, the new page of opinion was announced in the following editorial:

> Through the new page opposite the Editorial page that we inaugurate today, we hope that a contribution may be made toward stimulating new thought and provoking new discussion on public problems. All of the Times's regular Editorial page columnists will appear with their usual frequency on the new page, but they will be joined by two or more outside contributors six days a week, writing on the widest possible range of subject matter and expressing the widest possible range of opinion. . . . The objective is rather to afford greater opportunity for exploration of issues and presentation of new insights and new ideas by writers who have no institutional connection with The Times and whose views will very frequently be completely divergent from our own. (*New York Times*, September 21, 1970, p. 42)

For the *New York Times*, the creation of the op-ed page was intended to fulfill a number of different functions. First, the op-ed page provided a space in the paper for specialists and experts to participate in public dialogue about the issues of the day. About half of the guest columns were solicited by members of the op-ed page staff, who suggested topics to specific writers and then worked with them to get the column in suitable shape (Diamond 1993: 278). These solicited columns were written mostly by academic experts, think tank intellectuals, and political insiders. The remaining columns were selected from an "avalanche of unsolicited manuscripts," which quickly came to exceed 100 each day (Diamond 1993: 278). Of these unsolicited manuscripts, the successful ones often came from the same kinds of people as the solicited columns: Ivy League professors, think tank intellectuals, and freelance journalists. In other words, while the op-ed page was open to outsiders, its orientation—consistent with the paper's marketing strategy of the time—was toward a relatively elite and specialized audience (Diamond 1993: 283). But while these new voices may have been elite, they were still different from the politicians, government officials, and other official sources that dominated the rest of the paper's front section.

The establishment of the op-ed page also coincided with a strategy by the paper to bring in a more diverse range of columnists and to try to increase the visibility and autonomy of its own regular columnists. Previously, most regular columnists for the *New York Times* had been long-term editors and correspondents who came from the most well-established corners of the paper. These columnists fit the stereotype of the elite, insular, and liberal *New York Times* journalist, a complaint that many critics were launching against the news and editorial divisions of the paper in the post-Vietnam war years (Diamond 1993: 293). The new columnists were less likely to have such an insular career trajectory (Diamond 1993: 292–304). The best example of this new policy was William Safire, a conservative columnist and former Nixon speechwriter, who had never worked for the paper when he was hired in 1973. Other notable exceptions include Anna Quindlen, who was working as a deputy editor at the Metro desk and was about to quit the paper to become a novelist when she was hired as a columnist in 1990. Bob Herbert, an African American columnist who was hired away from the op-ed page of the *New York Daily News*, became a *New York Times* columnist in 1993. The inclusion of outsiders has continued with two of the most visible columnists hired in recent years: David Brooks, who came from the world of long-form journalism, and Paul Krugman, who came from the Economics Department of Princeton University.

The expanded op-ed page was an instant success, with audience studies showing that it was the most widely read part of the paper (Diamond 1993: 277). This is particularly impressive when one considers the additional economic efficiencies that the op-ed page presented. A column was less expensive to produce than a hard news story of a similar length, even if it was written by a celebrity syndicated columnist (Diamond 1993: 294). Even better, half of the columns were written by outsiders, who were thrilled to be published in the paper and happy to receive the $150 payment that the *New York Times* offered for their successful entry (Diamond 1993: 278). Better still, the paper was able to sell the bottom corner of the op-ed page to corporate advertisers who wanted to circulate their own public policy messages—and to place those messages next to the other op-ed columns of the day (Diamond 1993: 293).

Not surprisingly, the formula for the expanded op-ed page spread quickly to other newspapers. By 1975, the *Los Angeles Times*, *Washington Post*, *Boston Globe*, and *Chicago Tribune* had all expanded their op-ed pages, opening them to outside contributors much as the *New York Times* had done; so, too, had smaller, regional papers, such as the

Milwaukee Journal, Minneapolis Star, and others that wanted to open their papers to the voices of outsiders.[19] This orientation to outsider perspectives only intensified with the rise of the Internet and its incorporation into the content strategies of newspapers throughout the nation. We discuss the impact of the Internet later in the chapter. First, though, we turn to the other key event in the history of opinion: the rise of television.

Television Enters the Scene, 1950–1980

Since 1950, the history of media opinion must be understood in relation to the growing influence of television. While television was already coming to dominate the world of political discussion and commentary by the 1960s, this was not a development that was as obvious during the initial decade of national network television. Indeed, in the early years of television, most of the leaders in the industry sought to minimize their involvement with the news, which they viewed as a public service that was always a money loser. Slowly, though, television producers discovered that they could produce a more entertaining form of public affairs programming—as long as they concentrated on opinion and commentary, as long as they worked to create more entertaining formats, and as long as they turned their attention to politics and political personalities.

As network television completed its first full decade, most critics held its achievements in extremely low regard. To be sure, television had its supporters. Jack Gould, who wrote the television column for the *New York Times*, focused much of his energy on praising those programs that were "extraordinarily good," while reminding his readers that television very much resembled the rest of the arts, in the sense that its outstanding achievements were surrounded mostly by mediocre productions (see Gould 2002 for a selection of Gould's thoughtful commentaries on television). But most critics were far less generous, taking a viewpoint similar to that expressed by Lippmann in a 1959 column:

> The great offense of the television industry is that it is misusing a superb scientific achievement, that it is monopolizing the air at the expense of effective news reporting, good art, and civilized entertainment. The crux of the evil is that in seeking great mass audiences, the industry has decided that the taste of the great masses is a low one, and that to succeed in the competition it must pander to this low taste. (quoted in Rossiter and Lare 1963: 412)

The problem with this type of all-consuming condemnation was that it was made by people who tended not to watch television and who seemed uninterested in a careful examination of what was good and what was bad in television.

Gould was an exception in that his analysis of television was based on a careful consideration of the actual range of programming content. As such, his writings on 1950s television news are instructive. In a 1956 article published in the *New York Times Magazine*, for example, Gould provided an inventory of television's strengths and weaknesses (see Gould 2002: 221–227). At the top of his list were the special programming events, including broadcast productions of the leading dramatists of the day, as well as nonfiction media events, such as the coronation of Queen Elizabeth II, the World Series, and the national political conventions (Dayan and Katz 1992). At the bottom of his list were the television comedies, including the variety shows and the situation comedies, which Gould felt were produced too frequently to allow any sustained creativity. Gould liked the hour-long television dramas far more than the made-for-television movies, and he found the primary attraction of the quiz shows to be the low cost of their production. He was generally disappointed with television news, which offered "no sustained coverage in depth, little helpful evaluation of the significance of the headline, and virtually no interpretive commentary to stimulate the viewer to do some thinking for himself" (Gould 2002: 225). But he had higher hopes for the opinion formats that were emerging on many of the networks.

See It Now, Meet the Press, and the Development of Television Commentary

While Gould may have been disappointed with regular television news broadcasts, he thought much more highly of the weekly news reviews. By far the best of this group of shows was Edward Murrow's *See It Now*, which Gould described as the only news program that came close to the BBC's standard of "truly creative journalism" (Gould 2002: 213).[20] While *See It Now* is best remembered for a series of programs in 1953 and 1954 that criticized Senator Joseph McCarthy's anticommunist tactics, Gould was already praising its virtues after the first broadcast of the show in November 1951. He continued to applaud the show for its analysis and commentary, specifically for the fact that it was "less concerned with headlines than with the background of events" (Gould 2002: 207). *See It Now* was by far the most critically acclaimed news program during television's first decade, winning Emmy Awards every year it was broadcast.

By the time *See It Now* ceased production in 1958, the show had established a format for the serious news magazine show that has continued to this day. *CBS Reports* (1959), *The NBC White Paper* (1960), and *David Brinkley's Journal* (1961) all drew their format and their inspiration from Murrow's *See It Now*. So, too, did *60 Minutes*, which would become the most famous news magazine program in American television history. When CBS began broadcasting the show in 1968, its executive producer was Don Hewitt, who had directed *See It Now* for a number of years (McNeil 1996: 742).

The other important development in 1950s television was the establishment of the political interview shows, which Gould (2002: 225) described as "consistently interesting." Most praiseworthy among these shows was *Meet the Press*, which won a Peabody Award in 1952.[21] CBS developed its own political interview show, *Face the Nation*, in 1954, while ABC waited until 1960 to develop its version of the political interview show, *Issues and Answers*. Other early interview shows focused on business industry leaders (e.g., Dumont's *Meet the Boss*), athletes (NBC's *Meet the Champions*), and academics

(ABC's *Meet the Professor*).[22] But it was the political interview show that has proven to have the greatest durability. Perhaps more than any other, these shows demonstrated the promising contribution that television could make to the space of opinion.

Several factors help to explain why the political interview shows were adopted by all the television networks. First, and probably most important, was that the shows tended to feature political elites and policy makers. *Meet the Press* established this practice early on by stacking its guest list with important government officials; according to Bernhard (1999: 50), 85 percent of the show's guests during the 1950s were government officials. Because the programs were stacked with the official sources and government officials who are so highly prized by journalists, the shows quickly developed a journalistic prestige that was mostly withheld from the other television offerings. Additionally, and particularly during television's early years, there was a sense that politicians were not able to hide their true selves from the camera in the same way they might be able to do in newspaper interviews. As *Meet the Press* producer Lawrence Spivak commented, "TV has an almost infrared quality of getting beneath the skin of an interviewee" (quoted in Bernhard 1999: 52).

Another feature of the political interview shows was the way they put journalists and politicians into direct conversation with one another. This was important for the status and influence of the journalistic field because it brought journalism closer to the political field, while also guaranteeing a measure of autonomy from the state. In print media, as we have seen, columnists often had difficulties writing about the conversations they had with political officials without appearing too dependent on those officials. But television held out a promise to political figures that was lacking in print: namely, the possibility of directly addressing a national audience and thereby helping to cultivate their own political celebrity. This allowed the journalists moderating the programs to adopt a more critical and combative style without fear that their guests would stop accepting invitations to appear. Of course, all of this was framed in terms of the public interest. In the beginning of each episode of *Meet the Press*, for example, viewers were reminded that "questions do not necessarily reveal [the reporters'] point of view—it's their way of getting a story for you" (quoted in Doherty 2003: 85; see also Clayman and Heritage 2002).

To see an example of how the interview shows were able to maintain a critical, independent attitude while continuing to attract important political guests, we can consider the case of Senator Joseph McCarthy. McCarthy appeared on *Meet the Press* seven times between 1950 and 1954, in addition to multiple appearances on *Chronoscope*, *Face the Nation*, and *American Forum on the Air* (Bernhard 1999: 166–168; Doherty 2003: 85–89). From his first appearance to his last, the senator was consistently challenged to defend his record, his tactics, and his honesty, while being pressed to provide concrete details that might support his charges about communist infiltration into key American institutions. McCarthy was interrupted, corrected, and, by 1954, openly derided by the moderators of these programs. When the interview shows did not have McCarthy as a guest, they often asked the guests they did have about McCarthy, and they openly courted McCarthy's political opponents from the Senate to appear on the show (Doherty 2003: 88). Despite this challenging reception, however, McCarthy continued to return to the interview shows, as have politicians ever since.

By 1960, television had established itself as perhaps the most important place for political opinion and commentary. Indeed, every U.S. president since John F. Kennedy has appeared on *Meet the Press*; so, too, have the leaders of thirty-two different nations, as well as hundreds of politicians and journalists. The high-profile guests, the display of journalistic critique and autonomy, and the belief that the television interview is a window into the psyche of political leaders have all combined to create a situation where the interview shows are newsworthy events in their own right. The major newspapers write dozens of articles every week about things that are said on these programs and the guests who are scheduled to appear on them. In many ways, in fact, the political news cycle is set each Sunday by the events that take place on these political interview programs, and this has been the case since the early 1960s.

Conversations with Walter Lippmann

In light of television's increasing agenda-setting power, the print columnists who had previously dominated the space of media commentary were faced with a simple choice: either secure a spot on television or become more marginal in the space of opinion. This new state of play was signaled by Walter Lippmann's decision to appear on television. When he was approached by Fred Friendly in early 1960 and asked to participate on a CBS interview program, Lippmann initially declined the offer, since he believed that the only way to save television from its wretchedness was to establish a noncommercial public television network (Steel 1999: 516–517). Friendly persisted, however, and eventually managed to convince Lippmann to do a one-hour interview. For Lippmann's part, he managed to get Friendly to agree that the program would be broadcast only if Lippmann was happy with the finished product; Friendly also agreed, on Lippmann's insistence, that no commercials would interrupt the program (Steel 1999: 517).

CBS had modest goals for the program. Indeed, the primary interest was not to make money from the program or to attract a large mass audience. What CBS really wanted was the prestige payoff from a symbolic association with Lippmann. After all, CBS had ended production of its most prestigious news show, *See It Now*, and it was struggling to keep up with NBC, whose *Meet the Press* and *The Huntley-Brinkley Report* were the clear leaders in their respective genres. Howard K. Smith, the moderator of *Face the Nation*, was chosen to interview Lippmann, and the show was broadcast in August 1960. Ultimately, the public response to the Lippmann interview was much greater than CBS had anticipated: the program was lauded in front-page stories across the nation, with commentators suggesting that television might finally have come of age as a serious medium (Steel 1999: 517), and Lippmann received a Peabody Award for the program in 1962, adding it to the two Pulitzer Prizes he had won.

In light of this success, CBS persuaded Lippmann to participate in six more interviews, paying him $15,000 for each interview (Steel 1999: 517). And so it followed that between August 1960 and February 1965, CBS News broadcast a total of seven hour-length television interviews with Walter Lippmann. The setting was simple. The interview would take place in Lippmann's library or at his summer home in Maine. CBS would send one of its most esteemed journalists, such as Walter Cronkite or Eric Sevareid, who would ask Lippmann questions about the events of the day. Lippmann spent most of his time engaged in commentary about foreign affairs and the Cold War, but he also spoke about economic policy, race relations, domestic politics, and American history, as well as providing more abstract commentary on the nature of power and the qualities of effective leadership.

While the Lippmann interviews were never incorporated into regular programming, they nevertheless had a powerful impact on the development of television commentary. Symbolically, the power of the Lippmann interviews was their display of two journalists engaged in discussion about important public matters. There were no interviews of politicians. There was only discussion and commentary between journalists. This brought television commentary more into line with what was happening in the newspapers and the magazines, in the sense that it placed journalists at the center of the space of commentary. But television improved on print because it placed its commentaries within *conversations*, where two (or more) individuals were engaged in a public debate and discussion about the meaning and significance of the most important events of the day. In addition, the Lippmann interviews placed the print columnists and the television journalists into direct conversation with one another in a way that increased the autonomy, the prestige, and the influence of both.

By the end of the 1960s, television executives were trying to figure out how to incorporate commentary into their regular news broadcasts. ABC began adding commentaries to its nightly news broadcasts in 1967; in 1969, the network hired Howard K. Smith to coanchor the news and provide regular commentaries at the end of the program (Alterman 1999: 62). CBS quickly followed suit, relying on Eric Sevareid to close out the broadcast with political and social commentary (Alterman 1999: 62). These commentaries were a regular feature of the nightly news until the late 1970s, when they began to fall out of favor.[23]

Agronsky and Company and Other Early Pundit Shows

For a variety of reasons, the nightly news commentaries were not the best way to incorporate opinion into the television news space. For one thing, news executives were never entirely comfortable with the nightly television commentaries because the commentators were too unpredictable and their comments often provoked public complaint and criticism (Alterman 1999: 62). Furthermore, the appearance of commentators on the nightly news threatened television's practices of journalistic objectivity, which tended to rely on the visual naturalism of interviews and on-the-scene reporting to legitimate their authority (Fiske 1987; Lewis 1991; Jacobs 1996; Morse 2004). As a communicative style, the choice of direct address (as opposed to a more dialogical, conversational format) failed to take advantage of the distinctive innovations that television commentary had developed in its news magazine programs and interview shows. In this choice of communicative style, the nightly news commentators were no different than the print columnists. If anything, the television commentators were actually at a symbolic disadvantage because their New York location prevented them from establishing the insider connections that the Washington-based print columnists had so successfully developed and used to establish their authority.

To realize the potential that the Lippmann interviews had suggested, broadcasters needed to return to a format where columnists and other pundits argued among themselves about the events of the day. This was the best way to distinguish their product from print, and it was the best way to increase the journalistic autonomy and the public influence of television pundits. By 1970, there were already several different versions of this type of format in production. *Washington Week in Review* was established in 1967 as a weekly panel show where four journalists and a moderator discussed the major news events of the week. The program has been broadcast on PBS since January 1969, and it is the longest running public affairs program on that network. A few years earlier, in 1966, *Firing Line* had established a more political and partisan version of the panel show. Hosted by William F. Buckley, the conservative commentator and the founding editor of *National Review*, the show matched Buckley against leading political figures and intellectuals from the liberal-left, such as Noam Chomsky, John Kenneth Galbraith, James Farmer, and Sidney Hook. *Firing Line* demonstrated the entertainment value of more confrontational political talk shows, and when PBS picked the program up for national syndication in 1971, it became the first show of its kind to establish a national audience.

The television program that had the greatest influence on the future of broadcast commentary, however, was *Agronsky and Company*. The show was hosted by Martin Agronsky, whose previous credits as a journalist and commentator included stints as a reporter for the *Palestine Post*, as the foreign correspondent for ABC Radio who covered the Eichmann trial, and as a moderator for the CBS political talk show *Face the Nation*. He began hosting *Agronsky and Company* in 1969. The program was broadcast on commercial stations owned by the Washington Post Company and was also picked up by many PBS affiliates (Nimmo and Combs 1992: 126).

As compared with the other early pundit shows, *Agronsky and Company* did not bring guests onto the program, nor did it include anyone outside the journalistic field. The discussions were less orderly than those on *Meet the Press* or *Washington Week in Review*, with many more interruptions, arguments, and disputes (Nimmo and Combs 1999: 127). Additionally, the show was more character driven, in a way that increased its entertainment value and encouraged viewers to identify with specific characters. As Alterman (1999: 62) has described it, "the idea was that instead of merely relaying information, each pundit would portray himself as a stock character, thereby giving viewers a chance to identify, either positively or negatively, with an entertainment personality rather than just a boring journalist." Initially, there were four panelists, or "characters":

- James J. Kilpatrick wrote one of the most popular conservative syndicated political columns in the country, "A Conservative View." Kilpatrick was also the conservative commentator on the "Point/Counterpoint" segment of *60 Minutes*, from 1971–1979. On *Agronsky and Company*, he played the part of the "courtly Southern gentleman, proud-to-be-a-Confederate." (Alterman 1999: 64)
- Carl Rowan wrote a syndicated column for the *Chicago Sun-Times*, and had held positions in the Kennedy and Johnson administrations. Rowan, who was the most visible African-American journalist in the nation, was the show's Great Society advocate, and a frequent foil to Kilpatrick in discussion about domestic politics and race relations.
- Hugh Sidey, who was the White House correspondent for *Time* magazine, played the part of the Washington insider.
- Peter Lisagor was the Washington bureau chief and syndicated political columnist for *Chicago Daily News*. A regular guest on *Meet the Press*, *Face the Nation*, and *Washington Week in Review*, Lisagor played the part of the hard-boiled, old-school journalist. (Alterman 1999: 63)

More than any show before it, *Agronsky and Company* was able to establish a format that transformed the field of media commentary into an entertaining, synergistic, multimedia space. Print columnists played a central role on *Agronsky and Company*, and they were able to use their appearances on the program as a springboard to additional television appearances, better name recognition, and increased speaking fees on the lecture circuit. *Agronsky and Company* also presented the print columnists with a new way to build their reputations, which was different from the Lippmann era and its emphasis on scholarly detachment or insider connections. On *Agronsky and Company*, it did not really matter who you knew; what was valued was the pithy argument, the witty put-down, and the ability to talk about politics without actually talking to politicians. The regular appearances on television also helped—not only by introducing the columnists to a new audience but also by allowing their loyal readers to develop a deeper familiarity with the columnist.

Nowhere was the new communicative style and positioning of the multimedia celebrity columnist more apparent than with the rise of George Will.[24] Initially hired as an editor and Washington correspondent for Buckley's *National Review* in 1973, Will also had the good fortune, early in his career, to land positions as a syndicated columnist for the *Washington Post* and as a contributing editor for *Newsweek* magazine. In fact, Will was the first choice of the *New York Times* when they decided to expand their op-ed page and add a conservative columnist, ultimately settling for William Safire (Diamond 1993: 120). But Will's big break came in 1976, when, following the death of Peter Lisagor, he became a regular panelist on *Agronsky and Company*. Will soon came to dominate the show, perfecting his persona as the erudite and witty new voice of American conservatism. Will used his initial successes on television to secure even better television appearances. ABC hired him in 1981 as a regular panelist on *This Week with David Brinkley* and also relied on his expert commentary on *Nightline* and *The ABC Evening News*.

A comparison of Will and Lippmann helps to shed light on some of the key changes that had occurred by the 1980s in the field of media commentary. For the most part, Lippmann had developed his arguments in books, as well as in his contributions to longform journalism outlets such as the *New Republic*. His columns were a vehicle for conveying his public philosophy to a broader public audience and for demonstrating how that philosophy could be effectively applied to an analysis of the day's events. Television was something Lippmann entered with serious reservations, and it was an activity he kept largely separate from his other acts of commentary. George Will, by contrast, entered into television commentary without reservation, and he used his other media activities as a way of supplementing his television celebrity. Furthermore, even though Will had a doctorate in political philosophy from Princeton, he did not generally develop his arguments in books, relying instead on his columns and his television appearances.

The relationship between books, columns, and television was one of the most telling things that had changed by the 1980s in the world of commentary. While George Will has published eleven books, seven of them are collections of his *Newsweek* and *Washington Post* columns and serve primarily to enhance his intellectual authority rather than to develop his ideas in a more extended or reflective way. Two of his books are about baseball, and the remaining two are more serious and reflective books. To be fair, Lippmann also published many books that consisted of collections of previous articles, speeches, and columns: thirteen in total. But Lippmann published ten major works that were conceived and written originally as books. In addition, Lippmann published many of his original books before he had achieved fame as a columnist. Two of his books were published before he began his job as editor at the *New Republic*, four were published before he began writing his column for the *New York World*, and six were written before he began his Pulitzer Prize–winning column, "Today and Tomorrow." George Will did not publish his first original book until 1983, when he was already a famous columnist and a media celebrity. Furthermore, Lippmann's books were taken up by the leading philosophers and intellectuals of the day in a way that Will's have never been. What all of this demonstrates is the way that the practice of media commentary had, by the 1980s, become more separated from the academic world of books.

Television Embraces Opinion, 1980–Present

By 1980, then, television had managed to effect some significant changes in the structure and hierarchy of the world of media commentary. Print columnists were desperate to get regular spots on television and were primarily interested in magazine and book writing as part of a synergistic strategy for increasing their multimedia celebrity. The newspapers that employed these columnists were in on the game—led by the *Washington Post*, which owned *Agronsky and Company* and used the show as a platform for launching its newspaper columnists into multimedia celebrity (Alterman 1999: 152). These developments were in place well before the rise of cable news in the 1980s and 1990s, though the development of cable news networks certainly magnified and accelerated some of these trends.

While the basic formats for television commentary were already in place by 1980, however, the shows that carried them did not tend to be terribly powerful at generating viewer ratings and thus were not important to the programming strategies of television executives. In fact, with the exception of *Meet the Press* and the other Sunday morning talk shows, most of these new formats for television commentary were developed for a smaller and more exclusive market, and they were usually broadcast on public television. In other words, developments in the world of television commentary took place mostly under the radar, with the exception of the political (and, occasionally, intellectual) elites who were infatuated with the new programs. This began to change in the 1980s, however, as opinion and commentary became more important to the programming strategies of television industry executives.

Nightline

Nightline began in 1979 as a fifteen-minute nightly update on the Iranian hostage situation. Hosted by ABC's chief diplomatic correspondent, Ted Koppel, the ratings for this show were much higher than expected.[25] This led ABC executives to turn the program into a thirty-minute program broadcast every weeknight at 11:30 P.M.[26] As the hostage crisis dragged on, the show quickly broadened its focus to cover other crises, breaking news, and media events, both domestic and international. Notable episodes (often broadcast on-site) covered topics such as South African apartheid, the Arab-Israeli conflict, the student demonstrations at Tiananmen Square, the 1991 Gulf War, and the 1993 attempted coup in Russia. *Nightline* has won every major award in broadcast journalism, including nine Peabody Awards.

As a news format, *Nightline* combined elements of the panel show and the news magazine, while adding innovations of its own. Similar to the news magazines, topics would usually be introduced with a short background piece, written and produced by one of the news correspondents.[27] From there, the episode would usually move to a panel discussion between the host, one or more politicians or "newsmakers," and perhaps a few journalists or expert commentators. But *Nightline* added several new features as well. First, it relied on satellite technology to bring together guests from around the world in its panel discussion. Second, *Nightline* would often broadcast on location, in a way that borrowed from the most compelling feature of standard television journalism, yet modified for the purposes of discussion and commentary. Third, *Nightline* was quite successful in the periodic use of a town meeting format, which combined the panel discussion with live audience participation. All of these innovations would be adopted in subsequent years, particularly by the new cable television news networks.

Cable News Networks

From its beginning, cable television news has privileged commentary over reporting as a way to maximize the broadcast time it can extract from a single piece of reporting. This can be seen in the integral role played by commentary in the basic news format developed by CNN in the 1980s—the "rolling update." The rolling update had three parts (Hartley 2001: 121). First and most simply, CNN rebroadcast the same stories repeatedly over the course of two or three days. In addition, CNN treated each new development of a continuing story as a news event in itself. This involved reviewing the previous events in the story and then updating them with the new event. Finally, after the new event had been added to the ongoing story, CNN followed this with an extended studio discussion about the new event and its meaning, usually by CNN correspondents and the occasional academic expert. In this way, CNN was able to incorporate the panel show into its routine news broadcasts.

By the late 1980s, however, CNN had moved away from general news programs toward branded shows, particularly during the prime-time slots. The first big success came with *Larry King Live*, which premiered weeknights on CNN beginning in 1985 and has been among CNN's most watched programs ever since, with approximately 1 million viewers each evening. But even before Larry King's program, CNN had already created a number of prime-time programs devoted to political commentary, with many of these programs hiring talent away from the panel discussion programs on PBS. Rowland Evans and Robert Novak were hired right away, bringing their nationally syndicated *Evans and Novak* to the fledgling network, where it would be broadcast on Saturday evenings. Novak was also one of the original panelists for *The Capital Gang*, which was also broadcast on Saturday evenings beginning in 1988. Other panelists on this program included Pat Buchanan, who had been a regular on *The McLaughlin Group*, one of the most influential political talk shows broadcast on PBS in the early 1980s; Al Hunt, a *Wall Street Journal* political correspondent who was a regular on the PBS program *Washington Week in Review*; and Mark Shields, a liberal columnist for the *Washington Post* who was a regular commentator on PBS's *McNeil/Lehrer NewsHour*.

But the most important and influential of CNN's prime-time programs was *Crossfire*. The show was created in 1982 and initially hosted by Tom Braden and Pat Buchanan, who had created a radio version of the program in Washington, D.C., in 1977. Robert Novak became a cohost of the program in 1985, when Buchanan accepted a position as communication director in the Reagan White House. Braden was replaced in 1989 by Michael Kinsley, who at the time was editor of the *New Republic* and a columnist for *Time* magazine. Other cohosts of the show have included a number of individuals who seem to cycle in and out of the world of television commentary and political consulting.[28]

A typical episode of *Crossfire* would consist of liberal and conservative cohosts, as well as a liberal and a conservative guest. One of the cohosts would begin by reading a very short piece of news from the previous day's events, as a way of setting the context for the discussion to follow. The other cohost would then begin by addressing one of the guests, and the discussion would commence from there. In general, the liberal host asked questions of the conservative guest, while the conservative host would concentrate on the liberal guest. Questions were generally asked in a confrontational way, which emphasized the differences between conservative and liberal positions without leaving much room for overlap, agreement, or complexity. The hosts interrupted the guests frequently, rarely allowing them to speak for more than ten or fifteen seconds, unless the topic of the day concerned foreign affairs, in which case the guest list often included academic experts and foreign diplomats who tended to be given more time to answer the questions. After the discussion, the two hosts would end the show with a thirty-second summary of what had transpired, in the process translating the proceedings into two clear and opposing positions.

Crossfire managed to combine elements from previous shows in a new and compelling way, while creating a program that was more directly partisan in tone and explicitly connected to the political field. Like *Agronsky and Company* and *The McLaughlin Group*, it was a more raucous discussion, where hosts and guests interrupted each other frequently and arguments were made through exaggeration and hyperbole. Like the Sunday talk shows, it brought in guests directly from the political field, while supplementing those individuals with the occasional academic expert and journalist. Like the "Point/Counterpoint" segment of *60 Minutes*, it was organized around competing "liberal" and "conservative" viewpoints. Like *Nightline*, it was broadcast nightly, enabling it to remain current and to provide a real alternative to the nightly news.

As new cable news networks rose up to compete with CNN, they looked to *Crossfire* as the model for their prime-time programming. The most successful of the new cable networks was Fox News Channel, which was launched in 1996.[29] Led by Roger Ailes, who had served as a media consultant for Presidents Nixon, Reagan, and Bush, Fox News established a number of prime-time programs that resembled *Crossfire*. *Hannity & Colmes* was the most similar in format, with conservative and liberal cohosts, typically discussing politics and social issues with a liberal and a conservative guest. Unlike *Crossfire*, however, *Hannity & Colmes* ran for a full hour, allowing the show to cover several topics in a single evening. Fox News also allotted sixty minutes for the other key program in its primetime lineup, *The O'Reilly Factor*. Both shows attracted larger ratings than *Crossfire* within a relatively short time period; by 2002, both Hannity and O'Reilly had each established their own nationally syndicated radio talk shows, which helped them continue to build their brands and solidify the loyalty of their audience.[30] This move toward multimedia synergy would increasingly come to define the space of media commentary by the beginning of the twenty-first century.

Another factor that encouraged a shift in the genre practices of the television opinion programs—and that helped Fox News Channel's offerings in particular—was the industry trend toward audience segmentation. By the mid-1980s, audience fragmentation had led to a marked shift in programming and advertising strategies, away from general-interest media and toward "segment-making media" (Turow 1997). What this meant was that media executives (and the advertisers that supported them) began to tailor their programming for niche audiences, who would be more intensely committed to specific types of content. In the process, media channels often concentrated on a single type of content, hoping to cater to relatively homogeneous interpretive communities, who they imagined consumed little else beyond their favorite channels (Webster 2005: 369).

One of the most effective examples of this kind of niche programming strategy was the creation of a "conservative media establishment" in the 1980s and 1990s, which centered around the radio broadcasts of Rush Limbaugh, the television broadcasts of Fox News, and the editorial page of the *Wall Street Journal* (Jamieson and Cappella 2008). Aided by the elimination of the Fairness Doctrine in 1985, conservative radio talk shows had quickly established themselves as a major new genre, almost single-handedly reviving AM radio in the United States. Limbaugh's program was the most successful and influential of these new shows. Establishing his nationally syndicated radio show in 1988, Limbaugh already had a weekly audience in excess of 5 million by 1990, a large proportion of whom were intensely committed loyalists of the program.[31]

With Limbaugh's success pointing to the existence of a market for conservative opinion, Fox News adapted many of the key characteristics of conservative talk radio for its prime-time opinion programs. As Jamieson and Cappella (2008) argue, this included a defense of conservatism, the identification of the Reagan legacy as the sacred center of the conservative movement, a narrative that defined the "liberal elite" as the enemy of the nation, and a corresponding narrative about the liberal bias of the mainstream media. As we will see clearly in chapter 7, these features all figure prominently in the commentaries and debates that appeared on *Hannity & Colmes*.

For the opinion space as a whole, the most significant new discursive feature of conservative talk radio and Fox News's opinion programs was the narrative about mainstream media bias. This narrative introduced a certain kind of media metacommentary into the space of opinion, as a more central part of the discourse of television opinion programming. This discourse of media criticism proliferated, as it was incorporated into still newer formats that appeared on cable television. *The Daily Show with Jon Stewart*, which first appeared on cable television's The Comedy Channel in 1999, is in large part an extended critique of the opinion programs that appear on cable television, most notably those on CNN and Fox News. A spin-off from that show, *The Colbert Report*, is essentially a parody of Fox News Channel's most popular program, *The O'Reilly Factor*. Similarly, the resurgent program offerings on cable news channel MSNBC offer frequent criticisms of the opinion programs on cable television, most notably those airing on Fox News. We discuss this phenomenon of nested media metacommentary further in chapter 9. For now, what we want to emphasize is the way that the opinion space is expanding, diversifying, and becoming more densely (as well as more critically) interconnected. These trends have been supported by another development as well: specifically, the incorporation of the Internet into the space of opinion.

The Internet and Multimedia Synergy: The Second Golden Age of the Columnist

Since the late 1990s, the circulation of media opinion and commentary has benefited significantly from the growth of the Internet. With the 1993 release of Mosaic and the 1995 release of Microsoft's Internet Explorer, easy-to-use graphical web browsers became widely available, and the amount of Internet content exploded. Between 1993 and 1997, the number of Web sites increased from 150 to 2.45 million, and by the end of the twentieth century, more than 40 percent of the U.S. adult population was using the Internet (Boczkowski 2005: 7). Seeing this trend and noticing that online advertising revenues were increasing at a similar rate, newspapers looked to the Internet as a new and lucrative site where they could reinvigorate their product and grow their audience. By 1999, in fact, all but two of the largest 100 U.S. daily papers had established an online edition of their paper (Boczkowski 2005: 8).

While newspapers initially responded to the online possibilities by simply repackaging print stories for their online editions, they eventually saw that they could use their online papers to move away from fixed production cycles and produce content in a more constant way that would allow them to compete more effectively with television.[32] This began with the practice of adding news updates in the afternoons and during periods of breaking news.[33] Next was the establishment of online special features, which usually consisted of a more in-depth look (including analysis and commentary) at the major event of the day.[34] A third practice, spearheaded by Washingtonpost.com and quickly copied by the other elite papers, was the creation of new columns that were exclusive to the online paper and that focused primarily on politics and public policy. A fourth practice was the use of technology that allowed online readers to e-mail specific articles of interest to their friends and acquaintances. Fifth, newspapers created online spaces for user-authored content, typically in the form of Internet forums, chat rooms, and Weblogs.

Among the different online developments, the user-authored content proved to be the most consequential for increasing the influence and circulation of media commentary. Importantly, it was not just the mainstream newspapers and television stations that were creating forums and Weblogs for individuals to participate in discussion about the news of the day. Even more significant, perhaps, were the blogs that developed outside the established news organizations. Web sites like Daily Kos, Huffington Post, Instapundit, and Talking Points Memo created intensely interactive spaces of media commentary, which were updated almost continuously. Importantly, the initial point of departure for a new discussion was more often than not a comment on something that was said or written in the mainstream spaces of media commentary, with a hyperlink to the original provided (Johnson and Kaye 2004; Wallstein 2007).

The creators of the most influential blogs were drawn from many different points in the media space. For those interested in grassroots activism, the most exciting thing about the blog phenomenon has been the way that it has allowed important new voices to enter the space of opinion without having to pass through the gatekeepers of the establishment media. The best example of this phenomenon is Markos Moulitsas, the founder of Daily Kos, who has become an important voice for the progressive, grassroots wing of the Democratic Party and enjoys a daily readership in excess of 500,000. On the other side of the political spectrum is Glenn Reynolds, a University of Tennessee law professor and the creator of Instapundit, who has become an influential voice of conservative libertarianism, with an average daily readership of more than 250,000. But many other important blogs were created by individuals who already had a connection to the more mainstream spaces of media commentary. Arianna Huffington, the founder of HuffingtonPost.com, was a regular guest on radio and television political talks shows before her entry into the world of Internet commentary. Andrew Sullivan had worked at a variety of news magazines, including a stint as editor of the *New Republic*, before he created his extremely popular blog, The Daily Dish. And as political blogs became a generalized presence in the space of opinion, many of the leading columnists and television commentators established their own blogs, with notable examples including those of Chris Matthews (MSNBC), Paul Krugman (*New York Times*), and Dan Froomkin (*Washington Post*).

While the rise of blogs have clearly opened up the spaces of media commentary to new voices and created new venues for participation by ordinary citizens, another important effect has been to dramatically increase the visibility and the public presence of the major newspaper columnists, television commentators, and op-ed writers. Columnists writing for the major papers can now expect that each new column they write will be e-mailed by thousands of users and become the object of significant amounts of commentary in the major political blogs of the day. The same is true of the hosts of the most popular television commentary and interview shows, whose questioning styles and political talking points are interrogated endlessly on the Internet. More and more frequently, these blog commentaries are circulating back up to the major print and television media, in a way that turns commentary about their original commentaries into news events in their own right. The result is name recognition and a following for print columnists that have not been seen since the days of Lippmann, and name recognition for the television hosts that is probably unprecedented in media history.

But this second golden age of the columnist does not only show itself in the greater public attention paid to the major television pundits and newspaper columnists; it also extends to include the guest voices who get an article published on the op-ed page or appear as an expert (or an activist) on one of the prime-time television programs. Today, the well-placed op-ed or television appearance can provide far more than the proverbial fifteen minutes of fame. By the time it has been e-mailed among readers, incorporated into blog commentaries, and filtered back up into the mainstream media for a second round of publicity, the guest appearance in the world of media commentary may result in a decision to write more op-eds, to set up a Web site of one's own (including a blog, of course), to find an agent who can help with the possibility of another media appearance, or to abandon academia for one of the many think tanks that are more directly organized to get their experts and researchers placed into the world of media commentary and punditry.

The likely result of all this is a greatly expanded universe of people who want to participate in the space of media opinion and commentary. How this shapes (or does not shape) the world of opinion is a critical empirical question, which we take up in subsequent chapters. Before beginning our empirical analysis, however, we want to end this chapter by pointing to two points of tension that emerge from the history of opinion—tensions that are potentially consequential for understanding how mediated deliberation works in the space of opinion. These are the tension between complexity and connectivity and the tension between influence and autonomy.

Complexity and Connectivity

In Lippmann's vision of effective commentary, a crucial role of the columnist was to convey to his readers (including representatives of the state) the complexity surrounding an issue, the relative advantages and disadvantages of various approaches to the problem, and the unintended consequences of different policy choices. To be sure, Lippmann's vision has not always been followed in practice. It is probably more useful to think about a continuum of complexity, ranging from the nuanced to the formulaic—a continuum that also has a relational dynamic so that "more complex" is always defined in terms of a "less complex" media text. Historically, for example, the news magazines developed as a response to a perceived lack of complexity in the newspapers. A half century later, the rise of television gave newspapers an opportunity to offer their op-ed page as a relatively more nuanced set of commentaries than those one was likely to find on the screen. And during the last thirty years, the rise of more politically aligned television formats has allowed the more traditional television formats (the Sunday morning talk shows, the *Lehrer News-Hour*) to position themselves as the protectors of complexity. None of this is meant to suggest that complexity has disappeared from the spaces of media opinion or that the attribution of complexity has stopped functioning as a rhetorical marker of distinction. But it is likely, given the post-1980s history we have described in this chapter, that the ideal of complexity is now competing with other values, particularly in the television formats.

Perhaps the most serious alternative that competes with the ideal of complexity is the idea of connectivity, that is, that the most effective and important media commentaries are the ones that circulate widely as part of a broad public conversation. To be sure, it is possible to convey complexity while also achieving broad circulation. And there is also a continuum of circulation to be considered, which ranges from the op-ed column that disappears from public attention almost immediately to the comment that goes viral on multiple media platforms, including print, television, and Internet. But the rise of television does seem to have had the effect of encouraging circulation for its own sake, independent of the goal of complexity. This is not only because television has the largest audience but also because the figures who appear on television have tended to be the most successful at branding themselves as public commentators across a broad range of connected media platforms. Thus, while we see complexity and connectivity as analytically distinct views of what constitutes "effective commentary," and while the relationship they have with each other remains an open empirical question, prima facie, the history of opinion we have chronicled in this chapter suggests that there may well be a tension between them.

Influence and Autonomy

There are similar tensions discernible between the goals of influence and autonomy. One of the most compelling features of Lippmann's career as a columnist was his ability to be politically influential while maintaining his own intellectual autonomy. But this combination has proven to be difficult to master for most, and it is unevenly distributed across the opinion space. For example, politicians are clearly important actors in the opinion space, and they have a lot of political influence as state officials, but their status as party leaders places significant limits on their autonomy. Academics are careful to maintain their autonomy when they enter the opinion space, but their larger public influence is much less obvious. Historically, columnists seem to have been the most successful at combining autonomy and influence, but even here the range of action is limited by the format in which a columnist happens to be located, with autonomy generally declining as one moves from the elite newspaper column to the Sunday morning television program to the prime-time cable talk show. In general, the rise of television has increased the political influence of the opinion space, but it has tended to do so at the expense of autonomy. But here again, there are important differences that need to be explored since there is a range of possible combinations, depending on the speaker, the format, and—for the case of television—the other partners in conversation.

Just like the distinction between complexity and connectivity, then, influence and autonomy present two analytically distinct views of effective news commentary, and they have different points of connection to the history of media opinion. Indeed, the history suggests that these two principles have become increasingly differentiated; with the exception of the columnists, most other participants in the space of media opinion are forced to choose between influence and autonomy, and this choice is likely to shape the kinds of opinion formats in which they speak, as well as the nature of their speech. As the following chapter documents, there are concurrent processes of centralization and diversification in terms of who gets to speak, what they get to speak about, and how they get to make their arguments in the space of opinion.

Questions about autonomy, influence, complexity, and connectivity have clear implications for how we think about media, opinion formation, and processes of democratic deliberation. This is the central concern of the next chapter, where we trace understandings of the space of opinion as they have developed in debates about the relationship between media and democracy in a broad array of disciplines, including philosophy, political theory, sociology, and journalism. In particular, we ask why the model defined by journalistic objectivity continues to be so influential. More specifically, why does a model that emphasizes neutral media institutions and rational information-processing citizens continue to be so deeply held, despite the overwhelming evidence that it does a very poor job of explaining the way public communication actually unfolds in the space of opinion?

3 Media and Opinion Formation
TOWARD A NEW THEORY OF DELIBERATIVE POLITICS

IN HIS 2007 book *Assault on Reason*, Al Gore argues for the centrality of science and rationality for guiding public policy, and in this context, he emphasizes the importance of a robust news media to political democracy. This is an argument with which we agree; indeed, such an argument is familiar across the journalistic field, characterizing both the commercial mainstream media such as Fox News's claims to provide "fair and balanced" news and the critical stances of media watchdogs like Accuracy in Media (AIM), Fairness & Accuracy in Reporting (FAIR), and Media Matters for America (MMA). And although *Assault on Reason* is not primarily about the news media—rather, Gore criticizes the Bush administration for relying on political secrecy, a pervasive culture of anti-intellectualism, and calculated media manipulation to pursue the ideological and economic interests of a privileged few—nonetheless, the fundamental premise of the book is that the government of George W. Bush was profoundly antidemocratic because it undermined the ability of individual citizens to exercise their reason and make decisions that "contribute to the common wisdom" (2007: 100–102).

This idea—that citizens use their reason to deliberate and arrive at consensus on matters of common concern—is at the center of Gore's argument. In fact, he uses computers and parallel processing as a metaphor for representative democracy, describing how each individual "contributes to collective wisdom" by coming up with their own "portion" of the solution to social and political problems (2007: 102).[1] It is in this context that he decries media manipulation since the media's role is to provide facts so that self-determining individuals can deliberate about public matters. Our point is that Gore's argument represents a widespread moral assumption among political elites and broader publics; namely, that media should serve as a neutral vehicle for the dissemination of the information that citizens then use to act in political spaces imagined as being "outside" the media.[2]

From the perspective developed in this book, however, the paradox of Gore's position is that the public influence of *Assault on Reason* belies the ideas of both a neutral media and a rational, information-processing citizen. The impact of the book has much more to do with Al Gore's political biography and newfound personal charisma than with the information the book contributes. In fact, while *Assault on Reason* describes an idealized "marketplace of ideas" that selects the best and most useful ideas to inform the public good, Gore's actual practice points to quite a different dynamic of opinion formation. In publicizing the book in interviews for political talk shows and newspapers, for example, Gore has taken great pains to continue building the brand of Al Gore. This is a poignant narrative of a politician who, after losing the presidential election, manages to transform himself into an environmental activist, prize-winning author, and Nobel laureate, and who now serves as the embodiment of moral insight and personal redemption. Furthermore, when he appeared on television to market his book—typically, as a guest on one of the opinion programs rather than as an interviewee on the nightly news—Gore did not offer much in the way of neutral information. Rather, his appearances were marked by moral arguments, policy proposals, and compelling stories. The point is that Al Gore's media practices—the polemic, the publicity, and the performance—provide a superb example of an actually existing public sphere that works quite differently than the one based on an idealized image of a rational, deliberating citizen and a neutral media.

Why is there such a distance between Gore's normative vision and his actual media practice? We think the answer lies in the history of social theories about media, opinion formation, and deliberation, which we relate in detail in this chapter. This is a history of three waves of media theory—three models of media and deliberation—that have had very different public receptions.

The first wave of media theory defined much of the media scholarship produced prior to the 1960s. It emphasized the importance of objective news and neutral media for rational, information-processing citizens. The second wave of theory, which had roots at the University of Chicago in the 1920s, came to shape media research from the 1960s. This model emphasized the ways that small groups and social networks intervene between media and citizens to shape the nature of deliberation. It complicates the relationship between informal publics and media texts and suggests a variety of different roles and communicative formats through which journalism can fulfill its civic mission. More recent approaches have pushed this insight even further. In this third wave of media theory, a wide variety of aesthetic, agonistic, and performative structures are understood to help citizens identify with media intellectuals, which leads to increased levels of public involvement in the political public sphere. This cultural model of media and deliberation points to the importance of a variety of communicative formats for journalism, including the proliferating and innovative formats of the space of opinion.

Despite developments in theory, however, the small-group and cultural models have had little impact on public debates about media and deliberation. In fact, it is the rational, information-processing citizen model that enjoys the widest public acceptance, defining popular and professional perceptions of the appropriate role of the media in democratic societies, much as they are described in Gore's book. This is true despite the fact that this older model is sociologically thin and clearly does not describe the way people interact with the media in contemporary societies. Why is this so?

We argue it is because the model of the rational, information-processing citizen is central to the powerful project of professional journalism in the United States. That is why it continues to dominate public discourse despite the fact that its premises have long been falsified by empirical analyses. We sketch this history at the end of the chapter, describing how journalism responded to its uneasy professional status in the late nineteenth and early twentieth centuries by emphasizing its role in providing objective information to citizen-readers. We conclude that rather than a description of how democratic deliberation and opinion formation actually occur, the model of rational, information-seeking citizens is best understood as one intellectual position within a field of related intellectual positions, all of which compete to define the appropriate relationship between knowledge and power in large, complex democratic societies. When we make this analytical move, it becomes possible to comprehend the full range of media practices in contemporary publics and to consider how they might shape deliberation. It also becomes clear why the public journalism movement, which is the closest to the small-group model of deliberation and opinion formation, has been extremely controversial within journalistic circles (Benson 2009). The reason is that it challenges the dominant discourse that links journalism and democratic deliberation. No doubt a theory of democratic deliberation based on the cultural model would be even more problematic. If we do not balk at controversy, however, and if we recognize that the rational, information-seeking citizen model is only one vision of public communication among many that are available, then it becomes clear that Gore's normative vision simply mirrors the dominant public justifications for the media made by professional journalism, despite its obvious lack of fit with his actual media practice.

Direct/Indirect Deliberation and the Diversity of Media Formats

To organize our discussion of media and democratic deliberation, we pursue two related agendas in this chapter. First, we consider the relationship between mediated and direct deliberation. Like Habermas (1996: 373), Page (1996: 2–6), and Baker (2002: 125–128), we begin from the premise that direct deliberation, on its own, is insufficient to meet the demands of complex democracies and must be supplemented (if not, in fact, organized) by mediated deliberation. The empirical questions we ask in subsequent chapters of this book pursue this line of inquiry by assessing the structure and quality of mediated deliberation in a sample of opinion and commentary from the elite U.S. space of opinion. But our focus on mediated deliberation should not suggest that face-to-face communication is unimportant. Although we do not study direct deliberation empirically, it is critical to place an analysis of mediated deliberation in the context of all the different ways of thinking about the relationship between mediated and direct forms of public communication.

Second, since our research seeks to analyze the relationships between different kinds of journalistic practices and different kinds of media formats, our other goal in this chapter is to consider how the complexity of formats and practices influences mediated deliberation. As Page (1996: 125) has argued, an assessment of the success or failure of mediated deliberation requires "examining the whole range of communications media through which political ideas can flow." This means paying attention to the variety of formats, genres, and practices in the media field and the relationships between them.

We focus on opinionated news media formats as our central object, but this should not suggest that the space of opinion is the only place where mediated deliberation happens. Rather, we identify our analysis of the opinion space as one (albeit important) part of a wide range of mediated formats in which deliberation occurs. These include news reporting, as well as news commentary and opinion, entertainment formats, and social networking formats. Each of these different media formats has its own idealized conception of citizenship, its own way of defining civic responsibility or civic authority, and (typically) its own moral geographies that point to areas of perceived threat within the media space (Jacobs 2005: 83). Rather than uncritically reproducing received notions of civic worthiness and unworthiness, then, we seek to explore questions about changing moral geographies in the increasingly complex mediated publics of contemporary democratic life.

Media and Deliberation

For those who talk about communication and democracy, the value of public deliberation is central. This is the idea that democratic decisions require individuals to talk about matters of collective importance, so that after debating the merits of competing goals, commitments, and policies, they will be able to reach a reasoned consensus about the best course of action. The democratic value of deliberation of this kind is better public decisions, an increased level of public trust, and a heightened sensitivity toward competing perspectives.

Political theorists argue that deliberative practices must enact three principles of communication to be democratic: inclusion, reasonableness, and publicity (see Young 2000: 24–26).[3] For a public decision to be legitimate, it must include all who are affected by it, it must give a full hearing to all viewpoints, and importantly, those who participate must be reasonable. This last criterion means that participants must be willing to listen to others and be open to the possibility of being persuaded by the force of the better argument. Finally, discussions must also be conducted under conditions of maximum publicity within open and transparent forums, so that third parties can watch and hold speakers accountable for their arguments.

But these preconditions present a real problem for actual spaces of public communication. In the huge, complex democracies in which we live, the conditions for this kind of deliberation are extremely difficult to meet, since the possibility of any kind of widespread democratic deliberation is contingent upon the conditions and possibilities of widespread mediated communication (Page 1996: 4–5). Since it is the communicative capacities of mass media that connect the vast numbers of people of contemporary societies, the political question becomes: to what degree can democratic deliberation take place through the mass media? Or to put it another way, what is the role of the media in contemporary democratic deliberation?

On the question of transparency and publicity, there is probably no better place than the mass media for public discussions to take place. The media are stunningly powerful in their ability to publicize events, issues, and arguments.[4] On the issues of inclusion and reasonableness, however, the potential of mass media seems far more limited.

Media access is a scarce resource, and the ability to participate is distributed in an extremely limited and unequal way (see Bennett, Lawrence, and Livingston 2007, esp. pp. 46–57). This violates the principle of inclusion, because there are voices and perspectives that are consistently and nonrandomly left out. Inequality of media access also violates the principle of reasonableness, since even if participants are willing to be persuaded by the force of the better argument, most of them lack the regular access to the media that would allow such a possibility to be realized in practice. In addition, the lack of regular access makes it more likely that participants will put forth their position in the strongest form possible and without the expectation that they will become part of an ongoing deliberation about public policies or priorities. For the most part, this means that the media encourage serial monologue rather than dialogue. And when dialogue does emerge, it seems that participants are rarely open to the idea of being persuaded to adopt a different argument than the one with which they entered the conversation. This explains all the hand-wringing about the state of the media that one finds in current political criticism.[5]

But if the media are unable to support perfectly rational or perfectly inclusive deliberation, what role do they play in public opinion formation? What kind of political deliberation do they actually support? What kinds of civic practices do they assume for their readers and viewers? And how are the professional communicators that occupy most of the media space connected to the deliberative practices of ordinary citizens?

In part, the answers to these questions depend on which particular version of democratic theory one prefers. Different theories tell different stories and emphasize different elements in their prescription for the right relationship between media and deliberation. For participatory liberal theories of democracy, for example, it is desirable for the voices in the media to be as diverse and representative as possible—in terms of the information they provide, the different viewpoints they express, and the different interests that they represent (Ferree et al. 2002: 296–297). That is, journalists and their sources—as well as news commentators, columnists, and pundits—are expected to represent diverse interests and backgrounds in their persons and careers. This logic informs many of the critiques of mainstream journalism—specifically, its preferences for official sources and its dependence on the voices of the powerful (see, for example, Ericson, Baranek, and Chan 1989; Bennett 1990; Gans 1979). For the space of opinion, it is less clear whether this kind of criticism is valid. As we discussed in the previous chapter, the expansion of the op-ed pages of major newspapers, a policy that began at the *New York Times* in the 1970s, was designed to counter heavy reliance on journalists and official sources. The logic was that outsiders would make the opinion space more representative of wider public opinion. Whether this goal has been realized in practice is an empirical question we address in chapter 4. At the very least, though, the legitimating rhetorics of op-ed page editors seem to be consistent with the normative ideals of participatory liberal theories.

For representative and elitist theories of democracy, the diversity of public participation is a less important issue. These democratic theories understand that professional communicators and commentators are the major players in the public conversation. The role of professional communicators therefore should be to articulate the full range of official views on an issue. Ideally, the range of views presented will be proportional to the respective electoral power of each position. Elitist and representative theorists of democracy also prefer that professional communicators offer commentary and opinion in a detached style with the goal of encouraging a dialogue among the well informed (Ferree et al. 2002: 291–292; Baker 2002: 129–134). In other words, news professionals are expected to provide a fair and open space for the range of official views on an issue. In mainstream journalism, this amounts to a normative defense of the indexing theory of press-state relations (Bennett 1990), which argues that journalists calibrate their news coverage according to the range of views that are displayed by the key government officials for a given policy issue. The extent to which this kind of indexing occurs in the space of opinion is an empirical question to which we turn in the next three chapters. Our point here is that unlike liberal participatory theories, representative and elite theories of democracy typically envision practices of mediated deliberation where politicians, experts, and officials predominate.

Other theories of democracy evaluate the performance of mediated deliberation in still different terms, emphasizing the codes, narratives, and discourses through which media texts are produced. There are several threads of theory that converge around this idea. For republican visions of democracy, for example, mediated deliberation should maximize the production of common solidarities and collective narratives, a task that requires considerable collective reflection to reach a shared understanding of the collective good (Baker 2002: 138–143). Habermasian and neo-Habermasian theories of complex democracy also value these kinds of reflections about the public good, but they want to balance these reflections against the recognition that competing interests and competing groups are an inevitable part of public life, and thus they insist that nonideological forms of mediated deliberation must allow different groups to articulate their own discourses about the common good independently.[6] This is particularly important for groups that have been marginalized historically. Each group must be able to voice their own discourses independently and autonomously within the official mediated publics of civil society (see Baker 2002: 143–147; Fraser 1992; Jacobs 2000). Poststructural and critical theories of complex democracy also emphasize group autonomy and inclusion, but they extend this insight to include different forms of discursive creativity. In this way, they move beyond Habermas to insist that mediated deliberation must include more than rational-critical discourse and other expert rhetorics (Ferree et al. 2002: 306–315).

While these theories of complex democracy differ in important respects, what they all share is a vision of mediated deliberation that emphasizes that "the press should be thoughtfully discursive, not merely factually informative" (Baker 2002: 148). They also give greater weight to partisan styles of journalism than one finds in most normative arguments about media and democracy (Baker 2002: 163; also see Schudson 2008: 21–22). In our terms, then, these theories are interesting because they acknowledge both that there is a range of valuable media formats that can support democratic deliberation and that in the large culture we share, there is a complicated relationship between mediated and direct forms of deliberation. In so doing, they reveal a clear need to move beyond a model of neutral media and a rational, information-seeking citizen.

In what follows, we attempt to sort through these issues by outlining three ideal-typical models of media and deliberation. We begin with the model of the rational, information-seeking citizen, which continues to be publicly relevant even if it has little scholarly support. Our general criticism of this approach is that it is too rigid and sociologically thin. From there, we move to a model of small groups and informal publics, which does a much better job of thinking about the relationship between mediated and direct deliberation and points to the need for different communication styles and media formats. This model is consistent with the theories of complex democracy, which we discussed previously. Our main concern with this model is that it leaves the details of these different media formats underspecified, overly abstract, and insufficiently linked to the institutional and cultural history of the media organizations in which deliberation takes place. It also tends to place too strong a normative injunction against strategic communication, in a manner that is insufficiently attentive to the empirical realities of public communication or the current organization of the space of opinion. We correct for this with our third model, which offers a more cultural approach to the question of mediated and direct deliberation. This cultural model, which informs our own thinking about media and deliberation, connects the discursive creativity emphasized by some theories of complex democracy with the specific media formats that are available in the U.S. journalistic field.

The Rational, Information-Seeking Citizen

The first model of media and public opinion—and surely the most restrictive one—holds that rational citizens gather information from the news media and then deliberate with others about matters of common concern. The media's role in this process of opinion formation is to provide the informational infrastructure that supports individual decision making: individuals read newspapers, watch television, and browse the Internet to become better informed about public matters, to become better voters, to make more informed choices about public policies, and, occasionally, to more effectively engage in debate about public matters.

In many ways, the model of the rational, information-processing citizen emphasizes making decisions and choices. Deliberation may be a part of the process of making a decision, but ultimately what is important is that individuals decide what their preferences are and then act on those preferences. Voting, then, is probably the signal act for this model, by which all other civic and political activities can be judged. In voting, individuals gather as much information as they can about the competing candidates, they make a decision about which candidate they support, and then they act on that preference. The key issue is that they get accurate information, either from the media or from the discussions they have with others. In the end, the outcome of the vote is publicized, and individuals know how their own preferences compared with the preferences of others. This model of media performance is closely connected to the normative vision of liberal democratic theory, in which the extension and institutionalization of the vote is seen as the first and most important act of citizenship (see Dahl 2000; Held 2005).

While the model of the rational, information-processing citizen is clearly connected to the core democratic activity of voting, its logic was extended during the early decades of the twentieth century into many other parts of the public sphere through the development and institutionalization of polling techniques. With opinion polling, individuals are contacted and asked to state opinions or preferences about a particular issue, election, public policy, or product. These individual opinions are then aggregated and reported back, often through the media, as "public opinion." Polling extends the logic of the rational citizen into the everyday activities of civil society, at the same time that it links these activities to news media and to journalism more generally. Indeed, ever since George Gallup developed his scientific opinion poll in the 1930s, news media have funded these polling activities and publicized their results; Gallup's American Institute of Public Opinion was supported by 125 daily newspapers, and many other early pollsters also had financial arrangements with the press (Schudson 1998: 224). In the process, journalism discovered a ready source of newsworthy material, which also served as a daily source of civic and professional legitimation.

Sociologists have criticized the "public opinion poll" almost continuously since its emergence. Blumer (1948), Habermas (1989), and Bourdieu (1990) have all argued that it is both incorrect and dangerous to give the name "public opinion" to the aggregated opinions of individuals. After all, these opinions are generally elicited without serious reflection or deliberation on the part of the individuals giving them. Just as often, opinions are given about matters for which individuals have imperfect information. And most important, the aggregation of individual opinions into something called "public opinion" ignores the central idea of deliberation, which is that an opinion or an argument will be better if it emerges as the result of a serious discussion, in which all participants are willing to change their mind and all are willing to be persuaded by the force of a different argument. The practices of opinion polls (and the journalism that reports their results) do not display much concern with the existence or the quality of this kind of deliberation.

For his part, Gallup was unconcerned with the possibility that individuals gave snap opinions based on limited information or reflection, because he thought that the aggregation of these types of opinions would balance themselves out and that more informed opinions would rise to the top (Schudson 1998: 227). Furthermore, Gallup rejected what scholars today call mediated deliberation, arguing that it amounted to little more than ideological manipulation by propaganda and interest groups (Schudson 1998: 228). But this kind of argument shows the weakness of the model of the rational, information-processing citizen. "In fact," Schudson (1998: 228) argues in a critique of Gallup's theory of opinion formation, "democracy requires that private opinions are not the point of departure for public opinion; truly public opinion does not exist until it is arrived at through discussion and deliberative assemblies." To this, we would add that these deliberative assemblies should include mediated and direct forms of communication, as well as a way of linking the two.

Small Groups, Informal Publics, and Opinion Formation

Since the days of Robert Park and the Chicago School, sociological theories of media and opinion formation have rejected the model described previously, emphasizing instead how people use the news media to inform small-group discussions in informal social networks. Many political theorists have also moved in this more sociological direction, developing dual-track models of communication and opinion formation that emphasize the importance of both mediated and direct forms of deliberation, while still maintaining a normative privilege for the latter (Benhabib 2002; Young 2000). For these theories, small groups are the key locus for rational deliberation because they can more effectively control the information that is relevant to the discussion (see Barber 1984). Individuals bring information into these discussions from a variety of sources, including personal experience, expert knowledge systems, and the media. And because it is a small-group context, participants have the opportunity to critically assess each source of information and to introduce additional sources of competing (or complementary) information to the discussion. Each new piece of evidence is subject to potential criticism, as is each new argument made from that piece of evidence.

If deliberation is moved into small groups, however, how are these discussions linked to the larger spaces of public attention and debate that are organized by the media? While small groups are better able to support substantial processes of deliberation by minimizing the distance between actors and spectators in the discussion, this comes with a cost, namely, a decrease in the influence and force of the deliberation's outcome. The profile of media communication is the exact opposite. Although there is a large distance between actors and spectators and a therefore a reduced likelihood of full and inclusive deliberation, the opinions circulated in the media have much greater influence than those that remain limited to small-group discussions. Thus, in these theories of opinion formation, the hopes for a mediated public sphere reside in the degree to which (and the mechanisms through which) the media is open to inputs from smaller, informal deliberative spaces.

The work of Robert Park provides one of the earliest descriptions of how this more sociological model of media and opinion formation works. Park argued that news is different from other forms of knowledge because news is defined by its transient and ephemeral quality (Park 1940: 676). The key to news's liveliness, as compared with history, is that it is reported as a series of isolated incidents, rather than as a teleological sequence.[7] The reason for this is that news is a public commodity; it does not become news through any individual reading but rather through the fact that it is part of a public communication. Because news treats events as if they are isolated, this requires individuals to talk about them, and it is from these conversations that public opinion emerges:

> The first typical reaction of an individual to the news is likely to be a desire to repeat it to someone. This makes conversation, arouses further comment, and perhaps starts a discussion. . . . The clash of opinions and sentiments which discussion invariably evokes usually terminates in some sort of consensus or collective opinion—what we call public opinion. It is upon the interpretation of present events, i.e., news, that public opinion rests. (Park 1940: 677)

This description of news and public opinion rejects the image of the isolated individual who reads the paper alone, contemplates the meaning of current events, and develops an individual opinion about those events that is carried into public encounters. Instead, Park's media sociology provides a thoroughly social and public account of the news. If an item of news is interesting enough for an individual to reflect on it, then this reflection will usually be accompanied by—indeed, it is often preceded by—the desire to discuss the news item with another individual. And so the opinions that individuals develop from news items are almost always already public opinions, in the sense that they emerge from discussions with others. In the end, for Park, the issue of most importance is the degree to which the news encourages people to talk about current events in a way that will bring about public opinion formation, and thus the public character of the newspaper is the central sociological concern.

Park's ideas about the media were developed further by Freidson, Katz, and others, as part of a critique of mass society theory and its model of the isolated, socially disconnected media consumer. Freidson (1953: 317) insisted that the concept of the mass is not a useful way to describe the media audience. His work suggested that research should begin from a focus on "the local audience itself as a social group composed of individuals who have absorbed mass communications into their relatively settled ways of behaving and who . . . behave towards mass communication in an organized, social manner." Empirical studies by Bogart (1955) and Larsen and Hill (1954) supported Freidson's claim that the mass is not an empirically accurate way to talk about the media audience. Indeed, every sociological study of real audiences invariably reached the same conclusion that Katz and Lazarsfeld (1955) had made in their pathbreaking study, *Personal Influence*: specifically, that the effects of mass culture are always mediated through (1) the different uses individuals make of the media text and (2) the specific networks to which they belong, as well as the dynamics of influence that operate within those networks. In many ways, Katz's (1960) "Communication Research and the Image of Society" signaled the end of mass society theories and the victory of the Chicago/Columbia model of social networks, interpersonal communication, and public opinion formation in the sociological study of the media.[8]

While the theories of Park, Freidson, and Katz do a good job of describing how media are used within social networks as a part of the opinion formation process, they are not as useful for explaining how the opinions and arguments from these small-group discussions find their way back into the media. Katz's theory is a good example of this. During the earlier phase of a discussion, he argued, media have a good deal of influence, particularly among the early adopters and informational elites who constitute the opinion leaders of many social networks and who tend to be more intensive consumers of media information (Katz 1960). During the later periods of deliberation and decision making, however, interpersonal relationships and emergent conversations tend to have more influence over the collective opinion that emerges. This model provides a nuanced and detailed account of how media get absorbed into social networks and group discussions, but it does not provide any insight into how the outcomes of those discussions find their way back into the media.

Since the nature and form of this feedback are critical for a theory of deliberative politics, how can we think about the connection between small-group discussions and networks and the larger public conversations that occur in the media? The theories of Park and Katz do not get us very far here. Habermas's theory of official and informal publics, on the other hand, moves us closer to a theory of media, opinion formation, and deliberation.

Like Park and Katz, Habermas argues that opinion formation emerges from the overlapping networks of informal discussions that take place within subcultural publics and other associational spaces.[9] But Habermas extends this argument in several important ways. First, he argues that informal publics are actually more effective than official publics at perceiving new problems, developing new approaches to existing problems, and constructing new collective identities.[10] Second, and more important from the perspective of a theory of opinion formation, Habermas insists that there must be an interplay between official and informal publics. Without such interplay, it is impossible for the opinion formed in civil society to make any effective demands on the state or to have any steering influence over society. To be sure, opinion formation occurs in informal publics, but without access to the media, "the signals they send out and the impulses they give are generally too weak to initiate learning processes or redirect decision making in the political system in the short run" (Habermas 1996: 373).

Habermas recognizes that there is a complicated relationship between informal publics and the media. Any media text can be used, through a process of hermeneutic reconstruction, as the context for a further discussion within civil society (see Habermas 1996: 374). This is similar to the earlier arguments of Park, Freidson, and Katz, which emphasize the ways small groups and social networks use media texts to inform discussion. But Habermas is concerned about how these discussions can influence the official publics, in an environment where those official publics are organized through a highly centralized and market-driven media industry, which tends to limit the entry of new topics, rhetorics, and speakers into the official public sphere and to be dominated by administrative rhetorics and various forms of strategic communication. Given that "the sociology of mass communication depicts the public sphere as infiltrated by administrative and social power," Habermas (1996: 379) argues, there is reason to be "cautious in estimating the chances of civil society having an influence on the political system."

In times of relative social stability, Habermas argues that informal publics have a hard time gaining visibility or influence within the official publics of the mainstream media. During periods of mobilization, however, he argues that the balance of power will begin to shift to the informal publics of civil society (Habermas 1996: 379). He sees this happening in two general ways. In the first instance, actors within the political system recognize that the only way to advocate successfully on a particular issue is to mobilize support from informal publics. In this type of action, the initiative and the power to place an item of concern on the public agenda remain with the political center, but success in doing so requires the identification and mobilization of an already-formed public opinion within civil society. In other words, this is a feedback mechanism from civil society to the official public sphere, but it does not allow actors in civil society to enter the official public sphere with a significant level of autonomy, on their own terms. In fact, this type of feedback mechanism is similar in many respects to the model of mediated deliberation described by representative theories of democracy.

In the second feedback mechanism, the initiative emerges from civil society itself, during moments of crisis usually associated with successful social movement activity. Habermas clearly favors this second type of mobilization—not only because it grants more autonomy and legitimacy to informal publics but also because he thinks that the issues that emerge in this way display greater sensitivity and heightened reflexivity (see Habermas 1996: 381). The picture here is one of varying levels of attention within official publics to the interests and concerns of civil society. From the perspective of social movements and informal publics, this is essentially a theory about the political opportunity structure of the public sphere. Movements and other civil society actors need to pay attention to political developments and changes in public opinion and be ready to mobilize for collective action when the public or political environment maximizes their chances for success (McAdam, McCarthy, and Zald 1996; McAdam 1996).

What does this model suggest about the media? Normatively, Habermas shares a media ethics put forth by Gurevitch and Blumler (1990), who argue that journalists should maintain a continual surveillance of the social political environment, looking for emergent issues of potential concern. Journalists should identify the key issues of the day, including the major actors who are most likely to be involved in the resolution of these issues. They should provide a platform for dialogue between those who represent official publics (i.e., representatives of the state, as well as major stakeholders from the largest bureaucracies) and those who represent civil society (i.e., representatives from social movements, nonprofit organizations, and other associations and interest groups). They should insist that representatives of the state participate in these dialogues. They should seek to uncover and unmask all forms of strategic communication, what today is commonly called "spin." Finally, they should speak to their readers as citizens who are capable of making sense of these issues. In other words, as Habermas (1996: 378–379) argues:

> The mass media ought to understand themselves as the mandatary of an enlightened public whose willingness to learn and capacity for criticism they at once presuppose, demand, and reinforce. . . . According to this idea, political and social actors would be allowed to "use" the public sphere only insofar as they make convincing contributions to the solution of problems that have been perceived by the public or have been put on the public agenda with the public's consent.

Although Habermas himself does not attempt to concretize his theory by applying it to actually existing media institutions, it is clear that his normative model emphasizes not only aspects of "objective journalism" but also opinion, commentary, and editorial. Objective journalism would focus on what the major stakeholders and the representatives of civil society have to say about the resolution of the major issues of the day. They would insist that representatives of the state respond to the demands of civil society, and they would protect themselves against undue influence from administrative power. On the other side of the newsroom, columnists would focus on identifying what were the most important issues of the day, they would provide commentary and context about competing proposals to deal with social issues, and they would make proposals of their own for dealing with these problems, written to an audience who was invited to participate in the critical discussion. Finally, editors would focus on making space available for all representatives of civil society—and not just the representatives of official publics—to bring new issues before the public and to suggest possible resolutions to these issues. The space of opinion is particularly important in this model as the location from which citizen voices and interests are represented back to elites by journalists and columnists.

With Habermas's more recent interventions, then, we have a theory of media and deliberation that places more attention on the spaces of opinion and commentary, as those are the spaces where it is possible to stage a dialogue between official and informal publics—either by allowing representatives of civil society to speak for themselves about the issues of the day or by allowing others (e.g., columnists, intellectuals, and other expert commentators) to challenge official stakeholders on behalf of civil society. While useful, however, we think that Habermas's theory of deliberative politics still has not moved far enough toward an analysis of the "actually existing public sphere." In the first place, his model of the media is presented largely as a normative vision rather than an empirical description. Habermas (1996: 377–378) recognizes this limitation, acknowledging that "it is by no means clear how the mass media intervene in the diffuse circuits of communication in the political public sphere." But such clarity is required. If we discover upon empirical examination that media do not affect the political public sphere in the way that Habermas's normative theory suggests they should, we still need an empirical description of how media actually organize public debates. And this empirical description is likely to point to a number of communicative processes that go beyond dispassionate, rational debate and analysis.

In fact, if we put Habermas's normative model to a series of empirical tests, we are likely to find that his theory of political deliberation misunderstands the cultural, aesthetic, and performative aspects of public life. Among contemporary theorists of civil society, Alexander (2006: 44–45) has made this critique most forcefully. By translating the philosophical vocabulary of the Enlightenment into a theory of rational speech acts, Alexander argues, Habermas has unnecessarily limited his empirical analysis of public discourse to a consideration of how reasonable, how reciprocal, how transparent, and how nonstrategic that discourse is. For Alexander, however, a signal feature of public discourse is that it is organized into cultural codes and dramatic narratives, which divide the world into good and bad, pure and impure, trustworthy and suspect, sacred and profane. Criteria such as "reasonable" and "reciprocal" are not very helpful analytical tools for understanding these kinds of symbolic codings. Alexander argues that a stronger cultural vocabulary will prove useful for the analyst who is interested in understanding the actual empirical contours of public debate. To this suggestion, we would add that these codes, narratives, and performances will be inserted into mediated deliberations within specific media formats and genres, which have their own histories and their own cultural inertia. The role that these media formats play in public deliberations must also be considered—not only for how they affect mediated official publics but also for how they shape the interactions between official and informal publics.

A Sociocultural Model of Media and Deliberation

When cultural sociologists engage questions about civil society and deliberation, they emphasize the ways that political communication is always narrated and performed and that there is therefore always an aesthetic dimension to public deliberation (see Alexander 2006; Jacobs 2000; Jacobs and Sobieraj 2007; Smith 2005; Eyerman 2006, 2008; Polletta 2006). This is more than a mere supplement to existing theories because it forces us to rethink the relationship between mediated and direct deliberation and to reconsider the communicative styles that shape such a relationship. For Alexander, the process of deliberation consists not only of a critical debate about the propositional content of competing arguments but it also involves the attempt to develop a shared understanding—developed through cooperative as well as competitive processes—of the dramatic and aesthetic dimensions that surround the issues of the day. This includes debates about a variety of cultural issues. For example, what is the central dramatic conflict that defines the issue? Who are the central protagonists and antagonists in the battle to resolve the issue? What are the character attributes of these protagonists and antagonists? Who is to be trusted to act in the public interest? What kind of attitude or subject position should members of the public adopt, as the audience to the deliberation? To what extent do new events, new evidence, new voices, and new arguments work to realign these types of symbolic orderings?

What are the consequences of this cultural model of media and opinion formation? First, it is necessary to understand how the cultural codes and rhetorical structures of media discourse are connected to the conversations that individuals have about matters of common concern. People do not only get facts and information from the media. Arguments and opinions, discourses and narratives, scripts and performances—all of these can be found in the media, and all of them find their way into the conversations individuals have with others about matters of common concern. In this view, citizens are cultural actors who rely on the forms, genres, and values of mediated public life to achieve the intersubjectivity required to deliberate about matters of common concern.

Thus, the media are central not only because they are purveyors of objective information to individual citizens poised to vote or debate but also because they provide a common cultural repertoire that makes deliberation possible (and even desirable) in the first place. To be sure, a part of this repertoire includes the expectation of an objective news media for the conduct of democratic politics. But this cannot be the whole story because it cannot account for the enjoyment people receive from their (mediated) civic involvements. For Habermas, one is compelled to participate in the public sphere out of a sense of duty. As a member of the public, one has a responsibility to demand that the state justify its legitimacy in a transparent way. And yet, as Bauman (2003: 151) argues, any moral dialogue requires that both parties enjoy the other person's company and take pleasure in what that person has to say. In the absence of this kind of pleasure, we are likely to invest most of our energy in trying to disqualify our adversaries from participating in the dialogue (Jacobs 2004).

Drawing on recent developments within cultural sociology (Alexander 2006; Eyerman 2006; Apter 2006; Goldfarb 2005; Jacobs 2005, 2007; Smith 2008), we argue that the pleasures of public participation are premised on an acceptance of a variety of aesthetic and performative structures. These include rational argument and the presentation of evidence, as traditional models of media and the public sphere would expect. But they also include more playful forms of argument, such as the clever use of dramatic techniques to place moral conflict into bold (and usually overstated) relief, the careful cuing of recognizable genres, and the elaborate identification of contemporary public figures with mythic archetypes—all of which increase the level of civic involvement, in official as well as informal publics. Returning to the case of media opinion, we want to suggest that if an individual "hates" George Will or Paul Krugman or Bill O'Reilly, it is more likely that that person will participate in the public sphere. Indeed, without an attachment to some of the regular characters of the space of opinion, it is unlikely that most individuals will sustain a regular level of participation in (or enjoyment in) the informal publics of civil society. In fact, an activated and mobilized set of informal publics is much more dependent on the media than Habermasian theories of complex democracy suggest. In particular, we would suggest that the mobilization of informal publics is often connected to those media formats that are organized around a regular cast of compelling characters.

A cultural model of public deliberation also argues that the feedback circuits that connect informal and official publics operate much more regularly than Habermas recognizes. This works in a number of different ways, some direct and others more indirect. In terms of direct feedback, we can begin by revisiting the two-step flow model of Katz and Lazarsfeld (1955), which found that the more influential members of most discussion networks tend to be the same people who have the highest level of media consumption. What does this fact mean for a cultural model of opinion formation? First, high-level media consumers are likely to know the most about the regulars in the space of opinion— the politicians, the elite correspondents, the newspaper columnists, and the television talk show hosts—and they are likely to have arranged them into a symbolic hierarchy of those they like, those they trust, and otherwise. This symbolic identification means that the discussions taking place in informal publics are likely to begin from a discussion of the regular characters—including the arguments they make but also the friends and enemies they identify, and the relevant characteristics of those friends and enemies. And the feedback from these informal publics back to the media—which once came primarily in the form of letters to the editor but increasingly includes monitoring blog discussions by the major media organizations—tend to focus on commentary about these regular characters and the narratives they are circulating in the media. To be sure, this is an empirical question, which suggests a different research agenda than the one we have chosen to pursue. But we raise it because, if these kinds of cultural dynamics are prevalent in the current mediated environment, then this provides an additional rationale for studying the space of opinion. Recent research on political blogs does in fact suggest that a good deal of the discussion that takes place focuses on the characters and narratives of the space of opinion (Burroughs 2007; Davis 2009).

There are also feedback loops between official publics and other kinds of more specialized public conversations in the institutionally separate fields of publishing, entertainment, the academy, and politics. These types of communicative interactions often find their way into the media, but they are not limited to those spaces. Indeed, while journalism has long claimed the right to organize the space of opinion in the public sphere, journalists have never controlled the public conversation completely. As the next chapter will demonstrate, there are other important sources of opinion, including powerful elites from politics and the academy, as well as a range of advocacy and service organizations in civil society. Each of these cultural and political fields contains more or less official conversations that are also connected to the elite social space of opinion and the official public conversation of democracy it mediates. Representatives from these spaces collaborate and compete with journalists and others in the media to represent, reflect, and shape public opinion. They do not need to be activated or mobilized during moments of crisis consciousness, as Habermas suggests. Motivated by the institutionalized sources of media access in newspapers, radio, television, and the Internet—primarily in the opinion spaces of those media—they are always activated.[11]

In this more empirically nuanced, culturally informed understanding of the role of the mass media in public opinion formation, then, it is not only factual information that is important. Official opinion and news commentary in the form of op-eds, television and radio talk shows, or blogs are equally if not more determining of the shape of informal and official public opinion. With this focus, it becomes possible to see that opinion authors do more than explain and clarify the elite conversation or triage public issues for citizens as the rational information model would suggest. They also do more than represent social interests that are otherwise unrepresented in the public conversation—the normative model that Habermas presents—although many columnists in fact do such representative work. In addition to the modes of opinionated speech that the first two models of public opinion formation would define, the cultural model of mediated deliberation also expects news commentators and opinion columnists to render compelling narratives of the central characters in political and cultural life and also to construct themselves as compelling characters in their own right. To the extent that they do this, they will almost always rely on various rhetorical styles that Habermasians would dismiss as strategic communication. But a cultural model is not so quick to dismiss these communicative styles. That is, a cultural model will be attentive to the ways that opinion authors unfold dramas of intrigue and honor, articulate and defend central social values, and present themselves and others as more or less heroic characters in the struggle for the good—be it freedom, democracy, equality, integrity, or the United States itself. In this context, the ideal of rational dialogue and dispassionate deliberation is only one of several performative modes available to media intellectuals, even if we recognize that the model of rational dialogue is a historically and politically important mode of deliberation. But the point is that it is one rhetoric among many.

Finally, a cultural model of deliberation emphasizes how different media formats tend to encourage specific kinds of speakers and performative styles. In the news interview, for example, readers and viewers expect journalists to ask questions, and they expect the interviewees (typically, government officials) to provide informative answers (Clayman and Heritage 2002). When reading a newspaper opinion column, they expect experts to evaluate competing policy proposals and to provide the background context that makes those competing proposals more understandable. When watching the cable television talk programs popularized by *Crossfire* and *Hannity & Colmes*, they expect that the dueling hosts and their guests will compete to heap symbolic pollution on the opposing political party. To be sure, these are generalizations, and any given format will display greater variation and complexity in the communicative styles they display, as we demonstrate in the empirical chapters that follow. For the moment, what we want to emphasize is the way that each media format creates its own genre expectations. As with all genres, viewers and readers (as well as critics and creative personnel) evaluate the effectiveness of a given media text in a way that is consistent with the genre expectations of that particular format (see Turner 1993: 85–89; Bielby and Harrington 2008: 66–100; Mittel 2004). A cultural model recognizes that this is an important part of the connective tissue that holds together mediated and direct deliberations.

By pointing to the importance of media formats and their corresponding genre expectations, it becomes possible to link the normative commitments of the three ideal-typical models described here with their different degrees of tolerance and preference for specific parts of the media space. For the rational information model, the preferred media format is limited to the news interview and the descriptive news report. For Habermasian theories of informal publics and complex democracy, we can see an expanded list of preferred media formats, including watchdog journalism, opinion columns, and some of the newer experiments in public journalism (Ettema 2007; Glasser and Craft 1998). These theories allow for a more diversified space of mediated public dialogue, while still trying to protect the public sphere from too much strategic communication. Cultural models of complex democracy expand the list of preferred media formats even further, recognizing that drama, disagreement, and strategic communication do not necessarily undermine democratic deliberation. Indeed, these theories are open to the possibility that disagreement can actually improve deliberation (see Price, Cappella, and Nir 2002), that an inclusive public dialogue is likely to require more partisan journalism formats and more strategic communication (see Baker 2002: 163), and that civil, detached forms of public deliberation may not be the best way to maximize popular inclusion or popular participation (see Ferree et al. 2002: 315; Young 2000: 63–70).

The point is that, as we move away from the model of the rational, information-processing citizen, we begin to imagine practices of mediated and direct deliberation that involve a much fuller range of communicative styles and media formats.

To be clear, we are not arguing *against* the importance of objective news, which has become a stable expectation of the space of opinion, as well as a wide array of political and cultural actors. However, we do want to historically contextualize the importance of objective news. The project of journalistic objectivity is only one intellectual project, albeit a particularly influential one, in the history of the U.S. political public sphere. Once it is viewed as such, the existence of other projects becomes easier to see. Or to put it a different way, it becomes easier to see these other projects as something other than a threat to civil society.

Rational Information-Processing Citizens? Redux

If our argument is correct that the actually existing public sphere is culturally embedded and fully mediated, then why does the sociologically thin theory of the rational, information-processing citizen dominate normative theories of democracy and media? Why, in place of the rich, complicated, interconnected networks and institutions of public communication, have theories of democracy emphasized the abstract citizen of democratic theory? The answer lies in the particular way intellectual and political life is organized in U.S democracy, especially the part played by professional journalism.

The story of professional journalism is important for several reasons. First, the journalistic field, especially in its mainstream general publications, is the major repository out of which the common stock of cultural resources circulates to form the basis of shared social meaning. Ideas and information that originate in other parts of society are circulated through the media and shaped by their framing and presentation by authors in the media, thus often by journalists (McCombs 2004; Bennett, Lawrence, and Livingston 2008). The major media frames—especially how journalism understands the relationships between state and citizen, knowledge and power, fact and value—are also likely to shape wider public understandings of these relationships (Entman 2003a). Second, where it overlaps the political field, the journalistic field introduces independence and intellectual autonomy into the political field; that is, it is an important place where knowledge and power meet in public (Benson and Neveu 2005). The elite space of opinion in the journalistic field is particularly important in this regard since it is the focus for a wide array of social actors who enter the official public sphere to speak on matters of common concern; these social actors include politicians, activists, academics, social movement advocates, writers, and educators. This is also why Bourdieu's analysis of intellectuals and power focuses on the intersection of the journalistic, academic, and political fields, because this intersection influences all of these powerful cultural fields. For all these reasons, then, journalistic understandings of public communication, citizens, and the political process have been widely influential.

Like other intellectuals and professionals, journalists also draw on cultural understandings of individualism to define their social role in terms of the wider public good.[12] Typically, too, they position themselves between elites and citizens, on behalf of citizens.[13] In the first instance, journalists report the activities of elites so citizens know what is going on and can make the political and economic decisions that affect their lives. This is at the core of the civic learning model of the rational, information-seeking citizen, described previously. In addition to this, journalists also reflect and represent public opinion to elites, serving as critics and discussants of a wide range of policies (see Lichtenberg 1990; Rosen 2001). This journalistic role is central to the small-group discussion model, model two, which we described earlier. In this role, journalists help to call the public into being; they literally mediate the relationships between elites and the huge populations affected by elite policies. Third, however, as our sociocultural model of mediated deliberation would emphasize, in both of these roles, journalists use and create the cultural repertoires through which elites and citizens understand themselves as democratic actors and act like democratic citizens (see Alexander 2006: 80–85).

Despite the relational and culturally embedded nature of journalism, however, most journalists continue to rely on the idea of the abstract individual of the civic learning model to frame their professional practice. The idea is that objective journalism provides the information required for democratic deliberation of individual citizens and is therefore crucial to democracy.[14] Thus, journalists need to be autonomous from powerful social interests to ensure that what is published is reported as objectively as possible. Where did this idea come from?

Facts and Values

As journalists professionalized in the early part of the twentieth century, they drew on and contributed to emerging social understandings of the relationship between facts and values (Hallin 1992; Gordon 1994; Schudson 1978). As it was famously expressed in the philosophy of the social sciences (Weber [1918] 1946), questions of value were for those who pursued politics as a vocation, while those interested in scientific truth needed to limit their arguments to facts produced using scientific methods under the rule of reason. This distinction was difficult to uphold in practice, however—even for scientists. As Weber acknowledged, the scientist is always committed to the value of the scientific endeavor itself. While the sphere of scientific activity may be separate from a value-laden domain like politics, the scientist always retains a stake in the conditions of the scientific enterprise and thus a connection to the world of values. To take another example from the sphere of law, while liberal jurisprudence has long made a distinction between matters of law and matters of fact, it is jurists who make arguments about how the facts and the law are connected. In both of these examples, there is an intellectual interpreter positioned between matters of fact and matters of value. This is true in the history of journalism, too, where professional opinion columnists came to occupy a position mediating between facts and values.

Journalism professionalized in a context of deep anxieties about modernity. As Schudson tells the story, these anxieties included a loss of faith in the functioning of capitalist markets, widespread concerns about democracy in a context of increasing social difference with the massive influx of new immigrants and the expansion of suffrage to women, and a growing distrust of "simple facts" that emerged out of the experience of propaganda during World War One and the growth of public relations professions in the 1920s. Journalists responded to these pressures in several ways. One response was to separate fact-based journalism from editorial and thus to assert the difference between journalists and the capitalist owners of the media. This was reflected in the organization of the newspaper, where from the 1920s onward, news and editorial were strictly segregated: editorial opinion was published on the editorial page of the newspaper, while the rest of the paper was devoted to objective reporting understood as a realistic and descriptive recounting of the previous day's events (Schudson 1978: 179–181; Schiller 1981). Second, contemporaneous theorists of journalism like John Dewey and Robert Park argued that newspapers were a way of integrating new populations into American democracy by providing common sources of information and cultural resources (Park 1940, 1941; Dewey 1991; Whipple 2005; Jacobs 2009). Thus, the role of the newspaper was crucial to democracy since newspapers provided the resources for a common democratic life under conditions of social fragmentation and increasing difference.

Third, journalism responded to anxiety about the trustworthiness of facts by developing a sophisticated idea of objectivity based on "rules and procedures" for producing facts and for distinguishing facts from opinions (Schudson 1978:7). These rules and procedures included guidelines about sourcing, quotation, and authorial voice and are still relied on by journalists today. In the 1920s, this idea of objectivity was used by professional journalists to distinguish themselves from the emerging public relations field in particular, where the goal was to promote a particular point of view. But even this more sophisticated understanding of fact-based reporting, which could be clearly separated from editorial, propaganda, and public relations, came into question as the decade of the 1920s wore on. More complex questions began to emerge about how objective journalism, on its own, was to produce informed and effective citizens. As we described in chapter 2, newspapers responded to these issues by introducing the syndicated political columnist to provide analysis to help readers better understand the meaning, context, and significance of the day's events.

Importantly, while political columnists were a new kind of media intellectual, they did not develop a significantly different civic justification for journalism but instead relied on the model of the information-processing citizen and its preference for objective facts and dispassionate analysis. Typically a journalist by training, the columnist shared a concern for journalism's uncertain professional status. Similar to other professions (e.g., science, medicine, law), journalists based their professional legitimacy on the idea that their work was in the public interest. Unlike those more successful professions, however, journalists and columnists were less able to secure their professional autonomy by creating market closure in the form of clearly established credentials, specific trajectories of training and education, or enforceable professional memberships. For journalists and political columnists, then, professional institutionalization was much weaker, and their professional autonomy became linked to the idea that only journalism could provide the accurate and objective information that democratic citizens needed.[15] The new political opinion columnist, by extension, offered a commentary based on the facts but at no time challenged the basic distinction between facts and values.

So, although political columns were different from objective reporting, professional journalistic values of objectivity and autonomy shaped their development nonetheless. What was distinct about professional political columnists was that they presented independent analyses and commentary on the news of the day; the political column was neither news nor editorial but reasoned analysis based on the news. Indeed, early disputes between celebrity columnists and editors revolved around the independence of political columnists from editors and newspaper owners (Gordon 1994), cementing a definition of objectivity and autonomy as freedom from censorship from powerful economic and political actors.

To be sure, this commitment to objective journalism has weakened significantly in today's world of media intellectuals, at least in some quarters, as the space of media opinion has become more diverse. Today, there are many regular voices that do not come from the traditional worlds of journalism. Many come from politics, particularly on television, where the hosts and regular guests of political talk shows are increasingly likely to be former speechwriters and political advisers (Chris Matthews, Pat Buchanan, Tim Russert, George Stephanopoulos), former political consultants and strategists (Paul Begala, James Carville, Mary Matalin), and former politicians (John Sununu, Joe Scarborough). Others come from previous careers in entertainment (Keith Olbermann, Jon Stewart) and tabloid journalism (Bill O'Reilly).

With the diversification of formats and of the career trajectories of the main characters in the opinion space, the belief that the primary goal for media is to provide information for the putatively rational citizen has come under challenge. Some new voices in the opinion space criticize the "mainstream media" for bias, while others question whether it is necessary or even possible to segregate facts from opinions in a meaningful way. Still others defy the idea that a public-minded media should avoid being entertaining. Rather than simply denouncing these developments and attempting to "search in vain for a purity that only exists outside society," we follow Eliasoph's (2007: 94) suggestion for cultural sociologists, which is "to grasp the moral materials that are already in use." That is, after all, what the readers and viewers of media opinion are doing.

4 Who Speaks in the Space of Opinion?

IN A 1994 opinion column, unusual for its support of President Bill Clinton's foreign policy, William Safire begins with a statement that describes his view of the political conversation in which he and other columnists are speaking:

> From diplomats in the Quai d'Orsay to powerplayers in the Kremlin to forgetful editorialists in the U.S., the drumbeat has begun: why not end "intrusive inspections" and do oil business with Saddam? (*New York Times*, May 2, 1994, p. A17)

Safire's figure of speech, the drumbeat, is suggestive. It conjures an idea of public opinion as a palpable force pressing in on decision makers at the highest political levels. At the same time, Safire's list of influential actors—French diplomats, Russian policy makers and U.S. newspaper editors—maps a particular circuit of elite political opinion and suggests at least one other that includes those like Safire himself who continue to support economic sanctions against Iraq. Safire is an undisputed master of his craft. In this one simple opening sentence, he effectively sketches a geography of the public conversation, as well as his place within it. He positions himself as an opinion leader in U.S. politics and aligns himself with the grand tradition of U.S. opinion columnists who have the power to frame debate on foreign and domestic policy matters alike.

Safire's columns and the responses to them also provide ample evidence of the central place he has occupied in the formation of political opinion in the United States. They are full of references to conversations, personal interviews, and informal banter with U.S. presidents and other world leaders. Such references display his insider status, the pundit's stock in trade ever since the days of Reston, Alsop, and Krock. A superb stylist, Safire gives the impression of being a key player in the decision-making process. Take, for example, his account of a 1993 interview with then President Clinton about anti-Israeli boycotts. Safire actually quotes *himself* saying to the president that he thinks Clinton's reasoning is a "little fuzzy." He then chronicles Clinton's reply:

> . . . the word fuzzy got to him. Asked about his lack of leadership on Bosnia, he responded: "There is a Security Council. And some people on it have a veto. And the people on it who have a veto have vetoed what I think is appropriate to do in Bosnia." Then he turned to the scribes, his visitor included, who have been blistering his hide: "And I have yet to read a compelling case for why the United States on its own should either send a large number of troops or start a bombing mission all by ourselves. . . . Every one of these articles," he warmed to his subject, "is very, very fuzzy about what specifically we should do in the face of French, British and Russian opposition—every last one of them," he emphasized, so as not to overlook mine. (*New York Times*, September 16, 1993, p. A23)

Here Safire indicates that Clinton has read and is responding to political opinion columns, and this is not atypical; on the wall of Safire's Chevy Chase home "is a framed Safire column vigorously annotated by then-President George Bush" (Alterman 1999: 136).

As a last example, consider a column that Safire wrote in which he adopts the voice of a political speechwriter—a position for which he had extensive experience, having served in such a capacity for both President Richard Nixon and Vice President Spiro Agnew. In this column, Safire writes the speech Bill Clinton *should* have delivered on the need to intervene in Bosnia (*New York Times*, April 4, 1993, p. A23). As all these examples show, Safire was a figure who fully embraced his influence as a powerful Washington insider. He wrote critical opinions for and about presidents. He expected to be heard, and in fact he was.

Safire may be uniquely influential in his generation, a true heir of Lippmann, Reston, and the rest, but he is also an exemplar of a particular kind of elite media intellectual—the professional columnist. For those at the top of this field—people like William Safire, Paul Krugman, George Will, Thomas Friedman, David Brooks, and Maureen Dowd—their opinion columns are virtually required reading in the elite political conversation of the United States. This is not to say that professional columnists are narrowly political. Rather, elite columnists claim to identify themselves with ideas rather than ideology, with opinion rather than partisanship, with disinterest rather than disengagement. This understanding draws on long traditions, in the history of journalism as well as the philosophy of the social sciences (e.g., Lippmann 2000; Weber 1946; Arendt 1967), all of which enshrine an ideal that attempts to combine a detached intellectual vocation with a deep commitment to political life and common values.

To be sure, this ideal does not describe all speakers in the space of opinion, nor does it describe every professional columnist, nor every column they write. Ideals are rarely fulfilled in practice, and the professional opinion columnist is under pressure from a variety of changes in the media environment. New media, differentiation within the news industry, and evolving genres and formats have all transformed the landscape of political opinion, altering the conditions under which opinion is produced, circulated, and interpreted. In this context, not everyone who offers opinion draws on the tradition exemplified by Lippmann, nor do all speakers enjoy the full privileges of the elite columnists. As we documented in chapter 2, the history of opinion in U.S. media reveals a variety of different conditions under which people speak and write, as well as marked differences in autonomy, influence, and proximity to power. Not everyone gets to be like William Safire.

This chapter begins to examine the range of different contemporary practices and positions in the space of media opinion and commentary. To set the scene, we chart the institutional and communicative geography of media opinion, so we can tell the story of who gets to participate. Before turning to our empirical analyses, however, we briefly discuss the difference between *access* and *autonomy* in the space of opinion.

The Need for Autonomy: Public Spheres and Cultural Fields

Up to this point, we have framed our study of media opinion in terms of the ongoing debates about the public sphere and mediated deliberation. Our historical argument is that the opinion columns and televised political commentaries that comprise the space of opinion have been a tremendously influential part of the political public sphere in the United States for most of the twentieth century. More generally, we have argued that any theory of public opinion formation or mediated deliberation needs to account for this space of opinion. As with all publics, it is normatively desirable if these spaces of opinion offer opportunities for a variety of voices, perspectives, and cultural formats. This helps to maximize the representativeness of the largest publics, at the same time that it improves the feedback mechanisms that link official and informal publics.

Empirically, then, a central question for this book is the degree to which the space of opinion is open or closed to the range of voices in civil society, politics, and other cultural organizations outside the media. This is a question of *access*, and it rests on a distinction between media insiders and media outsiders. Media insiders are those whose careers and livelihoods are rooted primarily in the journalistic field, such as journalists, professional columnists, editors, owners, and television talk show hosts. Media outsiders, by contrast, are those whose careers, identities, and livelihoods are primarily located outside the journalistic field. Outsiders include groups like politicians, academics, lobbyists, representatives of professional and trade associations, lawyers, and writers. In this chapter, we ask: to what degree is the space of opinion open to media outsiders? And for those media outsiders who do gain access to the space of opinion, do they face the same conditions of speech as media insiders?

These questions about access to the space of opinion are connected, in turn, to a second central issue in the public sphere tradition that concerns the *autonomy* of speech. That is, do those who speak in the space of opinion speak in their own voices, or do they represent other powerful social interests? Are media insiders or media outsiders more autonomous when they speak in the space of opinion? Is it true that the tradition of the autonomous elite columnist exemplified by William Safire is in decline? As more partisan opinion formats appear in the space of media opinion, do they change the organization of access and autonomy? These are critical questions, because they speak to the ability of the opinion space to operate as an arena of opinion formation and deliberative politics, rather than as a simple front for business or political interests.

For normative theories of public deliberation, of course, it is desirable for speakers to have as much autonomy as possible, as this is the best way for speakers to assume dialogue roles, to be self-reflective, and to challenge any competing viewpoint from a principled standpoint (Cohen and Arato 1992, esp. pp. 356–357). As an empirical matter, however, questions of autonomy are complicated by the fact that the space of mediated opinion also operates according to the logic of cultural fields (Bourdieu 1993). Thus, spaces of opinion are also defined in large part by struggle to define the principles on which the autonomy of the field itself rests.

In general, there are two competing principles that can be used to claim distinction within a cultural field. On the one hand, it is possible to achieve success according to structural logics operating outside the cultural field itself: for example, market success, proximity to economic or political elites, or alignment with the values or the rhetoric of a specific cultural or social movement.[1] On the other hand, cultural producers can achieve distinction by appealing to principles of classification that are internal to that specific cultural field. This involves considerations about what constitutes good art, literature, journalism, or science, as well as a consideration of the history of debates about these matters within the field.[2] For Bourdieu (1991: 661, 664), internalist principles of distinction define the "privileged social universes" constructed by specific cultural groups who have established both the right to control the "means of cultural production and diffusion" and also "the power of evaluating themselves according to their own criteria." It is these internalist principles of distinction that are related to the demand for autonomy. In other words, within a cultural field, the quest for autonomy will be driven at least as much by a concern for professional and intellectual control within the field as it is by, say, an interest in critical rationality or a commitment to demographic representation (although these principles are not necessarily mutually exclusive).

If a normative theory of the public sphere asserts that the intellectual autonomy of speakers is always desirable and important, then a theory of cultural fields contributes the insight that the demand for autonomy will always be asserted against a range of alternative positions. This is the first sense in which the field metaphor is a relational one. Within the journalistic field, there are extremely powerful alternative positions that compete with high-end professional understandings of journalistic autonomy. Such alternative positions rely on external sources of distinction such as circulation size, audience ratings, and advertising revenue. In addition, because the journalistic field overlaps the political field, there is an important alternative position that comes from a journalist's proximity to political elites or to official representatives of the state (Bourdieu 2005; Darras 2005).[3] In fact, Bourdieu argues that journalism is a "weakly autonomous" field, precisely because it is more easily steered by external sources of distinction than are other cultural fields, like the academy or literature (Bourdieu 2005: 33). What this means is that journalism, at least in its dominant tendency (i.e., general interest media), is more susceptible to the influence of money and power than are many other fields of cultural production (Benson and Neveu 2005: 5). To be sure, the internalist principles of distinction are important, too, and they are associated with the exercise of autonomy in the form of high-quality in-depth reporting and incisive commentaries on the op-ed page. Such marks of distinction are also usually sanctified through prestigious journalism awards, such as the Pulitzer Prize or the Peabody Award (Benson and Neveu 2005: 4). But the point is that the commitment to these principles of distinction is a contested one. Indeed, media mogul Rupert Murdoch has always been highly critical of the pursuit of Pulitzers, dismissing them as "journalists writing stories to impress other journalists" (Bowden 2008: 111).

The idea of fields is relational in a second sense as well, in that fields are related to each other. Thus the journalistic field is shaped not only by the structure of its internal relationships but also by its proximity to adjacent fields. The most significant of these adjacent fields are the political field and the social science field, because actors in these three fields are in competition to define the legitimate vision of the social world (Bourdieu 2005: 40). For the United States, we would also add the increasing number of think tanks, which are situated in a field (or fieldlike space) somewhere between politics and social science and present new challengers in the competition to define the social world (Medvetz 2007). For Bourdieu, the primary concern is the increasing influence of the journalistic field in structuring the distinctions of other cultural fields, primarily by establishing a connection between media publicity and principles of distinction and success in those other fields (Bourdieu 2005: 41–45; also see Bourdieu 1998, esp. pp. 68–78).

If journalism is influencing other cultural fields, however, it is certainly also the case that these other fields affect the journalistic field, particularly in the spaces of media opinion and commentary. When politicians, academics, lawyers, novelists, or other cultural producers participate in the opinion space, they can introduce alternative definitions of truth, competing claims of authority, different topics of discussion, and different rhetorical styles of argument. These alternative styles enter into a symbolic competition with the styles put forth by journalists and columnists and challenge the dominant definitions of what constitutes good commentary or opinion. To the extent that such challenges are successful, there will be important consequences for the kinds of arguments that get made in the space of opinion.

Remembering that journalism is a type of cultural field is useful, then, because it reminds us that media are more than just the communicative environment of political and cultural conversation. That is, it reminds us that media are shaped by social, cultural, political, and economic factors that do not involve the normative ideals of civil society or deliberative democracy that are so central to the public sphere tradition. And importantly, it allows us to realize this without reducing the analysis to a political economy of the media industry (Benson 2007). The main problem with the political economy approach is that it weakens the analytical power of the public sphere concept as a vehicle for doing empirical media research. Indeed, Habermas's own public sphere theory is weakened by a reductionist political economy of the media, in the sense that he tends to read the degree of public sphere autonomy directly off the level of commercialization in the media industry (Benson and Neveu 2005: 9–10; Benson 2012).

Our research is premised on the possibility that autonomy is a more complex phenomenon than the political economy approach allows and that it requires much closer empirical investigation. Thus, we ask how spaces of media commentary are characterized by varying levels of autonomy, differing commitments to the value of autonomy, and different understandings of what an effective and autonomous voice looks like. We investigate whether differences in autonomy are associated with different kinds of media insiders and media outsiders. And we ask whether competing principles of autonomy are distributed in patterned ways across the opinion space. That is, we suspect that autonomy will look different on the op-ed page of the *New York Times* than it will on Fox News Channel's prime-time television program *Hannity & Colmes*, and we also think it is likely that autonomy looks different for academics who enter the opinion space than it does for politicians, columnists, representatives of advocacy groups, or public relations specialists.

The analyses that follow investigate variations in autonomy. They rely on data from large random probability samples of opinion from the *New York Times, USA Today*, the *NewsHour, Face the Nation, Crossfire*, and *Hannity & Colmes* from 1993 to 1994 and from 2001 to 2002, the first two years of the last two U.S. presidential administrations ($n = 1,819$).

Data

We drew a 12.5 percent sample of days from two twenty-four-month periods—1993–1994 and 2001–2002—and collected all the op-eds published in the *New York Times* and *USA Today* for those days from the full-text database provided by *Nexis*.[4] As we outlined in chapter 1, the *New York Times* was chosen because it is the paper of record, and *USA Today* because it is the most widely circulated newspaper in the United States.[5] The unit of analysis in the newspaper sample is the op-ed ($n = 910$).

Television transcripts were sampled using the same logic we followed for newspapers; thus we took a random sample of days from the same two time periods, 1993–1994 and

2001–2002, and collected transcripts from *Face the Nation*, *Crossfire*, *The NewsHour with Jim Lehrer*, and *Hannity & Colmes* as representatives of the range of political talk shows on Sunday morning and daily television that are aired on network, public, and cable channels. *Hannity & Colmes* appears in the 2001–2002 sample only, reflecting an overall expansion in the number of television talks shows aired over the period. Television transcripts are much longer than individual newspaper op-eds, so we sampled fewer transcripts than op-eds—selecting fifty days from each period—with the goal of producing a sample size roughly comparable with the newspaper sample, which was evenly balanced between Sunday morning and weekly political talk shows. The basic unit of analysis in the television sample is the speaker-show ($n = 909$), that is, the speech of an individual speaker on a particular episode of a television show. At this level, we can compare characteristics like occupation and sex of the speaker and overall length of speech between opinion authors in print and on television.

Along with quantitative variables describing regular features of the opinion space, there are approximately 10,000 pages of text data in the newspaper sample and 10,000 pages in the television sample, about 20,000 pages overall. Our goal is to draw connections between the social space of opinion described by the quantitative measures on the one hand—thus, the analysis of authors' occupations, the range of content, length of speech, number of turns, and other characteristics of format—with an in-depth cultural analysis of the narrative features in particular cases, on the other. This underlies the extended case studies in chapters 7 and 8. Together, the materials we use from these newspapers and television shows help us shed light on some of the most important institutions of elite political opinion in the United States; that is, they are general topical spaces that are central to an ever-expanding plethora of news and opinion networks that, taken all together, constitute an important part of the political public sphere.

The media institutions of this wider public sphere include newsletters, pamphlets, local and progressive television, radio, and newspapers, newsmagazines, and Web-based information sources, including blogs, message boards, and citizen-compiled news. This wider world of news, commentary, and opinion has expanded massively in the last few decades. There has been a proliferation of forms, styles, and genres, as well as an increase in specialized markets for information delivered rapidly via the Internet. These are big changes, and their full effects are as yet unknown. Like others, we expect them to be far-reaching changes. However, for reasons we outlined in earlier chapters, we also think it is likely that elite spaces of opinion will continue to exercise significant influence over this wider public sphere. Elite institutions with large educated publics like the *New York Times* and television shows with mass viewing audiences like *Face the Nation* will continue to serve as central points of reference in the formation of political public opinion for some time to come. They are also among the most influential parts of the journalistic field, identifying the most sanctified positions in the field, as well as the most visible and talked-about challengers. Indeed, rather than declining in importance, there are good reasons to suspect that the elite spaces we study are becoming increasingly central to this larger and more densely networked public sphere. If we are right, then it is crucially important to understand the dynamics of these spaces—to understand who speaks and under what conditions they speak.

Changes and Trends since the 1970s

William Safire may have written at length and in his own voice as an established political insider with undoubted influence in the U.S. government, but there are many others in the space of opinion who enter from outside the profession of journalism and who occupy positions quite different from Safire's. One important group of these media outsiders is politicians, who typically enter the space to promote or defend particular political positions. This group is primarily elected politicians but includes executive branch officials such as cabinet appointees, high-level civil servants from various government agencies, and local government officials, like mayors and city police chiefs. Others who speak in the space of opinion include academics, writers, artists, film directors, comedians, athletes, lawyers, representatives of business and the professions, and those who work for a range of civil society organizations, including lobby groups, policy institutes, and think tanks.

There are several reasons to think that the influence and the presence of these media outsiders in the elite space of opinion have been growing in the last two to three decades. As we saw in chapter 2, one major change from the 1970s onward is that the newspaper op-ed page has been opened to outsiders by powerful gatekeepers, most notably the editors of the *New York Times* op-ed page (Diamond 1993; Page 1996). When the *New York Times* expanded its op-ed page in 1970, the explicit rationale behind its policy was to allow a wider set of voices into the paper, in the service of democracy. The change was also motivated by the desire to protect the perceived autonomy of the paper; the *New York Times* was sensitive to charges of liberal bias and used its new op-ed page to provide a wider range of political positions (Rosenfeld 2000: 7). Another advantage of the expanded op-ed page was the ability of newspaper editors to more effectively distance themselves from the opinions published in their paper. Finally, the expanded op-ed page reduced costs, since outside authors were happy enough with the honor of getting published in the *New York Times* and therefore did not need to be paid more than a nominal sum.

A second reason for the growing presence of media outsiders is the general shift within journalism away from news gathering and toward commentary. Television has been a big source of this shift, as we saw in chapter 2, since it introduced format innovations within the newsmagazine programs and political talk shows that highlighted commentary, using traditional reporting only when it was necessary to set up the discussion that followed. This has been particularly true of the cable news channels. Similar trends have occurred in newspapers, as the rise of the Internet has tended to emphasize user-generated content, particularly opinion pieces, and the commentary that swirls around those opinion pieces. All of these changes have created a much larger opening for

policy experts, academics, and political insiders, who, together with the regular columnists and talk show hosts, increasingly form the cast of characters that take center stage
in official as well as informal publics.

A final factor shaping who speaks in the elite opinion space has been the various
threads of the public intellectual movement. The discourse of the public intellectual
draws on a venerable intellectual tradition, but in its specific use in the cultural politics of
the 1980s and 1990s in the United States, it emphasized a media strategy of trying to enter
the elite space of opinion to influence government policy and cultural values (Townsley
2006). In the political field, a range of civil society organizations developed highly successful media strategies to influence elite opinion. This was not only true of neoconservative think tanks and lobbies and the burgeoning, highly profitable political consulting
agencies they midwived. As they succeeded in getting their message across, others across
the nonprofit sector adopted their strategy. In turn, in the academy—in literature, history, and social science disciplines especially—a wide array of voices called for more "publicly relevant" scholarship, which was often translated into writing op-eds for newspapers
or appearing as a commentator on television (Jacoby 1987; Burawoy 2005; Said 1994).

Together these changes have redrawn the map of elite opinion and commentary in
significant ways. Although columnists, talk show hosts, and other journalists continue to dominate, there is evidence that a larger number of paths are now being
carved between the spaces of media opinion and other spaces that lie adjacent to the
journalistic field.

Places in the Public Sphere

The elite space of political opinion is not synonymous with the political public sphere,
but it is a very important part of it. As we argued in chapter 1, the space of opinion is best
understood as a chaotic intersection of several cultural fields. Using data from our samples from 1993–1994 and 2001–2002, we can draw a sociological map like figure 4.1,
which identifies the different fields, institutions, and occupational orders that constitute
the space of opinion. Underlying the space of opinion are the dynamics of the three most
important institutional fields as they intersect and overlap: namely, the academic, political, and journalistic fields. Inside the space of opinion, we have made the name of each
group roughly proportional to the number of authors coming from different occupational backgrounds in our sample. It is immediately apparent that the territory accounted
for by lawyers (2.2 percent) or writers (3.7 percent) is much smaller than that occupied by
professional columnists, who write 44.5 percent of all the op-eds in our newspaper
sample, or television talk show hosts, who account for 30.6 percent of all opinion segments in the television transcripts (also see table 4.1). Clearly, media insiders occupy a
large amount of territory in the space of opinion.

At the same time, however, the space of elite political opinion is also surrounded by a
cultural beltway, that is, an array of elite institutional spaces that are adjacent to the

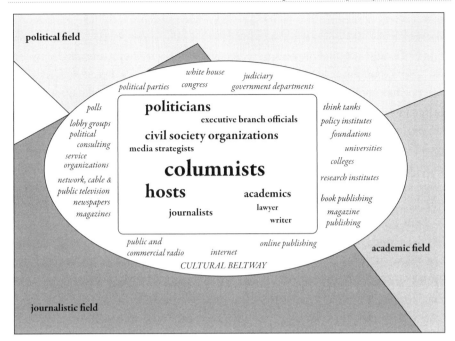

FIGURE 4.1 The space of opinion.

space of opinion. This cultural beltway is made up of the more public parts of other in-stitutions, such as the university, government institutions, and a range of advocacy orga-nizations from political parties to policy institutes, and the publishing and other mass media industries.

So although media insiders like professional columnists and television hosts clearly dominate the space of opinion, they do not account for the majority of all opinion; others are connected to the space of opinion through the political and intellectual net-works of the cultural beltway. Take successful bloggers, for example. Their opinions get picked up and circulated in more mainstream publications through Web sites associated with major newspapers or television shows. Repeated connections of this type may yield opportunities in the mainstream media, as the traditional distinctions of the journalis-tic field come to organize newer forms of media opinion, and traditional journalistic institutions begin to recruit the authors writing within them.[6] At the same time, estab-lished journalistic voices now maintain active Web presences as part of multimedia career strategies. In short, the connection of new media networks with more traditional spaces have both transformed those older spaces and effectively expanded their reach.

Another kind of trajectory organized through networks of the cultural beltway runs through political institutions like political parties, government departments, consulting agencies, and think tanks. The career of Paul Begala provides a good example of this kind of movement. Begala began as a political consultant and staffer in the Clinton ad-ministration and eventually became a television talk show host and an academic. Along the way, he contributed to *George* magazine, founded a highly successful political consulting firm with James Carville, began to appear as a guest on television opinion shows, and then became a regular on the television talk show circuit. Eventually, Begala came to host several talk shows, hold a position at a policy institute, and also occupy a research professorship at Georgetown University. This movement in and out of the space of opinion and political and academic spaces increasingly defines the elite of the new punditry.

There are also several paths from the academic field through the cultural beltway to regular positions in the elite space of opinion, although these are somewhat less traveled than the career paths for those from parapolitical careers or the new media. Consider Olivia Judson, for example. She is an evolutionary biologist trained at Stanford and Oxford who published a popular book entitled *Dr. Tatiana's Sex Advice to All Creation*. The book became a television show in Britain in which Judson starred as Dr. Tatiana. On the strength of this, Judson was asked to write a few opinion columns for the *New York Times*, most notably, columns on sex differences in animals following the Larry Summers controversy at Harvard in 2005. On the strength of these, Judson was recruited to write a regular blog on evolutionary biology for the *Times* Web site.

These stories describe the career paths of various pundits as they have moved from different institutional positions on the cultural beltway to the center of the opinion space and out again. Thus, a central question for this chapter asks about the composition of the space of opinion, through a comparison of media insiders and media outsiders. In the first instance, how diverse is the population of opinion authors, and has the geography of opinion changed in significant ways over time?

Differentiation and Degrees of Autonomy: Media Insiders

There is significant occupational diversity among opinion authors in the space of opinion, but in many other respects, they are stunningly similar. The majority of contemporary U.S. media intellectuals are members of political and cultural elites—establishment insiders. Their sociodemographic profile underlines this fact: U.S. media intellectuals are mostly white, male, native-born, and middle-aged to elderly—fortyish to seventy plus—very few opinion authors in our sample are of color, and only one in five is a woman.[7]

One thing that does distinguish different opinion authors, however, is their relationship to the media itself. The space of opinion is dominated by those from the journalistic field. That is, the majority of opinion authors are media insiders—columnists, talk show hosts, journalists, correspondents, editors, and media owners—and many boast careers that include several of these positions.[8] This is not surprising. If the institutions of the mass media form the material conditions for the circulation of opinion in mass publics, it makes sense that professionalized news broadcasters and those who deal in the business of public information will also be heavily represented among those who specialize in news commentary.

This also confirms the long-held understanding that elite opinion columnists emerge from the journalistic ranks (table 4.1). Someone gathers significant experience as a Washington and/or foreign correspondent and then goes on to become a respected, veteran opinion columnist. While this recruitment pattern shows signs of change in recent years, the idea that opinion writing is the crown of a long journalistic career continues to shape the field, reinforcing the internalist principles of distinction we described earlier.

Looking more closely at the data shows that the dominance of journalism, and specifically elite opinion columnists, is incontrovertible. Sixty percent of all opinion columns in the *New York Times* and *USA Today* in 1993–1994 and 2001–2002 were written by authors from the journalistic field—professional columnists, journalists, and media strategists (table 4.1: 44.5 + 6.8 + 7.9 + 0.9 = 60.1 percent).[9] And within this group, there is massive concentration, with nearly 40 percent of all opinion columns produced by a select group of thirteen authors, ten of whom write for the *New York Times* as

TABLE 4.1

OCCUPATIONAL BACKGROUND OF OPINION AUTHORS,
NEWSPAPERS AND TELEVISION 1993–1994 AND 2001–2002

	Newspapers	TV	Total
Talk show host	0.9%	30.6%	15.7%
Columnist	44.5%	5.5%	25.0%
Journalist	6.8%	6.6%	6.7%
Media strategist	7.9%	4.2%	6.0%
Elected politician[1]	5.3%	19.3%	12.3%
Executive branch official	3.1%	9.4%	6.2%
Civil society organization[2]	10.2%	10.9%	10.6%
Academic	11.6%	4.2%	7.9%
Lawyer	2.1%	2.3%	2.2%
Writer[3]	4.7%	2.8%	3.7%
Other[4]	2.9%	4.4%	3.6%
Total[5]	100.0%	100.2%	99.9%
	(910)	(909)	(1,819)

[1]Includes former politicians if they are writing on the basis of their incumbency or it's a master status (e.g., president of the United States).

[2]These speakers are from civil society organizations, primarily from political lobbies, advocacy groups, policy institutes, and think tanks but also from philanthropic, professional, and trade organizations.

[3]Includes freelance writers, nonfiction writers, and unaffiliated popular historians and biographers.

[4]These are occupations with five or fewer members, including artists, musicians, comedians, counselors, medical doctors, mothers, religious leaders, coaches, and athletes.

[5]Numbers may not add to 100 percent due to rounding errors.

professional columnists (table 4.2a).[10] Similarly, on the major political television talk shows, 46.9 percent of the opinion space was claimed by authors from the journalistic field: predominantly television talk show hosts but also "visiting" columnists, journalists, and media strategists from other newspapers, magazines, and television outlets (table 4.1: 30.6 + 5.5 + 6.6 + 4.2 = 46.9 percent). Here we see talk show hosts dominating, with 26.8 percent of all opinion segments accounted for by only thirteen talk show hosts (table 4.2b). Like columnists in the print media, then, talk show hosts dominate the space of opinion on television.

These columnists and talk show hosts are the celebrities of the journalistic field. In our sample, print columnists are represented by writers like Thomas Friedman, Russell Baker, Maureen Dowd, and Paul Krugman at the *New York Times* and Joe Urschel, Al Neuharth, and DeWayne Wickham at *USA Today*, all of whom enjoy massive audiences, often through the syndication of their opinion columns. On television, figures like Bob Schieffer, Jim Lehrer, and Sean Hannity are all celebrities of the opinion space at the center of the elite political public conversation. The importance of these celebrity voices in the opinion space can also be seen in crossover among media forms, where *New York Times* columnists like Thomas Friedman and David Brooks appear regularly on television talk shows. Similarly, a figure like Patrick Buchanan is a multimedia

TABLE 4.2A

COLUMNISTS APPEARING TEN OR MORE TIMES

Newspaper	Author	# Op-Eds	% All Op-Eds (n = 910)
New York Times	WILLIAM SAFIRE	57	6.3%
	BOB HERBERT	43	4.7%
	ANTHONY LEWIS	40	4.4%
	THOMAS L. FRIEDMAN*	27	3.0%
	RUSSELL BAKER	26	2.9%
	A. M. ROSENTHAL	23	2.5%
	MAUREEN DOWD	22	2.4%
	FRANK RICH	22	2.4%
	ANNA QUINDLEN	21	2.3%
	PAUL KRUGMAN	19	2.1%
USA Today	AL NEUHARTH	28	3.1%
	DEWAYNE WICKHAM	15	1.6%
	JOE URSCHEL	14	1.5%
Total		357	**39.2%**

TABLE 4.2B

TELEVISION PUNDITS APPEARING TEN OR MORE TIMES

TV Show	Author	# Appearances	% of All TV (n = 909)
Face the Nation	BOB SCHIEFFER	44	4.8%
	GLORIA BORGER	25	2.7%
The News Hour	MARGARET WARNER	23	2.6%
	JIM LEHRER	17	1.9%
	ROBERT MACNEIL	17	1.9%
	MARK SHIELDS	11	1.2%
	RAY SUAREZ	10	1.1%
Crossfire	MICHAEL KINSLEY	22	2.4%
	PATRICK BUCHANAN[*]	16	1.8%
	TUCKER CARLSON	12	1.3%
	PAUL BEGALA	10	1.1%
Hannity & Colmes	ALLAN COLMES	19	2.1%
	SEAN HANNITY	17	1.9%
Total		**243**	**26.8%**

[*]Thomas Friedman also appeared seven times on *Face the Nation*, and Patrick Buchanan also appeared as an op-ed author in *USA Today* in our sample.

presence: he edits his own magazine, writes op-eds for newspapers, and appears regularly on political talk shows. These individuals represent the most elite fraction of media intellectuals who develop fast-paced, institution-spanning careers that might include political appointments, academic posts, and honorary doctorates, as well as lucrative publishing deals or prestigious visiting fellowships at policy institutes or think tanks. The influential few are also personally famous (while others hope to be), and they contribute massively to the prestige, ratings, and profits of the mass media corporations that employ them. For this, they are rewarded with huge incomes to go along with their fame.

Given their fame and influence, however, how do these stars of the opinion space maintain their independence from power? This issue presents a conundrum for any author of opinion. How do you sustain a critical perspective when your livelihood relies on good relationships with powerful elite members? Historically, as we argued earlier, the answer to this question has required journalists to commit themselves to the professional project of objective journalism—to the impartial search for truth and intellectual autonomy from state and corporate power. This is at the core of professional journalistic ethics in the United States, a system that rationalized the way journalists—including opinion authors—related to the political process (Hallin 1994; Schudson 2005). Thus, while professional journalism has never been as autonomous from economic and political power as other intellectual fields like science or literature, it has nonetheless fiercely defended an independent press as essential to democratic civil society—as the main way that political actors are held publicly accountable.

How the reality of an autonomous, free press plays out on the ground, however, is a complex and uneven phenomenon. As Bourdieu has famously argued, while it is true the journalistic field has low levels of autonomy, nonetheless, like other cultural fields, it is internally differentiated between "those who are 'purest,' most independent of state power, political power, and economic power, and those who are the most dependent on these powers" (Bourdieu 2005: 41). We would observe, too, that this is true not only for the journalistic field as a whole but also of the spaces of opinion within it. That is, the opinion space is internally differentiated between those who are more or less dependent on their proximity to political and economic power and thus between those who are able to remain closer to professional journalistic canons and those who cannot or who choose not to do so. Of course, even those commentators who are closer to the field of power can mobilize the rhetorics of autonomy that historically have tended to emphasize a more adversarial and critical posture toward politicians and other powerful actors. But their proximity to power means that these commentators are always vulnerable to challenges that they lack autonomy. Within any cultural field, proximity to power can always be identified with complicity and thus with a transgression of the purity of the field.

Of course, proximity to power is defined relationally, and within the journalistic field, there is variation in how autonomy is organized, which is associated with who speaks in a specific medium or a specific format. For example, opinion in the *New York Times* is much more the province of professional opinion columnists than it is in the more popular *USA Today*, where activist media owners, public relations experts, and other media strategists are more likely to write columns. Indeed, table 4.3 shows that in the *New York Times*, professional columnists account for 60.4 percent of all columns, while they write only 12.3 percent of columns in *USA Today*. In contrast, *USA Today* has a much higher proportion of media strategists writing op-eds than the *New York Times*: 20.6 percent of all op-eds in *USA Today* are authored by media strategists, compared with only 1.6 percent in the *New York Times*.

The dominance of professional opinion columnists is a marker of autonomy, distinction, and investment in the *New York Times*. This kind of investment is not present on the op-ed page of *USA Today*, where efficiency and cost cutting play a stronger role. While the regular columnists for the *New York Times* are salaried employees of the paper writing columns several times a week, *USA Today* has chosen instead to create a "board of contributors," composed of syndicated columnists, journalists, freelance writers, and academics, each of whom contributes an op-ed column five or

TABLE 4.3

OCCUPATIONAL DISTRIBUTION OF OPINION IN NEWSPAPERS,
1993–1994 AND 2001–2002

	NYT	USA Today	Total
Talk show host	—	2.7%	0.9%
Columnist	60.4%	12.3%	44.5%
Journalist	5.7%	9.0%	6.8%
Media strategist	1.6%	20.6%	7.9%
Elected politician	4.4%	7.0%	5.3%
Executive branch official	2.5%	4.3%	3.1%
Civil society organization	4.6%	21.6%	10.2%
Academic	13.5%	8.0%	11.6%
Lawyer	1.1%	4.0%	2.1%
Writer	3.9%	6.3%	4.7%
Other	2.1%	4.3%	2.9%
Total	99.8%	100.1%	100.0%
	(609)	(302)	(910)

six times per year. Approximately half of the op-ed columns in *USA Today* are written by the board of contributors, which represents an obvious cost advantage when compared with the system of salaried professional columnists employed by the *New York Times*. Not surprisingly, the different levels of investment in full-time professional columnists can be seen in the different levels of distinction achieved by the op-ed pages of the two papers. Indeed, of the ten most prolific columnists in the *New York Times* during our sample period, all but two have received Pulitzer Prizes for Commentary. By contrast, no columnist writing for *USA Today* has ever won a Pulitzer for Commentary.

Similar distinctions can be made between the television talk shows. For example, *The NewsHour with Jim Lehrer*, which began broadcasting on U.S. public television in 1975, draws more clearly than its competitors on the traditional rhetorics of journalistic autonomy. Airing for sixty minutes each weekday evening, the *NewsHour* is known for its measured pace of dialogue and its careful separation of news and opinion. It has also created clear paths to the elite newspaper columnists, using them as commentators more frequently than we see on the other television shows. Almost 9 percent of all opinion on the *NewsHour* is spoken by professional opinion columnists from prestigious print outlets, compared with 4.4 percent on *Face the Nation*, 3.8 percent on *Crossfire*, and 3.4 percent on *Hannity & Colmes*.

Somewhat different from the *NewsHour* is *Face the Nation*, the venerable Sunday morning political talk show that first aired on CBS in 1954. Running for sixty minutes on Sunday mornings, *Face the Nation* and its equivalents on the other networks have tended to rely on the more adversarial rhetoric of journalistic autonomy. Their goal is a critical investigation of political affairs in which the primary format is an interrogation of politicians—although the ability of the format to accomplish this goal is uneven at best, as we show in subsequent chapters. Given this format, it is unsurprising that *Face the Nation* has by far the highest proportion of elected politicians and executive branch officials among the four shows surveyed (table 4.4: 30.6 + 12.1 = 42.7 percent), as well as the highest number of journalists: 11.7 percent of opinion on *Face the Nation* is spoken by journalists compared with 6.7 percent on the *NewsHour*, 4.7 percent on *Hannity & Colmes*, and only 1.9 percent on *Crossfire*. Indeed, journalists are much more heavily represented on *Face the Nation* than on the other shows surveyed, even edging out the *NewsHour*, which has a slant toward print columnists. Overall, however, the point is that the occupational composition of speakers at the *NewsHour* and *Face the Nation* suggests that these programs are more likely to rely on the traditional claims of journalistic autonomy than newer programs, such as *Crossfire* and *Hannity & Colmes*.

TABLE 4.4

OCCUPATIONAL DISTRIBUTION OF OPINION SPEAKERS ON TELEVISION, 1993–1994 AND 2001–2002

	The News Hour	Face the Nation	Crossfire	Hannity & Colmes	Total
Talk show host	28.0	27.0	41.8	25.7	30.6
Columnist	8.7	4.4	3.8	3.4	5.5
Journalist	6.7	11.7	1.9	4.7	6.6
Media strategist	1.3	0.8	6.6	12.2	4.2
Elected politician	12.0	30.6	18.3	16.2	19.3
Exec branch official	10.3	12.1	5.6	8.1	9.3
Civil society org	15.3	3.6	11.3	13.5	10.9
Academic	7.3	2.8	1.4	4.1	4.2
Lawyer	1.0	0.8	4.7	4.1	2.3
Writer	3.3	3.2	1.4	2.7	2.7
Other	6.0	2.8	3.3	5.4	4.4
Total	99.9%	99.8%	100.1%	100.1%	100%
	(300)	(248)	(213)	(148)	(909)

The more modern shows follow the adversarial tradition of *Face the Nation*, but they have adopted different techniques for demonstrating their autonomy. For example, *Crossfire*, which aired weekdays on CNN between 1982 and 2005, was a show where the host played a much more active role in making arguments and responding to guests than had occurred previously in political talk formats on commercial television. Shorter than the other shows at thirty minutes, *Crossfire* adopted a more aggressive tone, which is now synonymous with the "talking heads" style of U.S. television opinion and news commentary.[11] In other words, the hosts on *Crossfire* created their autonomy by dominating the space of debate and controlling the nature of contention within it. Thus we find on *Crossfire* that more than 40 percent of all opinion was spoken by the hosts, compared with around 25 to 28 percent on the other shows. There are reasonably high proportions of elected politicians and executive branch officials on *Crossfire*, too (18.3 + 5.6 = 23.9 percent), but much smaller numbers of columnists (3.8 percent) or journalists (1.9 percent) than on the *NewsHour* or *Face the Nation*.

While *Hannity & Colmes* has a substantial representation of speakers from the political field (16.2 + 8.1 = 24.3 percent) and (like *Crossfire*) a reasonably low representation of professional columnists (3.4 percent) and journalists (4.7 percent), its most distinctive demographic feature is the larger proportion of media strategists among its guests than on the other shows. These media strategists are media owners, editors, pollsters, political consultants, and party strategists, and on *Hannity & Colmes*, they account for 12.2 percent of opinion. *Crossfire* is the next highest, with 6.6 percent of all opinion spoken by media strategists. The *NewsHour* at 1.3 percent and *Face the Nation* with less than 1 percent of media strategists have much lower rates.

Taken all together, these findings indicate that there are marked distinctions between and among print and television outlets in terms of who speaks within them. The data on occupational composition suggest strongly that newspapers, and especially the *New York Times*, are associated with the traditional autonomy of the professional political columnist, while television formats are associated with the less autonomous pole of the journalistic field and are more closely linked to the political and economic fields. There is important variation within print and television formats, however, with the *New York Times* more strongly associated with traditional markers of journalistic autonomy than *USA Today*, and *Face the Nation* and the *NewsHour* more likely to host speakers from more autonomous parts of the journalistic field than *Crossfire* or *Hannity & Colmes*.

The key analytical distinction here is one of autonomy, that is, the ability of the shows and the speakers on them to develop positions independent from and even critical of the dominant narratives, characters, and interests in the political and economic fields. If the elite opinion space is to be more than an echo chamber that amplifies known positions on a limited set of preframed issues, then the journalists who dominate the space need to claim—to both display and exercise—their autonomy from powerful and moneyed interests.

Media Outsiders and the Expansion of the Opinion Space

Alternative, external sources of news and opinion can also be a powerful way to make claims of autonomy. Voices from outside the journalistic field are potential sources of new ideas and fresh thinking, and these are represented by those from nonjournalistic backgrounds such as academics, lawyers, writers, and those from a range of civil society organizations, including policy institutes, think tanks, professional organizations, and lobby groups.

Like media insiders, however, media outsiders have varying levels of autonomy from political and economic power. Lobbyists and political consultants are typically closer to powerful elites than academics or freelance writers, and as a result, they have a harder time creating the image of autonomy. We can also see elective affinities between different kinds of media outsiders and different parts of the opinion space. For example, academics are more likely to publish opinion in high-end journalistic opinion spaces than in formats with less traditional markers of journalistic autonomy. There are more academics represented in newspaper opinion than in television opinion (table 4.1: 11.6 compared with 4.2 percent), and this distinction is replicated between newspapers and among television shows as well. Comparing the newspapers (table 4.3), we see that 13.5 percent of opinion columns in the *New York Times* were written by academics, compared with 8 percent in *USA Today*. Similarly, the *NewsHour* hosted many more academics, 7.3 percent, than the other television shows (table 4.4)—*Hannity & Colmes* had 4.1 percent, *Face the Nation* had 2.8 percent, and *Crossfire* had only 1.4 percent of opinion spoken by academics.

A very different relationship exists with the advocacy groups and think tanks, whose presence in the opinion space appears to be inversely correlated with traditional markers of journalistic autonomy, at least in print. More than 20 percent of the op-eds in *USA Today* were written by those from civil society organizations, compared with only 4.6 percent of columns in the *New York Times*. In other words, writers from civil society organizations were four times more likely to write an op-ed in *USA Today* than in the *New York Times*. Similarly, on television, opinion from civil society organizations was marked everywhere except *Face the Nation*, which is the traditional redoubt of professional political journalism, especially Washington and foreign correspondents. So, while less than 4 percent of opinion was spoken by those from civil society organizations on *Face the Nation*, on the *NewsHour*, 15.3 percent of opinion was spoken by those from civil society organizations; the proportions for *Crossfire* and *Hannity & Colmes* were also quite high at 11.3 and 13.5 percent, respectively. (Notice that this is a particularly high proportion of speakers from civil society organizations for the *NewsHour*, which otherwise draws from the most autonomous positions and occupations in the journalistic field.)

One way to think about these differences is in terms of the proportion of autonomous positions relative to less autonomous positions in the space of opinion over time; for example, if we find there is a decline in professional opinion columnists producing opinion compared with media strategists or political operatives, this is a sign of declining journalistic autonomy. A second indicator of declining autonomy would be if there is evidence of increasing interpenetration between politics and media, for example, if there are signs of increasing overlap between political and journalistic functions for speakers in the space of opinion.

On these measures, the evidence for declining autonomy is mixed: our data show an overall pattern of heightened division as well as expansion, what sociologists call differentiation. That is, there has been an increase in the size of the elite opinion space in all formats, at the same time that a large influx of different kinds of media outsiders has accentuated differences internal to the opinion space. This is shown in the following analysis, which documents the distribution of opinion authors by media outlet and occupation over time.

Expansion

The first major trend to notice is the overall increase in the size of the opinion space between the early 1990s and the 2000s. In part, this is accounted for by the proliferation of television opinion shows, especially cable television shows during the 1990s, which we described in chapter 2. We have built this into our research design by including an extra television show in the second sample period that did not exist in the first: *Hannity & Colmes*. But even if we discount the new show, the evidence indicates an overall increase in the amount of opinion produced between 1993–94 and 2001–02, *in already existing formats*. On the television shows that were broadcast in both sample periods, there was a 25 percent increase in the number of individual speakers of opinion between 1993–1994 and 2001–2002. At *Crossfire*, it was an increase of 20 percent, at *Face the Nation* the increase was 32 percent, and at the *NewsHour*, there was a 24 percent increase in the number of distinct speakers between the sample periods. Although this was partly accounted for by changing conditions of speech on each of these shows, as we show in chapter 5, it nonetheless represents a real increase in the volume of opinion on the three shows we sample in both periods.[12] This increase did not come at the expense of the traditional opinion formats in print, which also experienced a modest increase in the number of columns published between 1993 and 2002.

Growing Diversity

The second trend we observe is a change in the composition of who speaks in the elite opinion space. The important finding here is that the expanded terrain of elite opinion has not been evenly distributed among purveyors of opinion. Rather, much of the new space has been taken up by those from outside the journalistic field, notably academics at the newspapers and lobbyists and think tank intellectuals on the television shows.

At the *New York Times*, the proportion of academics writing op-eds increased markedly, rising from 6.6 to 17.9 percent between 1993–1994 and 2001–2002. At *USA Today*, the proportion of academics writing op-eds also rose steeply from 1.7 to 12 percent. Much of this gain came from academic writing in law, policy, and especially social science disciplines, mostly from elite academic institutions. Similarly, table 4.5 shows that freelance writers increased their representation at the *New York Times* from

TABLE 4.5

OCCUPATIONAL COMPOSITION OF PRINT OPINION, BY NEWSPAPER AND SAMPLE PERIOD

		1993–1994	2001–2002
New York Times	Host	—	—
	Columnist	74.3	51.4
	Journalist	4.1	6.8
	Media strategist	1.7	1.6
	Elected politician	5.4	3.8
	Executive branch	2.1	2.7
	Civil society org	2.9	5.7
	Academic	6.6	17.9
	Lawyer	1.2	1.1
	Writer	0.8	6.0
	Other	0.8	3.0
	Total	99.9%	100.0%
		(241)	(368)
USA Today	Host	4.2	1.6
	Columnist	13.6	11.5
	Journalist	11.0	7.7
	Media strategist	29.7	14.8
	Elected politician	8.5	6.0
	Executive branch	3.4	4.9
	Civil society org	16.9	24.6
	Academic	1.7	12.0
	Lawyer	6.8	2.2
	Writer	0.8	9.8
	Other	3.4	4.9
	Total	100.1%	100.0%
		(118)	(183)

less than 1 percent to 6 percent and at *USA Today* from less than 1 percent to 9.8 percent. Together, these changes represent an increase in the voices of media outsiders in the space of opinion.

From one perspective, these changes might appear to signal a relative decline in the dominance of professional columnists in the journalistic field in favor of less professionalized journalistic authors. We would emphasize, however, that much of the new opinion territory in print formats is being occupied by speakers from the highly autonomous academic field and from the very elite ranks within it. In other words, newspapers seem to be building wider paths connecting their op-ed pages to highly prestigious writers coming from the most autonomous adjacent cultural fields.

As a group, the academics who write for the opinion pages and appear on television are more likely to hail from elite institutions like Harvard and Yale or the Washington, D.C. academic establishment represented by universities like Georgetown and George Washington University than from lower status institutions (figure 4.2a). The dominance of the D.C. institutions is especially marked for television. Note, however, that there are increasingly more academic representatives from elite non-D.C. institutions, foreign institutions, and other institutions in our second sample period, which represents an opening of the opinion space to less elite ranks (figure 4.2b). This trend appears to have been particularly marked on television, although the numbers get too small to make precise statements.

Academics who publish opinion in the elite space of opinion are also more likely to come from the social science and professional disciplines than from the natural sciences or humanities (Figure 4.3a), and this pattern has, if anything, become more marked over time (Figure 4.3b). These findings about academic discipline confirm previous sociological research on the distribution of the faculties, illuminating the intersections

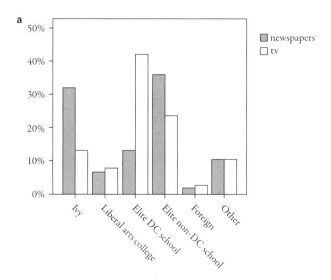

FIGURE 4.2A   Academic authors, by institution and format.

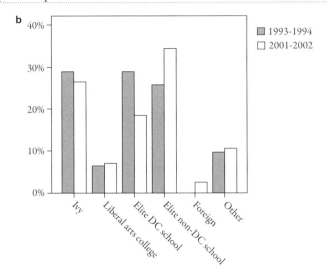

FIGURE 4.2B   Academic authors, by institution and period.

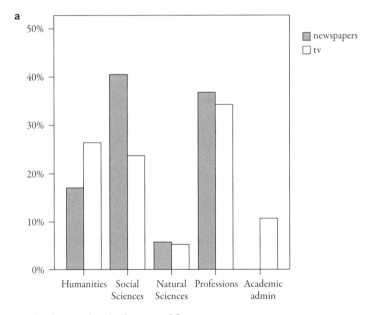

FIGURE 4.3A   Academic authors by division and format.

of the academic, political, and journalistic fields, where humanities and social science academics compete with pundits and think tankers to define questions of broad social and cultural meaning (Townsley 2000).

Despite their growing representation, however, academics are not columnists, and they do not enjoy all the prerogatives of professional columnists. Although a few academic authors like Richard Rorty or Alan Wolfe wrote about religion, philosophy, and democracy

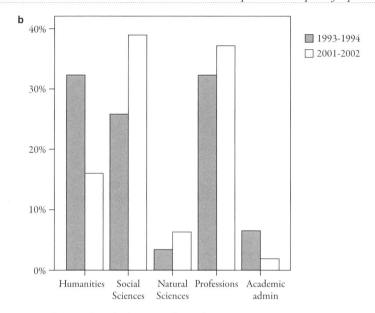

FIGURE 4.3B   Academic authors, by division and period.

more regularly than most media outsiders in the space of opinion, for the most part, academic authors appeared only once in our sample. Among these, there are historians (academic and popular) who appear as experts about a particular time and place. Many of these academics write about the political and democratic history of the United States. Biographers of founding fathers or presidents are particularly popular. We also find opinion authors from the ranks of applied administrative research—demographers, criminologists, and education professors—who do work that is directly relevant to general social policy. These authors might be understood as specific intellectuals whose expertise is sought when an issue emerges in the general public space that falls into their area of interest (Foucault 1980; Bender 1997). On this basis, some authors try to build a more general profile as an opinion author, but very few academics are repeat opinion authors (see appendix B). In other words, the op-ed page is managing to benefit from the autonomy of the academic field without providing enough regular access to any specific academic or group of academics to develop visibility as regular characters in the opinion space.

On television, however, the story is somewhat different. Table 4.6 shows that of the three shows that aired in both periods—*Face the Nation, Crossfire,* and the *NewsHour*—one of the most marked increases between 1993–1994 and 2001–2002 was the proportion of speakers from civil society organizations, mainly from think tanks and lobby groups. On *Crossfire,* speakers from civil society organizations increased from 7.2 to 14.7 percent, and on the *NewsHour,* they more than doubled their representation between 1993–1994 and 2001–2002, from 9.0 to 20.5 percent. *Hannity & Colmes* was similar to *Crossfire,* with 13.5 percent of speakers in 2001–2002 coming from lobby groups, think tanks, and other civil society organizations.

TABLE 4.6

OCCUPATIONAL COMPOSITION OF TELEVISION OPINION,
BY SAMPLE PERIOD

		1993–1994	2001–2002
The News Hour	Host	29.1	27.1
	Columnist	6.7	10.2
	Journalist	9.0	4.8
	Media strategist	0.0	2.4
	Elected politician	17.9	7.2
	Executive branch	7.5	12.7
	Civil society org	9.0	20.5
	Academic	6.0	8.4
	Lawyer	2.2	0.0
	Writer	5.2	1.8
	Other	7.5	4.8
	Total	100.1%	99.9%
		(134)	(166)
Face the Nation	Host	19.6	32.6
	Columnist	3.7	5.0
	Journalist	22.4	3.5
	Media strategist	1.9	0.0
	Elected politician	29.9	31.2
	Executive branch	13.1	11.3
	Civil society org	5.6	2.1
	Academic	1.9	3.5
	Lawyer	0.9	0.7
	Writer	0.0	5.7
	Other	0.9	4.3
	Total	99.9%	99.9%
		(107)	(141)

continued

		1993–1994	2001–2002
Crossfire	Host	47.4	37.1
	Columnist	8.2	0.0
	Journalist	3.1	0.9
	Media strategist	3.1	9.5
	Elected politician	15.5	20.7
	Executive branch	4.1	6.9
	Civil society org	7.2	14.7
	Academic	3.1	0.0
	Lawyer	4.1	5.2
	Writer	2.1	0.9
	Other	2.1	4.3
	Total	100.0%	100.2%
		(97)	(116)
Hannity & Colmes	Host	—	25.7
	Columnist	—	3.4
	Journalist	—	4.7
	Media strategist	—	12.2
	Elected politician	—	16.2
	Executive branch	—	8.1
	Civil society org	—	13.5
	Academic	—	4.1
	Lawyer	—	4.1
	Writer	—	2.7
	Other	—	5.4
	Total	—	100.1%
			(148)

Authors from civil society organizations have a higher degree of autonomy than others in the political field, but they tend to have much less autonomy than journalists or academics since they are usually speaking on behalf of a particular group that usually has a known ideology. Considered in this context, an increase in the proportion of opinion authors from these less autonomous origins—such as we see with *Crossfire* and the *NewsHour*—is a sign of declining autonomy in that part of the opinion space. *Face the Nation* is different in this regard because it actually saw a decrease in participation by those from civil society organizations, from a small 5.6 percent in 1993–1994 to 2.1 percent of speakers in 2001–2002. And if an increase in the representation of academic speakers is a sign of increasing autonomy—which we also see on *Face the Nation* (from 1.9 to 3.5 percent) and the *NewsHour* (from 6 to 8.4 percent) but not on *Crossfire* (moving from 3.1 percent to zero)—then we can conclude, on balance, that authors from more autonomous occupations increased their representation at *Face the Nation* and to some extent at the *NewsHour*, while those from the less autonomous civil society organizations increased their representation at *Crossfire*.

Politics, Power, and the Space of Opinion

Elected politicians and high-level executive branch officials together form the largest group of speakers in the opinion space who do not come from the journalistic field, and it is striking that they are more than three times more likely to appear on television than in print; as table 4.1 shows, political actors account for 28.7 percent of all television opinion and only 8.4 percent of newspaper op-eds. This suggests that the television opinion space is more closely tied to the political field than print opinion is. Comparing print sources in table 4.3, it is also true that politicians are more likely to write an op-ed in *USA Today* (11.3 percent) than in the *New York Times* (6.9 percent), reinforcing the argument that *USA Today* is closer to television formats than the *Times*.

The import of these differences, however, is not straightforward. Indeed, the presence of politicians and political actors in the space of opinion complicates the question of autonomy in a number of respects. There are crucial distinctions to be made between politicians who enter the space of opinion to support or defend a policy, on the one hand, and the domination of the opinion space by political operatives, on the other. The first model recalls Habermas's classical description of the public sphere, where rulers open themselves to democratic criticism and the exchange of ideas; the second turns the opinion space into a vehicle for propaganda to manipulate citizens. To be sure, these may not always operate as hard-and-fast distinctions in practice. Indeed, they may overlap to some extent, with politicians proffering propaganda and political operatives strongly committed to democratic policy debate. Nonetheless, there is an important distinction to be made between elected politicians who are publicly accountable through the ballot and political operatives who are not. To look more closely at what is going on, we ask: who are the politicians who enter the opinion space? How do they do so? And has there been change over time?

Analyzing the pattern of participation by politicians in the opinion space shows that most are elected politicians or high-level executive branch officials who appear only once in the sample (figure 4.4). This is true in both time periods, and it is also true of the small but significant cohort of foreign politicians who enter the U.S. opinion space to explain or defend policies that either originate in the United States or affect U.S. interests abroad.[13] Of those few politicians who appear more than once in our sample of the elite opinion space, most are congressional leaders who enter the space of opinion to explain a particular event or promote a particular policy. The majority of this group, then, appears to be democratic leaders who enter the space of opinion to discuss matters of common concern. This is precisely the function of the opinion space in a democratic society, where politicians are expected to engage in critical debate with representatives of the public to justify particular positions and try to reproduce their political legitimacy. If there is a decline in journalistic autonomy, then it must be elsewhere.

A second possible indicator of growing interdependence between journalistic and political functions in the space of opinion is the extent of traffic back and forth across the boundary between politics and journalism. There is some evidence of such traffic, typically for mid-level cabinet appointees, speechwriters, and political advisers who transit from political positions into careers as pundits and political consultants. Good examples are Paul Begala, Pat Buchanan, and John Sununu, and they appear to represent a growing trend. The primary destination for former political appointees appears to be television, which underlines the fact that opinion authors on television no longer

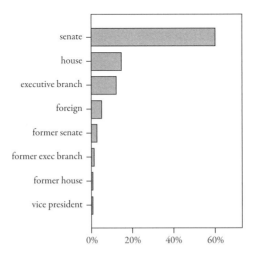

FIGURE 4.4 Institutional position of political opinion authors, appearing at least twice in the space of opinion.

need to come through journalistic careers to have a big impact. Notice, too, that at this point, traffic seems to run mainly one way. Once someone leaves the White House or Congress to become a media intellectual, a "regular contributor," or a pundit, they cannot easily transit back into elected politics proper. Instead, they become parapoliticians and quasi journalists whose main qualification to speak opinion is political and strategic experience rather than professional journalistic credibility. Indeed, this new characteristic of the opinion space provides support for those who speak of "the media" as a political player in its own right (cf. Cook 1998). There is a sense that these kinds of speakers are closely bound up with the narratives and agendas of mainstream politics, so much so, in fact, that "the media" becomes an actor in the drama. So there are signs that being a former political operative is increasingly a qualification for political punditry, at least on television, and this supports the argument that the political and journalistic fields are increasingly interpenetrated.

A third point of intersection between the political field and the elite opinion space is in civil society organizations like think tanks, advocacy groups, and policy institutes, a sector that expanded dramatically in size and influence in the last quarter of the twentieth century (Medvetz 2007). Our data confirm this, showing a rise in both the absolute number and the relative proportion of opinion speakers from civil society organizations between the early 1990s and the 2000s. This can be seen for newspapers (from 7.5 to 12 percent), as well as television (from 7.4 percent to 12.9 percent). At first glance, this suggests a close relationship between the space of opinion and the political field since, as we observed earlier, speakers from the civil society organizations tend to be associated with the less autonomous pole of the opinion space in print and on television.

As was the case for journalistic authors, however, opinion authors from civil society organizations are internally distinguished by how closely they are connected to official political institutions. There is a clear difference between an organization like the Red Cross, which is a universal nonpartisan service organization, and a lobby group like Missionaries to the Unborn, whose central mission is to shape legislation around abortion. To capture these differences, we distinguish three main categories of civil society organizations. The largest group is political lobbyists, advocates, and social movement activists (44.8 percent). Opinion authors from these organizations all seek to shape the political agenda directly, engaging in overtly political communication to promote their point of view. The second group is think tanks and policy institutes, which account for just over a third of opinion authors from civil society organizations (39.6 percent). These are nonprofit organizations that pursue more or less independent research in the public interest. These organizations might be further distinguished in terms of how partisan they are, but for our purposes, what they share is some kind of guiding philosophy, as well as the explicit goal of influencing and/or informing government policy discussions and the wider political conversation. Third are foundations, service organizations, and professional and trade associations (15.6 percent). Opinion authors from this group may promote a particular point of view or represent their members across a broad range of issues, but as a group, they tend to be not as politically focused or partisan as either advocates or think tankers (see appendix C for a list of organizations). With these categories in hand, we can now ask: where do opinion authors from different kinds of civil society organizations publish their opinion, and has that changed over time?

The answer is that there is a marked difference in the distribution of opinion authors from different civil society organizations across media formats. First, in contrast to the expectations of those who see input from civil society coming primarily from social movement organizations (e.g., Habermas 1996), we find that the preponderance of opinion speakers come from the most overtly political category of civil society organizations, namely, registered lobby groups and political advocacy organizations (appendix C).

Second, we find that the distribution of speakers from different kinds of civil society organizations changed dramatically between our sample periods. In the early 1990s, table 4.7 shows that speakers from civil society organizations were represented in print and television in roughly similar proportions, with somewhat more think tankers in print than on television and somewhat more professional organization representatives on television than appeared in print. Those from the most political category of civil society organizations, namely, lobby groups and activists, accounted for about half of the opinion authors from civil society organizations in both print and television formats.

TABLE 4.7

PERCENT OF CIVIL SOCIETY ORGANIZATION AUTHORS,
BY FORMAT AND PERIOD

		Print	TV	Total
1993–1994	Lobby, advocacy, or social movement group	51.9%	52.0%	51.9%
	Think tank or policy institute	44.4%	32.0%	38.5%
	Foundations, professional, trade or service organization	3.7%	16.0%	9.6%
	Total	100.0%	100.0%	100.0%
		(27)	(25)	(52)
2001–2002	Lobby, advocacy, or social movement group	19.7%	62.2%	42.1%
	Think tank or policy institute	56.1%	27.0%	40.7%
	Foundations, professional, trade or service organization	24.2%	10.8%	17.1%
	Total	100.0%	100.0%	99.9%
		(66)	(74)	(140)

By the early 2000s, however, this balance had changed dramatically. By 2001–2002, think tankers and those from professional organizations improved their representation in print at the expense of television. The biggest change by far, however, was that the representation of lobbyists and advocates was drastically reduced in print, accounting for less than a fifth of authors from civil society organizations, while at the same time on television, we find a huge 62.2 percent of all opinion authors from civil society organizations are lobbyists and activists.

We find this changing pattern repeated among newspapers and between television shows in ways that reinforce now-familiar themes. *USA Today* was more likely than the *New York Times* to publish the most political speakers from civil society organizations; on television, *Hannity & Colmes* and *Crossfire* were more likely to air lobbyists than the *NewsHour* (on *Face the Nation*, the numbers are too small to be meaningful). Overall across the television shows, the number of lobbyists remained around 60 percent of all civil society organization authors, which is considerably higher than in print.

We also find that the elite speakers from civil society organizations we capture in our sample tend to have careers in which they circulate between formal government institutions, think tanks and policy institutes. and lobby groups. For example, in the first sample period, 1993–1994, William Bennett spoke as a fellow at the American Enterprise Institute, but by 2001–2002, when we took our second sample, he spoke on behalf of an advocacy group titled "Empower America." His colleague at the American Enterprise Institute in the earlier period was Dick Cheney, who had been secretary of defense in the administration of George H. W. Bush. By our second sample period, of course, Cheney appeared on *Face the Nation* as the vice president of the United States in the administration of George W. Bush. This indicates that the most political civil society organizations are part of the cultural beltway through which individuals circulate between political and parapolitical institutions. When your party is out of office, you join a think tank or work for the party, only to reenter government again when your side wins. This is a pattern that has intensified with the burgeoning of political think tanks and lobby groups since the 1960s, but it has long been a part of U.S. politics (Townsley 2000; Medvetz 2007).

In the big picture, then, we think the evidence on the composition of opinion speakers suggests that at least some significant part of the space of opinion has moved closer to the political field in the last twenty years. Although elected politicians and incumbent cabinet appointees enter the public conversation in traditional ways to support or criticize particular policies, it is also the case that as the opinion space expands and television formats proliferate to become the ascendant format for the political field as a whole, less autonomous speakers come to dominate in the role of media outsider in the space of opinion. This is documented in the changing patterns of social backgrounds among opinion speakers, as well as in the increased interchange of personnel between television opinion and parapolitical institutions like think tanks and political lobbies. Together, these findings suggest quite strongly that the part of the opinion space that operates through television is closer to the political field than it once was. Or to put matters differently, on television those who enter the opinion space from the political field are increasingly being drawn from positions that lack any real autonomy. Elected politicians and appointees may be defending an established position, but at least they are speaking for themselves. Lobbyists and other advocates do not even pretend to speak for themselves.

This is not true of print formats, however, where there is little evidence of declines in autonomy. In fact, the picture is nowhere near as stark as Bourdieu and other critics paint it, since there are good reasons to believe that a highly autonomous model of journalism and political opinion will continue to prevail as the ideal in the journalistic field. Indeed, there are signs that autonomous traditions of journalism have gained ground in some places, most notably at the *New York Times*. Here, some new voices have entered, mostly from the academy and the ranks of freelance writers, but these authors do not dominate. Instead, it seems likely that the intellectual purchase of elite journalism is expanding and that it is reinforced by the entry of academics into print opinion spaces. In at least one optimistic future for professional journalism, the worlds of the Web, trade and university publishing, academe, and journalism are becoming not only more closely connected but also more professionally autonomous. Finally, to the extent that the space of opinion on television remains strongly connected to these more autonomous news print formats, there is reason to believe that the traditions of autonomous journalism will continue to shape journalistic practice across all opinion formats: print, electronic, and digital.

Conclusion: Expansion, Elongation, Attenuation

It is far too simple, then, to say that the space of opinion—or journalism as a monolithic whole—is moving closer to the "field of power" (Bourdieu 2005). Rather, our data show that in the last two decades, the space of opinion has become more differentiated. That is, it has expanded and elongated, with the result that its internal distinctions have deepened. Its external boundaries with other spheres of action have also become attenuated. This is evident in the overall growth of the space of opinion and the influx of new voices in every format. It can also be seen in the deepening of internal distinctions within the field, one part of which remains anchored in the traditions of journalistic autonomy and independent opinion most closely identified with the elite professional columnist at the *New York Times*, while another part—the political talk show—moves closer to the political field. This is precisely the pattern of elongation: the less autonomous part of the opinion space moves further and further away from the traditions of old-time journalism at the same time as the traditions of journalistic autonomy are intensified and reinforced in highly professionalized spaces like the *New York Times*. While it is unclear what a new vision for journalism might look like in this context, and while there are many anxious voices proposing different ideas, it is clear that there are competing definitions of what it means to be an influential voice in the space of opinion in the early twenty-first century. Importantly, as we have shown, there are different understandings of autonomy, newsworthiness, and journalistic distinction, some of which do not rely on the traditional professional understandings of objective journalism.

If this is an accurate picture of the space of opinion, what does it mean? Is the changing composition of authors altering the nature of opinionated speech? Do media outsiders and media insiders speak in the opinion space under different conditions? Do they use different rhetorics and styles of speech? Or do the norms of the journalistic field constrain the voices of media outsiders so that they are indistinguishable from journalistic ones? We address these questions in detail in the two chapters that follow, describing the formats, communicative models, rhetorical styles, and claims to authority made in different parts of the opinion space over time.

5 Formats and Norms in the U.S. Space of Opinion

AS POLITICAL SATIRE shows, *The Colbert Report* and *The Daily Show* on cable's Comedy Central channel are the current standouts of the genre.[1] On *The Daily Show*, host Jon Stewart boasts that his is the best "fake news" show on television. Much of the show is a parody of CNN, with cast members acting as commentators and experts who provide ridiculous, exaggerated, and comically polemical interpretations of the day's political news. On *The Colbert Report*, host Stephen Colbert has created a parody of Fox News, particularly the headlining show, *The O'Reilly Factor*. Colbert surrounds himself with an infinitude of American flags (and eagles), overtly manipulates his audience as well as (some of) his guests, elevates pandering self-aggrandizement to the point that the host becomes the main character of every story, and avows feelings over facts; it was Colbert who coined the term *truthiness*. Dominating the much-sought-after eighteen-to thirty-nine-year-old television demographic and boasting an audience in the millions, these shows are clearly understood as important to the political process. Indeed, every competitive candidate for the U.S. presidency appeared on *The Colbert Report* during the 2007–2008 campaign season, a clear statement that the joke is well understood by Washington insiders, as well as young viewers.

What is the joke? The joke seems to be that those pundits, commentators, and powerful media institutions that are expected to uphold the journalistic values of objectivity and autonomy merely simulate critical independence. Rather than reflecting and parsing widely held public sentiment, they have become political insiders themselves.

Not only is the journalistic field becoming more integrated into the field of power, the argument goes, it is more and more an insider's game. As a consequence, news commentary is increasingly partisan: opinion is intellectually entrenched, rhetorically unreasonable, and lacking in critical intellectual substance. Some contrast the current situation with a lost ideal of reasoned, civil democratic debate (e.g., Gore 2007), but such arguments tend to overestimate the level of purity among journalists in the past and to underestimate the degree to which commitments to objectivity and balance continue to inform much contemporary journalistic practice. Stewart and Colbert lade their critiques with heavy irony that underlines this fact, too. But the joke is still funny—there *is* reason to believe that the conditions and norms of opinionated speech have changed in recent decades. Indeed, it is hard to imagine a parody of Walter Cronkite or Eric Severeid having the same effect, as *media criticism*, that the Colbert and Stewart shows have had. But if the conditions of opinionated speech have changed, how exactly have they changed? Have the changes occurred uniformly across the broadcast spectrum? What about the space of opinion and commentary in newspapers?

Communicative Conditions and Speech Norms

This chapter investigates these questions by looking at the different formats of opinionated speech across the range of print sources and television shows analyzed in the previous chapter: the *New York Times*, *USA Today*, *The NewsHour with Jim Lehrer*, *Face the Nation*, *Crossfire*, and *Hannity & Colmes*. Here we focus on two main features of these formats. The first is the *communicative conditions* under which opinion is produced and spoken, such as length of speech and average length of conversational turn. Second and connected is the *communicative norms* associated with a particular format, by which we mean differences in expectations about the purpose and nature of speech.

To take the broadest example, newspapers and television shows tend to have different communicative conditions. In newspapers, columnists write as individuals and are not subject to interruption as a condition of their speech. This is also true of those few news commentators on television who make an individual statement directly to the television camera. Typically, however, television opinion is far more circumscribed. Although the amount of speech for an individual in the newspaper and on television is almost identical—the average length of the opinion columns we study is 707 words, and the average length of speech for an individual on the television shows we survey is 706 words[2]—on many television talk shows, speech is subject to conversational norms of interruption, criticism, and editing. For example, talk show hosts on the four shows we survey speak 826 words per show on average, but this speech is broken across twenty-six turns per show, making any single turn an average of thirty words long. These kinds of differences are built into the conditions of opinionated speech at different newspapers and television shows, and they have effects on the nature of speech. Consider, too, that since television was the fastest growing part of the opinion space between the early 1990s and the

2000s, this means that the conditions of television's more circumscribed formats account for an increasing share of the opinion space.

Connected but distinct from communicative conditions are communicative norms; these are the cultural expectations that inform the nature of speech within various formats. One communicative model is dialogic speech, which organizes a rational interchange between discussants, as part of a larger search for truth (Gouldner 1979; Habermas 1985). The goal is to arrive at some kind of truth or best analysis to inform a decision. The mode is calm and deliberative, and the guiding principle is that the force of the better argument should ultimately prevail—an outcome that is guaranteed under rational rules of conversation governing turn taking, interruption, summaries, and conclusions. A second model invokes the rules of political contest and competition. The goal is to win the argument or score points, and ideally to do so in a way that is dramatic and entertaining. In this case, speech norms tend to dictate a situation that is more conflictual, that has more interruptions and faster talk, and where the most powerful voice wins. Tellingly, on television programs such as *The O'Reilly Factor* and *Hannity & Colmes*, talk show hosts refer to many of their most partisan, contentious, and most heavily advertised segments as "shoot-outs," rather than discussions or interviews.

While the distinction between rational deliberation and partisan competition is helpful, and while it is linked in useful ways to theoretical debates about deliberative democracy, it needs to be specified further if it is to provide analytical purchase on the empirical nuances of communication within the space of media opinion. Thus we offer the following four distinctions as a guide for thinking about the communicative norms that inform the opinion spaces of newspapers and television:

a. Is the dialogue designed to promote complexity or reduction as the best way for understanding the issue under consideration?
b. Is the dialogue motivated by the desire to arrive at a new and better position on the issue or rather to identify with an established position (or set of established positions)?
c. Is the dialogue focused on a search for common ground and consensus, or is it focused on identifying points of difference and disagreement?
d. Are the speakers interested in hearing the other's position or in talking over the alternative voices and positions?

These four distinctions also inform chapters 7 and 8 by helping us tease out the way different formats shape the complexity of speech in different parts of the opinion space. While some formats are more strongly associated with certain conditions and norms of communication than others, this is by no means a perfect correlation. Evidence of different communicative norms can be found across the range of contemporary newspapers and television shows, and there are contingencies and innovations across formats and across time. Nonetheless, there are striking patterns among and between opinion formats, which we believe shape the nature of the speech they publish.

Newspapers

Looking first at formats in *USA Today* and the *New York Times*, it is clear that columnists who publish in the *Times* write at greater average length (716 words) than those at *USA Today* (434 words), and they rarely engage in direct head-to-head debate. *New York Times* columnists do take political positions in their columns, but they tend to work in a less structured political format than those who write columns for *USA Today*.

Al Neuharth at *USA Today* is a good example of the latter group. He became a columnist following a long career on the business side of media as an executive and manager for the Gannett group. As cofounder of *USA Today*, Neuharth committed himself to provoking controversy in his columns. He is known for the for-and-against format of his editorial page and his willingness to print one-sentence rebuttals from critics. Neuharth's columns are different than columns in the *New York Times*, then, because although they encourage exchange, they do so in a more delimited way since they deliberately invoke the genre of political debate, where the goal is to present competing arguments, on an already defined proposition, and against an identifiable debate opponent. This is one reason that critics have observed that *USA Today* columns—Neuharth's among them—are more like fast-paced television talk shows than traditional print opinion. Columnists in the *New York Times* are less likely to engage in direct debate with other columns on the same page; instead, they tend to write their columns as interventions in ongoing public debates, engaging a variety of different voices and positions in the process.

To give a more detailed sense of how these differences in format play out on the ground, in what follows we compare several examples of opinion on the energy plan proposed by the Bush administration in 2001. Energy policy was a theme of several important connected conversations in the U.S. opinion space during our second sample period, 2001–2002. These included questions about the links between high-ranking members of the Bush administration and the energy industry, the unfolding California energy crisis, the relationship of the United States with foreign oil producers particularly in the aftermath of the September 11 attacks, and questions about U.S. national interests and the oil supply in the lead-up to the wars in Afghanistan and Iraq. Opinion pieces were selected from the day the Bush energy plan was announced, May 17, 2001, or on the next day closest to it.

Looking at the newspapers, we see that both papers opposed the Bush energy plan. Editorials in both papers criticized the plan, and opposition was also asserted forcefully on the op-ed page of the *New York Times* and in the debate sections of *USA Today*. Despite these similarities in position, however, the two newspapers organized their commentaries about the issue in very different ways.

On the day the energy plan was announced, the editorial page of the *New York Times* criticized it, and opinion columnist Paul Krugman also wrote a blistering critique. Titled "Burn, Baby, Burn," Krugman's column focused in particular on Vice President Dick Cheney, whom he characterized as ideologically misguided and morally suspect. Krugman argued that the so-called energy crisis was manufactured by the Bush administration using "greasy" math to support their "lust for tubular steel." Citing the "the libertarian Cato Institute," Krugman asserted that the plan was a "smorgasbord of handouts and subsidies for virtually every energy lobby in Washington." In fact, Krugman concluded, the Bush energy plan was exactly backwards:

> The truth is that the administration has things exactly the wrong way around. It claims that we face a long-run energy crisis, and that there are no short-term answers. The reality is that in the long run the forces of supply and demand will take care of our energy needs, with or without Mr. Cheney's expensive new program of corporate welfare. What we need is a strategy to deal with the temporary problem of sky-high prices and huge windfall profits. But we're not going to get it, at least not from Washington. (*New York Times*, May 20, 2001, Section 4, p. 17)

As a *New York Times* opinion columnist, Krugman writes his column as a critical dialogue with policy makers and frames his argument as part of a discussion about what policies will most effectively respond to the economic issues facing the nation. In this specific column, as in many others, Krugman challenges the underlying assumptions of the Bush-Cheney energy plan, questions the evidence that the administration has presented in support of its plan, and criticizes the motives of the key policy makers involved. In writing this type of column, Krugman continues a long tradition of newspaper commentary in which the columnist takes the role of a policy adviser. These types of columns are careful to describe the alternative position and its underlying assumptions, even if they ultimately focus on identifying points of difference rather than consensus. They also tend to emphasize complexity and, correspondingly, the search for a new and better position on the issue.

Krugman's column differs from those in *USA Today* in several respects. First, the signed columns in *USA Today* are shorter and, as a result, are not able to develop their argument with the same level of detail. Second, and more important, the signed columns in *USA Today* are typically organized in a for-and-against format, where columnists are writing against the official editorial position of the paper rather than making a more general intervention into the ongoing debate. This particular debate format makes it more likely that *USA Today* will select guest columnists who have a well-known and established position on a defined topic rather than guests who offer new or innovative positions. It also makes it more likely that *USA Today* columns will emphasize single-issue frames, where the goal is to advocate on behalf of a particular policy rather than to provide a larger context from which to understand the issue. In other words, *USA*

Today's debate format encourages reduction over complexity, disagreement over consensus, and alignment with established positions.

There were three energy "debates" in this format in *USA Today* following the announcement of the Bush energy plan on May 17, 2001. The first, published on the day the plan was made public, offered an editorial argument titled "Higher Energy Prices Fuel Changes to Ease Crisis," with the subtitle "Bush Plan, Due Today, Can Help. But Be Wary of Giveaways." Similar to Krugman in the *New York Times*, the unnamed editorial writer argued that market forces of supply and demand would eventually "heal" the energy crisis. But the main argument of the *USA Today* editorial had less to do with an evaluation of the Bush administration's policy-making process and instead focused on the general problem with government regulations (in this case, environmental regulations), subsidies, and "pet projects and giveaways." The opposing view, "Reduce Gasoline Taxes: Funds Go to Pork-Barrel Road Projects, Consumers Could Use Relief," was written by Pete Sepp of the National Taxpayer's Union, an advocacy group. Sepp made the case for cutting the gasoline tax to give consumers relief and, like the editorial, argued: "Big government, not Big Oil, is behind many price surges at the pump." As in the *New York Times*, then, the editorial position of *USA Today* was critical of the Bush energy bill. But whereas Krugman's column was a detailed criticism of a specific policy, *USA Today* columns provided more general and sweeping criticisms of government, drawn from well-known political positions and frames.

On May 24, one week after the plan was announced, there was a second debate on "gasoline prices" in *USA Today*. The editorial was headlined "How You Pay at the Pump to Protect Corn Growers" and argued against environmental regulation in its subtitle: "Federal Rules Push Prices Up. Environmental Protections Backfire." Against the editorial was a shorter column written by Eric Vaughn, the president of the Renewable Fuels Association, the national trade association for the ethanol industry. Vaughn's column was an advocacy piece titled "Ethanol Is Good for USA. . . . It Helps Meet Clean-Air Standards and Cut Dependence on Foreign Oil." Similarly, in a third debate from May 30, Energy Secretary Spencer Abraham was invited to write against the editorial position that "wasteful handouts skew energy plan's benefits" and "subsidies for energy firms add cost, ignore lessons of history." Abraham offered a column headlined "Incentives Are Good Policy" with the inset "Energy Crisis Demands Serious Efforts to Boost Efficiency." Abraham argued that *USA Today* "has it wrong. Unlike congressional energy plans, President Bush's energy plan is not largely premised on tax breaks and subsidies for industry." He then goes on to emphasize that subsidies are limited and targeted to provide incentives for developing alternative, cleaner technologies. Abraham attempts to reject the editorial frame of "corporate welfare" but was only partially successful. By this time, the corporate welfare trope had become definitive for this issue in the opinion space. Abraham, like Vaughn and Sepp, also had substantially fewer words in which to make his case—405 words compared with the editorial's 668 words.

In fact, this pattern was typical of *USA Today* debates: editorials were half as long again on average at 668 words than the opposing column, which averaged only 434 words. Typically, too, they took a particular position on a single-issue topic. Moreover, those positions tended to pose questions in well-understood issue frames: for example, in the frame of "citizen-consumers versus government environmental regulations" or "citizen-consumers versus big greedy government-subsidized corporations." Indeed, the frames are so well known that one does not even have to read the debate to understand the contending positions of the authors. The structure of headlines, subheadings, and snatch quotations makes it immediately clear what is at issue and what the positions are.

The overall effect of this format is to keep opinion in *USA Today* tightly tied to already-existing and preframed positions in the political landscape. Thus, as we show in the following chapter, opinion columns in *USA Today* are more commonly for or against some specific existing policy than columns in the *New York Times*, which are more likely to tell bigger stories, make wider moral arguments, or introduce new arguments into the conversation. In our example of opinion about the Bush energy plan in 2001, the particular focus of the debates in *USA Today* on incentives or gas prices tended to limit the scope of the conversation to a single issue rather than open it up to how issues might be linked to tell a larger story. Certainly, there was little global critique of the type Krugman made in the *New York Times*. Rather, different issues tended to be dealt with in separate and distinct debates, with different voices speaking to the editorial voice on preselected topics. In this structure, *USA Today* editors take the role of permanent moderator in the national conversation, which is understood primarily as a debate. This is similar to the role of the talk show host participating in a for-and-against format of television opinion.

Television

On the political television talk shows, representatives of more or less well-known political positions are typically asked to address an issue as part of a panel discussion. This is a major structural difference between the formats of print and television opinion: on television, people interact in vivo, with accompanying risks of complexity and contingency. As a result, the television shows have developed distinct styles to organize interaction between participants. As we shall see, however, the conversation unfolds in a variety of different ways, depending on the particular program.

Some television shows have formats and follow speech norms that are more like print opinion in the *New York Times* than debate formats in *USA Today*. For example, on the *NewsHour*, news commentary is preceded by the presentation of straight news, factually reported and kept separate from the opinion segments that follow. The ensuing discussion tends to be wide-ranging, with heavy representations from journalists, print columnists, academics, think tanks, private research firms, and trade associations charting out different positions in the form of a scholarly roundtable. For example, on the day the Bush energy plan was announced, Ray Suarez moderated a discussion between six speakers who represented a variety of energy industry groups, environmental organizations, and policy organizations. Suarez opened the segment by introducing his guests:

> Here to help us walk through the Bush energy proposal are Jane Houlihan, research Director at the Environment Working Group; Michael Marvin, president of the Business Council for Sustainable Energy, which represents wind, solar, and natural gas producing companies; Lynne Church, president of the Electric Power Supply Association, the national trade association for competitive power suppliers; Red Cavaney, president of the American Petroleum Institute, representing the major oil companies; Karl Rabago, managing director of the Rocky Mountain Institute, a research and education group focusing on energy efficiency; and Phil Verleger, an energy economist and president P.K. Verleger, a consulting firm.

Suarez then asked each guest in turn what they thought of the energy plan, posing his questions in a nonevaluative, neutral manner. To open the discussion, he asked:

> Well, Red Cavaney, let's start with you. An overview of the Bush [plan], does it make sense to you?

Cavaney briefly stated his position, and then Suarez turned to each of the guests in turn, asking for their statements by asking simply "Lynne Church?" or "Jane Houlihan, how about you?" "Karl Rabago, your review of the plan?" "Now, Phil Verleger, what did you make of the Bush plan?" In the next conversational round, Suarez introduced a prompt and asked each of the guests to respond, starting this time with Karl Rabago.

> RAY SUAREZ: Karl Rabago, let me read you a quote from the report that was released today. "The United States is facing the most serious energy shortage since the oil embargo of the 1970's, a fundamental imbalance between supply and demand." Is that the way you see it?

There are several interesting communicative features of this discussion. First, the moderator of the discussion, Ray Suarez, limits himself to asking short, neutral, "seeking information" types of questions. Not only does Suarez allow each guest time to state a position but also he allows them to frame their answers in any way they wish and to elaborate any themes they choose. The guests do not engage each other directly but direct their comments to Suarez as the chair of the panel. The pace is calm and the tone deliberative. As the segment unfolds, points of agreement among the panelists are noted, and points of difference are made through the introduction of new information and different perspectives. In the process, many different specific arguments are made in a comparatively short time: these include an analysis of the policy details, a discussion of the political process surrounding the bill as well as potentially useful additions that might have been added to the bill, a consideration of what is being said about the proposal in other media, and a historical analysis that contextualizes the present crisis against previous similar crises. The overall effect of this format is to encourage complexity over reduction.

These features of the *NewsHour* contrast sharply with the conditions and norms of speech at a show like *Hannity & Colmes*, where a more overtly political and contentious style of commentary is the defining characteristic. At *Hannity & Colmes*, the hosts dominate the conversation and usually display a clear preference for one side of a debate over another. Guests rarely speak for long and are subject to constant interruption by other guests and by the host. The overall effect is frenetic. Indeed, while the average conversational turn for a speaker on the *NewsHour* is 84 words, on *Hannity & Colmes* it is less than a third of that at 27 words (median turn length is 68 words at *Face the Nation* and 38 words on *Crossfire*). Commitments to scholarly rationality, to the force of the better argument, or to the identification of points of agreement are not central values in the exchanges on *Hannity & Colmes*.

The *Hannity & Colmes* broadcast from May 17, 2001 on the energy plan provides a good example of these differences in communicative conditions and speech norms. There were five segments on the show that day, including one on the Bush energy plan, one on the California energy crisis, and a prerecorded interview from show archives on drilling in Alaska.[3] The remaining two segments concerned praying students being asked to leave the White House and a discussion of a wrongful death case concerning a fetus in Arkansas. Of the energy segments, the first, which we excerpt here, accounted for more than a third of the show and was the main segment for the day.

ALAN COLMES, CO-HOST: First, leading our debate across America this Thursday: Will there be fall-out from President Bush's energy policy? Some Democrats have already criticized the president's plan. House minority leader Richard Gephardt said, "The president's energy plan is out. It's slick. It looks like the annual report of Exxon/Mobil. It's a deficient plan." Is this the new line of attack for Democrats?

Joining us now, former speech writer for President Reagan, Fox News political analyst Peggy Noonan. I like the shades!

Peggy Noonan, former Reagan speech writer. Thank you.

COLMES: Very nice.

HANNITY: Looks like a liberal.

COLMES: Oh, that's what they look like?

HANNITY: No, I'm kidding. He has—he has dark shades. That's why.

COLMES: All right. Look, you have to have them if you're a liberal.

(laughter)

COLMES; Now, listen, this energy—these energy meetings, Peggy, that Dick Cheney conducted were conducted in private. When Hillary Clinton—granted, not an elected official—did that with the health care plan, she was blasted by conservatives. Why is it OK when Cheney does it that way?

NOONAN: You know, that—of all the criticisms . . .

COLMES: Keep them on. Keep them on.

NOONAN: . . . of this plan—I can't see you that well . . .

COLMES: OK.

NOONAN: . . . with them. Look, of all the criticisms of this plan, I think that is one of the stranger ones. This administration has come in after eight years of essentially no energy policy. They are trying quickly to put together an energy policy that will answer the essential question, "How do we get more energy?"

COLMES: All right, let's be fair here . . .

NOONAN: We got an energy problem. We got to get some more.

COLMES: Let's be fair. There was no energy policy . . .

NOONAN: They put it together . . .

COLMES: Going back to Carter there was no energy policy. . . . (*Hannity & Colmes*, May 17, 2001)

There are many features worth noting about this exchange. First, the show is organized explicitly around "conservative" and "liberal" positions. This is the primary function, for example, of the lighthearted banter about the guest's sunglasses, in which clothing choices are added to the list of easy-to-spot items that allow a quick identification of political identity. Second, rather than asking the guest about her evaluation of the proposed policy, the cohost of the show begins by providing his own evaluation and then asking the guest to respond to his evaluation. The question is posed with the full expectation that the response will be one of sharp disagreement, and the explicitly partisan political party framing of the discussion is maintained throughout the segment. It contrasts sharply with the almost painfully neutral delivery of Ray Suarez on the *NewsHour*, who asked questions about similar topics on the same day. Furthermore, the guest, Peggy Noonan, who is a former speechwriter for Ronald Reagan, is clearly someone who has been selected not only to defend the energy plan and the Republican position in all its details but also because she can be counted on to maintain the partisan framing of the discussion, which she does to great effect throughout the segment. Third, the segment as a whole is characterized by a comparatively high level of interruption. Interruption is fairly good-natured, with laughter and jokes accompanying the cross talk. Indeed, our reading indicates that these features appear to be standard on *Hannity & Colmes*, particularly if the guests are political insiders accustomed to such banter, as Noonan clearly is. For the most part, the interruptions are not intended to ask for additional clarification, detail, or justification; instead, they are designed to end the speaker's turn and to introduce a completely different argument.

Face the Nation and *Crossfire* fall somewhere between the formats of the *NewsHour* and *Hannity & Colmes*, but they each have distinct features. *Face the Nation* is the format for national correspondents, where politicians typically come to defend or criticize specific policy initiatives. Thus it is on *Face the Nation* that Vice President Dick Cheney, the architect of the energy plan, appeared to make the administration's case.

In that interview, the show's moderator and veteran political journalist for *CBS News*, Bob Schieffer, joined with Gloria Borger, also from *CBS News* and *U.S. News & World Report*, to interview the vice president. They subjected him to a series of questions about the energy plan, citing critics from policy institutes, the *New York Times*, and consumer polls, all of whom had criticized the substance of the plan, as well as the political process through which it was developed. It was as though Schieffer and Borger had collected every single criticism made in the elite opinion space over the previous three days to present to Vice President Cheney for a response on the Sunday morning after the plan was unveiled. At the same time, the show was a good choice as a forum for the vice president to make his case, since he was given the time and space to answer each question at length and without interruption. Indeed, Vice President Cheney's average turn length in the conversation was 95 words, and he took 24 conversational turns. This is much longer than the turns taken by the interviewers: Bob Schieffer averaged 25 words over 22 turns during the show, and Gloria Borger 26 words over 13 turns. In contrast to *Hannity & Colmes*, then, where the turn length for guests was significantly shorter, the overall pace of *Face the Nation* was measured. Although Schieffer and Borger asked far more critical, challenging questions of the vice president than Ray Suarez did of his guests on the *NewsHour*, like Suarez, Schieffer and Borger kept their questions brief and to the point. The main difference seems to be that unlike Suarez on the *NewsHour*, Schieffer and Borger's questioning was insistent in tone, with both interviewers firing questions at the vice president one after the other. But the questions asked on *Face the Nation*, while challenging, were shaped by the desire to hear the other's position, in its full complexity and most developed form.

After thanking the vice president for the interview, Schieffer and Borger then turned to the Democratic opposition in Congress for a critique of the energy plan. Democratic Senator Barbara Boxer condemned the plan roundly, speaking as a representative of California, where the energy crisis was most acute at the time. Indeed, the choice of Senator Boxer underlines the explicitly political format of *Face the Nation*, where political opponents are invited to make their competing cases to the nation in general and to Bob Schieffer and Gloria Borger in particular. The preeminence of majority party speakers is underlined by the fact that while Senator Boxer as a member of the party in opposition speaks at length—with an average of 106 words per turn—she takes only nine turns compared with the vice president's twenty-four turns. Finally, notice that the guests do not argue with each other directly in this format but make their case to the hosts. The hosts, in turn, are committed to pushing the guests to articulate their arguments in the fullest possible detail. In this spirit, Bob Schieffer sums up the show's raison d'être at the end of the second segment when he says: "Senator, thank you very much. I think we've really got both sides this morning."

The fourth show, CNN's *Crossfire*, is closest to *Hannity & Colmes* in its communicative conditions and speech norms. Hosts at *Crossfire* take partisan positions; there is a higher degree of interruption and cross talk and therefore much shorter average turns for each speaker. Correspondingly, there is a much higher average number of turns per show on *Crossfire* (25 turns) compared with *Face the Nation* (10 turns) and the *NewsHour* (8.5 turns), although not quite as high as that on *Hannity & Colmes* (27.5 turns).

What distinguishes *Crossfire* as a format is that for most of our sample period, at least one of the hosts on each show has been a political insider—either a former politician, a cabinet member, or a political consultant of some kind. The other host is usually a political journalist who takes a partisan position. For example, you see Patrick Buchanan or John Sununu teamed with Michael Kinsley, or Paul Begala or James Carville teamed with Tucker Carlson. There is also the straight journalistic team of Bob Novak and Bill Press.[4] Each of these figures is branded as either a liberal or conservative critic, and together they subject guests to the "crossfire" of competing questions from the "left" and the "right." In this respect, like *USA Today* and *Hannity & Colmes*, the orientation is toward the identification of (and the alignment with) established positions.

On the day the Bush energy plan was announced, the *Crossfire* hosts for the evening were Robert Novak and Bill Press, and the guests were two congressional representatives, Republican Billy Tauzin from Louisiana and Robert Wexler, a Democrat from Florida. The hosts editorialized as they asked questions, with each host interrogating the guest from the other side of the political spectrum (a format *Hannity & Colmes* also used to great effect). On the May 17, 2001, episode of *Crossfire*, the show began with host Bill Press taking the liberal position in asking questions of Representative Tauzin:

> BILL PRESS, CO-HOST: Congressman Tauzin, good to see you on CROSSFIRE. President Bush went out to unveil his plan today at a turkey manure plant, which I think sort of sums up the entire plan, beginning with this so-called crisis.
> You know, former President Jimmy Carter in the "Washington Post" this morning spoke about this crisis. I'd like to read you just a little bit of what the former president had to say, quote: "No energy crisis exists now that equates in any way with those we faced in 1973 and 1979. World supplies are adequate and reasonably stable, price fluctuations are cyclical, reserves are plentiful and automobiles are not waiting in line at service stations." Isn't it true? This whole crisis has just been manufactured to give the oil companies whatever they want?

Representative Tauzin replies with good humor:

> REP. BILLY TAUZIN (R), LOUISIANA: You spooked us out. That's exactly it. . . .
> Gasoline prices are not rising, there are no blackouts in California, it's all

made up, it's all fake. We're not shutting down petrochemical plants in Louisiana because the price of natural gas is too high. Farmers are not going to face incredibly high prices for fertilizer next year, because we're not manufacturing ammonium and nitrogen anymore at those plants. No, we don't have a crisis.

What we have is a crisis that's about to explode on this country, and if we don't start thinking about it as rational human beings instead of demagoguing it, we are going to be in trouble.

Notice how the *Crossfire* format is a combination of elements from *Face the Nation*, in that it questions political representatives about the specific details of the plan (i.e., a desire to hear the other's position) and from *Hannity & Colmes*—in particular, the use of dueling hosts and the framing of questions that are intended to elicit sharp disagreement. Given this hybrid character, it is not surprising to find that the average length of conversational turns at *Crossfire* falls roughly in the middle of the distribution of the television formats we study. The average length of conversational turns on the *NewsHour* is 84 words compared with 68 words on *Face the Nation*, 38 words on *Crossfire*, and 27 words on *Hannity & Colmes* (see appendix D for more detail). What is unusual about *Crossfire*, however, is that although the pace is fairly quick and the tone of the conversation is aggressively argumentative, speech tends to be far more evenly balanced between hosts and guests than on the other shows. Hosts on *Crossfire* participate as equal and partisan debating partners with their guests, but they do so without dominating the program. In the transcript for this particular episode of *Crossfire*, for example, Novak averages 41 words a turn over 28 turns, Press averages 49 words a turn over 17 turns, Tauzin averages 50 words a turn over 17 turns, and Wexler averages 38 words a turn over 25 turns. This contrasts sharply with the other shows, where either guests or hosts account for the majority of speech.

In addition to these structural features, the different choices of guests also distinguish the shows. For the Bush energy plan discussion in 2001, the *NewsHour* gathered experts from a range of energy and environmental institutions to assess the government's plan. The discussion was run like an academic panel, providing the various points of view and reactions of organized opinion outside the government. The host's role was performed in a neutral manner and aimed simply to direct the panel. In sharp contrast, *Face the Nation* was the place where the government (the vice president) and the opposition (the leading Democratic senator) were asked to make their cases for and against the plan. *Crossfire* and *Hannity & Colmes* also focused primarily on the politics of the plan, but they tended to do so in dialogue with lower level politicians and political consultants than one is likely to find on *Face the Nation*.

Finally, we observe that the differences in partisanship, pace, and tone of the shows we have described follow the patterns of journalistic autonomy and dependence we documented in the previous chapter. The *New York Times* and the *NewsHour*, which have higher proportions of speakers from more autonomous intellectual traditions like journalism and the academy, also tend to follow speech norms that are slower and less frenetic. *USA Today* and *Hannity & Colmes*, whose guests are more likely to be political strategists and representatives from advocacy organizations (i.e., with comparatively lower cultural autonomy) feature a faster pace with more frequent interruptions.

Changes in Print and Television over Time

Given these differences in the conditions and norms of speech across different opinion outlets, a second question this chapter raises is: to what degree have these less autonomous, more partisan, faster paced formats been growing at the expense of more traditional, deliberative, and dialogic news commentary and opinion? While our sample periods are only ten years apart, formats change quickly in broadcast media, and our data show change as well as continuity in conditions of speech between the early 1990s and the 2000s. Specifically, we find a pattern of relatively stable speech conditions in print in contrast to speedup, interruption, and increasing partisanship on television.

This builds on our earlier findings that the amount of opinion has increased in traditional formats as well as newer ones in the last two decades. It also parallels our findings for the composition of opinion speakers, which indicated that distinctions between more and less autonomous opinion formats have deepened. Stated another way, although there has been an increase in the amount of television opinion over time, we find that this has not occurred at the expense of print opinion but rather in tandem with it, as the entire opinion space has expanded. As chapter 4 documented, the median length of columns increased between 1993–1994 and 2001–2002, and while the increase was fairly modest at the *New York Times* (+1.7 percent, or an increase from 712 to 724 words), it was much more dramatic at *USA Today*, where median column length increased 86 percent, from 348 words to 648.

By contrast, at the three television shows airing in both sample periods, guests and hosts experienced a decline in the total amount of time they had available to speak. This was most marked at the *NewsHour*, where median total length of speech decreased about 27 percent, but there were also small decreases at *Face the Nation* (-6.5 percent) and *Crossfire* (-8 percent). Other indicators shown in table 5.1 confirm this general story. The number of speakers increased on all three television shows, a fact that certainly helps to explain the reduced time—and also the reduced number of conversational turns—that most guests and hosts had available to them. Again, these patterns were more or less marked at different shows, with the changes more pronounced on the cable news programs than they were on *Face the Nation* or the *NewsHour*.

At the *NewsHour*, the format did not change much. If anything, it became more like print in its commitments to noneditorial commentary, including a reduced role for the host. As at the other shows, there was a slight decline in the number of turns per speaker on each show, a decline that is straightforwardly explained by the small increase in the

TABLE 5.1

STRUCTURES OF OPINIONATED SPEECH, BY OUTLET AND PERIOD

		Median # speakers/ show	Median # turns/ speaker/ show	Median turn length*	Median total length
New York Times	*1993–1994*	—	—	—	712 words
	2001–2002	—	—	—	724 words
	Total	—	—	—	**716 words**
USA Today	*1993–1994*	—	—	—	348 words
	2001–2002	—	—	—	648 words
	Total	—	—	—	**434 words**
All print (median)	*1993–1994*	—	—	—	697 words
	2001–2002	—	—	—	715 words
	Total	—	—	—	**707 words**
The NewsHour	*1993–1994*	6	10	77 words	730.5 words
	2001–2002	8	7	91 words	534 words
	Total	7	**8.5**	**84 words**	**606 words**
Face the Nation	*1993–1994*	5	9	71 words	706 words
	2001–2002	6	10	65 words	660 words
	Total	**5**	**10**	**68 words**	**673 words**
Crossfire	*1993–1994*	4	32	26 words	898 words
	2001–2002	6	17.5	45 words	826.5 words
	Total	**5**	**25**	**38 words**	**863 words**
Hannity & Colmes	*1993–1994*	—	—	—	—
	2001–2002	8	27	27 words	704.5 words
	Total	**8**	**27**	**27 words**	**704.5 words**
All television (median)	*1993–1994*	5	14.5	52 words	780.5 words
	2001–2002	7	13	46 words	652 words
	Total	**6**	**14**	**50 words**	**706 words**

All differences are statistically significant at the .01 level.
*Median of average turn length for the category.

number of speakers appearing on each show in the second sample period. At the same time, however, the average length of each conversational turn actually increased (+20 percent) at the *NewsHour* between 1993–1994 and 2001–2002, which contrasts sharply with the other opinion shows on television. This is counterintuitive, given the increase in the average number of speakers on each show and the substantial overall decline in total average length of speech per speaker (-27 percent), which should have led to shorter average turns, all conditions being equal. What had occurred at the *NewsHour* was a reduction in the role of the host, who took fewer and shorter turns over the period. (Add) This trend was very different than what was happening with the hosts at the other shows. The effect, as we saw with the discussion of energy policy, was to place the guests into a common dialogue, where different analyses were compared, where points of agreement were noted, and where the ultimate goal was to reach a fuller understanding of the situation.

Similarly, at *Face the Nation*, there seems to have been minimal change in communicative conditions and norms between 1993–1994 and 2001–2002. Speakers had slightly more turns on each show in the second sample period, and there were very small declines in the total length of speech and the average length of turn for each speaker. As one of the oldest, most elite, and highly successful opinion formats on television, this is not terribly surprising. Designed as an extended conversation between a journalist and a politician, the program is intended to uncover the competing policy positions and personalities that make up the world of politics. Journalists get to ask tough and probing questions, while politicians have the opportunity to address a national audience. The key to the arrangement is that hosts do not dominate the program and that guests answer the questions that are asked of them. The goal is to identify the most important established positions on a given issue, but to do so in a way that establishes these positions in their fullest detail and complexity.

If *Face the Nation* and the *NewsHour* stayed fairly stable during these two time periods, however, *Crossfire* changed dramatically. The average number of conversational turns for the typical individual on *Crossfire* declined dramatically, from 32 turns a show in 1993–1994 to an average of 17.5 turns a show in 2001–2002 (-45 percent). This was associated not only with an increase in the number of speakers on each show but also with an *increase* in average turn length for each speaker (from twenty-six to forty-five words). Part of this is explained by the fact that *Crossfire* changed, in 2002, from a thirty-minute format to sixty minutes. But with such an increase, one might expect an increase across all speech indicators—number of turns, length of turn, and total length of speech. Instead, we find that the median length of speech for an individual on any particular episode declined over the period, from 898 words to 826.5 words (-8 percent). The number of conversational turns for each speaker declined even more dramatically, from 32 to 17.5 turns.

What accounts for these changes on *Crossfire*? One reason is that there were fewer elected politicians and executive branch officials appearing on the show during the second sample period (see appendix D for more detail). Typically, we find that when elected politicians and executive branch officials appear on television talk shows, they tend to speak at greater length and take more conversational turns than most other kinds of guests. At *Crossfire*, between the early 1990s and the 2000s, the proportion of opinion spoken by politicians dropped dramatically from 17.2 to 7.2 percent. And for those politicians who did appear on the show, their average number of conversational turns dropped precipitously, from 31 to 14.5 turns per show. Similarly, the average number of conversational turns for executive branch officials dropped from 27 a show to 14.5 turns a show. For the most part, however, these changes were pushed by changes in format, particularly the introduction of many more distinct episode segments (table 5.2).

These new episode segments, which emphasized the importance of the program's hosts, came to replace dialogue with elected politicians and executive branch officials. These new segments included periods of extended banter between the hosts, taking well-known positions on general topics, as well as a new "Fireback" segment, where the hosts responded to viewer e-mail. In both of these kinds of segments, there were no guests participating at all. On *Crossfire*, then, there was a recentering in the journalistic field between periods, with a heavier emphasis placed on the role of pundits, commentators, and especially the talk show host, rather than politicians or other high-status government representatives. At the same time, the hosts aligned themselves more and more clearly with existing well-known positions in the political field. This represented a movement closer to the communicative norms and conditions displayed on *Hannity & Colmes*, a program that was the closest direct competitor to *Crossfire*.

TABLE 5.2

NUMBER OF SEGMENTS BY SAMPLE PERIOD, *CROSSFIRE*

	1993–1994	2001–2002	Total
Segment #			
1	96.0%	33.5%	54.1% (166)
2	4.0%	27.7%	19.9% (61)
3	—	18.0%	12.1% (37)
4	—	17.5%	11.7% (36)
5	—	3.4%	2.3% (7)
	100.0% (101)	100.0% (206)	100.0% (307)

As a whole, then, these findings indicate that the conditions and norms of communication among television formats are also differentiating, with the *NewsHour* and *Face the Nation* reemphasizing the norms associated with high-end professional journalism, while *Crossfire* and especially *Hannity & Colmes* continue to innovate forms of speech that are centered on sharp, argumentative, short exchanges between media insiders and, to a lesser extent, between these media insiders and selected political insiders.

Insiders and Outsiders Revisited

Are the different formats and communicative norms of the opinion space so constraining that they determine the nature of speech, or can different kinds of speakers shape the nature of their speech *independently* of format? We explore this question by analyzing whether the occupational background or the gender of a speaker alters the nature of their speech in different television formats.

Occupation

The amount and frequency of speech varies widely between speakers from different occupations across the four television shows we have surveyed. Details are provided in table 5.3, which shows that talk show hosts (826 words), print columnists (790 words), politicians (807.5 words), and executive branch officials (720 words) tend to speak the most on television. Hosts take many shorter turns than columnists or political speakers, who speak at greater length at each conversational turn. Academics (517 words) and speakers from the civil society organizations (527 words) have the lowest total word length on average, and academics also have the lowest number of average turns per show. Note, however, that although academics speak less often than other kinds of speakers, when they do speak, they do so at greater length, averaging 101 words per turn: this is twice the median turn length of 50 words. Academics are followed by journalists with 84 words per turn, executive branch officials with 82 words per turn and print columnists with 79 words per turn.

Print columnists and academics became more similar to each other between the early 1990s and 2000s, too: there was a decline in turn length for academics with a small rise in overall number of turns; for columnists, there was a decline in number of turns combined with a substantial rise in average turn length. Even in the later period, where there were signs of speedup and reduction in turn length at most shows, columnists and academics continued to speak at comparatively greater length than others in the space of opinion.

In addition, academics and columnists were much less likely to be interrupted than other speakers. This was certainly due in part to the fact that when academics and print columnists appear on television, they are more than twice as likely to appear on the *NewsHour* (7.3 + 8.7 = 16 percent) than on *Face the Nation* (2.8 + 4.4 = 7.2 percent),

TABLE 5.3

CONDITIONS OF SPEECH ON TELEVISION, BY OCCUPATION

		Median # turns/ speaker/ show	Median turn length	Median total length*
Talk show hosts	*1993–1994*	28	29	821.5
	2001–2002	23.5	31	826.5
	Total	**26**	**30**	**826**
Columnists	*1993–1994*	13	58	959
	2001–2002	8.5	99	762.5
	Total	**10**	**79**	**790**
Journalists	*1993–1994*	7	87	550
	2001–2002	9	81	650
	Total	**8**	**84**	**612**
Media strategists	*1993–1994*	13	42	497
	2001–2002	24	21	611
	Total	**23**	**24**	**578**
Elected politicians	*1993–1994*	12.5	76	919
	2001–2002	10	75	794.5
	Total	**10.5**	**76**	**807.5**
Executive branch	*1993–1994*	10	82	843
	2001–2002	9	81	652.5
	Total	**9**	**82**	**720**
Civil society orgs	*1993–1994*	9	62	763.5
	2001–2002	8	68	508
	Total	**8**	**68**	**527**
Academics	*1993–1994*	4.5	120	620.5
	2001–2002	5	94	508
	Total	**5**	**101**	**517**
Lawyers	*1993–1994*	13	48	834.5
	2001–2002	12	40	630
	Total	**12**	**46**	**641**

continued

TABLE 5.3 (Continued)

		Median # turns/ speaker/ show	Median turn length	Median total length*
Writers	*1993–1994*	10	85	729
	2001–2002	9	70	622
	Total	**9.5**	70	**659**
Others	*1993–1994*	8	78	504
	2001–2002	6	73	559
	Total	**6.5**	77	**556**
Total median (television)	*1993–1994*	14.5	52	780.5
	2001–2002	13	47	652
	Total	**14**	50	**706**

All statistically significant at the .01 level.
*Median of average turn length for the category.

Crossfire (1.4 + 3.8 = 5.2 percent), or *Hannity & Colmes* (4.1 + 3.4 = 7.5 percent). See Table 4.4. This is evidence that different formats tend to select opinion speakers from different occupational backgrounds.

Despite this evidence that occupational differences matter, then, our data indicate that format is probably more important in shaping opinionated speech. Looking at average turn length—or how long someone speaks at each conversational turn—is a good indicator of the pace and tone of a show. Guests from different occupational backgrounds on *Face the Nation* and the *NewsHour* have longer average conversational turns, ranging from 80 to 130 words; guests on *Crossfire* and *Hannity & Colmes* have comparatively shorter conversational turns ranging between 20 and 60 words per turn. The possible exception here is lawyers, for whom median turn length is remarkably similar at the *NewsHour* (49 words a turn), *Face the Nation* (52 words a turn), and *Crossfire* (52 words a turn). Notice, however, that the deflating effect of the *Hannity & Colmes* format seems to work for lawyers as it does for guests from all other occupations: the median turn length for legal guests on *Hannity & Colmes* is 25 words a turn, which is very close to the median for all speakers on the show, which is 27 words (see appendix D for details of speech conditions by occupation and format).

The punch line is that while occupation does affect the length and frequency at which a guest speaks on television, it does so within boundaries set by the show's format. What this means is that we can predict turn length for an individual on television more effectively if we know whether the speaker is appearing on the *NewsHour* or on *Hannity & Colmes* than if we know whether she is an academic or a lobbyist. It also means that the relative autonomy of speech that some individuals enjoy in their own intellectual milieu—in the academy, the legal profession, or literature, for example—simply does not translate in a format like *Hannity & Colmes*. In fact, if you ask who Sean Hannity interrupts the most, it is guests who are academics, writers, and print columnists, and to a lesser extent, media strategists, lawyers, and his cohost, Alan Colmes. Clearly then, even the most autonomous (and long-winded) opinion speakers like academics are constrained by the norms and conditions of speech in a format like *Hannity & Colmes*. This is also true to some extent on *Crossfire*. And in both cases, it is connected to much lower representation of academics, print columnists, and writers on these more partisan shows, where the format seems to be more amenable to the styles and skills of media strategists and speakers from advocacy organizations, political lobby groups, and think tanks, who appear to be more likely to reduce an issue to an established position, to emphasize disagreements, and to be willing to talk over other guests.

Gender

If occupation has only a limited effect on the length and frequency of speech in different formats, what about gender? Again, the answer varies, depending on where in the opinion space someone speaks and how their occupational role positions them; in short, it depends on format and occupation.

The most significant fact about gender in our data is that the overall representation of women in the elite space of opinion is extremely low. At the beginning of the twenty-first century, only one in five opinion authors were women. This is the most important way that women speak less than men in the space of elite opinion, and it rests on the question of access.

By some measures, however, the situation has improved between our sample periods: the proportion of women who spoke in the space of opinion shifted from 14.6 percent to 19.9 percent between the early 1990s and the 2000s. Note, however, that all of this increase was concentrated in a single occupational category—the television talk show host category. Among television talk show hosts, the proportion of women more than doubled from 11.7 to 28 percent between 1993–1994 and 2001–2002, and this *entirely accounts* for the shift in the overall representation of women. This increase in women's representation was produced by just a few individuals on the *NewsHour* and *Face the Nation*—Gloria Borger, Charlayne Hunter-Gault, and Margaret Warner. These women are powerful voices in the elite opinion space, and like their colleagues in print—Gail Collins, Maureen Dowd, and Anna Quindlen—they occupy a significant proportion of the space of opinion (table 5.4).

There are reasons to suspect, however, that the success of these individuals does not harbinger a wider change toward gender equity in levels of representation in the elite space of opinion. Indeed, once hosts are excluded from the analysis, there is no statistically

TABLE 5.4

WOMEN HOSTS PUBLISHING OPINION, BY PERIOD AND OUTLET

	New York Times	USA Today	News Hour	Face the Nation	Crossfire	Hannity & Colmes	Total
1993–1994							
HUNTER-GAULT, C.	—	—	5	—	—	—	5
WARNER, MARGARET	—	—	8	—	—	—	8
2001–2002							
BORGER, GLORIA	—	—	—	23	—	—	23
CROWLEY, MONICA	—	—	—	—	—	1	1
ECHEVARRIA, LAURA	—	1	—	—	—	—	1
IFILL, GWEN	—	—	6	—	—	—	6
INGRAHAM, LAURA	—	2	—	—	—	—	2
MYERS, DEE DEE	—	—	—	—	1	—	1
WARNER, MARGARET	—	—	15	—	—	—	15
TOTAL	—	3	34	23	1	1	62

significant change in the *proportion* of women who speak in the elite space of opinion between the early 1990s and the 2000s.

Print and television outlets vary significantly in their recruitment of women speakers, however, and this appears to interact with occupation. Of all the shows, the *NewsHour* was historically the most hospitable to women: at the *NewsHour*, women were 22 percent of all opinion speakers in the early 1990s and nearly 30 percent by the early 2000s. And in the talk show host category on the *NewsHour*, women were particularly well represented, increasing their representation from a third (33 percent) in 1993–1994 to nearly a half (47 percent) in 2001–2002.

In contrast to the *NewsHour*, the proportion of women on *Face the Nation* started from a lower absolute proportion of 14 percent in 1993–1994, and climbed to 22 percent by 2001–2002. This is completely explained by the introduction of Gloria Borger as a host. Indeed, if the host category is excluded from the analysis, the proportion of women on *Face the Nation* actually declined over the period. The smaller increases for women at *Crossfire* (from 5.2 to 11.2 percent of all speakers) and the proportion of women at *Hannity & Colmes* (18.2 percent) are not accounted for by hosts. Instead, they seem to represent smaller across-the-board trends in specific categories, like speakers from civil society organizations where women are comparatively well represented. Women are far less well represented among professional opinion columnists, politicians and executive branch officials, lawyers, and media strategists. Overall, we can say that the comparatively higher proportion of women on *Hannity & Colmes* and in *USA Today* comes largely from civil society organizations, and the higher numbers on the *NewsHour* and *Face the Nation* are largely accounted for by the hosts. The proportion of women is conspicuously lower at *Crossfire* in both periods.

But in the end, does it matter? This is a fundamental question for any compositional analysis of the opinion space. "Speaking differently" can mean many things, of course, and a large research literature dating back at least three decades suggests that women do speak differently than men (see Ferber 1995 for a review). But is there any evidence that the sex of an individual affects the length or frequency of their speech in the elite space of opinion?

In print formats, we find no evidence of these kinds of sex differences. Rather, the data show that while there is a marked difference in the *representation* of women among opinion authors, with men taking up the majority of the territory, when women do publish their opinions, they appear to operate under the same communicative conditions as men. Both women and men who publish op-eds in the *New York Times* and *USA Today*, for example, write at similar lengths. Indeed, as we documented in the previous chapter, column lengths in print are remarkably stable across gender and other characteristics: in the *New York Times*, median column length for women and men was exactly 716 words. In *USA Today*, the median column length for men was 433 words and for women it was slightly higher at 442 words.

On television, however, there are systematic differences in total length of speech, average turn length, and number of turns per show that appear to be significantly associated with sex. First, women tend to take fewer conversational turns than men on every show but the *NewsHour*, where the substantial number of women hosts inflates average number of turns. This is true to some degree at *Face the Nation* as well, where women take 12.5 turns per show compared with 16.5 turns per show for men, which is a comparatively small difference. In fact, when hosts are excluded from the analysis, the number of conversational turns taken by women and men are identical at both the *NewsHour* and *Face the Nation*. In contrast, the sex difference in conversational turns is more pronounced at the newer shows: at *Crossfire*, women take 20.5 turns per show on average compared with 30.5 turns per show for men, and at *Hannity & Colmes*, women take an average of 26 turns per show compared with 58 turns per show for men.

Second, the average length of conversational turn tends to be longer for men than for women on every show. This difference is more pronounced at the *NewsHour* (86 words for men compared to 47 words for women) and *Face the Nation* (65 for men, 26 for women) than at *Crossfire* (39 for men and 37 for women) and *Hannity & Colmes* (26 words for men compared with 22 for women), which is explained again by the fact that the majority of women-authored opinion on the older shows is spoken by women hosts, and hosts generally take shorter, more frequent turns, as we have seen. There also appears to be some other variation across occupational categories by gender, but the numbers get too small to make further occupational comparisons robust.

Third, when we look at total length of speech, it seems clear that except for speakers at the *NewsHour*, where the situation is roughly equal (men 692 words and women 592 words), men tend to speak at greater length than women on television. At *Face the Nation*, men speak 834 words on average compared with 451 words for women. At *Crossfire*, men speak 969 words on average on each show compared with women at 688 words a show, and at *Hannity & Colmes*, men have 867 words a show on average compared with 565 words for women.

Our conclusion is first that although slightly more women appeared in the opinion space in the early 2000s than in the early 1990s, this improvement in representation has been double-edged. Women have gained ground mainly on television, and although those women who speak as hosts enjoy privileges in that central institutional role, in the other television formats where they speak, women's conditions of speech are worse than men's in both absolute and relative terms. This is true in nearly every occupational category. This finding provides evidence for those who point to a decline in dialogic and deliberative speech norms. Indeed, it is ironic that as women enter the opinion space, their advent is associated with an overall decline in autonomy and complexity in that space.

It is striking, however, that elite print formats and those television formats most associated with print have resisted this decline, and women have made gains here, too. While print formats have been affected by these changes, they do not appear to have been transformed by them in the same way television has. At the newspapers we surveyed, we see an overall expansion in the number of columns published, an increase in the proportion of women writing columns in both newspapers, and stable speech conditions, regardless of the sex of the opinion author.

Again, this underscores our argument that the opinion space as whole was growing and becoming more internally heterogeneous over this period. Women were part of both trends: expansion and differentiation. At the newspapers and the elite television shows, the conditions of women's speech started to look more like men's, and although overall representation remained distinctly unequal, it improved between the early 1990s and the 2000s, most markedly at the *NewsHour*. At the more partisan television shows, by contrast, and especially at *Hannity & Colmes*, the conditions of women's speech were even worse than men's, with short turn lengths and fewer conversational turns overall. At *Crossfire*, too, in particular, the representation of women remained particularly low, even in our second sample period.

The analysis of sex differences is revealing in several ways. First, it shows that while dynamics of sex and/or gender clearly structure the composition of who speaks in the space of opinion—that is, gender structures access to the space of opinion—the format of speech at different newspapers and television shows exercises a powerful independent effect on the nature of that speech. Second, to the degree that sex differences illuminate how other public identities, like race, region, and ethnicity, structure the opinion space, this suggests the absolute centrality of institutions and particular formats as they serve as resources for or constraints on how those identities operate in the U.S. space of opinion. We focus on sex and gender here because our data are the most robust for this dimension of social inequality, but connected questions could be asked, especially for race but also for region, age, nativity, and other factors.

Finally, our compositional analysis raises associated questions about how the conditions and norms that define formats are connected to the content and style of speech. This is the focus of the following chapter, where we ask: are different formats associated with different opinion styles? Are opinion styles associated with different audiences, variations in language use, or different claims to authority? In other words, what are the different narrative styles and rhetorics in the opinion space?

"Analysis, it's not ideology."

—PAUL GIGOT, *The NewsHour*, June 1, 2001

"Caution: You are about to enter the no-spin zone."

—BILL O'REILLY, *The O'Reilly Factor*

"Sarah Palin says she's got nothing to lose by playing rough with Barack Obama. John McCain may disagree. Let's play HARDBALL."

—CHRIS MATTHEWS, *Hardball with Chris Matthews*, October 14, 2008

6 Rhetorics in the Space of Contemporary U.S. Opinion

A RECURRENT THEME in the world of media opinion and commentary is that objective analysis is difficult and rare. Critics and commentators emphasize that the threats to good analysis are many: ideology, public relations spin, soft and unchallenging questions, one-sided political partisanship, emotion, dishonesty, venality, banality, tedium, and even insufficient levels of patriotism have all been presented as obstacles to an effective, insightful analysis of the events and issues of the day. Good analysis must be based on logic and reason, the argument goes. We do not disagree with this statement, but beyond this initial commitment, there is a range of competing rhetorics that shape *how* objectivity is envisioned and performed. On different issues and at different times, moral outrage, calm authority, professorial didacticism, or ironic humor can all powerfully inform the delivery and reception of opinion.

This chapter focuses on these performances by describing and analyzing the different rhetorical styles that are deployed within the contemporary U.S. space of opinion. Drawing on the cultural sociological model of public opinion we outlined in chapter 3, we identify how opinion authors draw on existing cultural styles and traditional narrative forms to express and authorize their speech. Many make moral and political arguments to intervene in ongoing debates; others attempt to alter the public conversation by reframing the issues. It is in these ways that opinion authors both summon the publics to which elites address their arguments and also hold those elites accountable in the name of such publics.

Data and Methods

As in previous chapters, we compare opinion from six outlets: the *New York Times*, *USA Today*, *The NewsHour with Jim Lehrer*, *Face the Nation*, *Crossfire*, and *Hannity & Colmes*. Unlike in previous chapters, however, here we compare newspaper op-eds with show *segments* rather than entire television episodes (n = 2,152). Television transcripts are considerably more complex than newspaper op-eds because they typically cover several distinct topics in different segments. Each segment takes the form of a conversation between separate groups of individuals, and while talk show hosts usually appear in every segment of a show, most guests do not. Looking at segments allows us to make more precise distinctions between the different styles of argument various speakers make (see appendix A).[1]

Similarly, the variables we develop for the analysis of rhetorics in this chapter are more complex than the traditional variables on social background, occupation, and gender, which we presented in chapter 4, or the inherently numeric variables describing turn length or median number of words spoken on a television show, which we presented in chapter 5. In those chapters, we could rely on established social science conventions to develop our variables. Here, however, because we want to explore rhetorical styles, claims to authority, and the use of different kinds of language and cultural references in texts, there are limits to how much our quantitative measures can tell us. To be sure, much can be gained from the formal analysis of the rhetorical features of speech: large amounts of data can be analyzed systematically, major structural features of the universe of opinion texts can be identified, and an overall sense of the context in which specific texts operate can be provided. What is lost with such an approach, however, is some capacity to explore complexity and to examine the multiple meanings that are circulating within a single stream of text data; there is always the tendency to treat the categories one has generated as more distinct and mutually exclusive than they really are. Our hope is to combine some of the strengths of both approaches; thus we have proceeded as far as possible to self-consciously ground our quantitative variables in a close, interactive reading of opinion texts.

For the variable measuring "primary opinion style," for instance, we spent a great deal of time immersed in and reading the opinion texts, and we used an iterative approach to identify dominant opinion styles. For this reason, we coded each text independently to develop a grounded list of styles. We met regularly to check the compatibility and reliability of our categories, and we played with different categories and reanalyzed the data in several different ways.[2] Through this process, we eventually distinguished five major opinion styles.

"Making specific arguments" refers to an opinion text that supports or criticizes a particular policy, piece of legislation, person, or event. Such texts typically refer to a particular, detailed, and ongoing dispute in which a specific outcome is in the balance. In this style, opinion is presented in a for-or-against format. Similarly, the opinion style "making moral arguments" relies on a for-or-against frame, but in contrast to "making specific arguments," those "making moral arguments" appeal primarily to universal social values or very general understandings about "who we are" and the "difference between right and wrong." The third opinion style we identified is "asking questions." Largely the province of interviewers and opinion show hosts, the "asking questions" style also has the effect of framing issues in particular ways, although there is variation in the degree of partisanship, position taking, and complexity in the "asking questions" style. The fourth style we identify is "reframing," which is a specific attempt to disrupt and alter existing conversational frames in the opinion space. "Reframing" typically asks readers to reexamine basic premises and/or tries to refocus the attention of elites and publics. The final opinion style we identify is "providing information." In this style, the primary intent of an opinion column is to present evidence, facts, or data in the context of an ongoing conversation. The rhetorical performance is one that judiciously refrains from taking a position or making larger political or moral claims. To be sure, the analytical distinctions between these five primary opinion styles are sometimes hard to maintain: it is very clear when reading opinion texts that there is often more than one opinion style in a given text. This is evident in the excerpts we present throughout this chapter. But it is equally clear that the vast majority of op-eds and television opinion segments are encoded through a dominant opinion style.[3] This is what we capture with our "primary opinion style" variable, which we use to map the distribution of opinion styles in the space of opinion as a whole.

We also used a grounded process to develop our "ideal reader" variable, coding texts independently and then meeting to consider conflicts and overlap. For this variable, we asked the open-ended question: who is the imagined audience this opinion author thinks she is addressing? The result was a long list of categories that included "mothers," "post-911 New Yorkers," "fans," "veterans," "voters," "police chiefs," "consumers," and "sports decision-makers." The final variable contained more than thirty categories. Looking more closely at this long list, we again experimented with different codes and ran the analysis in different ways. Eventually, we determined that the primary distinction was between those opinion authors who were writing *as if* they were engaged in a discussion with only political insiders and those authors who were speaking *as if* they were addressing a broader public audience of general citizens. This distinction draws on Umberto Eco's (1998) comparison between a model reader (i.e., the imagined reader in the author's mind) and the empirical reader who actually reads the text.[4] Our variable intends to capture the ideal or imagined reader and thus is an important dimension of how texts work in the contemporary space of opinion. That is, our "ideal reader" variable describes two competing visions of politics among opinion authors: one where politics is viewed as a game for insiders and one where politics is seen as a discussion among citizens.

We produced similarly long lists of categories when looking at those who claimed authority on the basis of experience. These included "terrorist hostage," "politician," "grieving mother," "athlete," and "baby boomer." These categories were eventually collapsed into a measure of claims to authority based on personal experience and claims to authority based on professional experience. Of course, experience claims are only one of several ways to make a claim to authority when presenting an opinion. So at the end of this chapter, we consider *direct* claims to authority, which include experience claims, as well as formal markers of social authority such as research credentials or political position. We contrast these with *indirect* claims to authority, which include the use of scientific discourse, historical discourse, and references to popular texts, including other news and opinion texts and also music, film, and television genres. This latter set of variables measuring references to other media texts underpins our preliminary discussion of intertextuality in the space of opinion and captures an important and growing dimension of mediated deliberation.

A final methodological observation in this connection is that the level of analysis of rhetorical forms should be understood as analytically separate from the analysis of the institutions, formats, and persons who populate the space of opinion. For example, although the opinion style that attempts to reframe an issue of common concern is most commonly used by the most autonomous speakers in the opinion space like academics and professional columnists, reframing is an opinion style that is available to all kinds of speakers in all kinds of formats, and we find it in all of the formats we study. Similarly, historical and scientific claims to authority are made by a wide range of opinion speakers in every format we study. The point is that the relationships between particular speakers, formats, and rhetorics are open empirical questions to be explored rather than foregone conclusions that can be inferred from a basic knowledge of format or speaker.

We conduct such an investigation in the analysis of rhetorics that follows, and it complicates the story we are telling about the expansion and differentiation of the space of opinion in several ways. First, the analysis of rhetorics shows that while it is true that the opinion space has expanded, formats have proliferated, and divisions between different principles of distinction have deepened, the opinion space as a whole has also become much more interwoven, more densely interconnected, and more textually self-referential. Second, the analysis of rhetorics suggests that the older, more traditional television shows play a particularly important role in this system, serving as a bridge between the more deliberative and autonomous opinion styles that characterize high-end print journalism and the faster, more partisan opinion styles that characterize the newer television and print formats. What is less clear in this connection is the degree to which the opinion space is a communicative arena that continues to addresses wider publics or if there are signs that it is becoming an increasingly exclusive space of communication oriented narrowly to political insiders.

Providing Information or Making Arguments?

When individuals publish opinion in newspapers and on television, they participate in the formation of public opinion in multiple ways. Certainly, one way is by providing new information to voters. For example, information is provided when a forensic psychologist discusses the possible motivations of a criminal (*Hannity & Colmes*, October 17, 2002), when a Washington correspondent analyzes the surprise reelection of Helmut Kohl as German chancellor in 1994 (*NewsHour*, October 17, 1994), or when Mushahid Hussain, a former newspaper editor and elected Pakistani senator talks about his experiences as a political prisoner (*New York Times*, February 12, 2001, p. A23). Without a doubt, some information is provided in every opinion text. But as a *rhetorical* matter, the type of neutral delivery that presents itself as only providing information—just the "straight facts"—is comparatively rare in the U.S. opinion space. In fact, among the different types of styles displayed by contemporary U.S. opinion authors, the "providing information" style is the one used the *least* often—only 12.7 percent of all opinion is in the style of "providing information" in a self-consciously neutral way.

Among formats, the more autonomous high-end outlets in print and on television are more likely to exhibit this opinion style than those formats characterized by less autonomous speakers and conditions of speech. This parallels our findings about autonomy and deliberation from chapters 4 and 5, and thus it is unsurprising that the "providing information" opinion style was more common in *New York Times* columns (13.5 percent) than in those published in *USA Today* (6 percent), and that it was more common at the *The NewsHour* (24 percent) and *Face the Nation* (16 percent) than at *Hannity & Colmes* (9.9 percent) or *Crossfire* (5.2 percent).[5] The big difference from previous chapters, however, is that the "providing information" style of opinion that self-consciously offered information in a neutral manner was much more common on television than in print, characterizing the older, traditional television formats in particular. It appears, then, that the traditional television formats remain strongly connected to the "providing information" commitment of professional journalism, at least insofar as this describes the rhetorical styles that characterize these formats.

By far the most common rhetorical style for commentaries and columns in the opinion space, however—and by a large margin—is an argumentative opinion style. More than half of all the opinion in our sample is expressed in this way: either as an argument for or against a specific course of action (31 percent) or as a moral argument that mobilizes specific social values on behalf of a particular cause (26.2 percent). We can see examples of the former type of partisan argument in the many debates about U.S. interests in the Bosnian conflict in the early 1990s. As the following excerpts demonstrate, the style of argument is similar, regardless of whether the analyst is arguing for or against U.S. entry into the conflict:

The Clinton administration seems determined to have Americans die in the Balkans. . . . Although revulsion at the struggle is universal, most people recognize that the world is full of horrid conflicts that would cost far too many U.S. lives to try to control. During the Cold War, the threat of Soviet aggression caused the USA to become, at enormous cost, the global guarantor of peace. But communism is now dead. The lack of strategic interest does not lessen the humanitarian concern, of course. However, those demanding that Washington intervene are not offering to join the fight, as did members of the famous Lincoln Brigade in the Spanish Civil War earlier in this century. . . . Washington policymakers quickly grow impatient when faced with intractable foreign problems. But they have no right to order young American men and women to die in the utopian pursuit of global stability. (Doug Bandow, Cato Institute, *USA Today*, May 17, 1993, p. A12)

Well, it's a U.S. show, Bob, in the sense that we've got to lead the West. We've got to lead our European friends in insisting upon that action. And as a matter of fact, it should be a NATO force. Now they'll m—be mostly U.S. planes that will do these air strikes. I think it's important to do two things, if I—don't mind my saying. One, this is a war of aggression. It is not merely a civil war. This is an aggression by Serbia across the Drina River into the independent country of Bosnia, run by a war criminal named Milosevic who happens to be the president of Serbia. That's what this is. And secondly, there is genuine, real live genocide. And it seems to me that we—there are things we can do. . . . I think it's clear that we have to set certain goals. We can't go in and bring peace in the Balkans, but there are certain things we can do right now that can raise the price of the committing—the commission of genocide by the Serbs. There are things we can do right now that enhance the humanitarian aid getting in, and there are things we can do right now to bring the prospect of the Serbs to the peace table, because n—if nothing changes, Bob, they're not about to go to the table. They've got everything they want and they continue to march on to divide up that country. (Senator Joseph Biden, *Face the Nation*, April 25, 1993)

In both of these examples, the commentators provide information and context, but they do so for the larger purpose of making a specific argument about why the government should or should not pursue a specific course of action. In the first case, Doug Bandow of the Cato Institute provides historical information in a metaphorical way to contextualize the present situation and make an argument about the dangers of entering the war. In the second case, Senator Joe Biden offers information about what is happening in Serbia to make an argument about the kinds of military action the United States should undertake. In neither instance is the information provided simply as a neutral aid for the rational citizen. Instead, the information is organized strategically in favor of a particular argument, either for or against military intervention.

While these examples make implicit moral arguments about specific policies, in other instances, the moral argument is the primary objective of the commentary. This style is evident in an op-ed in the *New York Times* written by Dennis DeConcini, Democratic senator from Arizona, who argued:

> President Clinton and our allies must take further steps, including military force, to stop the genocidal slaughter of civilians. . . . We must act because our moral integrity as the leader of the democratic world is at stake. The West must not turn its back once again on genocide in Europe. (*New York Times*, May 18, 1993, p. A21)

DeConcini goes on to argue that it is in the economic and political interests of the United States to intervene militarily in Bosnia, but he leads with the moral argument that the United States must oppose genocide. Clearly, in each of these examples, the reader or viewer learns information about the unfolding situation in Bosnia, but in each case, the argument about values or action—is it right or wrong? should we vote yes or no?—is as important as, or even more important than, the information conveyed.

Frequently, the moral argument dominates the commentary even more centrally than is the case in this example, serving as a general condemnation of a particular situation without the same kind of focused argument for or against a specific policy. Consider the following two examples, one from a discussion of tabloid news and the other from a discussion of the economy:

> Are serious news people who are supposed to be presenting us information about our world that's important to us, as we go about our lives, as government leaders try to lead, is that being sidetracked by tabloid? And I'll say that it is. When Diane Sawyer asks Marla Maples if Donald Trump is the best sex she's ever had, that is misusing her credibility as a journalist. (Ellen Hume, *Crossfire*, February 17, 1994)

> Well, I mean, when you read Goldman Sachs got 58 new partners, all of them got $5 million average bonus last year, at the same time middle-class income's going down, there's a problem in America, my friend. (Pat Buchanan, *Crossfire*, October 17, 1994)

In these two examples, there are certainly implicit policies that the speakers are supporting. Hume's comment can be seen as a plea for less tabloid journalism, whereas Buchanan's criticism can be seen as an argument in favor of policies that limit executive compensation. But it would be misleading to claim that this type of policy advocacy was the intention of either speaker. Rather, the main effect of these arguments is the moral criticism of a person or situation. Diane Sawyer and Goldman Sachs partners stand in for larger social groups, which are polluted because they are characterized as acting in a way that threatens the larger public good. In other words, those who speak in the space of opinion invest considerable energy narrating compelling dramas of intrigue, horror, and moral danger, in a manner that is consistent with the cultural model of mediated deliberation we introduced in chapter 3.

On balance, we find that moral argument was slightly more common on television than in print, while arguments for or against specific policies were much more common in print than on television. Here again, however, there was important variation among the television formats, with the older television shows, like the print formats, more likely to make specific arguments than moral arguments. Moral arguments were far more likely to predominate at *Crossfire*, where they accounted for half of all opinion, and also at *Hannity & Colmes*, where moral argument accounted for well over a third of all opinion spoken on the show. For all the print and television outlets we survey, however, making arguments of some kind is the dominant style in which opinion is performed, as Table 6.1 shows.

Imagining and Invoking Audiences

Specific and moral argument styles are both characterized by a for-or-against structure that assumes the opinion author is connected to a reader for whom the opinion matters. Opinion authors display this sense of themselves as influential players in the development of policy and public opinion by addressing their speech in a way that invokes third parties not actually present in the conversation. This is what Clayman and Heritage (2002) documented in their landmark study of the news interview, and we find it in the

TABLE 6.1

ARGUMENT STYLE BY OUTLET

	New York Times	USA Today	The News Hour	Face the Nation	Crossfire	Hannity & Colmes	Total
Specific argument	36.3	54.0	28.0	22.1	25.1	16.1	31.1
Moral argument	25.6	20.2	14.8	10.1	50.8	41.4	26.3
Asking questions	—	—	28.0	46.8	11.4	25.3	16.5
Reframing	24.6	19.9	5.3	5.0	7.5	7.3	13.3
Providing information	13.5	6.0	24.0	16.0	5.2	9.9	12.7
Total	100%	100%	100%	100%	100%	100%	100%
	(609)	(302)	(304)	(357)	(307)	(273)	(2,152)

opinion texts we examine too. In general, opinion texts invoke two basic types of third-party audiences: elite networks of political insiders and publics of general citizens.

Consider the following examples where opinion is clearly addressed to an audience of political insiders—policy makers, policy advisers, and policy analysts. In the first, Nicholas Kristof, a regular columnist at the *New York Times*, begins by providing information about growing nationalism in China, observing that many Chinese seemed to be enjoying the troubles the United States was experiencing in the aftermath of the World Trade Center bombings. This information is provided as a report of an essay written by a Chinese student, and so its authority is grounded in the evidence of the journalist and the expert. He then goes on to write the following:

> When President Bush visits Beijing next month, he needs to raise the matter with President Jiang Zemin. It was President Jiang who launched the effort in 1990 to cultivate nationalism as a new unifying ideology for China, and he needs to know that we find this abuse of the education and propaganda systems unacceptable. . . . President Jiang himself is not trying to nurture xenophobia. But his efforts to use nationalism as a new unifying ideology risk having that effect. One of the greatest challenges for the global community will be to manage the rise of China. President Bush must try to make Mr. Jiang realize that this process will go more smoothly if China modernizes not only its financial system and highway network, but also its propaganda apparatus, so that it promotes international harmony rather than hatred. (Nicholas Kristof, *New York Times*, January 22, 2002, p. A19)

Kristof's column provides information and context, but it is primarily written as a piece of advice to the Bush administration, which makes specific suggestions for Bush's upcoming trip to China. To be sure, the "we" he references—those who "find this abuse of the education and propaganda system unacceptable"—is an outraged public whose interests need to be articulated and protected. But the dominant mode of address is to political insiders. It is a specific recommendation for action written as though Kristof is a close foreign policy adviser to the president. And Kristof's elite mode of address is no fantasy; he can be confident that his column will be read by presidential aides in both countries and reported as part of an executive summary of the key political editorials of the day.

The second example is taken from an exchange between two columnists—William Kristol of the *Weekly Standard* and Thomas Friedman of the *New York Times*—who are debating the meaning of the Clinton administration's actions in Somalia on *Face the Nation*. Kristol says:

> Really, at the core of the failure in Somalia is the Clinton administration's belief that wishing can make it so, that if we talk a lot about working with the UN, . . . [if

we are] clever in our rhetoric, that somehow, these local warlords will stop be-having the way they've always behaved. And I think you see a lot of that in domes-tic policy, too: You give a speech, you have six phrases that everyone likes—security, responsibility—you have a huge PR blitz, there's no legislation, there are no details, a lot of the de—a lot of the details are covered up, that somehow that this is going to work, too. Both at home and abroad, this administration has a huge belief that rhetoric can substitute for—really for hardheaded sound policy." (William Kristol, *Face the Nation*, October 10, 1993)

Kristol's speech is intended to provide a general framework for criticizing Clinton's pol-icy-making approach as one with too much rhetoric and not enough "hardheaded" analysis. Like Kristof's column, it is directed primarily to political insiders, in this case to conservative intellectuals and policy makers who oppose President Clinton. The use of "we" in this example very clearly underlines this fact. Kristol sees himself as part of a conversation about politics among elite insiders. When he says "if we talk a lot about working with the UN . . ." and "You give a speech . . ." he seems to imply that he is the one giving the speech or talking to the UN.

To be sure, the audience for both of these pieces of commentary extends well beyond the elite political insiders addressed by the authors and includes many ordinary people. In important respects, though, the power and the influence of this mode of address come precisely from the fact that it is part of an elite conversation among important decision makers. Indeed, as we have argued in previous chapters, the leading newspaper columns and television talk shows provide some of the most important communicative spaces that constitute the elite political public sphere. But the elite mode of address has a more general influence as well. To the extent that ordinary readers accept the subject position being offered to them, they are encouraged to imagine politics and policy making as a discussion among elite political insiders and to identify with them. For the nonelites in the audience, their role is to line up behind their favorite elite commentators and decision makers and take their talking points from those individuals.

Of course, elite address is not the only one available. The other mode that character-izes the opinion texts we study addresses the reader as a citizen or as an ordinary member of the public. Consider the following exchange between Pat Buchanan and Andrew Sullivan, which took place on *Crossfire* on May 19, 1993:

BUCHANAN: What is the pedigree of the idea that a homosexual relationship is on an equal moral plane with traditional marriage? What is the genesis of—

MR. SULLIVAN: We're talking about a civil act. We're talking about the United States, which is a civil and secular society, in which all we're asking for is, not religious marriage, we're asking for equality in the civil sphere, where civil citi-zens coexist together. They may disagree about morals—

BUCHANAN: But what is your idea—

MR. SULLIVAN: —but they want equal rights, and that's what we're offering them.

BUCHANAN: What is your idea, even in the civil sphere, that these types of relationships are on the same plane and should be on the same plane as a traditional marriage, which society and law sanction in order for the basically the propagation of children and—

MR. SULLIVAN: Because I believe they are the same, because I believe that the emotional commitment of one man for another man or another woman for another woman is the same in terms of the love that they can have and the commitment that they can bring of a man and a woman, and not all heterosexual marriages create children either.

BUCHANAN: Right.

Both of these speakers are clearly elite. Buchanan has served as an adviser to three presidents and has worked as a political commentator for dozens of magazines and television shows. Sullivan, a former editor of the *New Republic*, is also a frequent commentator for print and broadcast media and currently writes one of the most influential and popular political blogs. But that is not salient in this exchange about gay marriage. In this back and forth, neither individual is speaking as a political insider, nor are they providing direct policy advice, nor are they even offering expert analysis. Instead, they are having a debate about whether religious or civic principles should guide how people think about gay marriage. Neither person claims any official expertise, nor do they suggest that this is a discussion that is reserved for expert analysts and decision makers. They are speaking as members of the U.S. public. Indeed, the conversation could be taking place in any living room in the country.

Another way in which commentary and opinion texts invoke the audience-as-citizen is when they seek to explain the significance of a particular issue or event. Typically, the goal is to try to suggest a counterintuitive or more complex understanding than is immediately obvious. This form of public address imagines the reader in the role of a student, typically a civics student. Lippmann used this style frequently in his columns in the first half of the twentieth century, but today this pedagogical style is most likely to be used by academics, as well as some think tank intellectuals and select columnists. An excellent example of this opinion style is a commentary in the *New York Times* written by Alan Brinkley, professor of history at Columbia University. The op-ed appeared in the midst of President Clinton's failed attempt to create universal health care in the early 1990s. Brinkley assessed the process of making effective policy by analyzing the history of the Social Security Act of 1935:

When it was enacted, its benefits fell much further short of universality than almost any health care measure now debated. Huge categories of people were excluded. When the first pension payments began, in 1940, they reached fewer than a quarter of all workers and virtually no one outside the paid labor force. Yet within four years, Congress began to expand the system. Today, Social Security pensions are the closest thing we have to a universal system of social insurance. Whatever its flaws, it is the most popular and politically unassailable social program the Government has ever produced.

The Social Security Act was successful because it established the principle that Americans were entitled to certain social protections. That principle quickly produced almost irresistible popular demands for continued expansion of the system. Surely, legislation establishing the principle but not the reality of universal health care would similarly generate substantial public pressure for expansion. (*New York Times*, August 12, 1994, p. A23)

Brinkley provides a historical lesson in the ironies of policy making, viewed from the long perspective. The opinion style provides information, suggests a change in policy focus, and in so doing tries to reorder the policy priorities in the health care debate. Thus he argues that it is less important for a new policy to be fully inclusive, as long as it establishes the principle of full inclusion. In the same column, too, Brinkley discusses the 1965 Medicare Act to argue that a policy will be more successful in the long term if it establishes a principle of financing and cost containment. By using these two historical comparisons, Brinkley offers readers a set of guidelines for understanding the future consequences of current policy debates. Rhetorically, the column reads like a college lecture that imagines an audience of student-citizens who need new information and more context to understand an ongoing policy discussion. To be sure, Brinkley may also hope to educate elites and sway the policy discussion, but the primary mode of address is to a public of general citizens.

As each of these examples demonstrates, opinion authors conjure an imagined reader—political insiders or general citizens—and in the same process direct their empirical readers to put themselves in the position of the protagonists in the text. They ask their readers to understand the situation from the point of view of a policy maker, a policy adviser, or a member of the public. When we assess modes of address more formally in Figure 6.1, we find that about half of all opinion is addressed to political insiders rather than to general citizens (51.7 percent versus 48.3 percent), but this varies considerably across outlets and opinion styles. About 60 percent of all opinion on the *NewsHour* and *Face the Nation* was addressed to wider publics of citizens, while opinion and commentary at the other four outlets was more likely to treat the conversation as one between political insiders. *USA Today* is striking in this regard, with nearly 70 percent of all the opinion it published addressed to political insiders; this compares with 58 percent at *Crossfire* and 54 percent at the *New York Times*, although note that *Hannity & Colmes* is much closer to the median with just under half—48 percent—of opinion addressed to political insiders.

This pattern of differences in mode of audience address replicates our earlier findings about the importance of the older television shows and highlights their continuing

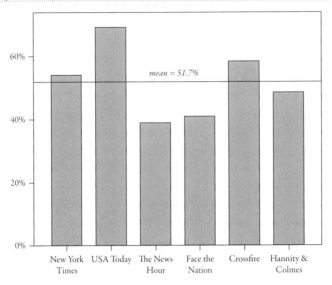

FIGURE 6.1 Percent of opinion texts addressed to political insiders rather than general citizens, by outlet.

connection to the traditions of elite professional journalism. Indeed, it is striking and not a little ironic that, despite the reputation of the newer television formats as popular, populist, and therefore appealing to wider audiences, speakers on *Crossfire* are significantly more likely than those at *The NewsHour* or *Face the Nation* to formulate their commentaries as conversations with elites and play the role of the political insider.[6] In the older television formats, by contrast, speakers are far more likely to address their comments to an imagined public of general citizens. When taken together with the finding that these older television formats are also the most likely to exhibit the opinion style of providing information, as well as results from chapters 4 and 5, which showed that print columnists, journalists, and academics are more likely to appear in the older television formats than the new ones, it seems clear that *The NewsHour* and *Face the Nation* are important bridges between the traditional and newer formats in the journalistic field, helping to anchor television opinion in the traditions of the high-end print values of factual reporting and an orientation to citizen publics who need to be informed to participate in democratic deliberation.

Forms of address are also clearly connected to differences in opinion styles between the formats we study, as Figure 6.2 shows. Thus, the high proportion of all opinion at *USA Today* was addressed to elite audiences because *USA Today* was much more likely than other outlets to publish opinion in a for-and-against opinion style organized around a predefined policy or political topic. Of all the different opinion styles, the for-and-against styles were the most likely to address an imagined audience of political insiders. In fact, more than 80 percent of those making or criticizing a specific policy presented their opinion as though they were participating in a conversation between political insiders.

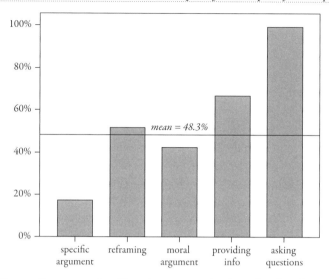

FIGURE 6.2 Percent of argument styles addressed to citizens rather than political insiders, by opinion style.

This is less true for the other opinion styles: moral argument, providing informa-tion, and reframing styles are more evenly split between those opinion pieces that position themselves as part of a conversation among political insiders and those that address themselves to a public of general citizens. By contrast, the opinion style of asking questions is almost entirely performed as a form of public address. Ninety-nine percent of the opinion texts that took the form of asking questions were spoken by talk show hosts, and in virtually every case, the hosts positioned themselves as reg-ular people—ordinary members of the public, speaking on behalf of regular citi-zens. This is a marked feature of the opinion style of asking questions; namely, those who ask questions attempt to shape the public conversation by representing publics to elites.

Asking Questions

Like the for-and-against styles, asking questions is a distinct performative style within the opinion space, and it occurs almost exclusively on television. Its purpose is to shape the political agenda, but it does so in a more indirect way than other opinion styles—by setting the agenda. The power of the questioner is in framing what is talked about, even though those who are questioned do not always answer questions directly. The fact that political leaders appear on television in large numbers to receive questions, however, demonstrates clearly that elites, as well as opinion authors, share an understanding that public opinion—as it is formed in and through the mass media—is an important part of the exercise of power (Clayman and Heritage 2002).

While "asking questions" constitutes a distinct style, it is also the case that new talk show formats have brought with them different substyles for asking questions. *Face the Nation*, one of the oldest formats in television opinion, is the example par excellence of asking questions in the classical style of the news interview. When *Face the Nation*'s host Bob Schieffer asked Senator Joe Biden in 1994 to explain why and how the U.S. military would go into Bosnia, Schieffer represented himself as asking the question on behalf of an interested public. Biden answered the question in the same spirit. It is clear that Schieffer's role as a representative of an interested public is the source of his authority for questioning political elites in this way, and we would emphasize that it is also the key to Schieffer's performance of journalistic neutrality in the exchange.[7] In fact, Schieffer's style of asking questions on *Face the Nation* is solidly grounded in the traditions of objective journalism and follows the standard form for the political news interview, described so well by Clayman and Heritage (2002). As we saw in chapter 5, too, questions on *Face the Nation* tend to be shorter than on the newer talk shows and much less evaluative. The *NewsHour* is similar to *Face the Nation* in this respect, with shorter, nonevaluative questions and a demonstrated commitment to rational, deliberative, objective news and commentary.

In contrast, on newer programs such as *Crossfire* and *Hannity & Colmes,* questions are considerably longer, and they are far more likely to contain propositional content aimed at eliciting disagreement. Take, for example, *Crossfire* host Tucker Carlson asking Governor Gary Johnson of New Mexico to defend his position on the decriminalization of marijuana:

TUCKER CARLSON, CO-HOST: Governor Johnson, legalizers such as yourself, or de-criminalizers, like to beat up on Prohibition. But the fact is, the little-known fact that Prohibition, like the current drug war, saved lives.

I just want to read you two statistics. These were compiled by Professor Mark Moore of Harvard. During prohibition when alcohol was not legally sold, death rates from cirrhosis of the liver dropped 60 percent among men. Admission to mental hospitals for alcohol-related causes dropped 50 percent. Of course, when Prohibition was repealed, alcohol consumption went up astronomically. Isn't the bottom line here that the drug war, whatever its problems, saves lives? (*Crossfire*, April 20, 2001)

Governor Johnson immediately disagreed and explained why Carlson's argument was incorrect.

This excerpt provides a good example of the difference in questioning styles between different formats. Unlike Schieffer's question to Biden, asking him, "Are you talking about us going it alone [in Bosnia]?" notice how the question Carlson asks Johnson first states a position and then asks Governor Johnson to disagree. This kind of question is characteristic of the two newer shows we study and reflects a shift away from an older

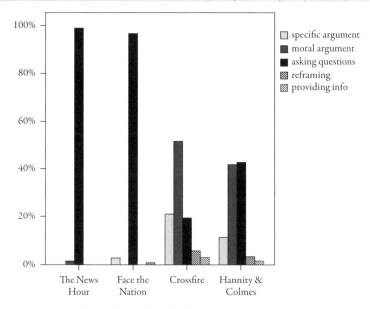

FIGURE 6.3 Argument styles of television hosts, by format.

tradition of dispassionate analysis where the norm is "that interviewers should (i) avoid the assertion of opinions on their own behalf and (ii) refrain from direct or overt affiliation with (or disaffiliation from) the expressed statements of interviewees" (Clayman and Heritage 2002: 126).

Not only are questions more loaded and argumentative on the newer shows but hosts at *Crossfire* and *Hannity & Colmes*, are also far less likely to use the asking questions style of opinion, as Figure 6.3 shows. At the *NewsHour* (98.8 percent) and *Face the Nation* (97 percent), nearly all of the opinion produced by hosts is in the style of asking questions, but at *Hannity & Colmes* less than half (42.6 percent) of all opinion spoken by hosts is in the style of asking a question, and at *Crossfire*, hosts asked questions only 19.3 percent of the time. In fact, at the newer shows, hosts were much more likely to make moral arguments or take a position for or against some specific policy. This is a significant departure from the role of the television talk show anchor and the traditional model of the political interview.

Reframing

The final opinion style we explore is reframing. Reframing is similar to asking questions in that it attempts to set the agenda for public conversation. And insofar as it is more likely than the argumentative opinion styles to engage general citizen readers rather than political insiders (see Figure 6.2), reframing is like providing information and asking questions as a style of opinion. Unlike asking questions, however, which is entirely the province of talk show hosts, reframing is a rhetorical style associated with media outsiders, such as academics, lawyers, and writers. Through reframing, these authors seek to alter the already established terms of conversation, to refocus attention, or to change the fundamental ways we think about our shared history, identity, and culture.

In its most basic form, then, reframing is an attempt to change the topic of the conversation. Alan Brinkley's op-ed on the history of health care legislation cited previously is a good example. Another comes from Representative Martin Frost of Texas, who appeared on an episode of *Crossfire* to comment on the "beltway sniper" who was terrorizing the Washington, D.C. area by shooting victims at random in 2002. Frost agreed with the hosts and other guests that the sniper needed to be caught but then went on to suggest that the Republican administration was using the sniper issue to deflect public attention from the worsening economy (*Crossfire*, October 15, 2002). After several attempts to change the topic of conversation, Frost's strategy was eventually successful, and the conversation shifted to the economy.

But reframing can be more than a topic change. It can also be an innovation in the opinion space, reflecting the possibility that a new argument can change the terms of debate. Take, for example, Richard Freeman's argument for buying weapons from militia in Northern Ireland (*New York Times*, July 28, 2001, p. A11). Freeman, an economist at Harvard and the London School of Economics, argued that disarming the militia by funding community development with the proceeds from decommissioned weapons was in the rational interests of all parties. Using the rational-choice logic of economic analysis, Freeman reframes the debate about disarming Northern Irish militias by shifting the discussion from the history to the future, and from redress for victims to rebuilding communities.

Or consider the following column written by Cornell economics professor Robert Frank:

> Traffic jams are a nuisance, but they are more than that. Studies have shown that compared with people who walk or take public transportation to work, people who face protracted commutes in heavy traffic are more likely to experience high blood pressure. They have more frequent disputes with their coworkers and families. They suffer more frequent and more serious illnesses. And they are more likely to experience premature deaths. . . .
>
> Although increased traffic congestion stems from many familiar causes (like population growth, cheap gasoline prices, increased urban sprawl and failure to invest in public transport), it is also the result of another factor that has received little attention—increased inequality in income and wealth.
>
> The basic mechanism at work is something we may call the Aspen effect. Wealthy residents have long since bid up real estate prices in Aspen and other exclusive resort communities to levels that virtually exclude middle- and low-income

families. Most of the people who provide services in these communities—teachers, policemen, firemen, laundry and restaurant workers—must therefore commute, often at considerable distance. As a result, all roads into Aspen are clogged morning and night with commuters, many of whom come from several hours away. "Greater Aspen" now has a radius of more than 50 miles. . . .

The current policy agenda in Washington not only promises little relief for harried commuters, but is likely to make matters worse. Start with the tax cut. In the proposed $1.35 trillion reduction, 40 percent of the benefits would go to families in the top 5 percent. By making the income gap greater than it is already, this measure is likely to push low- and middle-income families even farther from their jobs, thus increasing the length of their commutes. (*New York Times*, May 11, 2001, p. A35)

This is a complicated text. Frank begins in lecture mode, arguing to his audience of student-citizens that traffic congestion is a serious public health issue, an argument that is itself a reframing of sorts. He then offers an alternative argument for the causes of increased congestion, which he links to rising income inequality. Next, he uses this argument to reframe opposition to the proposed tax cut, arguing that it will increase traffic congestion at the same time that it decreases the money available for developing new urban transit programs. In the course of the column, then, Frank provides a good deal of information, and he makes arguments both for and against specific policies. The dominant style, however, is reframing, with the objective of placing the tax debate in the context of urban planning.

Of course, just because an author attempts to reframe an issue does not mean the reframing will be successful or influential. What it does suggest, however, is that the author *believes* that changing the terms of conversation on a public issue is possible through publishing good argument and opinion. This resonates with the value of rational-critical debate in democratic theory and with the associated idea that the persuasiveness of an argument can change widely held social ideas. It is for this reason, too, that we see the use of the reframing style of opinion as a rough indicator of the autonomy of opinion authors and their role as purveyors of innovation in the space of opinion. Why? Because when authors use the opinion style of reframing, they are performing their sense of their own intellectual autonomy, and they are projecting a perception of their power as agents of discursive innovation.

The occupational profile of reframing lends weight to this contention, since it is largely the province of highly autonomous opinion authors. It includes authors from intellectual occupations outside the media with strong traditions of intellectual autonomy, such as academics, lawyers, and writers, and although they are somewhat less likely to use reframing, it also includes high-end media insiders like columnists and journalists.[8] By contrast, the reframing style of opinion is perishingly rare among talk show hosts, and it is also uncommon among politicians, executive branch officials, and those from civil society organizations. Authors from these latter groups appear to be much more closely tied to the preexisting frames and alignments of the political field than those from groups where we see more frequent attempts to reframe public issues.

The distribution of the reframing opinion style across different formats also confirms our sense that the newspapers, especially the *New York Times*, enjoy high levels of autonomy in the social space of opinion. In the first place, reframing is far more likely to occur in print than on television: the *New York Times* led in the proportion of columns (24.6 percent) that deployed the reframing technique, with *USA Today* somewhat lower (19.9 percent). In contrast to the newspapers, the frequency of reframing was much lower on television at around 6 percent overall. Second, however, and unexpectedly, reframing was slightly more common on the newer television shows—*Crossfire* (7.5 percent) and *Hannity & Colmes* (7.3 percent)—than on the older shows—*NewsHour* (5.3 percent) and *Face the Nation* (5 percent), although these differences are small.[9] For the *NewsHour*, we believe the lower incidence of reframing is partly explained by the more frequent technique of "providing information," which is also a style used frequently by media outsiders such as academics. For *Face the Nation*, the lower proportion of reframing arguments is almost surely the result of the powerful presence of hosts, their singular use of the "asking questions" style, and the specific way that they tend to ask their questions, which are somewhat more extended and considerably more frequent than the kinds of questions that tend to be asked on the *NewsHour*.

In the end, the pattern of reframing styles that we find across formats, texts, and authors is somewhat contradictory, especially for the television formats. That is, while the older television formats appear to share the values and practices of the high-end print formats, boasting the most autonomous speakers and using the most autonomous styles of opinion on television, the low levels of reframing at *The NewsHour* and *Face the Nation* indicate that these formats may not be well suited to producing innovation or evoking new insights in the space of opinion. Moreover, to the extent that reframing is so much more likely to occur in print formats than in television formats, this underlines the role of print as an important communicative space for the innovation of opinion frames and narratives in the space of opinion.[10] We offer a closer analysis of these issues in the two case study chapters that follow. Before turning to those analyses, however, we conclude our analysis of rhetorics with an examination of claims to authority in the space of opinion.

Claiming Authority

In addition to using specific styles of commentary and particular modes of audience address, authors also make a variety of claims to authorize their opinions. Claims to authority are ways of asserting the right to speak on a particular topic, and they are also methods for asserting the quality and weight of that speech. Recall that normatively, most democratic theories of the public sphere prefer authority claims that are inclusive rather than exclusive, and they prefer modes of argument that are understood as universally valid rather than particular or specific. The crucial idea is that the better argument should win, regardless of who speaks it. We share an intellectual commitment to these positions, but our cultural model of complex democracy also prompts us to examine how claims to authority are also part of the *performance* of opinion, which is connected to a cultural pragmatics of claiming authority. In this view, the use of scientific language, the invocation of direct human experience, or the deployment of popular culture references is understood as the rhetorical means through which individuals authorize their speech; that is, they are the strategies that make speech persuasive, legitimate, or compelling. Widening the empirical lens in this way helps us see important variation between different kinds of authority claims in the contemporary space of U.S. opinion.

Direct Authority Claims

In the first instance, speakers can choose to make either direct or indirect authority claims. In direct authority claims, the speaker invokes authority on the basis of some specific experience or status that cannot be separated from their personal characteristics or biography. The most common form of direct authority claim is made to experience and appears in nearly a quarter (23.7 percent) of all the opinion texts we study. Experience claims are made more frequently in *New York Times* columns (48.8 percent) than in *USA Today* columns (35.9 percent), and although they are not as common on television, they nonetheless occur regularly, ranging in frequency from 15 to 22 percent of speaker segments, depending on the specific program.

The following two examples illustrate the two basic types of direct experience claim. The first example is an excerpt from Senator Richard Lugar on the *NewsHour* in 1994 about U.S. policy on North Korea's nuclear program:

> One reason why Sen. Nunn and I went over there was to have at least a bipartisan influence on the debate which we are certain is going to occur in the Senate on this, maybe even offer some advice to our President, because this is serious business. The reinforcement of our position there is technically something that can be done. We discussed very candidly with Gen. Luck and with the South Korean generals things that could be done to tighten things up. In many ways, the South Koreans perhaps were not as focused as they ought to have been for a while. I think they are now. We need to be. And so without forecasting what might occur, I think significant things may occur. Beyond that, we have to make certain we're determined and the American people understand that these negotiations must proceed until the North Korean nuclear program is terminated. (Senator Richard Lugar, *NewsHour*, January 27, 1994)

The second example is from a column by David Brooks that discusses airport security in the aftermath of the bombings on September 11, 2001.

Let me talk not as an expert, which I am about nothing, but let me talk just as a guy who travels and it's demoralizing. You go into these airports and it's always inconsistent what they ask for. I was roughing it in Key West this week. They made me unbuckle my belt as I walked through the magnetometer, and they never do that anywhere else. Sometimes they take your nail clipper, sometimes they don't. Everybody can see holes in the system we've got. They match the bag to the body on the first flight but not on the connecting flight. So you see the government taking on this big homeland security thing and they're transparently doing an ineffective job, they're pulling off every granny who walks through. And it's just demoralizing to see the government do something badly, something important, this badly. (David Brooks, *NewsHour*, January 18, 2002)

In both examples, references are made to direct experience, but they operate quite differently. In the first example, Lugar's personal experience is explicitly connected to his professional status as a politician. It is an expertise claim of sorts, and it reflects the position of the speaker as a political insider in a conversation between insiders. In this sense, then, it is a particularistic claim. In the second example, the experience claim is explicitly *not* based on the professional status of the speaker but instead is connected to the speaker's personal experiences as a typical member of civil society—in this case, as somebody who travels and has experienced the new security procedures implemented at airports. This is quite a complex form of authority claim and has a long history in professional journalism as "the man on the street" device. On the one hand, because it explicitly rejects any connection to expertise, its "authority" is fairly unclear, as it represents nothing more than the anecdotal observation of a single individual. On the other hand, because this kind of authority claim is almost always used to invoke the "ordinary citizen," it achieves a certain kind of universality that is much more appealing, and at least as powerful, as claims that refer to special expertise.

Another type of direct authority claim is when authors make reference to recent research or a book they have completed, or when they support their arguments through direct reference to the authority of an academic discipline. These claims are made overwhelmingly by academics and writers and to a far lesser extent by other speakers. They are much more likely to be made in print than on television, and among the newspapers in our sample, they are much more common in the *New York Times* than in *USA Today*. There are two ways that these speakers attach their arguments to their specific academic credentials and recent publications. The simplest way, and by far the most common, is to use the byline where the newspaper provides a short description of the writer. The following bylines, all from the *New York Times*, are typical:

Patrick Weil is a senior research fellow at the French National Center for Scientific Research, University of Paris 1–Sorbonne.
Stephen Jay Gould, a professor of zoology at Harvard, is the author of "Questioning the Millennium."

Bruce Ackerman and Anne Alstott, law professors at Yale, are authors of "The Stakeholder Society."

The second way to claim the authority of academic credentials is for authors to directly reference their research within the text of the op-ed or within the discussion taking place on the television show. Done briefly, such discussions function like the byline as a claim to authority based on status. Performed at length, however, this type of authority claim moves toward logical argument and the presentation and evaluation of evidence. This more extended scholarly claim is particularly common among academic historians, especially presidential historians, who are often asked to reflect on current presidents by comparing them with historical presidents. Jim Lehrer's 1994 interview with Doris Kearns Goodwin about the Clinton presidency is a good example.

> MR. LEHRER: Speaking of Roosevelt, your most recent book, your recent book is about Eleanor and Franklin Roosevelt. Are there parallels between their relationship and the relationship of the Clintons?
>
> DORIS KEARNS GOODWIN: It seems to me—maybe I'm so absorbed in Franklin and Eleanor—but it does seem remarkably so. I mean, in both cases the men are the more gregarious, Bill Clinton and Franklin Roosevelt, the more easy with people. The women are the moral, the more uncompromising, the more principled. In both cases, it seems to me, they were political partners. And you get an enormous benefit from being a political partner, you're a big figure. But on the other hand, I know with Eleanor, because she was his partner politically, she could never relax with him. He'd have these cocktail hours at night, and she'd come roaring in, wanting to talk about slum clearance or civil rights. And he just wanted to drink and gossip. After a while, there was a rumor in Washington, "Dear Eleanor, couldn't you be a little tired tonight?" It was Franklin Roosevelt's nightly prayer. Sometimes I have the feeling, can Hillary Clinton truly play with President Clinton when she's so involved and she's an inside figure just as much as anyone in the administration? (*NewsHour*, September 13, 1994)

In this case, Goodwin references her own research expertise to draw comparisons between the Clintons and the Roosevelts and to make a judgment about the Clintons. In this, she displays the basis for her opinion, rather than simply asserting her authority. But there is not really much extension past the byline in the opinion format: Goodwin's claim to authority rests on the description of her expertise as someone who has written books on the Roosevelts and Lyndon Baines Johnson, which is an assertion rather than a demonstration of her expertise. Furthermore, the elaboration of her position is made exclusively by reference to materials from her own books. Thus, while she defends her position by giving good reasons, the support she provides cannot be separated from her status or her research. There is no community of scholars or public opinion toward which she is making an intervention. Instead, the audience is getting a privileged peek into her private archival materials. In this case, then, as in the byline, a direct claim to authority is rooted in particularistic rather than universal standards of validity for opinionated speech.

Taken together, the different forms of direct claims to authority occur in just under a third (30.9 percent) of our opinion texts. Where they serve as a particularistic basis for claiming authority, direct claims to authority are problematic from the perspective of normative political theory. However, to the degree that direct authority claims make a more universal appeal, where they are associated with styles of opinion that are innovative and informative, and when they engage wider publics rather than political insiders, they are closer to those speech norms deemed the most valuable by theories of deliberative democracy.

Indirect Claims to Authority

In contrast to direct claims, indirect claims to authority tend to draw on modes of justification that are understood to be objective, scientific, logical, scholarly, or impersonal. This is less a claim to authority based on personal characteristics than one grounded in shared, public principles of dialogue and exchange. By definition, then, such claims approach the criteria of universal standards of validity and are preferred by democratic theories of deliberation. Here we examine three kinds of indirect authority claims: those based on scientific discourse, those that employ historical argument, and those that make references to popular media texts.

Scientific Discourse

References to research, evidence, experts, statistics, and particularly quantitative data are all indicators that authors are making claims to authority grounded in scientific discourse. In so doing, authors draw on what Alvin Gouldner famously called "the culture of critical discourse," which he described as

> an historically evolved set of rules, a grammar of discourse, which (1) is concerned to *justify* its assertions, but (2) whose *mode* of justification does not proceed by invoking authorities, and (3) prefers to elicit the *voluntary* consent of those addressed solely on the basis of arguments adduced. (1979: 28)

This is close to the normative understanding of public sphere theory, in the sense that support for an argument is detached from considerations of status, power, or personal characteristics. We can see a good example of this type of authority claim in the following op-ed, written by Virginia Ernster, a professor of epidemiology at the University of California:

Conflicting judgments about the value of routine mammography have left women in a quandary. Some experts say the evidence that mammography reduces breast cancer death rates by detecting cancer early is substantial, while others believe that routine mammograms provide very little, if any, benefit. As a fiftysomething woman and an epidemiologist tracking the data, I believe that for now women 50 to 69 should stay the course and continue to have regular mammograms. But we ought not to dismiss concerns about flaws in the existing data, and women should know why experts are not speaking with a single voice.

The evidence is far from perfect. That is not the same as saying there is good evidence that mammography doesn't work. Rather, the evidence that mammography does work is weaker than we used to think. We also need to recognize that each of us weighs benefits and risks differently.

A patient may reasonably ask what harm screening mammography can do, even if the evidence of benefit is flawed. While the downsides to mammography may seem minor, they are common. With each round of mammography, about 4 percent to 10 percent of women are found to have some sort of abnormal result; depending on the findings, the ensuing recommendations range from simply going for another mammogram to having a biopsy to rule out cancer. Various studies find that 80 percent to 95 percent of mammographic abnormalities turn out not to be cancer. Not having cancer is obviously good news, but with an estimated 28 million women having mammograms each year, that translates into hundreds of thousands going through the anxious experience of an abnormal test until the final result is known. One study estimated that after 10 mammograms the cumulative risk of a false positive result is 49 percent and the cumulative risk of biopsy in women who don't have cancer is 18.6 percent. Thus, false positives and follow-up tests are common. At the same time, we also know that about 15–25 percent of breast cancers are missed by mammography. (*New York Times*, February 14, 2002, p. A35)

By presenting an overview of the scientific evidence in favor of universal mammograms for early breast cancer detection, Ernster makes the case for continuing the broadly based public health policy despite concerns about its effectiveness. Her use of scientific language is particularly striking. She refers to evidence, statistics, tests, and several specific scientific procedures such as mammography screenings and biopsies. In this way, she effectively uses scientific language to invoke the culture of critical discourse. It is an academic move, using the language of science and the academy rather than that of the mass media or political affairs. At the same time, however, observe that the reader is also asked to accept the scientificity of Ernster's claims on the basis of her direct claims to authority, insofar as her status as a professor of epidemiology at the University of California is included in the byline of the column. Interestingly, too, Ernster also makes a more universal direct claim based on experience when she refers to herself as an ordinary citizen—"a fiftysomething woman" who is at risk for the very condition that mammography is directed to find. In this single column, then, we find multiple authority claims, a feature that is common to the opinion texts produced by media outsiders, especially academics.

Scientific words are not the exclusive province of academics but are commonly used by a range of speakers to invoke scientific authority across the opinion space. Indeed, claiming authority using scientific language is by far the most common authority claim in our sample, occurring in more than half of all the opinion texts we study. We can get a rough indication of how often scientific language is used by counting how often key terms associated with science appeared in our sample: *expert* (4.9 percent), *evidence* (10.6 percent), *study* (9.1 percent), *report* (19.9 percent), *research* (6.5 percent), *statistic* (2.8 percent), *percent* (20.4 percent), *survey* (1.5 percent), *experiment* (1.1 percent), and *laboratory* (1.6 percent). Combining counts to create a "culture of critical discourse score" (CCD score), we found that scientific words were used in 51.4 percent of all opinion pieces, ranging from a single mention up to 23 occurrences in a single piece of opinion. (Ernster's op-ed scored 15.)

That scientific discourse is employed in more than half of all opinion texts testifies to the broad social authority of science, but there are indicators that this broad social legitimacy may be less important in the space of opinion than it once was. As Figure 6.4 shows, the frequency of scientific claims to authority increased between the two time periods for both newspapers, but it decreased markedly on all three television programs that broadcast in both periods. The most striking decline was at *Crossfire*, where the proportion of opinion segments that contained scientific language dropped from 68 percent in the early 1990s to 43 percent in the early 2000s. This is particularly interesting, given that during the second time period in our sample, *Crossfire* was in competition (a competition it was losing) with *Hannity & Colmes*—the program in our sample that displayed the least frequent use of scientific discourse (39.6 percent of segments on *Hannity & Colmes* used scientific language). This suggests a declining value for scientific discourse in the new television formats over time, as *Crossfire* attempted to emulate some of the features of its more successful competitor.[11]

If the rhetorical use of scientific discourse is an indicator of the strength of the connection between the opinion space and the more autonomous and objective spaces of scientific rules, evidence, and argument, then the declining use of scientific language in all the television formats suggests a decline in the autonomy of these formats, at least insofar as autonomy is connected to the prestige and power of science. Similarly, if we take the use of scientific discourse as a rough measure of universal claims to validity and thus as an indicator of the inclusiveness so valued by theories of democratic deliberation, then the decline in the use of scientific discourse is also a decline in a certain kind of universalism.

Observing the declining use of scientific discourse, then, deepens our understanding of the pattern of attenuation and differentiation we have found throughout our data, since it shows how the differences in authors, conditions, and norms of speech play out

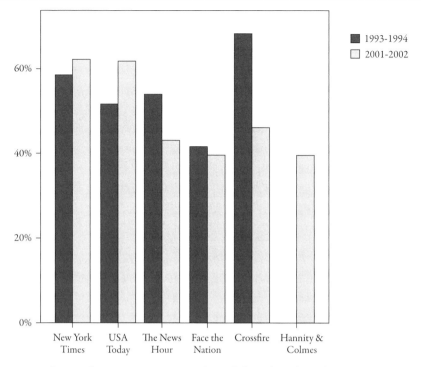

FIGURE 6.4 Percent of opinion texts using scientific words, by outlet and period.

at the level of rhetorical differences. Thus, differences in the use of scientific language correlate with known differences in the occupational composition of authors in print and on television, as Figure 6.5 shows. Academics and think tank intellectuals, who are more likely to appear in print, use scientific language the most. Media strategists, television talk show hosts, and executive branch officials, who are more likely to appear on the television shows, use scientific language the least. Columnists, journalists, lawyers, and elected politicians fall somewhere between these two extremes.

Historical Discourse

A second type of indirect authority claim is the use of historical discourse. In these kinds of authority claims, the speaker uses history as a guide for understanding current events and marshals detailed knowledge of the past to legitimate her authority as an expert commentator. This was one of the styles that Walter Lippmann used the most frequently, as we observed in chapter 2, and it remains an important feature in the opinion space today.

There are different levels of historical reference, which have correspondingly different performative effects and are associated with different speakers and audiences. The most common mobilization of historical authority is the cursory historical reference that relies on the performative effect of metonymy to suggest a simple correspondence

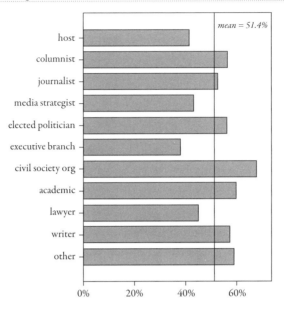

FIGURE 6.5 Percent using scientific words, by occupation.

between an event in the present and an event in the past. This form of historical discourse is more likely to occur in texts that address political insiders (36.6 percent) rather than general citizens (26 percent) and is used by a wide variety of speakers to authorize their opinions. Occurring in 31.5 percent of all opinion texts, this pattern of use suggests a wide social authority for historical argument.

Take, for example, journalist and famous hostage, Terry Anderson, who equates his kidnapping with another:

> Journalism can be a very dangerous profession. Daniel Pearl, after years of experience as reporter for *The Wall Street Journal*, must have known that before his kidnapping in Pakistan last week, as I did before I was taken hostage in Lebanon 16 years ago while working as a reporter for The Associated Press. (*New York Times*, February 1, 2002, p. A25)

Anderson then goes on to argue against negotiating with terrorists. He makes a powerful set of authority claims, combining personal and professional experience, logical argument, and the historical weight of the metonymy. The rhetorical force of his historical authority claim depends largely on the effectiveness of the metaphorical linkage between past and present events. It is especially powerful in this example because Anderson combines the cursory historical reference with a compelling claim from direct experience.

A more powerful mobilization of historical authority involves extended analysis of the past. Alan Brinkley's op-ed column about the history of health care legislation, which we discussed at length earlier, is a good example. Although this kind of extended analysis is far less frequent than the cursory historical reference—occurring in only 10.5 percent of all opinion texts—like a cursory reference, extended historical discourse can be used to create a metonymic effect. In addition, extended historical discourse can be used to provide an explanation of what caused a contemporary outcome. In both of these ways, the extended use of historical language establishes the speaker as an authoritative commentator and invokes the autonomy and power of systems of evidence, argument, and authority from outside the journalistic field to lend weight to opinion. In this, the authority of historical discourse is similar to the general authority of scientific discourse and reflects a more autonomous, academic claim of authority. Importantly, too, those opinion texts that contained extended historical discourse were far more likely than other texts to be associated with reframing opinion styles and thus also represent a point of potential innovation from outside the journalistic field.[12]

The kind of extended historical analysis we describe here is rare, however, and while it is concentrated heavily at the *New York Times*, where more than a quarter of the op-ed columns presented an extended historical discussion of some kind, extended historical argument is far less common at *USA Today* (10 percent) and rarer still on television, where only 2 to 4 percent of the television speaker segments use extended historical arguments. In fact, the opinion space in general, much like the news itself, is remarkably "presentist." Matters of common concern are typically discussed as occurring "in the current moment," "right now," or "as it is happening" and therefore without historical context or argument of any kind.[13]

This is particularly true of television opinion, where the presentism of opinion appears to have increased between our two sample periods: on the *NewsHour*, texts with no historical references were 58 percent of all opinion in 1993–1994, but by 2001–2002, they accounted for 70 percent of all opinion segments; on *Face the Nation*, the increase between sample periods was from a high of 80 percent in the early 1990s to an even higher 88 percent in 2001–2002; on *Crossfire*, texts with no historical reference moved from 53 to 74 percent of all opinion between the sample periods; and on *Hannity & Colmes*, 69 percent of opinion took place without historical reference of any kind. These numbers speak to the immediate quality of live television and the nature of news texts themselves, which commonly treat news events as isolated from previous events (Park 1940; Jacobs 2009). What they tell us, however, is that historical claims to authority are like other more academic strategies in the space of opinion in that they are associated with the high-end spaces of traditional print journalism, as they draw on the authority of academic discourse and intellectual life more generally.

This is confirmed in the occupational distribution for historical claims to authority, which shows that the use of historical discourse is also associated with the most autonomous speakers in the journalistic field, largely academics and writers but also columnists and journalists. Thus while many different kinds of speakers use *cursory* historical references in their columns and discussion segments, *extended* historical argument is the

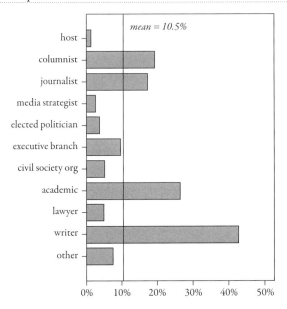

FIGURE 6.6 Percent using extended historical discourse, by occupation.

province of academic and literary opinion authors as Figure 6.6 shows. Writers (42.6 percent) and academics (26.4 percent) use this technique the most, followed by columnists (19.3 percent) and journalists (17.3 percent). The use of extended historical discourse is far less common for other speakers.

Like the use of scientific discourse, then, the overall pattern and changing use of historical discourse across formats, speakers, and texts add detail to our findings about patterns of change and continuity in the space of opinion over time. Less common than scientific discourse overall, historical discourse appears to be the special province of authors in the *New York Times* and of popular historians of U.S. history who are asked to provide commentary on the manners and morals of U.S. presidents.

Intertextual References

The final kind of indirect authority claim we consider is based on references to other media texts. Specific intertextual references can be thought of as a general claim to speak that is rooted in the ongoing public conversation organized through mass media. In our sample, such claims occurred in 40 percent of all opinion texts, which contained references to media as a general source of authority.[14] More significantly, we also find that in nearly a quarter of the segments in our sample (23.5 percent), authors made some reference to a *specific* news outlet, book, movie, or television show. Intertextual authority claims give force to a particular opinion or commentary by associating it with another media text. Intertextual claims work because "everyone" is presumed to understand the reference since they share a common stock of mass-mediated knowledge.

It is for this reason that intertextual claims share something of the universality of the "man on the street" device; they call on some presumably shared human experience both as a way to connect to an audience and as a way to invoke that audience as a public whose interests must be represented to elites. This is highlighted by the fact that while intertextual claims occur less often than scientific and historical claims to authority, they are significantly more likely than either scientific or historical claims to address an audience of citizens than an audience of elite insiders; 61.1 percent of all intertextual claims addressed themselves to audiences of general citizens, compared with 43.9 percent of those texts containing scientific claims and 42.9 percent of those texts containing historical claims.

Among intertextual claims to authority in the space of opinion, references to specific news texts are by far the most common, with the most important references being made to arguments appearing in specific newspapers, print newsmagazines, and television news shows. Together, these three genres account for 59.1 percent of all intertextual references in our sample, as Figure 6.7 shows.[15] A typical example of this kind of reference to another news text comes from an interview between Gloria Borger and Vice President Cheney in 2001 about the new energy plan proposed by the Bush administration, where Borger asked:

> BORGER: Mr. Vice President, let's talk about your energy plan a little bit. The New York Times this week called the plan, and I quote, "an alarmingly unbalanced piece of work whose main objectives seem to be to satisfy the ambitions of the

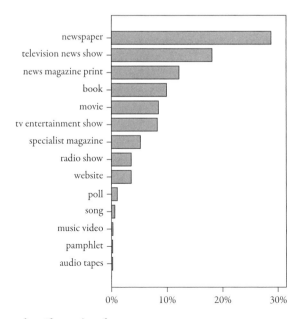

FIGURE 6.7   Genre of specific popular references.

oil, gas and coal industries." You also got the same criticism from the right in your party. The Cato Institute said that the plan is a smorgasbord of handouts and subsidies for virtually every energy lobby in Washington. How do you respond to that? (*Face the Nation*, May 20, 2001)

Borger cites criticisms that had already appeared in recognizably reputable outlets for the expression of public opinion to authorize her right to question the vice president of the United States on the details of his administration's policies. In this way, the intertextual claims serve as the basis of her authority to call the vice president to account for the energy plan on behalf of and in front of a wide viewing public.

Importantly, however, references to news texts are not the only kind of intertextual references we find in the space of opinion. Intertextual claims to authority are also made to movies, music, music videos, television dramas, comedies and documentaries, historical works, novels, pamphlets, and radio formats. While the specific intent of different intertextual references may differ substantially—that is, while different texts might intend to mobilize anger, compassion, nostalgia, or logic—what they all share as a claim to authority is a reliance on the media content that large publics have in common to make their argument. Consider the following op-ed by Maureen Dowd, which relies on well-understood popular culture imagery to parody the conservative cultural malaise of the early Bush administration.

Growing up with "The Jetsons," "Star Trek," the General Motors Futurama exhibit at the World's Fair with lunar colonies and underseas resorts, and Disney's "Tomorrowland Speedway," we imagined the 21st century as sleek and expansive, a cascade of creativity and invention in the arts, technology, science and medicine.

But the combination of the narrow Bush vision and shrinking economy is creating a climate where everything feels crimped, more about limiting expression than liberating it.

We face the jarring prospect that some of our top scientists may move to England, where they won't face the same strangling curbs on stem cell research, which is bound to go forward even without President Bush holding up his little "Stop" sign. Expatriate scientists are redolent of American artists in the 20's who flocked to sophisticated Paris, far from Prohibition and Calvin Coolidge.

We've had the Age of Enlightenment and the Age of Aquarius. Now we're in the Age of Arrested Development. Never mind the interplanetary cooperation presaged in "Star Trek." We're retreating from planetary cooperation. America has grown insular, isolationist, paranoid.

Nothing leaps ahead. Power clings to the passe, retreating from the cutting edge, running safe TV shows, choosing scientific stasis. Everything—from Washington's trashed international treaties to the coal-and-drill Bush environmental policy to Hollywood's tedious remakes and endless parade of World War II and Cinderella-themed movies—looks backward, not forward.

Our missile shield, more science fiction than science, has become a metaphor for our passive, defensive, retro crouch.

In the name of Captain Kirk, how did this happen? How did we end up charting a course to timidly go where every man has been before?" (*New York Times,* August 19, 2001, Section 4, p. 13)

Dowd draws readers into a shared world of memory and imagination by using popular references to *Star Trek* and even references to former intertextual parodies of *Star Trek*! "In the name of Captain Kirk. . . ." Arguably, this has the effect of rendering the serious criticisms she makes more palatable and reasonable. She provides a "universal" frame of reference to make her case persuasive by drawing on what "everybody knows" (or at least what her readers will know). She does not rely on scientific argument to talk about science, although she does make a cursory historical reference to Prohibition as a metaphor.

Overall, we find that media insiders like Borger and Dowd are far more likely to use intertextual references than media outsiders, as Figure 6.8 shows. Making intertextual references is much more common among talk show hosts (43.9 percent), journalists (43.3 percent), and media strategists (25.2 percent) and far less common among columnists (15.1 percent), academics (11.1 percent), and lawyers (10 percent). Intertextual references are the least common among politicians (5.7 percent) and executive branch officials (8 percent). The exceptions to this overall difference between media insiders and media outsiders is that print columnists look more like academics and

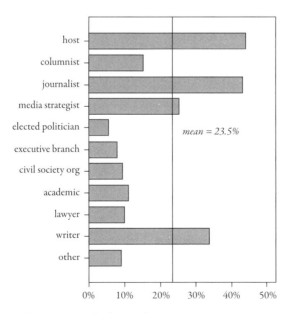

FIGURE 6.8 Percent making intertextual references, by occupation.

lawyers in their avoidance of intertextual claims to authority, while writers (33.8 percent) score high on our measure of intertextual references, largely because they write about their own and others' texts. The findings for format reflect these differences, too. Intertextual references are three times more likely to be invoked on television than in print (32.5 percent compared with 11.3 percent), and intertextual references are more common on *Crossfire* (39 percent) and *Hannity & Colmes* (34 percent) than on the *Newshour* (21 percent). In this, *Face the Nation* is like the newer television shows, with 35 percent of all segments containing intertextual references, which is largely explained by the show's format, which is designed as a summary of opinion and news commentary from the previous week. Taken together, these findings suggest that intertextual claims are indigenous to the media field; that is, they are a claim to authority that posits the mass media (and not just the news) as an independent source of social legitimacy.

There are also signs that the frequency of intertextual claims to authority has been increasing over time, from a fifth (20.4 percent) of all opinion texts in 1993–1994 to a quarter (25.2 percent) of all opinion texts by 2001–2002. Moreover, while rates of intertextual references were not significantly different in the three television formats that aired in both periods, the proportion of newspaper columns that made intertextual references increased at both the *New York Times* (7.9 to 11.4 percent) and *USA Today* (8.5 to 17.5 percent) between 1993–1994 and 2001–2002. This is an interesting finding, since it suggests that at the same time that the opinion space is expanding, that formats are proliferating, and that distinctions between styles and formats are deepening, the opinion space as a whole is becoming more densely interwoven and textually self-referential.

One way of thinking about these patterns is that intertextual references are an indicator of what we can think of as the media pole of the space of opinion, that is, an independent and separate form of social authority based on the common consumption of mass media, which is quite different than a claim to authority based in scientific or historical discourse. To investigate this idea, we explore the extent to which scientific, historical, and intertextual claims work together to authorize opinion. Since, as we have seen, opinion texts are likely to contain more than one claim to authority, we can ask: how likely is it that a claim to authority will stand alone or be used in conjunction with another claim? What evidence is there that intertextual claims are a distinct and separate form of authority claim?

Examined in this way, the distribution of claims to authority shows that scientific and historical discourse seem to share a cultural logic that is quite different than intertextual claims. First, we discover that direct or indirect claims to authority occurred in 82.9 percent of all opinion texts. Of those texts where claims to authority were made, about half contained two or more different claims to authority. Among these, we find that those containing scientific language are also more likely to use historical claims to authority and vice versa, while opinion texts that make intertextual claims to authority are far less likely to use either scientific or historical claims. In fact, when

TABLE 6.2

PROPORTION OF AUTHORITY CLAIMS THAT STAND ALONE, WITHOUT OTHER CLAIMS

Claims to authority	Proportion of claims that stand alone	1993–1994	2001–2002	
Direct	16.1%	19.4	14.3	↓
Scientific	29.2%	24.9	31.7	↑
Historical	20.6%	25.1	17.6	↓
Intertextual	52.4%	44.1	55.9	↑

compared with other kinds of claims to authority we measure, intertextual claims were by far the most likely to stand alone as a claim to authority (table 6.2). Fifty-two percent of all intertextual claims to authority appeared in opinion texts with no other authority claim, compared with 29.2 percent of scientific claims that were stand-alone claims and only 20.6 percent of historical claims (cursory and extended combined).

Moreover, these patterns are associated with formats and authors in by now familiar ways. Authors who are most likely to deploy scientific and historical discourse are the least likely to make intertextual references. And in formats where intertextual claims are highest, the incidence of scientific and historical claims is lower and vice versa.[16] Patterns of intertextual referencing appear to run in the opposite direction from all our indicators of the intellectual autonomy of traditional journalism—by occupation, format, and claims to authority.

Rationality and Rhetoric in the Space of Opinion

What do these findings tell us about the overall nature of the space of opinion, and what do they suggest about the democratic or critical qualities of the opinions and commentaries that appear within it?

First, there is evidence to suggest that the space of opinion is not only becoming bigger and more internally differentiated but also, conversely, becoming more textually self-referential and densely interwoven. This leads us to conclude that the mass media itself, and the public communication it makes possible, are coming to serve as an independent basis of social authority. What this means for the power and autonomy of the space of opinion is difficult to assess.

On the one hand, the growth in the size of the opinion space overall suggests its increasing importance as a form of journalism, cultural interpretation, and intellectual criticism. This is not necessarily a bad thing. We live in large societies, and media are the infrastructure of our widest solidarities—the platform for the possibility of shared agendas, cooperation, and peace. Similarly, intertextual claims to authority make reference to a real process of mediated deliberation in which people are able to build dialogue through a shared understanding of common cultural stories, codes, characters, and symbols. Thus it is unsurprising that opinion based on intertextual claims to authority are significantly more likely than those based on scientific or historical claims to address broad publics and to imagine public communication as a conversation involving regular citizens and not just powerful decision makers.

On the other hand, there are reasons to be concerned about a decline in intellectual autonomy as it is traditionally defined by the intellectual projects of professional journalists, academics, scientists, lawyers, and others. We want to suggest that intertextual claims to authority have an ambivalent relationship with these traditions of intellectual autonomy defined by older intellectual projects. That is, intertextual claims to authority have no necessary critical or logical element and can as easily serve to reinforce the status quo as to criticize it. From this perspective, intertextual claims run the risk of being superficially populist, ceding the right to that independent criticism of "the authorities" that was the raison d'être of classical conceptions of the public sphere.

Second, our analysis of rhetorics suggests that these traditional terms of evaluation might themselves be problematic. That is, our analysis shows that major styles and rhetorics in the space of opinion have uneven and contradictory relationships with the traditions of intellectual autonomy and critical rationality that are so central to classical theories of democratic deliberation and the public sphere. Thus, although it is true that we find that the distribution of rhetorical features in the space of opinion is associated with the differences between formats and differences between authors that we documented in chapters 4 and 5,[17] this is by no means a perfect correlation. Rhetorical features of speech are never simple reflections of the institutional location of an author, nor are they mechanical products of the speech conditions and norms provided by a particular format. Nor do particular rhetorical features occur together in predictable or straightforward ways. For this reason, we cannot simply follow Habermas and theories that assert that universal authority claims are better than particular ones, rational arguments are preferred over emotional or nonrational ones, and inclusive forms of speech are superior to exclusive forms of speech.

For example, if we examine the style of commentary that provides information, we can say that providing information is superior because it is more likely than more argumentative styles to address ordinary citizens. Addressing broader publics is also a feature of reframing and asking questions styles. The opinion style of providing information is also similar to reframing because it is more likely to use historical discourse to claim authority. Since historical argument styles typically make universal validity claims—that is, those associated with the logical and exhaustive analysis of evidence—they are preferred by democratic theories of discourse.

Despite these virtues, however, the major drawback of the providing information style is that overall it tends to make particularistic claims to authority. In particular, it is more likely than most other styles of opinion and commentary to claim authority on the basis of direct experience, and it is the least likely to invoke the universalistic authority of scientific language. In addition, the providing information style of opinion and commentary is the least likely of any style to rely on the general appeal of popular media references to assert its authority. To some extent, then, the goal of inclusiveness and addressing publics seems to run counter to the goal of using universal and scientific modes of speech—an argument that has been made by many poststructural and critical theories of complex democracy, as we argued in chapter 3.

We see this with the reframing style of opinion, too, which also has a complicated profile. Like the providing information style of opinion, reframing is most likely to rely on direct experience as a source of authority. At the same time, however, reframing styles are the most likely to draw on the authority of scientific discourse. So reframing styles of opinion tend to deploy several different authority claims: they are more likely to use historical discourse, to invoke scientific discourse, *and* to cite direct experience. Finally, as observed earlier, the reframing style is more likely than more argumentative for-and-against styles to address its audience in their roles as citizens. Rather than using either universalistic or particularistic claims to authority, then, reframers are likely to use them all, deploying every rhetorical tool in their repertoire to perform their opinion to the widest possible audience. The one exception is intertextual references. That is, reframing styles of opinion are the least likely to draw on the authority of the media field itself. In this, reframing has a tendency to move away from addressing wide publics and gestures back toward the distinctions and claims to authority in cultural fields beyond the media field, especially the academic field. Overall, however, reframing appears to be the most catholic and flexible in its attempts to use as many rhetorical forms as possible to achieve its aims.

In this, reframing styles contrast sharply with moral arguments and policy arguments, which are characterized by taking a position for or against some object, event, or thing. These more argumentative styles, which are the majority of styles in our sample, are the least likely of all opinion styles to address their audience as ordinary citizens and are by far the most restricted in their mode of address, speaking almost exclusively to an elite ideal reader. On the other hand, these argumentative styles are somewhat more likely to invoke scientific discourse than other argument styles, although they are less likely to rely on historical argument, and they invoke direct experience claims about a quarter of the time, which is about average for the opinion space as a whole. Moral argument is distinct from the opinion style of making specific arguments, since moral argument is much more likely to be associated with making intertextual references than specific arguments. In this respect, making moral arguments tends to be more presentist and more closely related to the authority claims of the media field as a whole.

Finally, the asking questions style of opinion—almost entirely the province of television talk show hosts—is very different from the other styles of opinion in the way it tends to make authority claims. Not only is the asking questions style by far the most likely to address a broad public audience but also it is the least likely to invoke any kind of authority claim, direct or indirect. That is, not only does the asking questions style make no direct claim to authority through experience or academic status but also it is less likely to deploy indirect claims that draw on the culture of critical discourse by using historical or scientific language. Instead, the asking questions style is heavily associated with making specific intertextual references to invoke authority and to frame opinion and commentary. Here, *Face the Nation* is the standout, as interviewers rely on media reports and commentary from the previous week to question guests on Sunday about the pressing issues of the moment.

Our final argument, then, is that these patterns are difficult to interpret from a strictly Habermasian perspective; different styles of argument are neither completely appealing nor completely unappealing when assessed against the procedurally rational standards of objective argument. Instead, each opinion style displays a complicated combination of characteristics, which are available to different speakers in different ways in different formats. In other words, the quality and effects of opinionated speech cannot be simply read off from the facts of format or occupation but interact in complex ways. More influential opinions—indeed, what many readers would consider better arguments—do not necessarily follow from the best, most rational, or objective argument. Rather, they are based in the successful performance of a particular style in a particular format. When opinion authors perform known characters using well-known styles and claims to authority, they enable readers to identify with the narratives they are telling.[18] To be sure, as we have seen, some rhetorics are more likely to be associated with specific formats and outlets than others and to display distinctions that are more or less important in the various intellectual fields that constitute the space of opinion, but it is their effects as persuasive performances that make the opinions work. This includes characters performing scholarly and scientific styles of opinion that invoke objective standards of speech, but it also includes performances that successfully make emotional appeals based on generalizing direct experience, invoking a common human situation, or referring to a well-understood popular icon. In this context, then, we want to suggest that it makes more sense to view the rhetorics that characterize the opinion space from the perspective of the cultural sociological model we outlined in chapter 3, and rather than asking simply if commentary is objective or nonobjective, or if opinion styles are inclusive or elitist, asking instead: how are different opinion styles used to persuasively shape the opinion narrative in particular cases?

In the next two chapters, we turn to such an analysis, focusing on two specific cases that received extensive discussion in the opinion space, the Enron scandal and what has come to be called the War on Terror. We examine how different characters and rhetorical styles interact within specific opinion formats and combine to produce collective interpretations and general public narratives about matters of common concern. In the process, the cases reveal the complexity of the relationship between opinion format and those markers of democratic deliberation that suggest that speech is autonomous, independent, and connected to genuine expressions of concern in civil society.

7 The Enron Scandal

SIGNIFICANT CHANGES OCCURRED in the world of media commentary between 1993 and 2002. Newspapers continued to lose circulation as readers moved increasingly online, and with the less lucrative revenue formula for online ad sales, most papers began to eliminate news bureaus and reduce the numbers of journalists they employed. In contrast to the retrenchment that was taking place in most of the newspaper, however, on the opinion page, there was a general expansion in the amount of space available for commentary and debate. At the *New York Times*, there was a significant infusion of new talent, with Maureen Dowd, Thomas Friedman, Nicholas Kristof, and Paul Krugman becoming regular columnists for the paper. Dowd, Friedman, and Kristof had taken recognizable paths to their positions, having previously served as high-profile correspondents. Krugman was an innovative addition, coming to the paper as a well-known professor of economics from Princeton University.

In television, the big change was the rise of Fox News, which launched in 1996. Fox News quickly caught up to CNN in its number of viewers, and by 2002 it had surpassed CNN in the competition for ratings. This had a number of effects. First, because Fox News devoted more of its evening lineup to opinion programs, it pushed all other cable outlets to increase these types of offerings. The second effect was a shift in the balance of performative styles that were on display on television talk shows in favor of the more political and partisan formats. These formats were already well established on CNN's *Crossfire*, but they proliferated further with the arrival and quick success of Fox News.

Additionally, because Fox News had such rapid and dramatic success, the structural features of its programming formats became the object of intense discussion among media critics and political commentators, who sought to decode the true meaning behind the mercurial rise of Bill O'Reilly and Sean Hannity.[1] This critical focus magnified the cultural influence of the new network—and its opinion programs, in particular—far in excess of the actual size of its audience.

As we will document in the following two chapters, these changes in the space of opinion have had complicated and contradictory effects. Contrary to the claims of some media critics (e.g., Alterman 2003; Kovach and Rosenstiel 1999; Fallows 1997), we want to suggest that it is far too simple to interpret the rise of these new formats in terms of an overall loss of journalistic autonomy or a decline in the quality of public deliberation. On different issues and at different times, as we shall see, the newer formats arguably did a better job at providing a wider range of representative points of view and new information on an issue than the more traditional formats did. In other instances, of course, the new programs offered little more than screaming, bombast, and politically polarizing sound bites. Sometimes they challenged their guests with hard-hitting, critical questions and free-flowing dialogue; in other instances, they reinforced the idea that the answer to every question depends on which political side you are on. The empirical challenge is to determine when they encourage deliberation and what kind of deliberation they encourage, as compared with other opinion formats.

To consider the deliberative quality of the opinion narratives we analyze, we ask:

(a) How do different opinion formats organize their discussions about issues?
(b) How open are different opinion formats to a diversity of voices, narratives, and rhetorical styles? And how flexibly do different formats respond to issues, events, and different kinds of guests?
(c) How are different narratives positioned in terms of the larger political field? For example, how much control do political principals have in framing public debate?
(d) To what extent does opinionated speech in different formats attempt to assert new principles of distinction within the journalistic field, that is, new ideas about what constitutes good journalism or good opinion? In this connection, to what degree are other types of media intellectuals able to assert their own critical interpretation of events?

As these questions indicate, we bring format differences to the center of our analyses in these final chapters. The increasing internal differentiation of the opinion space has meant that different kinds of outlets have developed their own narrative preferences, their own distinctive rhetorical styles, and their own cast of characters. But how does this type of format differentiation influence the types of access and deliberation that are available in the space of opinion?

The empirical analyses we have presented so far have offered some possible answers to this question. Specifically, we have found that columnists and academics are more likely to participate in the more traditional formats, while advocacy groups and think tank intellectuals tend to be drawn to the newer formats. We also found that the newer formats tend to offer much different communicative conditions and norms, which are organized in a more frenetic and polarizing manner. They encourage frequent interruptions, and their questions are designed to elicit and highlight disagreement. In many respects, these developments are cause for concern because they point to a possible fragmentation of the space of opinion.

But the rhetorics of the newer formats also provide interesting new possibilities. Compared with the more traditional television opinion formats, the newer formats are more likely to reframe the meaning of an issue, more likely to include historical discourse, and at least as likely to include scientific discourse. They are by far the most likely to rely on moral argument, a style of discourse that is favored by republican versions of democratic theory. Even the partisan framings have a role to play insofar as they recognize that there are real conflicts in values and interests and that real public debates about many issues are organized around popular struggles and established social divisions (Baker 2002: 163). This is not to say that nonpartisan forms of journalism and commentary should be banished from the space of opinion. The point is rather that partisan styles capture some of the real dynamics of civil societies.

To explore these format differences and the consequences they have for mediated deliberation, the following chapters offer a close examination of two of the biggest events that occurred during our research period. The Enron scandal emerged in December 2001 when Enron filed for bankruptcy. Enron was a consistent topic of debate throughout 2002. The "War on Terror" was taken up in the space of opinion immediately after the September 2001 attacks on the World Trade Center. It then continued with the war in Afghanistan, beginning in October 2001, and intensified throughout 2002 with the buildup to the Iraq War.

While these two events are unusual and even extraordinary in certain respects, they offer several advantages that help bring the larger cultural map of the space of opinion into bold relief. One advantage is that both events occurred after the creation of Fox News, the consequences of which, as we have already suggested, have reverberated throughout the space of opinion. Another advantage is that the sheer density of discourse that surrounded these two events presents a large corpus of textual data that can be used for cultural analysis. Debate about the War on Terror was particularly rich, accounting for nearly a third (30.5 percent) of all published opinion in our 2001–2002 sample. This kind of extended focus allows us to probe more deeply into the different rhetorics and cultural styles that are available in each format. It also allows us to consider how commentaries change in response to ongoing events, which gives our cultural analysis a diachronic sensitivity that would be lacking in more limited cases.

Another advantage of focusing on these particular events is that the large amount of discourse was accompanied by a much greater variety of guest voices than we saw in some of our other case studies. For example, the 1990s debates about what to do in Bosnia also involved a large amount of commentary, but this commentary was completely dominated by politicians and professional columnists. To be sure, there were interesting format differences during the Bosnia debate. The *New York Times* was more likely than the others to emphasize the complexity of the issue and more likely to criticize government policy.[2] CNN's *Crossfire* was more likely than the other formats to directly challenge and criticize foreign leaders. But there was a fairly narrow range of speakers and perspectives presented in all media formats. In contrast, discussions of Enron and (especially) the War on Terror displayed a greater variety and openness to outside voices. To be sure, the voices who typically dominated the commentary space continued to have the largest presence: columnists in the newspapers and elected politicians and talk show hosts on the television programs. But there were also multiple commentaries by academics, think tank intellectuals, advocacy groups, lawyers, writers, and media professionals. Importantly, this variety of speakers was seen not only on the printed page but also on television. This feature of these two events allows us to examine the operation of the space of opinion in a better than average setting, at least as judged according to the normative principles about mediated deliberation and democracy that we discussed in chapter 3.

Finally, and more generally, we want to suggest that major public crises such as Enron or the War on Terror have a far-reaching impact on journalism, as well as on civil society itself. This means that major events and crises are particularly important to study, precisely because they are unusual. For the case of journalism, Schudson has made a similar argument, insisting that social scientists need to recognize how the "anarchy of events" shapes the practice of journalism:

> Journalists make their own stories but not from materials they have personally selected. Materials are thrust upon them. A preoccupation with unpredictable events keeps something uncontrollable at the forefront of journalism. The archetypal news story, the kind that makes a career, the sort every reporter longs for, is unroutinized and unrehearsed. . . . And it is built into the very bloodstream of news organizations, it is the circulatory system that keeps the enterprise oxygenated. (Schudson 2008: 88)

Because journalists orient to unusual, big events as career makers, these events tend to be connected to innovations within the journalistic field, and as a result, they tend to have a lasting effect on journalistic practice. This is true in a more general way throughout civil society, in the sense that crises and other events have a lasting effect on the cultural performances and narrative styles that actors adopt in the public sphere. Indeed, there is a long line of research in cultural sociology that explores the cultural practices that public actors rely on to narrate a social crisis, to script a social drama, or to offer an authorized interpretation of a major public event (see, e.g., Eyerman 2008; Alexander 2006, 2010; Wagner-Pacifici 2000; Cottle 2006; Jacobs 2000; Kurasawa 2007; Mast 2006; Smith 2005). The point is that a special energy and a collective attention surround major public events like Enron and the War on Terror, which have powerful cultural consequences for the organization of the space of opinion.

The rest of this chapter focuses on the Enron scandal, as it was discussed in the space of opinion. The Enron scandal provides clear evidence of the important role that newspapers play for improving the quality of mediated deliberation. Newspaper commentaries about Enron tended to be the least politicized, and they offered the greatest diversity of speakers, providing good visibility for experts who did not come from the political or journalistic fields. For television commentaries about Enron, evaluations about mediated deliberation are more complicated, particularly if we are interested in the differences between the older and newer opinion formats. As we will see, the older formats did a better job of emphasizing complexity, but they did so in an environment in which politicians were granted almost complete interpretive freedom. The newer formats more consistently challenged politicians to justify themselves, but they did so in a cultural environment that emphasized simplification and moral division. In addition, we can see specific instances where skilled guests who refused to play by the rules of the newer formats were able to interrupt the overarching cultural organization of those programs, introducing new and more complex perspectives into the discussion. We explore the significance of these format differences at the end of the chapter and then again in chapter 8, in our analysis of commentaries about the War on Terror.

Enron: Anatomy of a Scandal

Enron emerged as a major public issue shortly after the energy conglomerate declared bankruptcy in December 2001. Concern had been mounting within the investment community throughout the second half of that year, as the company's stock price began to fall and as some financial analysts complained that the unusually opaque accounting practices of the company made it difficult to determine how much money Enron was actually earning. As the stock continued to lose value through October 2001, questions swirled about Enron's accounting practices. Moody's downgraded Enron's credit rating, and in November, the SEC launched a formal investigation into the company. When Enron filed for bankruptcy on December 2, it was the largest bankruptcy in U.S. history to that point, with liabilities estimated at $23 billion. The fallout from the Enron scandal also ultimately led to the dissolution of Arthur Andersen, one of the largest accounting firms in the world.

Two different types of narratives emerged in the commentary surrounding the collapse of Enron. The first, which was more common on television commentary shows—on the new cable talk formats, in particular—was a narrative about political corruption and the need for campaign finance reform. The second narrative was expressed predominantly in newspaper columns and emphasized economic corruption and the need for better regulation of the finance industry. Each narrative was framed as a debate with two competing sides: for or against increased government oversight of corporations, for or against greater limitations on corporate donations to politicians. Surprisingly, though, the two narratives were not often linked together.

Enron, Cable Television, and the Narrative of Political Corruption

The Enron case was discussed on television first and initially on the cable talk programs. In our sample, the first mention of the case occurs on December 31, 2001, on year-in-review segments of *Crossfire* and *Hannity & Colmes*. Both of these programs inserted the Enron case into one of their dominant ongoing narratives, connecting Enron to corporate political donations and posing the question of whether Democrats or Republicans were more corrupt.

We can see how this narrative developed by examining a December 31 debate on *Hannity & Colmes* between Alan Colmes, the cohost; Robert Weiss, an attorney and Democratic Party strategist; and John Fund, a *Wall Street Journal* columnist. The exchange is illuminating because of the way it continually circles back to the conflict between Democrats and Republicans. All three parties involved in the debate agreed quickly that there should be a Senate investigation of the accounting irregularities that emerged in the aftermath of the Enron meltdown. But this question was secondary to two more substantial issues: (1) whether the Enron case could be linked to corruption within the Bush administration and (2) whether the Enron case was equivalent to the Whitewater scandal of the Clinton administration.

The debate about political corruption on *Hannity & Colmes* is an excellent example of how the newer, more political shows organize their political commentary. Colmes begins the discussion by observing that Enron gave nearly 70 percent of its political contributions to Republicans. This was followed by an extended debate among the guests about the meaning of this fact.

FUND: And that shows—and that shows what?

COLMES: It shows that, clearly, they were giving much more to Republicans.

WEISS: The George Bush administration was bought and sold.

COLMES: Right. We also know . . .

WEISS: What an . . .

(CROSSTALK)

COLMES: Robert, we also know that Kenneth Lay was the single largest contributor to Bush. He helped Bush 41, Bush 43. And look at the board of directors.

WEISS: The board of directors at Enron consisted of Jim Baker, former secretary of the Treasury; Robert Mosbacher, former secretary of Commerce; and Wendy Gramm, former head of the CFTC. Five weeks before . . .

COLMES: Right. Phil Gramm's wife.

WEISS: . . . the—Senator Gramm's wife. Five weeks before Wendy Gramm resigned from the CFTC, she initiated a policy exempting commodity traders, which included Enron, from the anti-fraud provisions. Five weeks later, she was on the board of Enron.

COLMES: So how do you call this a bipartisan scan . . .

WEISS: It's really not a bipartisan . . .

COLMES: What's bipartisan about this?

WEISS: . . . scandal.

COLMES: How is it bipartisan? (*Hannity & Colmes*, January 15, 2002)

As the discussion continued, debate turned to a comparison with Whitewater, with Weiss and Colmes suggesting that Republicans were a lot more eager for investigations of Clinton than for investigations of Bush, while Fund and guest host Monica Crowley dismissed this suggestion.[3] A brief debate ensued about whether the editorial policy of mainstream newspapers resulted in a persistently biased coverage of the issue, before concluding with another expression of unanimous support for investigations of Enron.

This particular episode of *Hannity & Colmes* was somewhat unusual because the dominant host, Sean Hannity, was not on the program. Hannity has an unusual style, where he tends to break away from the ongoing discussion to criticize the mainstream media or defend the Bush administration. The following discussion about the Bush administration's energy policy with Democratic Representative Elliot Engel of New York provides a good example of Hannity's style:

ENGEL: But I'll tell you one thing. Vice President Cheney met with Enron many, many times when he had his task force developing energy policy for the Bush administration . . .

HANNITY: That's right. That's right.

ENGEL: . . . and I think that Vice President Cheney should disclose who he met with, how many times he met with, and what influence . . .

HANNITY: They already have disclosed.

ENGEL: . . . and what influence Enron had in formulating Bush energy policy.

HANNITY: Wait a minute. This—this has not been pointed out by the media, and I find this a little disheartening because I think there's some intellectual dishonesty on the media's part.

He met at a time where gas prices and energy prices were going through the roof and he met at a time when we had rolling blackouts in California with the third largest energy company in the country. Doesn't that make good sense to you?

ENGEL: Well, it's no crime to meet with them, but he ought to disclose it. There's been a shroud . . .

HANNITY: He has. He mentioned it this week that . . .

ENGEL: Well—no. There's been a whole cloud of secrecy, and we don't know whom he met with, we don't know how many times, we don't know what they discussed, we don't know what influence Enron had in formulating energy policy, and we ought to know.

HANNITY: All right, but if we're going to go down that road, then we're going to go through all the trade junkets that the Clinton administration had with their top officials from Mickey Kantor to—their connection to Mr. Rubin and also. . . . (*Hannity & Colmes*, January 15, 2002)

From this point in the discussion, the other guest, Republican Congressman Chris Shays of Connecticut, attempted to reframe the issue as having to do with the illegality of soft money and corporate contributions, while Hannity tried to maintain the position that every senator who received money from Enron should recuse himself from an investigation. Colmes tried to redirect the discussion back toward the issue of political corruption, asserting that Enron had too much influence over energy policy appointments in the Bush administration. But after a short debate about whether the Enron case might actually lead to legislation banning soft money, Hannity ended the show with the following comment:

HANNITY: All right. We've got to run, but the Bush administration couldn't be bought. They made the call, and they wouldn't bail them out. That's a big part of this story. Thank you all for being with us.

As we see in these two excerpts, discussions emerge in a particular way on the newer cable shows like *Hannity & Colmes*. To begin with, the hosts almost always ask questions in a way that encodes a narrative of their own and that challenges the guest to agree or disagree with the narrative. This gives the hosts an unusual framing power, which is exceptional in its ability to maintain a critical autonomy from politicians and also in its ability to reduce all issues to two opposing and polarized positions. To take another example, consider the following exchange between *Crossfire* host Bill Press and Republican Congressman J. D. Hayworth, where Press connects Enron to the Bush administration and Hayworth responds by referring to ethical lapses of the Clinton administration.

PRESS: I hate to be the one to bring you the bad news, but we know that Ken Lay is one of the president's—the chairman of Enron—is one of President Bush's closest friends. We also know he's President Bush's biggest campaign contributor. Over $2 million, he and the company [contributed] to the president's various campaigns for governor and president over the years. So isn't it clear, congressman, that any investigation of Enron, necessarily has to go right to the Bush White House, indeed, right to the Oval Office?

HAYWORTH: Well, of course, that's what you very much hope for, Bill. But let me walk you through this for a second, I know it's difficult for you, after eight years of ethical difficulties that you had to sidestep and ignore, it's tough to know that we finally have a president who knows what the meaning of is—is who has come in to try to change the tone in Washington. You want to remain tone-deaf. The fact is Enron has given thousands of dollars politically to thousands of candidates, both Republicans and Democrats, thousands to Tom Daschle the lead recipients in the House this year are Sheila Jackson Lee and Ken Benson, both Texas Democrats. (*Crossfire*, January 10, 2002)

From the perspective of a theory of mediated deliberation, what kinds of commentaries are these? In the first place, they are narratives by political insiders and about political insiders, where the assumption is that politics is a game of influence and access. Arguments are generally not motivated by the desire to offer policy advice or to explain to citizen-viewers the underlying factors that helped to create the crisis. Scientific and historical discourse is almost entirely absent. Instead, the stock in trade of this narrative is partisan argument in the guise of moral critique, designed to encourage the audience to line up behind one of the political parties in defense against the dangers presented by the other. And this is true regardless of which position the hosts and guests take about who is more corrupt.

A key feature of these formats, then, is their lack of flexibility in responding to attempts to reframe existing issues. Consider the following exchange, between Sean Hannity and Lanny Davis, who was the White House special counsel under President Clinton:

HANNITY: I want to talk about Joe Lieberman and his ability to conduct a fair investigation with at least not having the appearance of impropriety here.

We know that Joe Lieberman took $250,000 from Enron, Arthur Andersen, the accounting firm, and Citigroup. We know Lieberman's former chief of staff is an Enron lobbyist who met with members of his staff. We know Daschle's biggest contributor is Citigroup. Chuck Schumer's one of the biggest recipients of Enron.

How do these guys sit there in judgment of this case when they're up to their eyeballs in Enron donations themselves? They should recuse themselves like Ashcroft, shouldn't they?

DAVIS: Because Joe Lieberman is not making an issue of a lot more money that was taken by President Bush and other Republicans from Enron, and he shouldn't make the issue, and accepting campaign donations from Enron is OK for Joe Lieberman, it's OK for President Bush. The focus of Joe Lieberman is fixing the problem that caused . . .

HANNITY: I don't believe that. I—this has been political from day one, and by your own admission, you've been—you've been critical of the Democrats that have been out there trying to turn this into a political issue. The whole reason for these hearings is that they think they can make the White House look bad and embarrass the president. Isn't that true? And yet this is coming back to haunt them. Joe Lieberman cannot conduct a fair and objective and balanced hearing when he himself has received those kind of dollars from Enron and those groups associated here.

DAVIS: I have—I have a feeling there's a little wishful thinking, Sean, that you want Joe Lieberman and other Democrats to act the way the Republicans acted towards Bill Clinton.

HANNITY: I want them to recuse themselves because they can't—there's a conflict of interest. It has the appearance of impropriety.

DAVIS: We're not going there. (*Crossfire*, January 3, 2002)

As in the previous examples, the debate is primarily moral critique, focusing on the question of whether Democrats possess the moral purity required to investigate political corruption. Hannity makes this case by referring to prominent Democrats who received large contributions from Enron, an argument he made in every discussion he had about Enron on his television program. Davis parries this charge by referring back to Republican actions during the Clinton presidency, suggesting that the Democrats could not possibly act as poorly as Republicans had during that time.

For a theory of mediated deliberation, however, the most important feature of this exchange is Davis's inability to shift the debate away from the initial narrative of political corruption. Davis attempts to link the Enron scandal to a narrative about economic corruption, when he ends his comment about Lieberman by arguing that Lieberman's focus "is fixing the problem that caused." But before he can even finish this argument, Hannity cuts him off, explicitly rejects the economic argument, and asserts that "this has been political from day one." Davis never returns to the economic theme, and in fact when he finishes his exchange with Hannity, Colmes begins a new line of questioning about Enron's undue policy influence. There could not be a clearer indication that the primary interpretation of the Enron case on *Hannity & Colmes* is to be a political one. The attempt to reframe the event as an economic issue is rarely made, and when it is attempted, it fails quickly.

Interestingly, we see the same redirection in a January 28 episode of *Crossfire*—one of only two episodes of *Crossfire* where a guest attempted to tell a story of economic corruption in the context of the Enron scandal. Most of the discussion took place with Senators McConnell and Durbin and covered the well-worn territory regarding how much influence Enron had over energy policy (including a debate about whether Vice President Cheney had a responsibility to disclose more about the meetings he had with Enron). After this discussion, however, there was a segment with Stan Brand, who was an attorney for Arthur Andersen.

PRESS: Stan, I believe that what Andersen is accused of doing with the other accounting firms is worse than what Enron is accused of doing, because I was living under this myth that the accounting firms were there to protect people like us, like investors. And it seems to me, the core problem here, getting away from the people to the policy, is that, if you look at Andersen last year, they made $25 million auditing Enron's books, but they made $27 million serving as consultants to Enron.

They got even more money by helping them with their business. That's the conflict that Arthur Levitt tried to get the Congress to change. It never happened. Don't you realize—or are you willing to admit now, speaking for Andersen, that that dual role for accounting firms is wrong and must be changed?

BRAND: Well, first, on the numbers, they didn't make all that money off consulting. There were tax returns prepared. There were registration . . .

(CROSSTALK)

PRESS: Well, other work, let's say.

BRAND: Other work, not consulting. Consulting was actually a very small part of that. Joe Berardino, the CEO of Arthur Andersen, has said changes need to be made. And Andersen will be part of those changes and part of the reforms. And if that's ultimately where it leads, then Andersen will be part of that change and part of that reform.

PRESS: Fifty-three million dollars the five accounting firms gave members of Congress since 1990. Andersen alone gave money to 94 out of 100 United States senators. The reason that rule wasn't changed is because Andersen and other companies bought off the Congress, didn't they? (*Crossfire*, January 3, 2002)

The rest of the discussion focused on the question of political influence and whether Arthur Andersen had corrupted the process of economic regulation through its political donations. Brand's attempt to reframe the issue as a story of economic regulation and Arthur Andersen's cooperation completely failed to interrupt the overarching narrative of the *Crossfire* format.

Other Versions of the Political Narrative

The narrative of political corruption dominated the commentary about Enron on *Crossfire* and *Hannity & Colmes*, but it was much less visible in the other parts of the opinion space. The *NewsHour* and the *New York Times* almost completely ignored the political narrative, focusing instead on the economic dimensions of the issue. Commentary on *Face the Nation* was evenly split between the political and economic narratives. Commentary at *USA Today* was mostly economic, though there were a few columns that contributed to the narrative of political corruption. We will turn shortly to the economic narratives, but before doing so, we consider how the political narrative developed in these other outlets.

On *Face the Nation*, the political narrative developed as a dialogue between the hosts of the show and a series of elected politicians, and it centered on the question of policy influence. Starkly different from the cable news programs, these discussions were explicitly framed around the need to find out what happened and explicitly *not* about which political party was to blame. Consider, for example, the following exchange between Gloria Borger and Senator Daschle:

> BORGER: Can I just ask you to follow up on the Enron scandal and campaign finance? I mean, aren't Democrats trying to have it both ways? Democrats and Republicans received an awful lot of money from Enron. Democrats and the Republicans received an awful lot of money from the accounting industry. Is— isn't it difficult for you to lay the blame all on—all on one party and not on both?
>
> SEN. DASCHLE: Well, we're not laying any blame. We're simply trying to get the facts. We're trying to—to understand what happened. And we've got to remember that one of the lessons out of this is that we've got to do something with the incredible mismanagement of employee pension funds. We cannot allow that to go unaddressed this year. So in addition to campaign finance reform, Gloria, we've got an array of other corrective reform measures that must be taken. There's a lot that can be learned, but I don't think either party ought to try to lay blame. Let's just let the facts speak for themselves. (*Face the Nation*, January 27, 2002)

While Borger asks a question that is similar in content (if not in form) to the types of questions that Sean Hannity asked of his guests, it is not framed in a way that suggests political hypocrisy by Democrats. The result is that Daschle does not have to spend any time rejecting such an implication. In fact, he is able to reject the argument that assigning political blame is a primary task to be accomplished, and he is able to redirect attention back toward the kinds of economic regulations that need to be put in place to ensure that similar scandals do not occur in the future. Daschle has more control over the framing of the issue, even while the narrative he chooses to tell rejects the focus on political corruption or the assumption of polarization. A similar exchange occurred between host Bob Schieffer and Senator Lieberman:

> SCHIEFFER: Clearly many of the people in Enron were supporters and political contributors to the Bush administration. The Bush administration says it did nothing out of the ordinary in connection from this. What do you need to know from the White House?
>
> LIEBERMAN: Well, Bob, let me stress that the focus of our investigation is going to be what hap—the corporate scandal, what happened in Enron, but—but since we're the Governmental Affairs Committee and we're a government oversight or an investigative committee, we've also got to ask: What could the federal government have done? And in asking that, we've got to ask, where was the federal government and its agencies? Not only back to January 20th when the Bush

administration with all its contacts with Enron took over, but before that, and not only about the executive branch, but about Congress itself.

There—there—we don't know—look, it's obvious, and a fact, that the—that the Enron executives were major contributors to the Bush campaign. We know that Mr. Lay and other executives of Enron were right in the middle of the formulation of the Bush administration energy policy and energy appointments that were made. But we don't know enough to know whether any of that influence in any way stopped the administration or agencies of our federal government from protecting average shareholders who lost their life savings when Enron collapsed. And that's the question we're going to ask. (*Face the Nation*, January 13, 2002)

The focus on finding information is more easily linked to the economic regulation narrative, which we turn to shortly. In fact, in a February 10 episode of *Face the Nation*, Congressman Tauzin explicitly rejected the political narrative when he was asked whether he thought Enron was a political scandal, and he proceeded to reframe the issue as an economic one, arguing that "this is primarily a scandal of corporate greed and corruption, the likes of which I've never seen in any corporation in America." The discussion then turned to the question of how typical Enron's accounting practices were, compared with other corporations.

In the *New York Times*, we see a similar reframing of the political narrative, which largely avoids the focus on political insiders and moves toward a reframing of the political dimensions of the crisis as legal ones. A good example of this is a column written by Akhil Reed Amar, a professor of law at Yale University. Amar's column argued that the ability of individuals to impede congressional investigations through repeatedly invoking the Fifth Amendment—as Enron executives were doing at the time—was based on a mistaken interpretation of the Constitution (*New York Times*, February 18, 2002, p. A15). Specifically, Amar argued that the reading of the Fifth Amendment that was institutionalized by the Supreme Court in 1892 "warped the separation of powers" and unreasonably constrained congressional action, as could be seen in the inability to prosecute Oliver North following the 1987 Iran-Contra hearings, as well as in the decision not to compel testimony from John Huang in the 1997 investigation of campaign finance abuses. Amar concluded the op-ed by making a specific policy suggestion: namely, that the Supreme Court review its interpretation of the Fifth Amendment.

Amar's column is notable for its use of extended historical argument and the way that it ties this historical narrative to a specific policy recommendation. Compared with the other political narratives about Enron—and particularly those on television—Amar's column emphasizes judicial actions over legislative ones. These kinds of alternative perspectives are precisely why the *New York Times* created the op-ed page, and they constitute a major difference between the space of commentary in newspapers and the more restricted opinion space of television. Narrative diversity, complexity, and openness to

voices from outside the media or political field were also features of the economic narrative that dominated the op-ed treatment of Enron on the *New York Times* op-ed page.

The Economic Narrative in the New York Times

> It was a shocking event. With incredible speed, our perception of the world and of
> ourselves changed. It seemed that before we had lived in a kind of blind innocence,
> with no sense of the real dangers that lurked. Now we had experienced a rude
> awakening, which changed everything. No, I'm not talking about Sept. 11; I'm
> talking about the Enron scandal. (Paul Krugman, *New York Times*, January 29,
> 2002, p. A21)

This quote, from columnist Paul Krugman, effectively captures the main elements of the
New York Times commentary on Enron. Cleverly taking advantage of all the commen-
tary about the War on Terror, Krugman asserts that "in the years ahead Enron, not
September 11, will come to be seen as the greater turning point in U.S. society" (*New
York Times*, January 29, 2002, p. A21).

The goal of Krugman's comparison is not really to compare Enron and September 11
but rather to reject others' attempts to diminish the significance of Enron or to characterize it as a normal risk that exists in a market society. Specifically criticizing Vice
President Cheney, Treasury Secretary O'Neill, SEC Chairman Pitt, and Republican
Party Chairman Racicot for failing to understand that "the old laxity is no longer
acceptable" (*New York Times,* January 29, 2002, p. A21), Krugman formulated two
questions that would be the primary focus of the economic narrative: How many other
Enrons were out there? And what new regulations needed to be put in place to prevent
future Enrons?

On the first question, Krugman wrote, "I'd be very surprised if we don't have two,
three, even many Enrons in our future" (*New York Times*, February 1, 2002, p. A25). He
then proceeded to outline three developments that emerged in the late 1990s, which he
felt "opened the door for financial scams on a scale unseen for generations." First, Krugman argued, the new technologies that emerged with the rise of the Internet economy
created financial confusion, because financial experts did not yet know how to value the
"new economy" companies in a reliable way. Second, the stock market bubble created a
"natural Ponzi scheme," creating "an environment [where] it's also easy to run deliberate
pyramid schemes." Third, there was a decline in legal oversight, for which Krugman
blamed Republicans in Congress:

> Once upon a time, the threat of lawsuits hung over companies and auditors that
> engaged in sharp accounting practices. But in 1995 Congress, overriding a veto by
> Bill Clinton, passed the Private Securities Litigation Reform Act, which made
> such suits far more difficult. Soon accounting firms, the companies they audited

and the investment banks that sold their stock got very cozy indeed. (*New York Times*, February 1, 2002, p. A25)

Krugman's Enron columns were laced with scientific discourse, making repeated references to books and studies by academic economists. Krugman's own writings about Enron were supplemented by other guest columns about Enron published in the *New York Times*, too, which included a heavy representation of academics and other financial experts who focused on the question of what regulations needed to be established to prevent events like Enron from occurring in the future. For example, Robert Frank, a professor of economics at Cornell University, argued for stricter accounting regulations, coupled with harsh sanctions for those who violate the regulations (*New York Times*, August 24, 2002, p. A13). Citing Adam Smith, Frank argued that it was both unrealistic and unreasonable to expect business leaders to practice voluntary compliance in the absence of stiff sanctions. In a similar vein, accounting professors Granof and Zeff traced the causes of Enron back to the 1970s, when members of Congress declined to enact tougher standards for financial reporting, and when they began an assault on the regulatory authority of the Financial Accounting Standards Board (FASB), which continued throughout the 1980s and 1990s (*New York Times,* January 21, 2002, p. A19). Their solution was a complete overhaul of the existing accounting model, as well as an increase in autonomy for the FASB. Jeffrey Sonnenfeld, dean of the Yale School of Management, also traced the problem back to the 1970s. Rather than blaming accounting practices, however, Sonnenfeld placed the responsibility on changed management practices: specifically, the growing focus on immediate financial returns, the focus on acquisition as an end in itself, and a general disregard for sound management practices, the primary focus of which should be to produce better products and services.

> These serial acquirers did not build businesses around core competencies but were scavengers for good deals, a strategy that rarely pays off in the long run. (A study done for The Wall Street Journal by Thomson Financial found that in the current weak economy the stocks of the top 50 acquirers have fallen three times as much as the Dow Jones industrial average.). . . .
>
> The academic research on diversified firms is unambiguous. They generally do not beat the market. The executives could not possibly remain knowledgeable about the changing technological and market requirements for such disparate businesses. It has been reported that Gary Winnick of Global Crossing, for example, so little understood his telecom businesses that he relied on a Salomon Smith Barney telecom analyst, Jack Grubman, to guide financial and strategic moves. (*New York Times*, June 12, 2002, p. A29)

Like the Granoff and Krugman columns, Sonnenfeld's op-ed makes extensive use of scientific and historical discourse, repeatedly referencing academic studies and research reports. In the course of his column, Sonnenfeld identifies two basic types of executive. The preferred type is the manager, who is an expert in the delivery of a specific product or service, who tends to value teamwork, and who tends to believe that management is something that is learned over time, through careful reflection and experience. The profane type of executive is the serial acquirer, who is interested in acquisitions rather than services, who is not much of a team player, and who believes that leadership is an innate quality that cannot be learned. And having done this analytical work, Sonnenfeld ends the column in characteristic academic fashion, by highlighting historical continuity and the importance of better collective wisdom:

> None of this is really new. The fall of the most recent corporate acquirers provides spectacular reminders of lessons we've seen decade after decade. (*New York Times*, June 12, 2002, p. A29)

The Economic Narrative in USA Today

While the Enron columns in the *New York Times* were written primarily by academics, the economic narrative in the *USA Today* was penned primarily by representatives from think tanks, advocacy groups, and professional associations. Correspondingly, we see a lot less scientific language or historical discourse in the *USA Today* columns, and a much larger number of specific policy proposals. Furthermore, the economic narrative in *USA Today* emerges as a dialogue between business insiders and members of Congress, written primarily from an insider's perspective. Consider the following column, written by James Castellano, chairman of the board of directors of the American Institute of Certified Public Accountants:

> As the national professional association of CPAs, the American Institute of Certified Public Accountants (AICPA) is deeply disturbed by the collapse of Enron, a failure that has shaken confidence in our capital markets. The personal tragedy to the company's employees and shareholders goes far beyond the jobs and dollars they've lost. The AICPA is committed to working with Congress to develop meaningful reforms.
>
> All interested parties—including the accounting profession, the investment community, public companies, creditors and the financial industry—should be actively engaged. In the weeks since the Enron collapse, various parties have put forth proposals to reform the accounting and auditing system and, more broadly, the financial-reporting model. . . . The AICPA recently endorsed a petition to the SEC, calling for more disclosure about a company's liquidity, off-balance-sheet entities, related party transactions and hedging contracts. Congress should carefully consider these proposed reforms, as we all endeavor to restore investor faith in the U.S. financial-reporting system. (*USA Today*, February 14, 2002, p. A16)

This column is different in a number of respects from what we saw in the *New York Times*. First, it is written almost as if it were a press release, announcing the work that the AICPA has been involved in to fix the crisis and the specific proposals it has made to Congress. There is no attempt to explain the causes of the crisis or even to assign blame; rather, the goal is to identify specific policy proposals and make sure that the professional association of accountants is included in the list of key policy players dealing with the situation.

For the think tank intellectuals writing Enron columns in *USA Today*, however, there are two central messages. First, the crisis is not as bad as people think. And second, increasing government regulation will not do anything to fix the problems that do exist. Thus, James Glassman, a fellow at the American Enterprise Institute, argued that Enron was an exceptional and unusual case, which tended to obscure the fact that most financial analysts did an excellent job and that the market was generally effective at eliminating underperforming analysts (*USA Today*, March 25, 2002, p. A14). As a result, there was no need for new government regulation. Similarly, for Peter Vandoren, writing on behalf of the libertarian think tank the Cato Institute, the lesson of Enron is that there actually needs to be *less* government regulation.

> With the collapse of Enron, companies will now have to go to extra lengths to convince investors of their financial integrity. And auditors will need to rebuild the public trust they have lost. But increased government regulation is unnecessary. . . .
>
> If Congress and the SEC can refrain from new laws and regulations, companies will actually have to go to greater lengths to regain investor confidence. And investors will learn to rely less on government regulation and more on other voluntary mechanisms to ensure economic integrity. (*USA Today*, March 7, 2002, p. A11)

What about the academics who wrote Enron columns for *USA Today*? Here, we see a reliance on some of the same discursive features that academics for the *New York Times* used: specifically, the greater reliance on scientific and historical discourse, as well as the general goal of *explaining* the significance of the crisis, for citizen-readers, as well as elites. At the same time, however, we also see the same narrative tendencies that the think tank intellectuals deployed, in the sense that they tended to downplay the significance of the crisis and to discount the likely benefits of additional regulation. In other words, academics writing Enron columns for *USA Today* relied on the displays of expertise that were connected to their academic status, without deviating from the overarching narrative line that was developing in the paper. Consider the following column written by Douglas Branson, a law professor at the University of Pittsburgh:

> To suggest that the federal government should impose negligence standards for corporate officers is blunderbuss. The American business-judgment rule says that if directors are proactive, making decisions, they will be liable only for gross negligence, for good reason. We want to encourage directors to undertake informed

risk-taking. We want directors, rather than courts, to manage corporations' business and affairs. And for directors asleep at the switch, who do nothing, the state-law standard of conduct already is negligence.

Then, too, states permit corporations to amend charters to relieve directors of liability for negligence. Nearly every state has followed Delaware in allowing adoption of these clauses allowing the limitation of director liability. More than 60% of the USA's large corporations have adopted them, making enactment of a negligence standard a grandstanding play. . . .

In the United States and around the world, we are in the midst of a good-governance movement that has seen vast improvement in the governance structure and practices of large corporations. The federal government should not muck around with it.

Take testimony, separate auditing from consulting in accounting firms, consider narrow reforms, but come to the realization that Enron is the very sick child of a very healthy corporate-governance system in the United States. (*USA Today*, March 1, 2002, p. A9)

The attempt to explain the underlying context that informs the regulation debate is typical of the academic style, as is the use of multiple forms of expertise—in this case, an explanation of the relevant legal standard, a mobilization of statistical data, and even the use of a global-comparative perspective. To some extent, then, Branson's column introduces some complexity into the economic narrative in *USA Today*. On the other hand, the policy implications of the column, which emphasize the dangers of regulation and the benefits of doing nothing, are quite similar to the arguments being made by the think tank intellectuals and other guest columnists for *USA Today*. By separating the structural and thematic elements of the argument in such a way, Branson's column is able to draw on the kinds of authority claims that one expects from an academic while at the same time making an argument that is consistent with the general tone of the op-ed page of that specific paper. Both strategies increase the likelihood of getting the column published.

A Hybrid Narrative: Enron Commentary on the NewsHour

While the political narrative of Enron dominated the discussion of the cable talk programs, economic interpretations were much more visible on the *NewsHour*. This reinforces previous findings throughout the book that indicate that opinion on the *NewsHour* is more like print opinion than cable television opinion. The people who made commentaries about Enron on the *NewsHour* also overlapped with the world of print opinion, with a substantial proportion occurring in the regular discussion of key issues of the day, which took place between the host of the show and two syndicated columnists, David Brooks and Mark Shields. At the time, Brooks was senior editor at the *Weekly Standard* and a contributing editor at *Atlantic Monthly*, but he would go on to join the staff of the *New York Times* in 2003 as a regular columnist for the paper.

Shields had been a regular commentator for the *NewsHour* since 1987 and wrote a nationally syndicated column that he had started with the *Washington Post*.

Although Enron commentary on the *NewsHour* was voiced largely by print columnists, the format of their commentaries differed in interesting ways from the kinds of economic commentaries we saw on the op-ed page of the *New York Times*. Specifically, when the columnists appeared on television, they were much more likely to include political interpretations as part of their commentary. For the case of Enron, the result was a hybrid commentary, which discussed the issue of economic regulation but focused almost exclusively on actors from the political field. Consider the following exchange between Brooks and Shields:

> MARK SHIELDS: Let me just first say, I have not seen a better piece on Enron in print or anywhere than Paul's done this week. I just really . . . Terrific. "Take the money 'Enron'" is going right into the language. This was marked by regulators who didn't regulate, directors who didn't direct, and you can see the transformation. Will the Congress act? We've got born-again regulators, we've got watchdogs on Capitol Hill now. The President himself is a born-again populist this week. He belatedly discovered his populist roots in the form of his wife's mother having lost money on Enron. He was furious—enraged by it. So, yes, will they act? Yes, they'll act. What they will do I think is unclear at this time. There is a resistance, obviously, and strong resistance from large corporate interests to do too much, but at the same time I think there will be . . . Arthur Levitt, who was the chairman of the SEC in the last administration, a reviled figure in the American accounting industry and Wall Street as well, is now revered on Capitol Hill. . . .

> MARGARET WARNER: But, David, for instance, Arthur Levitt's proposal came to naught because 13 Senators in different ways pressured the SEC to back off. Is that kind of thing really going to stop? Are we going to see a rolling . . . A reimposition of the same controls that they fought all along?

> DAVID BROOKS: I think it may actually—I think what we've seen this week is that Enron turned into sort of a Whitewater-Watergate political scandal, which it is not. It is, however, an important cultural and political moment. And I think the moment is this: We're going into an information-age economy where people have 401(k)s, where most people are involved in the stock market, and people are willing to go into that sort of privatized, deregulated world. They don't want to go back into the 1950s with big pension plans and big Social Security programs. But if they are going to go into this world, the bargain has to be, it has to be fair. There has to be fair competition; there have to be rules safeguarding my entry into that world of private stock ownership, and people are going to demand that. They're not demanding it as anti-capitalists; they are capitalists; but they're going to demand some sort of rules. So what people in Congress have to decide,

and especially Republicans, "am I pro-business or am I pro-competition?" Because, as we just saw in that report, the two are not the same thing. (*News-Hour*, January 25, 2002)

Like the political narratives we saw on other television programs, this commentary describes the Enron events mostly in terms of the actions of politicians. But it is not a narrative of political corruption, hypocrisy, or influence. Like the economic narratives we saw in the newspapers, the *Newshour* commentary tells a story about the workings of the financial market and the kinds of regulations that are needed to ensure that investors receive good information. Unlike so many of the print columns, however, Shields and Brooks do not describe the issue as one that can be resolved through the self-correcting nature of the market or through the more civic-minded and empowered actions of business leaders and accountants. Instead, the viewer gets the sense that politicians will enact the correct regulatory policy changes, even if they do so for the wrong (i.e., for political) reasons.

What we see with television commentary about Enron, then, is that the heroes of the narratives are almost always politicians, regardless of whether the focus of the narrative is on the economy or the political system. This is perhaps not surprising, when we consider how the guests of these programs are dominated so thoroughly by people who come from the political or journalistic field.

Conclusion: Format Differences in Commentary about Enron

For the case of Enron, the newspaper op-ed page seems to have offered the most diverse and the least politicized forms of mediated deliberation, and the newspaper discussions included a greater variety of voices from people who came from outside the journalistic and political fields. This is an interesting fact, when combined with the realization that newspaper commentaries were also more likely to offer specific policy proposals. This would seem to suggest that the presence of outside voices—in this instance, including those from outside journalism as well as outside politics—helps to decrease the likelihood that media commentaries will emphasize "horse race" or "political strategy" frames, as they so often do in their "objective" news reports.[4]

While the newspaper commentaries included a greater diversity of voices, however, this diversity was stratified, with more academics writing in the *New York Times* and more speakers from think tanks and professional associations writing in *USA Today*. This had consequences for the types of arguments that were made and the forms of authority that were mobilized. In general, the *New York Times* columnists narrated the Enron scandal in a way that emphasized greater complexity, with more reframing, more historical discourse, and more scientific discourse. Columns in *USA Today* emphasized a narrower range of policy proposals, most of which questioned the effectiveness of government regulation. Still, op-ed columns in *USA Today* highlighted a greater number of relevant issues than were found in television commentaries, and the issues they identified were less narrowly tied to the organization of the political field.

For the television commentaries, taken as a group, one of the most striking features was the central role that politicians played in the narratives. This was equally true whether the speaker was a talk show host, a politician, a political adviser, or a print columnist. This is true even in the *NewsHour* commentaries on Enron, which took place mainly among print columnists. In their composition of guests, then, as well as the narratives they privileged, television commentaries about Enron were more closely tied to the narratives and frames of the political field than newspapers were.

The preference on television for political narratives rather than economic ones is an intriguing pattern that merits further research. One thing that seems certain is that the circulation of economic narratives is more likely in those parts of the space of opinion where academics are present. It is not always the academics that are actually making the economic argument, but their inclusion in the debate did seem to produce more narrative diversity in the space of opinion. On the television programs, where academic voices were largely absent in the discussion of Enron, the heroes and villains of the narratives were almost exclusively politicians, and the terrain of symbolic action was restricted largely to the political field.

Which television formats are more or less closely tied to the political field, however, is far less clear. On *Face the Nation*, which is the oldest television format in our sample, the discussion was completely dominated by politicians, who had virtually unlimited interpretive authority. This interpretive freedom was connected to the style of the talk show hosts, who limited themselves to asking questions and avoided any moral argument or partisan communication. In other words, the objective and nonpartisan practices of *Face the Nation*'s hosts had the effect of turning the program over to politicians. And yet, by doing this, the political narrative that developed on *Face the Nation* was less dominated by horse race themes than the newer formats were. Indeed, the discussions on *Face the Nation* allowed politicians to disavow assigning political blame, to suggest that their main motivations were to find out what happened and prevent it from happening again in the future, and to connect their political actions back to the economic dimensions of the crisis. In other words, the interpretive freedom granted to politicians allowed more complexity in their commentaries, at least as compared with the newer television formats.

Indeed, when we examine the commentaries about Enron on the newer cable programs, one of their most striking features is the way they emphasized simplification over complexity. The debates on *Crossfire* and *Hannity and Colmes* contained lots of moral argument, but it was framed around disagreement rather than common values. In fact, most of the moral arguments on these programs were connected to ongoing political divisions and to the ongoing narrative of political corruption.

How we evaluate these simplified moral narratives of political division is not altogether obvious. To be sure, a communicative space that rejects complexity and reduces everything to politics creates real problems for mediated deliberation. If these communicative spaces are inventing political divisions where they did not exist before, then that is even worse. If the narratives of political division reflect actual social divisions and social struggles, however, then such a framing would seem to reflect the political organization of actually existing civil society, and the attempt to paper over or ignore such differences could easily be interpreted as ideological (see Baker 2002: 161–163; Ferree et al. 2002: 315). Indeed, the newer formats make it much more difficult for politicians and other guests to maintain their own narrative autonomy, given that they are generally responding to a morally charged question. This reduces the ideological power that politicians have on these programs, even if this comes at the expense of increased ideological power for the talk show hosts. But even here, how we evaluate the host's ideological power is somewhat contradictory because of the way the newer formats pay such persistent attention to the media's framing power in public debates and the possible ideological biases that one can find in other media formats. This feature introduces a degree of public reflexivity in the form of media metacommentary, a point we return to at the end of the book.

In those instances where television expands to include other types of voices, there tends to be a corresponding opening up of the narrative features of their commentaries. This was clearly the case in the only episode of *Crossfire* in our sample that featured guests from outside the political field: a January 18 episode that featured Ralph Nader and Fred Smith as guests. While Nader had been a political candidate in 2000, he is better known as a consumer advocate and social critic. The other guest, Fred Smith, worked at the time for the Competitive Enterprise Institute, a think tank that focuses on economic policy research. Smith and Nader both discussed the need to protect the small investor, particularly by introducing reforms and greater transparency in employee investments and pension plans. Smith also argued for greater caution and research by small investors, suggesting that "if people can't explain to you how they're making money, you maybe shouldn't invest in those areas" (*Crossfire*, January 18, 2002). And despite the talk show hosts' repeated attempts to turn the issue back to the narrative of political corruption, Smith and Nader maintained the focus on economic commentary and the need for reform.

In this episode segment of *Crossfire*, then, it appears that the particular mix of voices allowed the guests of the program to resist the overarching interpretive preferences of the hosts (i.e., the narrative of political corruption) and to put forth their argument in an effective, detailed, and forceful way. The absence of any elected politicians or political strategists on the segment made this possibility more likely too, because those types of guests are much more willing than other guests to "play the game" of political polarization that the *Crossfire* hosts want to play. In other words, the ability of the newer formats to provide a more diverse communicative environment requires an ensemble of guests that extends beyond the political and journalistic insiders who so often dominate the programs.

To explore more fully how the variety of narratives circulating in television commentaries are related to the mix of guests appearing on those programs, we would need a case with a much greater density of discussion and a correspondingly larger diversity of guest voices. We see this greater diversity in the commentary that surrounded the War on Terror.

I think there are really interesting questions that have come up during this period of the last two months—of to what extent is a journalist a citizen—in your hierarchy of responsibilities. Is it citizen first and then journalist? Is it journalist first and then citizen? In my view: it's citizen first, but I say that with . . . there's a little bit of a catch in my throat when I say that because we still need to be able to challenge what Washington is telling us and we still need to ask the tough—the toughest questions we possibly can—but you can't stop being an American at the same time. These are some very, very . . . I mean, some of these things many of us as journalists have never confronted.

—CNN'S JUDY WOODRUFF, in Jones (2002), pp. 6–7

8 The War on Terror

THE EVENTS OF September 11 presented a significant challenge to the journalistic field and especially to its professed stance of journalistic detachment (Rosen 2001). In the weeks immediately following the tragedy, most reporters eschewed detachment and opted instead for a journalism of consensus and solidarity (Schudson 2008: 77–81; also see Hallin 1994: 53). In many respects, this was a temporary shift; dissent and contention could be found in *New York Times* coverage of the global crisis by the end of September 2001, and its special "A Nation Challenged" section was discontinued at the end of that year (Schudson 2008: 77–80). By the beginning of the Iraq War in 2003, most American television networks had adopted a neutral tone in at least 90 percent of their coverage; Fox News was the least detached, but even its coverage maintained a neutral tone in more than 60 percent of its news stories (Aday, Livingston, and Hebert 2005). The return to detached news coverage did not bring about a return to the same distinctions that had characterized U.S. journalism before September 11, however. The detached stance of objective journalism had been challenged, leaving new questions about what should count as authentic journalistic practice.

Much of the scholarship about post-9/11 journalism has pointed to the limitations of standard journalistic practice and its ideals of detachment and objectivity. Waisbord (2002), for example, argues that U.S. journalism is poorly equipped to serve the needs of democracy during times of global crisis because of its reliance on sensationalism and its inability to talk about structural issues without relying on "news hooks." Ultimately, he argues, journalists turn to narratives of patriotism because their ideals of objectivity and detachment do not provide the resources that would allow them to respond effectively to large-scale trauma. Sreberny (2002) makes a similar argument about the inability of objective, detached journalism to respond effectively to collective trauma; looking at the commentary section of the British press, she examines how a new sense of collective understanding was created through the affective and creative work of guest columnists (specifically, novelists). The point is similar to Baker's (2002) argument about mediated deliberation in a complex democracy and reinforces an argument we have been making throughout the book. That is, in societies defined by real social division and conflict, the practices of detached and objective journalism must be supplemented by the more partisan and argumentative discourse that one finds in the space of opinion.

We see this in a study by Robert Entman (2003b) that examines how arguments in the space of opinion affected the wider landscape of mediated deliberation after September 11. Entman was interested in how challenges to the Bush administration's framing of the War on Terror had emerged and how they had become increasingly visible throughout 2002. In his model of "cascading activation," Entman (2003b: 425) finds that the initial challenges to the dominant frame came from the editorial and op-ed pages of newspapers, which were "freer of the constraints of standard newsbeats and news definitions that render journalists dependent on official discourse." Specifically, Entman identifies elite columnists Thomas Friedman and Seymour Hersh as the initial disseminators of the counterframe, which placed more critical scrutiny on Saudi Arabia than on Afghanistan or Iraq. Once elite discord began to emerge, particularly among Republican politicians, then political elites who were interested in challenging the Bush administration's definition of the situation were able to use these columns to create an alternative frame, which they repeated in their interviews with journalists. In this way, the arguments initially formulated in the space of opinion found their way back into standard news reports, which were now reported in the voice of official sources.

To be sure, the fact that Friedman and Hersh were able to challenge the Bush administration in their columns does not mean that the space of opinion served the public interest unproblematically. As Entman (2003b: 427–428) points out, the question of Iraq was the dominant public focus throughout 2002, and Saudi Arabia was "never destined to be more than a sidelight, albeit a nagging one from the Bush administration's perspective." Furthermore, as Friel and Falk (2004) have argued, the op-ed page of the *New York Times* has consistently ignored international law arguments about the conduct of war by

American leaders, despite the fact that editorials and columnists frequently cite international laws in criticism of foreign governments. This inconsistency has had disastrous consequences, they argue, culminating in the refusal by authorities writing in the op-ed page to cite international law in an evaluation of the Bush doctrine of preemptive war. In other words, while the space of opinion provides a forum where influential speakers can introduce new interpretive frames into the public debate, its power to do so effectively is often limited by political and ideological factors.

Following Entman, Baker, and others, we analyze the major narratives that emerged in the opinion space about the War on Terror during 2001 and 2002. There were three key events that helped to shape commentary. The first was the attacks of September 11, 2001, when hijackers used commercial airplanes to destroy the World Trade Center buildings in New York City. The second key event was the October 2001 invasion of Afghanistan, and the third major event was the vote by Congress, in October 2002, to authorize U.S. military action in Iraq. As the congressional vote drew near, public commentary turned increasingly to the question of the impending invasion of Iraq and the larger question of the Middle East, and away from more general issues involved with international terrorism and domestic security.

For these events, we return to the four major dimensions of analysis we outlined in chapter 7:

(a) How do different opinion formats organize their discussions about issues?

(b) How open are different opinion formats to a diversity of voices, narratives, and rhetorical styles? And how flexibly do different formats respond to issues, events, and different kinds of guests?

(c) How are different narratives positioned in terms of the larger political field? For example, how much control do political principals have in framing public debate?

(d) To what extent does opinionated speech in different formats attempt to assert new principles of distinction within the journalistic field, that is, new ideas about what constitutes good journalism or good opinion? In this connection, to what degree are other types of media intellectuals able to assert their own critical interpretation of events?

In what follows, we examine each outlet separately to identify the ways in which specific speakers, opinion styles, and claims to authority combined in particular formats to shape the narratives that developed about the War on Terror. There were five major narratives: (1) a narrative about American unity and strength; (2) a narrative about the Middle East and the Islamic world in general; (3) a narrative about security, liberty, and Constitutional rights; (4) a narrative about military strategy, concerning a possible invasion of Iraq; and (5) a narrative about political polarization, cynicism, and unprincipled dishonor. These narratives developed with different levels of complexity in different opinion formats, with some emphasizing difficulty and contradiction and others highlighting a clear set of binary moral distinctions.

USA Today

While *USA Today* published considerably fewer commentaries about the War on Terror than either the *New York Times* or the television programs in our sample, nevertheless, several narratives emerged on the paper's op-ed page. The initial columns emphasized the general safety of airplanes and the need for Americans to continue flying. These were written by Al Neuharth, owner of the paper, and also by Phil Boyer, the president of the Aircraft Owner's and Pilot's Association. Neuharth suggested that the Federal Aviation Association should spend more money to increase security at airports and on airplanes (*USA Today*, September 21, 2001, p. A25). Boyer suggested that the small airplane operators he represented were not a significant security risk, and he argued that increasing security at the airports that serviced these planes would be a waste of money (*USA Today*, October 2, 2001, p. A12).

A second type of narrative that was repeated frequently in the months right after September 11 was one that emphasized the "end of normalcy" and stressed the need for intelligence and resolve. These narratives were most common in October and November but disappeared from the *USA Today* op-ed page after December 2001. It was not uncommon in these narratives for comparisons to be made with Israelis, who had been dealing with terrorism for decades.[1] Other columns stressed the need to avoid panic and to adopt an intelligent and sensible approach to security issues.[2] Less common in *USA Today* were columns that used an academic form of historical irony to narrate the end of normalcy.[3] In this type of interpretation, which we will see more frequently in the *New York Times*, the roots of insecurity are traced back to a previous foreign policy decision and its unintended consequences.[4]

The third and dominant narrative emerged after the October invasion of Afghanistan. At this point, debate in *USA Today* turned to a consideration of liberty, security, and military strategy in a time of war. These debates were carried out largely among columnists, academics, and think tank intellectuals. Here, the early columns were extremely aggressive, dismissing diplomatic efforts and political sensitivity as ineffective and dangerous. Peter Schweitzer, a fellow at the conservative Hoover Institute who wrote several columns about the War on Terror for *USA Today*, argued that diplomacy with the Taliban should be avoided as much as possible and that the overriding goal should be absolute military victory.[5] A similar kind of column was written by Amitai Etzioni, an academic sociologist and think tank intellectual who founded the Communitarian Network in 1990.[6] For Schweitzer, the relevant comparison was the 1991 Persian Gulf War, whereas for Etzioni, it was Bosnia. Otherwise, the columns were very similar: critical of the intrusion of political considerations into military strategy, counseling an extremely aggressive posture, and suggesting that things like political diplomacy or cultural sensitivity were a dangerous waste of time. As Etzioni wrote:

> The United States has been scaling back its bombing on Fridays, the Muslim Sabbath. And only after much public agonizing has the Bush administration decided to continue bombing during the Muslims' holy month of Ramadan. All of this even though the other side has given us no indication that it would curb its attacks on the days holy to us—or to them.
>
> The reason? We fear offending the sensibilities of Muslim nations that support us and further inflaming the enmity of the others.
>
> Is this any way to win a war? Political considerations are severely hampering our military's ability to oust the Taliban from power. . . . Some might say that I should not second-guess our leaders. But the art of war is not rocket science. And I am not second-guessing the military, but objecting to the micromanagement of the war by politicians.
>
> One reason the war in Kosovo—also fought against a small country, Serbia— took so long was that initially a 19-member committee composed of political representatives of various nations had to approve each bombing target. We won once the general in charge was given guidelines and freed to proceed within their confines. . . .
>
> Our willpower is being tested. If it continues to be questioned—because of excessively political dillydallying and curtseying to Muslim sensibilities—we shall lose much more than the coalition: The war against terrorism will turn into another 100-year war, with unimaginable human toll and misery on all sides. (*USA Today*, November 7, 2001, p. A15)

This aggressive posture began to soften as the invasion of Afghanistan ended and as concerns about Constitutionally guaranteed liberties began to assert themselves more forcefully.[7] As attention turned away from Afghanistan toward Iraq, opinion columns in *USA Today* also became increasingly focused on the Bush administration's foreign policy decisions. The majority of these commentaries were written by think tank intellectuals, columnists, and other freelance writers who wrote regular columns for the paper as members of its board of contributors. Most of these columns were written in the "Opposing View" space of the op-ed page, meaning that they were written in opposition to the official editorial position of the paper. And almost all of these commentaries were written to criticize or support specific policy proposals. For example, two scholars from the Brookings Institution, Ivo Daalder and James Lindsay, argued that the decision to invade Iraq would fracture the international coalition that had been put together to combat terrorism; a more effective approach, they suggested, would be to intensify sanctions and weapons inspections in Iraq (*USA Today*, November 29, 2001, p. A15). James Bamford, a member of the board of contributors and the author of a book about U.S.

intelligence agencies, criticized the Bush administration for the way it was placing political pressure on intelligence agents, arguing that this would imperil the effectiveness of U.S. foreign policy in the future (*USA Today*, October 24, 2002, p. A13). Richard Deats, a minister, academic, and international peace activist, criticized the Bush administration's policy of preemptive war; citing Martin Luther King Jr., Deats suggested: "The way to peace is not through waging war" (*USA Today*, February 1, 2002, p. A11). And Pat Buchanan, the syndicated columnist and ubiquitous television pundit, criticized the Bush administration's goals in Iraq as a misguided and misconceived effort at creating an American empire, which would surely fail:

> For some among our Beltway elite, even a U.S. invasion that effects regime change in Baghdad isn't enough. Their vision: a MacArthur Regency in Baghdad, a Pax Americana, a benevolent American empire in the Middle East. As with Hitler's Germany, we must "de-Nazify" all of the "Islamo-fascist" states—Iraq, Iran, Syria, Saudi Arabia, Sudan, Lebanon and Libya—and tutor their people in the blessings of democracy and free markets.
>
> What is wrong with this vision? Only this. It is a century too late. Jefferson's idea, that "all just powers come from the consent of the governed," and Wilson's idea of the self-determination of peoples have taken root in the souls of men.
>
> The West long ago lost the will to colonize, civilize and "Christianize" what Kipling called the "lesser breeds without the law." The age of Western empires is over....
>
> American empire is an intellectual construct of scribblers and think-tank denizens more familiar with the hazards of graduate school than of gunnery school. Americans won't send their sons to die for an empire concocted by talking heads whose boys won't be patrolling that empire.
>
> Look at what became of the British in Palestine, the French in Algeria. Do we really want our own Battle of Algiers in Baghdad? Our own intifada? An American empire in the Islamic world would put us at endless war in that most volatile of regions, and with its most violent forces: Arab nationalism and Islamic fundamentalism. Calls to jihad on America would echo in every mosque from Morocco to Malaysia. (*USA Today*, November 15, 2002, p. A21)

Offering a moral critique of the "Beltway elite" and the think tank intellectuals who seemed to be influencing them, Buchanan's column reframed the question of Iraq as a drive for empire rather than security. Drawing out a historical narrative that equated the Bush administration's goals with the actions of failed empires of the past, Buchanan lists a string of instances where those past empires were brought down by the resistance and resentment of colonized populations.

With the *USA Today* commentary, then, we can see a shift from an initially aggressive narrative of military retribution without negotiation or compromise, toward a concern about civil liberties, and finally to a concern about how a military invasion of

Iraq would damage international coalitions, weaken U.S. foreign policy, and embolden enemies trying to bring down the American empire. Elected politicians and political strategists were largely absent from the discussion, allowing the columnists, academics, and think tank intellectuals who dominated the discussion a large measure of autonomy and critical distance from the political field. Indeed, as concerns increased about the possible encroachment of the state against civil society, the critical narratives increased in force, as did the use of indirect authority claims such as historical discourse and intertextual references.

New York Times

As is the case with most big foreign policy debates, commentary about the War on Terror in the *New York Times* was framed by the regular columnists and supplemented with historical and analytical pieces by academics and think tank intellectuals. The columns can generally be divided into two types: (1) columns that debated military and political strategy and (2) columns that debated intelligence gathering, war, and Constitutional liberties. Embedded within many of these debates was a more abstract discussion about the civic modernization of the Middle East.

The discussions about intelligence gathering and civil liberties were taken up primarily by columnists and law professors. In these op-ed columns, writers emphatically and uniformly rejected the Bush administration's treatment of prisoners, as well as its elevation of security needs over Constitutional liberties. Columnist Nicholas Kristof's initial grappling with the issue is a good example of the commentary we see in the *New York Times*:

> When I first wrestled with this issue, I thought I was going to wind up endorsing President Bush's view that the prisoners are, as he put it today, "killers" rather than P.O.W.'s. But as I read the convention and talked to legal experts, it became clear that the administration's arguments, while initially persuasive, have the disadvantage of being wrong.
>
> To be more precise, they conflict with the letter and spirit of the convention. Moreover, as some in the Pentagon are quietly trying to point out, they set a terrible precedent for our own Special Operations soldiers.
>
> "It is in the American interest to see the Geneva Convention applied," said Steven R. Ratner, a scholar of international law at the University of Texas. (This kind of thinking isn't confined to eggheads in the Boston-Washington corridor.) "Who knows when the day will come when our soldiers will be held by people in some kind of a murky conflict and we will want the protections of the Geneva Convention to apply?"
>
> The contrary argument is that the Taliban and Al Qaeda prisoners do not meet the tests set by the Geneva Convention, such as wearing uniforms and obeying the laws of war.

That is simply wrong. Anyone who bothers to read the convention will see that those tests apply to "resistance movements" outside a country's armed forces. The tests do not apply to military units within a nation's armed forces—such as all Taliban soldiers and perhaps also Qaeda's "Arab Brigade" in the Taliban army. Under the Geneva Convention, all these fighters within the Afghan armed forces are P.O.W.'s whether or not they wear uniforms or obey the rules of war. . . .

But the law is clear: We should presume that detainees are P.O.W.'s and then convene a tribunal to sift among them and exclude those who did not fight in the Taliban army. This corresponds to what we did in the gulf war, when the first Bush administration meticulously followed the Geneva Conventions. (*New York Times*, January 29, 2002, p. A21)

Kristof's column begins from personal experience, recounting an initial sympathy with the Bush administration position. It then subjects that initial impression to empirical and critical scrutiny. Reading the law and consulting with legal experts, Kristof comes to the conclusion that the administration's interpretation is wrong. The column is then able to conclude with a specific policy recommendation for the treatment and classification of prisoners of war.[8]

Given the fact that the commentary in the *New York Times* privileged legal evidence and legal expertise, it is not surprising to find guest columns written by law professors that provided a more extended legal and historical rejection of the policies of the Bush administration. Thus Stephen Gillers, a law professor at New York University, cited a 1984 Supreme Court decision that required all trials to create "a reliable adversarial testing process" to support his argument that defense lawyers who agreed to represent defendants in military tribunals would be violating the ethics of every state bar in the country (*New York Times*, December 3, 2001, p. A19). David Cole, a law professor at Georgetown University and a regular voice on op-ed pages around the country, likened the Justice Department's domestic war against terrorist "sleeper cells" to the anti-Communist laws of the McCarthy era. Quoting a 1967 Supreme Court decision that declared these laws unconstitutional, Cole ends his column by declaring "it would indeed be ironic if, in the name of national defense, we would sanction the subversion of one of those liberties—the freedom of association—which makes the defense of the Nation worthwhile" (*New York Times*, October 19, 2002, p. A17). In all of these discussions, columnists and academics were able to maintain a consistent and critical position against the Bush administration's policies, supporting their arguments with the authority of legal precedent, historical evidence, and a close reading of international agreements.

In contrast to the debates about intelligence gathering and international law, debates about military and political strategies offered different kinds of arguments, opinion styles, and evidence. Most important, concerns about military and political strategies were held together by an overriding narrative about the transformation of the Middle

East. What was needed, according to this argument, was a political, cultural, and civic revolution in most nations of the Middle East. More openness, more tolerance, and more self-criticism of fundamentalism would empower the progressive elements of these countries and begin a modernization of the region, which would ultimately disempower the extremist and anti-Western forces that had gradually been building strength for the past thirty years. To be sure, there were important differences of opinion about how easy it would be to bring about such a transformation, and about what American actions would most effectively help such a change to occur. But the competing opinions about military and political strategy all shared the assumption that the civic modernization of the Middle East was the best way to win the War on Terror.

The primary debates in the *New York Times* involved two competing theories of civic modernization in the Middle East and their consequences for military and political strategies. One of these theories was advanced by columnist Thomas Friedman. Stylistically, Friedman wrote from the subject position of a foreign policy adviser or a policy analyst. He also made extensive use of personal and professional experience claims, based on the many years he spent as a correspondent in Jerusalem, and based on the journalistic, political, and scholarly contacts he had cultivated during his time in the Middle East. Relying on these experiences and contacts, Friedman's columns were distinctive in the way that they tried to paint a picture of the motivations and the mind-set of Islamic terrorists and in their insistence that understanding these motivations was necessary for any effective foreign policy response. More than any other voice providing commentaries about the War on Terror, Friedman identified the people living in the Islamic world as the central protagonists in his narrative.

Friedman's column of September 13, 2001, titled "World War III," provides an excellent example of the distinctive features of his commentary. Written from Jerusalem, the column begins with the following account:

> As I restlessly lay awake early yesterday, with CNN on my TV and dawn breaking over the holy places of Jerusalem, my ear somehow latched onto a statement made by the U.S. transportation secretary, Norman Mineta, about the new precautions that would be put in place at U.S. airports in the wake of Tuesday's unspeakable terrorist attacks: There will be no more curbside check-in, he said. I suddenly imagined a group of terrorists somewhere here in the Middle East, sipping coffee, also watching CNN and laughing hysterically: "Hey boss, did you hear that? We just blew up Wall Street and the Pentagon and their response is no more curbside check-in?" (*New York Times*, September 13, 2001, p. A27)

As the column continues, Friedman asks plaintively, "Does my country really understand that this is World War III?" and then proceeds to describe the inner mind of the enemy:

And this Third World War does not pit us against another superpower. It pits us—the world's only superpower and quintessential symbol of liberal, free-market, Western values—against all the super-empowered angry men and women out there. Many of these super-empowered angry people hail from failing states in the Muslim and third world. They do not share our values, they resent America's influence over their lives, politics and children, not to mention our support for Israel, and they often blame America for the failure of their societies to master modernity.

What makes them super-empowered, though, is their genius at using the networked world, the Internet and the very high technology they hate, to attack us. Think about it: They turned our most advanced civilian planes into human-directed, precision-guided cruise missiles—a diabolical melding of their fanaticism and our technology. Jihad Online. And think of what they hit: The World Trade Center—the beacon of American led capitalism that both tempts and repels them, and the Pentagon, the embodiment of American military superiority.

And think about what places in Israel the Palestinian suicide bombers have targeted most. "They never hit synagogues or settlements or Israeli religious zealots," said the Haaretz columnist Ari Shavit. "They hit the Sbarro pizza parlor, the Netanya shopping mall. The Dolphinarium disco. They hit the yuppie Israel, not the yeshiva Israel."

So what is required to fight a war against such people in such a world? (*New York Times*, September 13, 2001, p. A27)

This is a typical Friedman column, in the way that it builds a detailed descriptive interpretation of the Islamic Middle East, while reinforcing that interpretation with references to Middle East journalists and scholars. The rest of the column, as well as most of the columns that Friedman would write over the next several months, provided a number of different (yet related) answers to this question of how to wage a war "against such people." For American policy makers and American citizens, Friedman stressed that it was important not to underemphasize the depth of the hatred of Israel and the United States among certain parts of the Islamic population.[9] Friedman also suggested that American leaders needed to take a tougher line with American allies in the Middle East, emphasizing that it would no longer be acceptable for them to maintain cordial relationships with terrorist groups.[10] Finally, in a suggestion directed to foreign politicians (as well as American diplomats), Friedman insisted repeatedly that Arab countries needed to be more tolerant of dissent and more willing to criticize the anticivil elements mobilizing within their countries.[11]

Because his main preoccupation was the inner psyche of actual and potential terrorists and the structural factors that activated such a consciousness, Friedman did not spend much time engaging the debate about invading Iraq, which took place during the second half of 2002. To the extent that he did write about this debate, he did so by contrasting "the deterrables like Saddam" with the "'undeterrables'—the kind of young Arab-Muslim men who hit us on 9/11, and are still lurking." Friedman continued by suggesting Americans would pay virtually any price to eliminate the threat from the undeterrables—the terrorists who hate us more than they love their own lives, and therefore cannot be deterred.

> I share this view, which is why I think the Iraq debate is upside down. Most strategists insist that the reason we must go into Iraq—and the only reason—is to get rid of its weapons of mass destruction, not regime change and democracy building. I disagree.
>
> I think the chances of Saddam being willing, or able, to use a weapon of mass destruction against us are being exaggerated. What terrifies me is the prospect of another 9/11—in my mall, in my airport or in my downtown—triggered by angry young Muslims, motivated by some pseudo-religious radicalism cooked up in a mosque in Saudi Arabia, Egypt or Pakistan. And I believe that the only way to begin defusing that threat is by changing the context in which these young men grow up—namely all the Arab-Muslim states that are failing at modernity and have become an engine for producing undeterrables.
>
> So I am for invading Iraq only if we think that doing so can bring about regime change and democratization. Because what the Arab world desperately needs is a model that works—a progressive Arab regime that by its sheer existence would create pressure and inspiration for gradual democratization and modernization around the region. (*New York Times*, September 18, 2002, p. A31)

For Friedman, then, the debate about invading Iraq was best resolved through the careful hermeneutic reconstruction of "angry young Muslims," in a sort of cultural reframing that Friedman himself was best able to provide and had been providing in repeated columns written over the previous twelve months.

The competing theory of "Middle East democratization" was developed most frequently in the columns of William Safire. For Safire, the War on Terror was presented as an epic struggle of good against evil, where the eventual victory of freedom over extremism was foreordained. In this narrative, the main threat to the successful transformation of the Middle East was the danger of "appeasement" by U.S. political leaders. Equally dangerous was the possibility that U.S. leaders would fail to recognize the deep interconnections between the different conflicts and challenges that confronted them in the War on Terror.

This combination of moral certainty and policy advice characterized Safire's commentary about the War on Terror throughout the period we studied. His columns identified the Israeli-Palestinian conflict as the central front in the War on Terror, and consistently sided with the Israelis, all the while sharing with readers Safire's private conversations with Israel's Prime Minister Ariel Sharon. Connected to these arguments were other columns that counseled against any diplomatic engagement with terrorists, arguing that the time had come for the United States to stand firmly on the side of freedom and against tyranny. We can see these suggestions in columns written about Iran, about Israel, and about the Palestinians:

> In Iran as in Iraq, Saudi Arabia and Syria, local tyranny and global terror go hand in hand. That's why we should resist strange antiterrorist bedfellowship with Iran's tough-cop-nice-cop rulers. Iran is becoming ripe for democratic revolution. We should not ally ourselves with the cruel clerics whom secular Persian patriots will one day throw out. (*New York Times*, November 29, 2001, p. A35)

> No nation or international group can be an honest broker between a democracy under attack and a terrorist coalition on the march. The time for such misguided U.S. "evenhandedness" is long past. The time for Palestinians to decide their own fate is now—antiterrorism and a peaceful state of their own, or terrorism and defeat. (*New York Times*, December 3, 2001, p. A19)

> No appeasement of Palestinian terrorists will persuade Arab rulers to help defeat Saddam; they want his defeat but cravenly want no part of defeating him. The Iraqi tyrant openly subsidizes Palestinian suicide bombing while he secretly aids Al Qaeda, which is why Palestinians danced in the streets of Ramallah on Sept. 11. (*New York Times*, March 25, 2002, p. A21)

On the one hand, Safire's columns can easily be read in a similar way to many of the aggressive early columns in *USA Today*, as arguments for punishment and retribution against Middle East terrorists and their enablers. This type of argument was also made forcefully and repeatedly on television (particularly on the cable programs), as we will see later in the chapter. But Safire's narrative is also a narrative of the inevitable civic transformation of the Middle East, which distinguishes it from the more vengeful *USA Today* narratives, bringing it more closely into line with the overarching message that the reader could find in the op-ed page of the *New York Times*.

For Safire, all of his arguments about the War on Terror are held together by two propositions: (1) that every aspect of the War on Terror is ultimately reducible to the Arab-Israeli conflict and (2) that freedom will eventually win out over tyranny, unless the United States interferes with this inevitable process by failing to take a hard line against the antidemocratic forces in that region. Thus, Iran's people are "ripe for democratic revolution," except that the United States sends out confusing signals by maintaining cordial diplomatic relationships with Iranian leaders. Palestinian extremists are emboldened by a U.S. position that tries to encourage Israeli leaders to negotiate with "terrorist appeasers." Saudi Arabia is beset by dissension and popular resentment against the royal family and would stand a good chance of democratic transformation if only Western leaders would stop pretending that the Saudi royal family was a trustworthy ally (*New York Times*, September 12, 2002, p. A27). Taken together, Safire's columns told a story in which a hard-line U.S. position would hasten the inevitable transformation of the Middle East toward freedom, openness, and civil society. Not surprisingly, then, Safire's position on the potential Iraq invasion was equally unambiguous and closely connected to the larger narrative of Middle East transformation.

But while Friedman and Safire were generally supportive of the Iraq invasion—Friedman guardedly and Safire without reservation—the extended debate about the potential invasion was not really the dominant preoccupation among the columnists and guest columnists writing for the *New York Times*. Instead, as we have suggested, the dominant theme was the question of civic modernization. This reframing was also evident in the guest columns, written largely by academics and think tank intellectuals. For these media outsiders writing about the War on Terror, reframing tended to emphasize the difficulties associated with the military strategy and the corresponding need to link any military efforts to a serious diplomatic engagement with civil society in the Islamic world.

We can see this emphasis on diplomacy and civil society in an early column written by Michael Walzer, professor of social science at the Institute for Advanced Study at Princeton. Walzer distinguished between "real war" and "metaphorical war," arguing that the metaphorical war was more important in the struggle against terrorism. The metaphorical war consisted of three related strategies: "intensive police work across national borders, an ideological campaign to engage all the arguments and excuses for terrorism and reject them, and a serious and sustained diplomatic effort" (*New York Times*, September 21, 2001, p. A35). Writing about Saudi Arabia, University of Maryland professor and Brookings Institution fellow Sibley Telhami suggested that the United States needed to consider reducing its military presence in Saudi Arabia because the large military presence there could be easily used to inflame anti-American sentiment and to destabilize Saudi Arabian civil society (*New York Times*, January 29, 2002, p. A21). Political scientist Alan Wolfe, who defined the War on Terror as a struggle between "two different ways of believing," offered a historical lesson about how the United States had managed to progress from a Puritan sense of "Protestant triumphalism" to a more modern configuration that managed to combine individualism, faith, religious diversity, and a largely secular civil society based on tolerance (*New York Times*, October 14, 2001, Section 4, p. 13). The message of all of these columns, while implicit, was clear. What was necessary was to allow the full development of a differentiated civil society in the Islamic world.

For the most part, the guest columnists were closer to Friedman's narrative of civic transformation than to Safire's, in the sense that they emphasized the contingency of the outcome and the need to engage Islamic civil society in a serious and sustained way. What they added was a comparative-historical sensibility. Thus, in the midst of the Afghanistan invasion, Nazif Shahrani—professor of anthropology and Central Asian and Middle Eastern studies at Indiana University—offered a history of Afghanistan, suggesting that part of the problem could be traced to British desires in the nineteenth century to create centralized Pashtun rule in the region.[12] For Shahrani, the only way to create a stable and nontotalitarian Afghanistan was to encourage a decentralized form of self-governance, with autonomy at the village and provincial levels. Michael McFaul, a political scientist at Stanford University and a fellow at the Hoover Institute, also drew on comparative-historical evidence to imagine the process of Middle Eastern democratization. McFaul's column was about the lessons that could be learned from the post-Communist transitions in Eastern and Central Europe after 1989. Noting that fewer than half of the post-Communist states had become liberal democracies and that many of them "teeter between democracy and dictatorship" (*New York Times*, November 24, 2002, section 4, p. 13), McFaul pointed to the factors that seemed to predict success in the transition to democracy: large infusions of money from the United States and international finance organizations, a quick resolution of any territorial disputes, and the inclusion of the new nations in U.S.-led international military alliances.

The message of these guest columns was clear: success in the War on Terror would require the active participation and diplomatic engagement of the United States, so that the resources devoted to democratization would match the rhetoric of "promoting freedom and liberty."[13] In the absence of this kind of engagement, suspicion and resentment of American motivations would rule the day in the Middle East. Fawaz Gerges, a professor of international affairs at Sarah Lawrence College, captured this overriding argument clearly in a column that recounted his experiences at a recent academic conference in Beirut. At the conference, Gerges wrote, he had encountered deep suspicion about American aims in the Middle East, the proliferation of conspiracy theories to explain what had happened on September 11, and a deep ambivalence about participating in the American-led War on Terror. The only way to overcome this situation, Gerges argued, was to engage in a sustained cultural, political, and economic dialogue with Islamic civil society:

American diplomats, even on the eve of war, have remained distracted and distant from the Muslim public. American embassies in the Middle East have long been impenetrable castles separated from the local communities. American ambassadors hardly venture out to participate and interact with the intellectual and cultural life in those countries.... The United States needs to invest directly in Middle Eastern civil societies to improve governance, education, health and quality of life. The challenge in gaining greater understanding in those societies will not be easy, but American diplomats can help by overcoming their own bunker mentality. The use of force against the Taliban and Osama bin Laden was unavoidable given the terrorist threat. But the long-term aim of reducing anti-American fervor among Islamic extremists will still best be achieved by directly engaging with the Muslim people. The military response that began yesterday only makes the hard nonmilitary work, in the next weeks and years, more necessary than ever. (*New York Times*, October 8, 2001, p. A17)

What was distinctive about this and other *New York Times* columns (with the exception of Safire's columns) was the way they took seriously the attitudes and beliefs of different populations in the Middle East, in the way they sought to explore the possible reasons for anti-American attitudes, and in the way they refused to stereotype or hypostatize Islamic populations as uniformly fanatical and irrational.

To be sure, there were significant limitations in the overall narrative environment at the *New York Times*. These become apparent when considered through our cultural model of mediated deliberation. Because Safire and Friedman were the two dominant voices, and because the main question was the potential civic modernization of the Middle East, the resulting debate was quite narrow. Moreover, to the extent that columnists and guest columnists engaged in historical and cultural analyses of different attitudes and beliefs in the region, they tended to do so within an Orientalist framework that viewed Muslim populations and Islamic beliefs as problems that Western policy makers needed to overcome.[14] Nevertheless, when compared with the columns in *USA Today*, the debate in the *New York Times* was less narrowly focused on domestic political considerations. This difference is even more marked when we turn to television, where debates were even more narrowly confined to the domestic politics of the War on Terror.

The Debate on Sunday Morning Television

If the goal is to find a variety of television voices speaking about the War on Terror, the Sunday morning programs are not a good place to look. Of the 122 speaker-segments from *Face the Nation* in our sample, all but four are authored by speakers from the political or journalistic fields. In fact, 107 of the speaker-segments are taken up by talk show hosts, elected politicians, and cabinet members. The remainder is accounted for by *New York Times* columnist Thomas Friedman, who appeared on five separate episodes of *Face the Nation*, as well as celebrity journalists Bob Woodward and David Halberstam. Academic representatives are also of the celebrity variety: the ubiquitous law professor David Cole and the Pulitzer Prize–winning historian Gary Wills.

In addition to the lineup of elite political insiders and academic and media celebrities, most episodes dealing with the War on Terror on *Face the Nation* exhibited a similar structure. The first guest was usually a cabinet member representing the position of the government. This was usually a representative from the Bush administration, but it was not uncommon for this opening segment to feature representatives from the Israeli or Palestinian governments. These guests usually presented their commentaries dispassionately, using the opinion style we describe as "providing information." When the guests were representatives of Middle Eastern states, it was also common to see commentaries presented in the form of moral critique. Following this segment, there would then be interviews with elected U.S. politicians, usually from the Senate but occasionally from the House of Representatives. This segment included members of both major political parties. Sometimes they appeared on the show together; at other times they appeared serially. The general focus of these elected politicians was to support or criticize specific foreign policy proposals. Finally, if there was time left in the program, there would be a final roundtable segment with journalists, columnists, former cabinet members, and the very occasional academic or expert analyst. This tended to be a wider ranging discussion, covering a greater variety of topics and employing a greater diversity of argument styles. In other words, each segment moved progressively further away from the political field, though the total distance traveled was rarely very far. A key issue for the discussions on *Face the Nation*, then, concerns the extent to which the program's hosts and non-political guests managed to achieve some critical autonomy from the official narratives of state representatives.

With such a heavy representation by politicians, it is not surprising to find different kinds of commentaries on *Face the Nation* than we saw in the newspapers. Rather than cultural engagement with the Muslim world, modernization projects in the Middle East, or concerns about civil liberties, the debate on *Face the Nation* focused centrally on official government policies and strategies in the War on Terror, and it typically focused on some actual or potential theater of operations. During the time period of our analysis, these discussions began with a consideration of Afghanistan, turned to the Israeli-Palestinian conflict and its role in the War on Terror, and then considered the question of the Iraq invasion during the second half of 2002.

Consider, for example, a September 2001 interview between *Face the Nation* host Bob Schieffer and Defense Secretary Donald Rumsfeld, shortly before the invasion of Afghanistan. It is worth exploring this particular conversation in some detail, as it is emblematic of the other discussions that took place, as well as of the general structure that subsequent programs about the War on Terror took on *Face the Nation*.

SCHIEFFER: The Taliban now says that Osama bin Laden—they're—they're seeking him to see if they can issue the request to tell him to leave. But they also say they don't know where he is. Should we take them at their word?

SEC. RUMSFELD: Of course not. They know where he is.

SCHIEFFER: And what should we do, or what should—what are we saying to them?

SEC. RUMSFELD: Well, I think we have to think about Afghanistan in a—in a different context. First of all, there are many Afghan people who are repressed, who are starving, who are fleeing from the Taliban. There are any number of factions within the Taliban that don't agree with Omar, the man who contends that now they can't find the person they've been harboring for years. There are many in the Taliban who prefer that the Taliban not harbor Osama bin Laden and the al-Qaida network. So it is not as though there is a front, and that there are good guys and bad guys. There are many tribes. There is the northern alliance, there are tribes in the south. And it is a very different kind of a conflict and a problem. What we have to do is to see that those who have been harboring terrorists stop harboring terrorists.

The interview begins with the host of the program asking Rumsfeld to comment on an official statement of the Taliban. As an opening question, this gives Rumsfeld an opportunity to reject the Taliban's claim, after which he proceeds to make the case that the Taliban does not represent a good portion of the Afghan population. In this way, the interview offers a platform for the Bush administration to describe its policy objectives. It is, in effect, asking for an official statement of policy. Fair enough to start. But no evaluation or critical deliberation ensues. In effect, then, the interview is a platform for the Bush administration to describe its policy objectives. The interviewer provides the space for a series of official proclamations—more "representative publicity" than rational-critical deliberation. Indeed, if there is any question that Rumsfeld is being asked only for a statement of policy, the next two questions that Schieffer asks remove any doubt. Scheiffer asks:

> SCHIEFFER: When you said that, "They know where he is," you sound very certain of that. And how can you be so certain?
>
> SEC. RUMSFELD: They know their country. They have been fighting against the Russians there, the Soviets there, for years. They have been fighting among themselves and the tribes. They—they have—they're hearty, tough people. They have networks throughout the country. And it is just not believable that the Taliban do not know where the network can be located and found and either turned over or expelled.

This second question does not really challenge Rumsfeld's initial statement as much as it asks for additional supporting information. In his response, Rumsfeld fails to offer any real evidence to support his argument, other than a superficial historical reference and a general statement about Afghan character. And yet, Schieffer decides not to press the question any further. Instead, he follows up with a third general question about military strategy, asking:

> SCHIEFFER: You have been understandably reluctant to discuss any kind of troop movements. Certainly, that's understandable. Let me just ask you the general question: Is the United States now in a position to strike?
>
> SEC. RUMSFELD: What we have been doing since the day of the attack is getting our forces positioned in various places around the world. This is not an Afghan problem; this is a worldwide problem of—of terrorist networks. And let there be no doubt about it, the—the al Qaida network is in at least 60 countries, and they are just one of many networks. And what we've been doing is getting our

capabilities for—located, positioned, arranged around the world so that at that point where the president decides that—that he has a set of things he would like done, that we will be in a position to carry those things out. And second, the United States government, e—even more importantly, has been getting itself arranged across the government. The Department of Treasury and—and the State Department and the Central Intelligence Agency, as well as the defense establishment, to help the world understand that it is a broad-based effort, not—not a military effort alone, but a—but it's going to have to go after political and diplomatic and—and economic interests, financial interests. (*Face the Nation*, September 23, 2001)

This third question, then, gives Rumsfeld a further opportunity to state the official government position, which is that Afghanistan is just the first step in fighting a global war against terrorist networks. Indeed, subsequent questions in the segment allow Rumsfeld to mention Iraq, Syria, North Korea, Libya, and Cuba, all as potential targets in the global War on Terror.

The Rumsfeld interview was followed by a short segment with the Pakistani ambassador to the United States, Maleeha Lodhi, who was given the opportunity to present the Pakistani government's official position as a U.S. ally in the War on Terror, and then the next two segments were discussions with senators, where the general focus was to evaluate the administration's foreign policy. The first of these featured John McCain, a Republican who generally supported the administration. The second featured Bob Graham and John Kerry, Democrats who were more critical of the administration's policies and who worked hard to turn the debate toward economic matters. In contrast to the opening questions posed to Rumsfeld, the questions asked of the senators solicited evaluative responses. Consider the following examples.

SCHIEFFER: We're back now with Senator John McCain, the chairman—or I should say now the ranking Republican on the Senate Commerce Committee, but a very influential person on—in Congress on economics, the airline industry. The first thing I must say to you, Senator McCain, is: When I hear a government official say, "Every option is on the table," and he says, "We've never ruled out the use of nuclear weapons," that's a sobering thought. Your comment? . . .

BORGER: But from a military standpoint, does it worry you that we could get bogged down in Afghanistan in—in the same way, say, that we—that we did in Vietnam? . . .

SCHIEFFER: Senator Graham, let me just begin with you. There are—there have now been report after report that the FBI, the CIA knew that there were followers of Osama bin Laden trying to get into flight schools, trying to take flight training, where they said, "We don't need to know how to take off and land an airplane. We just need to know how to steer one." These—these reports keep going around. H—what happened here? Why—why was not some action taken on this? (*Face the Nation*, September 23, 2001)

So here each question prompts the guest for criticism and evaluation, rather than simply providing a forum for representing the official state position, as Rumsfeld had done in the earlier segment. In general, McCain focused on supporting President Bush's foreign policy choices, praising the capabilities of the U.S. military, and downplaying the risks of invasion. Kerry took a different approach. Rather than focus on military strategy, Kerry shifted the focus to two other areas where he was more comfortable criticizing the policies of the Bush administration: specifically, the organization of intelligence gathering and the commitment to economic policies that help the unemployed. In both areas, Kerry suggested that the origins of the present crisis were to be found well before September 11, thus refuting the administration's claims that 9/11 was a fundamental historical disjuncture.

For the final segment of this particular episode of *Face the Nation*, attention turned to the analysts and the experts. This was by far the most wide-ranging, analytical, and prognostic portion of the program. There were three guests: the foreign affairs expert was Thomas Friedman, the *New York Times* columnist; the military expert was William Cohen, the former defense secretary; and the economic expert was Abby Joseph Cohen, a financial analyst at the Wall Street investment firm Goldman Sachs. Each guest provided commentaries that relied on their own specific forms of expertise, reinforced by frequent references to personal and professional experience. Friedman recounted an interview he had done with an Egyptian television station, reporting how he had to explain to them why Americans were so upset about the World Trade Center attacks and why he thought that politicians in the Middle East were underestimating how serious the U.S. response was likely to be. William Cohen provided a lesson in how to decipher U.S. military statements, actions, and silences and why he was convinced that some elements of the Pakistani military were providing information to bin Laden. Abby Joseph Cohen described how Wall Street bankers and analysts had already accepted the economic losses that would occur for 2001 and how they were focused on fiscal policy for 2002.

Comparing these three different types of segments, we can see that the levels of critical discourse and autonomy from the state have more to do with the ensemble of guests than with the host's or the format's commitment to journalistic objectivity. For instance, when interviewing a representative of the administration, the host limits his questions to requests for information and largely avoids any evaluation or critique. This is "objective journalism," to be sure, but it is almost completely dominated by the frames and narratives of state representatives. When interviewing elected politicians, the host tends to ask more evaluative questions, prompting the guests to offer judgments of state policies and their own analyses of the situation. Here there is more critical and analytical dialogue, but because of the ensemble of guests, the analysis maps pretty closely onto political party divisions and the emerging Washington consensus to go to war—note that there is never a suggestion that going to war is *not* an option—and speech is largely addressed to an imagined audience of political insiders and elite decision makers. Finally, when convening a roundtable discussion with experts and analysts, the host allows the guests to develop a collective interpretation of the situation, which is wider ranging, tied less closely to existing political divisions, and addressed to an imaginary audience of citizen-viewers who desire a more complex and multidimensional analysis of the day's events. But even here, the types of voices that are heard and the narratives that are developed are much more restricted than what we see in newspaper op-eds and, as we shall see, more restricted than the discussion that took place on public television or the cable talk programs. In other words, while the discussions that took place on *Face the Nation* provided lots of information, they were organized within extremely restrictive formats, the limitations of which become quite obvious when viewed from the perspective of a cultural model of mediated deliberation.

As the focus on the War on Terror continued on *Face the Nation*, it turned gradually away from the military operations in Afghanistan and toward the conflict between Israelis and Palestinians. Of all the discussions about the War on Terror, these were the narrowest in terms of the diversity of voices, as well as the rhetoric of the commentaries. There were two different parts to most of these programs. The first part consisted of separate interviews with representatives of the Israeli and Palestinian governments, each of whom provided information about their official policy on the conflict and offered moral condemnation of their opponent. The second part of these discussions included U.S. politicians, either senators or cabinet members. The U.S. politicians all emphasized the need for increased U.S. involvement in the peace process throughout the entire region and reinforced the Israeli contention that the peace process would move forward more effectively if Arafat were no longer the Palestinian leader.

The third area of extended discussion on *Face the Nation* concerned the debate about invading Iraq, which increasingly came to occupy the program throughout the second half of 2002. Like the other topics of discussion, the debate about Iraq was dominated by politicians, with some additional analytical work provided by columnists and journalists. The main difference was the reduced role for members of the cabinet and the larger representation of senators and members of Congress in the policy debate. The lack of executive voices in the discussion allowed more critical discourse, even if it remained largely within the confines of existing political divisions.

Among the politicians, there were two competing narratives about Iraq. The first, articulated by people like Senator John McCain, was in favor of doing whatever it took to remove Saddam Hussein from power. The second narrative, more common among Democratic senators, was also concerned about the threat from Iraq and generally favored an eventual military invasion. In this second narrative, though, there was serious concern expressed about the consequences of such an invasion, particularly if the United States acted unilaterally and failed to build a broad-based international coalition before the invasion.

While different in content, these two arguments shared important similarities in their underlying narrative structure. Both presented the situation as a conflict between the United States and Iraq. Both presented the "international community" as the central obstacle that the United States would have to face to achieve its objectives. Both proposed specific policy positions. And both relied on two primary sources of authority to support their proposed positions: (1) the conversations they had had with other politicians and (2) the policy proposals that other politicians had made. These features can be seen in the following interview excerpt:

> SEN. BIDEN: The president's looked me in the eye and said, "There is no plan on my desk. There's been no decision made." And—but I agree with John. There's obviously plans on other people's desk. What—what, not concerns me, but what I think has to be focused on is: Is there one plan? I know of several plans having spoken with several elements of the administration, each having their own point of view. I don't know which one the president has adopted or I don—my guess—what I'm saying is I don't think the president's decided on which plan yet. But, look, once Saddam is down, I don't know a single solitary informed person in the country or abroad who does not understand that there's a need to know what's going to follow Saddam so that we don't end up with a circumstance that is not worse but is chaotic. And I think this could be a win-win situation with the Russians. Lugar and I spoke to Putin about this. I mean, look, there—there—there are ways to generate consensus. And I think the first step is go for a hard regime of inspections. We know they're not going to go for that. At least make the case to the public at large, the world at large, that this is not just fiat on our part, and then we begin to build a case to have a consensus, not that anybody else is going to help us, but that we have the support, in effect, of the rest of the world to do what we have to do . . . so we don't have to worry again about all that debate about the street—the Arab street and all the rest. There's ways to do this. And I think we should. (Senator Biden, *Face the Nation*, June 16, 2002)

In this interview, which was relatively early in the debate about Iraq, Senator Biden begins his statement by agreeing with a statement made earlier on the same program by Senator John McCain. Next, Biden reframes the debate around the question of what is going to happen after the inevitable overthrow of the Iraqi government, citing knowledge of "every informed person in the country or abroad," as well as specific conversations he has had with Senator Lugar and Russia's leader, Vladimir Putin. Finally, he makes a number of specific policy proposals, focusing on the need to begin with inspections, to provide the moral foundations for building an international coalition.

Five months later, discussing the congressional vote authorizing the use of military force in Iraq, Senator Lieberman made the following argument on *Face the Nation*:

SEN. LIEBERMAN: I'm very glad that the president went to the United Nations. I
    think it's critically important that we not be in a position where we have to take
    military action against Iraq alone. It's clear to me now that we will not have to.
    I think if—if there is this violation that I expect, although I'd be pleasantly
    surprised if Saddam suddenly has a death-bed—or a UN-bed conversion—but
    we—we would immediately go back to the UN, challenge them to live by the
    words in the resolution because Saddam's failure to comply would have been a
    material breach calling for serious consequences. If the UN doesn't act, we have
    to put together our own international coalition and—and change that regime
    in Baghdad. (*Face the Nation*, November 24, 2002)

In this narrative, the international community is still the major obstacle. Here, though,
Lieberman supports the Bush administration speech before the United Nations, arguing that this has satisfied the moral requirement that the United States try to build
international support for its military objectives. Lieberman places Saddam Hussein
and the United Nations in a position of symbolic equivalence—assuming that both
will fail to act in ways that they have agreed to in prior UN resolutions. Signifying both
as untrustworthy and dishonest, the suggestion is that U.S. action is required to protect
the international moral order. This is an even more restricted and nationalistic narrative than we saw on the newspaper op-ed page, where the international community in
general and the UN in particular were more likely to be represented as honest, good-
faith actors.

Discussions with expert analysts supplemented the arguments being made by political
principals on these episodes of *Face the Nation* and provided some additional complexity.
For example, while these expert analysts shared the politicians' focus on the politics of
the Iraq questions, they were much more willing to explore the domestic political challenges that the Bush administration faced in its buildup to war. These analysts were also
much more likely to construct an intertextual dialogue between print and television
commentaries—not surprising, perhaps, since most of these analysts were print columnists and print journalists. Consider the following exchange between Gloria Borger (one
of the hosts of *Face the Nation*), Robin Wright (from the *Los Angeles Times*), and Richard Berke (of the *New York Times*):

BERKE: And—and, Gloria, I think we're already seeing the beginning of a—of a
    PR offensive from the president himself. We saw him at his ranch the other day,
    coming out and saying, "Wait a—whoa. Let's wait a minute. I'm a very patient
    man." He said patient, patient, patient, again and again, because he wanted to
    drive home the point that we're not going to rush into war. We're—we're think-
    ing about what we're doing, which is a—a—a—quite a contrast to what his
    statements were before about the evil Saddam Hussein and we're going to go
    after him.

BORGER: Well, speaking of frenzy, this administration has also said that it's us in the press, and particularly your own paper, Rick, The—The *New York Times*— that has overplayed the differences within this administration publicly about the question of whether to invade Iraq. What's your take on that?

BERKE: I think—I think we're reflecting the churning that's actually going on inside the administration. I—we're talking about an invasion—and this is— this is no small potatoes here, and I think it's only natural that we're going to— we're going to want to hear all sides. And as I said before, the debate is healthy. When people like Scowcroft come out and prominent Republican allies of the administration come out and say, "Wait a minute here. Let's think about this. Let's—let's talk about that," I think that's significant.

WRIGHT: And I think you've also begun to see people ask that important question: Is Iraq part of the war on terrorism, or is it a—another agenda? Is it a holdover from a war a long time ago? And I think that's what you see many of the top former administration officials, be they Republicans or Democrats, begin to ask. (*Face the Nation*, August 25, 2002)

This discussion is different from the interviews with politicians in the way that it highlights the public relations challenges involved with building a case for war. Earlier in the discussion, the guests had commented on specific op-ed columns written in the *New York Times* and the *Wall Street Journal*, as well as opinion polls describing American attitudes about Iraq. In all cases, the opinions and commentaries were presented as challenges and obstacles facing the Bush administration, which were just as important as developing military strategies or building international coalitions. This attention to the space of opinion itself added a level of understanding that was largely absent from the narratives that political principals were making. At the same time, however, it was still quite narrow because it framed public opinion as an additional problem that the Bush administration would have to manage. We conclude, then, that mediated deliberation on *Face the Nation* was reductive because it presented all aspects of the War on Terror discussion as challenges facing the Bush administration. This is a major limitation of these narratives, since they treat the Bush administration as the only real protagonist in the story. Identifying how these and other limitations were distributed across the space of opinion is a central goal (and, we think, an advantage) of our cultural model of mediated deliberation.

The Debate on the Cable Talk Programs

If the commentaries on the Sunday morning programs were dominated by elected politicians and cabinet-level appointees, it was the hosts who dominated the talk on programs like *Crossfire* and *Hannity & Colmes*. Indeed, one of the distinguishing features of these programs is the way that they can regularly feature elected politicians without letting those politicians dictate the cultural framing of the commentaries. Furthermore, the cable programs exhibited a greater diversity of speakers than the Sunday morning programs, with regular appearances by political consultants, public relations specialists, think tank intellectuals, representatives from advocacy groups, lawyers, and academics. With such a wide variety of guests, what did the debate about the War on Terror look like on cable television?

To begin with, the cable talk programs focused on the War on Terror to a much greater extent than the other media outlets we studied. As a result, there were many different areas of focus and many different narratives that emerged on the programs. The dominant cultural framework was the political narrative, which, like the discussion in the Enron case, was organized as a moral contest pitting Republican Party principles against Democratic ones. This had the effect, we will argue, of dramatically increasing the political polarization of the space of opinion—a polarization that continues today.

While the discussions about the War on Terror on the cable programs displayed striking and often alarming limitations, their deliberative deficiencies were different from those of the op-ed pages of the newspaper or the Sunday morning television talk shows. Furthermore, while the cable programs' overriding narratives of political polarization may have presented significant challenges to those guests who wanted to maintain some distance from the political field, they did not block out other topics, nor did they prevent a variety of different perspectives from emerging about the War on Terror. Before moving to a consideration of the political narrative that dominated these programs, then, we would like to explore some of the other commentaries and topics that they covered. They included the following topics, among others:

- A discussion with Jody Williams, Nobel Peace laureate, about whether land mines were a useful resource for U.S. military forces in Afghanistan (*Hannity & Colmes*, January 15, 2002)
- A discussion with nuclear scientists and investigative journalists about nuclear proliferation in India and Pakistan and the potential consequences that had for the larger War on Terror (*Hannity & Colmes*, December 31, 2001)
- A debate about the diffusion and integration of surveillance cameras throughout Washington, D.C. (*Crossfire*, February 15, 2002)
- A debate between a human rights activist and a neoconservative think tank intellectual about the Geneva Convention and the prisoners being held at Guantánamo Bay (*Crossfire*, January 15, 2002)
- An extended discussion with a New York congressman and a representative of the Arab-American Institute about the Arab-Israeli conflict and its relationship to the War on Terror (*Crossfire*, April 17, 2002)

These are complicated and contradictory discussions, the analyses of which are more difficult than it might at first appear. One the one hand, the discussions on these programs display certain features that are valued by traditional theories of deliberation. For instance, the shows are actual debates between individuals with different perspectives, rather than (as is the case in most of the space of opinion) serial opportunities for individuals to present their positions. In other words, these are communicative spaces where people are forced to defend their arguments against criticisms. In addition, they are discussions that include a variety of speaker types, a diversity of viewpoints, and the presentation of a variety of different types of evidence and authority claims. These would all seem to represent deliberative advantages, particularly when compared with the exceptionally restrictive communicative environment that characterized the Sunday morning talk shows.

On the other hand, these debates and their guests are repeatedly forced into the overriding narrative of political polarization between Republicans and Democrats, which is the defining feature of these cable programs. The hosts of the show insistently press their guests with ideological statements and questions that demand an agree/disagree response and thus continually push the discussion toward more polarized positions. The guests do not always take the bait, nor does this cultural organization of the program always prevent the guests from presenting arguments that escape the binary logic of polarization. But it is a crucial feature of the shows, even when the guests themselves do not play along.

We can see how this contradictory cultural dynamic plays itself out by examining one of the discussions mentioned: the *Hannity & Colmes* segment with Jody Williams, the founding coordinator of the International Campaign to Ban Land mines and the 1997 recipient of the Nobel Peace Prize. The discussion began with five questions from cohost Alan Colmes, which provided Williams with the opportunity to present basic information about the mission of her organization and to define the problem in her own words. Alan Colmes asks:

COLMES: Jody, I have a very basic question. What is a land mine? . . .

COLMES: And there are nine million of them in Afghanistan, as I understand. . . .

COLMES: Now, the U.S. Defense Department has recommended that our country abandon all efforts to join the mine ban treaty, the 1996 treaty that was forged in Oslo. Why is that? . . .

COLMES: So, what happens is, after a war ends, civilians, innocent women, children, men, they are walking, living their lives as civilians, and they unknowingly step into a mine and lives are lost. Do know how many lives are lost in this way? . . .

COLMES: Now, there is mine-detection technology, is there not?

WILLIAMS: There is, but, unfortunately, for the most part, the mine-detection technology is from World War II. The technology to detect the mines and take them out of the ground has not kept up with the technology to create new and more harmful weapons. (*Hannity & Colmes*, January 15, 2002)

These questions, then, were not terribly different from the "providing information" requests that dominated the question-asking style on *Face the Nation*. But about halfway through this segment, the questioning is taken up much more aggressively by cohost Sean Hannity:

HANNITY: Hey, Jody, listen, I've read a lot about you. And I really believe your heart is in the right place. I really do.

The first question I have for you is, do you believe groups like al Qaeda and the Taliban, groups that have as their goal, their stated goal, to kill innocent men, women, and children that they disagree with, do you think they would abide by any such agreement?

WILLIAMS: I don't think that is the reason why laws are formed. Nobody believes that anybody should commit homicide, for example, and yet there are laws to stop people from killing each other.

HANNITY: So, they wouldn't honor any ban on land mines, would they?

WILLIAMS: I'm not sure that that's the case. I think, if you take all of the mines away from the fighting people of the world, you destroy the stockpiles, you make it anathema, you make it harder and harder.

HANNITY: You believe that the al Qaeda network wouldn't use mines against armed Marines? Do you really believe that? Because there's a so-called international ban? That's pretty naive, Jody. Come on.

WILLIAMS: I believe that they might, but that isn't the point here.

HANNITY: It is the point.

WILLIAMS: The point is that the international community believes that we can make the world a better place if we ban this weapon, if we destroy the stockpiles, if we destroy production. That doesn't mean that individuals cannot create a land mine, just as the individual took the plane . . .

HANNITY: No, that's not the point.

WILLIAMS: Yes, it is.

HANNITY: The point, in my view, is, as with gun control, the problem of banning mines is that the good guys will comply with the ban and the bad guys will never comply with the ban.

So you have a situation where, in war, where a lot is at stake—and war is a very ugly thing, but sometimes it's a necessary evil—where our men are put at an advantage. And I'll give you a scenario. If we have U.S. Marines that are under fire and they need to retreat to a safe haven and they need to slow down the opposition, land mines are an effective tool to stop troops from advancing that would ultimately kill U.S. soldiers in a war situation. That's the good use of a mine, in my view, as horrible as that sounds.

WILLIAMS: None of us in the campaign have ever said that mines don't have some utility. The point is that the long-term consequences to civilians and our own soldiers far outweighs the immediate benefit of that weapon. (*Hannity & Colmes*, January 15, 2002)

From the perspective of any theory of political communication that we choose to apply, there are obvious problems with this exchange. Hannity's line of questioning applies the same logic he has used before in his opposition to gun control, which is that criminals and other "bad guys" will ignore the ban and that to think otherwise is "naïve." The criticism is not really directed at Williams herself but rather is connected to a larger critique of "liberals," a label used as a pejorative signifier for the Democratic Party. Williams repeatedly tries to reframe the discussion, suggesting that Hannity is missing the real point, which is that a ban would ultimately reduce the availability of land mines. Rather than debating the relative merits of these two competing interpretations, however, Hannity relies on a variety of nondeliberative tactics, which are increasingly inflammatory. Indeed, Hannity's next three questions to Williams invoke what Jeffrey Alexander has called the "sacred evil" of the Holocaust and effectively closes down the possibility of dialogue about land mines.[15]

> HANNITY: Well, maybe we should just ban war. Why don't we just ban war, then, Jody? Why don't we say all war ends tomorrow? Didn't they try and do that in 1928? . . .
>
> HANNITY: Well, in 1928 they banned war. Ten short years later, Hitler annexed Austria. And the rest is history. . . .
>
> HANNITY: Well, how do we overcome Adolf Hitler if we don't fight back harder than him and defeat his army by whatever means necessary? (*Hannity & Colmes*, January 15, 2002)

The point here is that despite the obvious deliberative challenges associated with forcing every discussion into the political polarization narrative, it remains the case that a skilled and patient guest of these programs has an opportunity to present her interpretation of a public issue. Despite the attempts by cohost Sean Hannity to force the debate about land mines into the same polarization narrative that he frequently used to talk about the gun control debate, Jody Williams still managed to provide a short history of land mines, an argument about their long-term effects on civilian populations, and a suggestion about how to minimize their destructive impact in the future. Similarly, on an episode of *Crossfire*, human rights activist Bianca Jagger and defense policy expert Ken Adelman managed to have an extended and nuanced discussion of the Geneva Convention and the treatment of prisoners of war, despite repeated attempts by the show's cohosts to reframe the debate as a referendum on the Bush administration's antiterrorism strategy (*Crossfire*, January 15, 2002).

But while it is possible for skilled guests to maintain some measure of control over their cultural performances, it nonetheless remains the case that the bulk of cable talk show opinion about the War on Terror was connected to the larger narrative of political polarization. This was particularly the case when the guests on the program were elected politicians, cabinet members, and others located primarily within the political field. As we will see, these discussions were dramatically different from the kinds of discussions that took place on the Sunday morning talk shows, illustrating how it is the interaction between the opinion format and the ensemble of characters that shapes much of the discourse that emerges from the television opinion space.

In the immediate aftermath of September 11, the discussions between politicians and cohosts largely avoided the political polarization narrative, focusing more on the binary moral distinction between American purity and Islamic pollution. We can see this in a September 20 episode of *Hannity & Colmes*, which was unusual in its size and composition, which included four members of Congress, two members of the Senate, and two former congressmen. The dominant theme of the discussion was shared by Republicans and Democrats alike, who, without exception, praised President Bush's leadership and extolled the strength and unity of the American people. In such a unity narrative, there was no room for political polarization. The following exchange is typical of this episode:

> ALAN COLMES, CO-HOST: Congressman, it's Alan. Welcome to the show. You and I have had our political disagreements.
> DELAY: True.
> COLMES: I look forward to the day we will have them again, but tonight, America stands united.
> DELAY: That's right. (*Hannity & Colmes*, September 20, 2001)

The message was clear. Future episodes would return to their dominant format, which pitted Republicans and Democrats in a battle for moral purity. For the time being, though, in the midst of the national trauma, the only reasonable responses were unity and patriotism. Even the "mainstream media," a frequent target of Hannity and many of his guests, was given a temporary reprieve from standard accusations of mundane perfidy. Witness the following commentary by Newt Gingrich, the former speaker of the House of Representatives and a frequent guest of the show:

> GINGRICH: Sean—Sean, the most amazing thing to me of this whole experience has been reporters not just on Fox, where you might expect it, but on a number of networks saying they don't want to know until it's over. They want to protect our troops, and they want to make sure they get the job done. I thought that was a sign that we may be more united than at any time since Pearl Harbor. I don't remember any time in the last 60 years that we were as united as we are right now. (*Hannity & Colmes*, September 20, 2001)

As the events of September 11 began to recede from direct experience, however, the cable programs returned to their usual narrative of moral division and political polarization.

As we have seen before, the performative display of these divisions works best when the guests on the show are people who come from the political field. For the most part, these kinds of political guests are more receptive to the cues that force discussion into the polarizing party-based framework. In addition, the hosts of the show rely more directly on the party-based distinctions when their guests are politicians, as the following two examples illustrate:

> PRESS: Congressman Hayworth, today "The Washington Post" announces that the—we have moved the Army, replacing the Marines into Kandahar at the base, and that they're going to be there for a long occupation of Afghanistan. Of course during the campaign last year, George Bush said we should not have occupied troops in Kosovo and Bosnia. He's going to bring them home. He also said we should have nothing to do with nation-building. Doesn't today's announcement mean that, in fact, Clinton was right all along? Bush was wrong all along? And Bush is now doing exactly what Bill Clinton did in Bosnia and Kosovo? (*Crossfire*, December 31, 2001)

> HANNITY: Congressman Greg Meeks, look, I know you Clinton sycophants, and I call them Clinton Kool-Aid drinkers, the man has done nothing wrong. But you got to admit, he adopted a policy of appeasement [in North Korea]. He believed them. He didn't insist on inspections, just like he didn't insist on inspections in Iraq. (*Hannity & Colmes*, October 17, 2002)

Both of these "questions" from the shows' hosts directly contrast political party policies to elicit a response that is linked to political party position.

While we found clear similarities in the basic structure of the political polarization narrative that characterized the cable talk programs, there were also some important differences between them. On *Crossfire*, arguments remained closely tied to the binary political narrative that had animated the show through its history; that is, issues were read as a comparative referendum on the Clinton and Bush administrations. In this referendum frame, almost every statement was like a partisan intervention in an ongoing political campaign. On *Hannity & Colmes*, by contrast, the debate was organized in a way that emphasized the need to invade Iraq; this was justified by two supporting narratives: (1) that all strategic calculations were different after September 11 and (2) that the Clinton administration's failed actions in Iraq were partly responsible for the current situation. As we will see later, these differences had the ultimate effect of making *Crossfire* look less authentic than *Hannity & Colmes*.

We can see this emerging difference between the two shows most clearly in the debate about whether to invade Iraq. The following exchange is a good example of the kind of debate that took place on *Crossfire*. Paul Begala is one of the cohosts of the program, while Congresswoman Susan Molinari and Democratic Party strategist Vic Kamber are the guests.

MOLINARI: Well now, listen, I mean are you trying to suggest that there is no rationale for this war? That the Democrat . . .

BEGALA: There is. There's an election in 41 days.

MOLINARI: And the Democratic party and the Democrat leaders are just following?

BEGALA: Yes.

MOLINARI: Or is it the fact that we now know that there is a man who, if the Clinton administration was doing their job, we would have nuclear arms inspectors in there so we would know just how much he has been able to develop . . .

BEGALA: And so Bush didn't do his job for two years until we had an election.

(CROSSTALK)

KAMBER: We're going to blame Clinton.

MOLINARI: Arms inspectors were denied access to Iraq during the Clinton administration. I mean that is a fact.

BEGALA: And in retribution for that he launched air strikes. And what did you say when he did it?

MOLINARI: Are you actually making the accusation that the president of the United States, with the majority of Democrat leaders in this country, are willing to commit young men and women to war as a political issue?

KAMBER: I'm saying to you—I'm willing to say on television and to you this president is willing to play politics with America to elect people he cares about.

MOLINARI: That's an outrageous charge. (*Crossfire*, November 27, 2002)

In this exchange, the debate about invading Iraq is treated as part of an ongoing *Crossfire* script in which Democratic and Republican Party operatives treat each other with suspicion and contempt. While two competing perspectives are presented, the character demands of these performances have the effect of encouraging hyperbole over evidence. Indeed, information, evidence, and other authority claims are brought in only when they play into the script.

By comparison with *Crossfire*, the debate about Iraq that took place on *Hannity & Colmes* was more one-sided, but it also exhibited greater narrative complexity, and it managed to achieve a greater sense of authenticity. To be sure, the partisan alignment of moral purity and pollution was still an important part of the discussion, and it was still connected to the comparative referendum on the Bush and Clinton administrations. But there were two additional elements to the *Hannity & Colmes* episodes, which complicated the presentation of arguments about Iraq. The first of these was the binary distinction between a pre- and post-9/11 world, which suggested the need for a fundamental rethinking of prior actions and positions. Consider the following exchange between cohost Alan Colmes and former Congressman Joe Scarborough:

COLMES: Let me go back to Congressman Scarborough for a second here.

Look, President Bush number 41 did not go and take out Saddam Hussein because he knew that would destroy the coalition he brilliantly built up. That coalition is still important to us, will continue to be important to us down the road, but could be permanently destroyed by an attempt to go after Saddam Hussein now, don't you think? If it wouldn't have worked then, why would it work now?

SCARBOROUGH: Well, the—you know, the reason why it wouldn't have worked then is because President Bush number 41 built that remarkable coalition based on the promise we'll liberate Kuwait, then we'll get out. He kept his word.

Bush 43, though—he faces a completely different world, and the bottom line is we can continue to have a government that tries to take away civil liberties from all Americans, but bottom line is this: We will not stop terrorism, we will not stop a dirty bomb from being dropped somewhere across the United States, unless we cut terrorism off at the source.... (*Hannity & Colmes*, May 29, 2002)

In this exchange, the 1991 decision not to invade Iraq is initially presented as a smart decision that can offer a lesson for how to act in 2001. It is rejected as a legitimate comparison, however, because it had taken place before September 11 "in a completely different world." This distinction was used regularly on *Hannity & Colmes* as a strategy for rejecting the validity of a historical argument.[16]

There was one historical argument, however, that was elaborated repeatedly and in great detail on *Hannity & Colmes* over the same period, namely, that the Clinton administration bore a large responsibility for the situation in Iraq, indeed, that Clinton's failures provided a justification for invasion. Consider the following exchange between cohost Sean Hannity and Alexander Haig, secretary of state during the Reagan administration:

HANNITY: Let me move on. Bill Clinton allowed Saddam Hussein to defy these resolutions for the entire eight years he was in office. What's the point of having them?

HAIG: Yeah. Well, I'm glad you said it that way because a lot of people blame a lot on the United Nations, and they are limited in what they're capable of doing. But, when we don't lead in that world body, don't expect anyone else to do it.

HANNITY: That's a great point.

HAIG: The failure is right...

HANNITY: Great point.

HAIG: ... here in Washington. (*Hannity & Colmes*, September 12, 2002)

This argument was reinforced with another criticism that Hannity made repeatedly about the Clinton administration's diplomatic strategy in North Korea. The following exchange with former Congressman John Kasich is typical:

KASICH: I think North Korea is the perfect example why we cannot trust corrupt regimes. I mean just think that in the 1990's, we traded some very valuable assets that we gave to the North Koreans in exchange for them not developing a nuclear program. How naive that we were able to trust a regime that had been run by some madman in North Korea?

COLMES: Should we threaten more . . .

KASICH: Now compare that to Iraq, now when you look at Iraq, the last thing we want to do is to have trusted Saddam Hussein over 11 years and trust him longer, so he can acquire a nuclear weapon. Listen, we have dug ourselves in a hole in North Korea. And I'll tell you, they're working all night long and they're going to be working, you know, until we can figure out a way to disarm North Korea of those nuclear weapons. . . .

HANNITY: Congressman, I want to get into this North Korea issue here, because it's something that we've got to delve into. I think probably one of the worst foreign policy blunders, the policy of appeasement that was adopted by Bill Clinton when he was president.

KASICH: Unbelievable.

HANNITY: Now Chris Cox had a study and he conducted a panel of Clinton administration. And what happened was North Korea under Bill Clinton became "the largest recipient of U.S. foreign aid in the Asia Pacific region." In an astonishing reversal, they write, "of nine previous U.S. administrations, the Clinton-Gore administration in '94 committed not only to provide aid to North Korea, but they earmarked that aid primarily for the construction of nuclear reactors worth up to $6 billion." The U.S. funded light water reactors in North Korea accumulated plutonium and spent fuel at the rate of 17,300 ounces a year, enough to produce 65 nuclear bombs a year.

They were supposed to have inspections. They got all that money that no other administration would give them. They licked the boots of dictators. They never followed through on the inspections, just like they never followed through on inspections in Iraq. And we have the result, a nuclear bomb in the hands of North Korea today. (*Hannity & Colmes*, October 17, 2002)

On *Hannity & Colmes*, we see the development of a complex and nested set of narratives. First, there is the epic struggle against the terrorist enemy, which requires resolute leadership, the unified support of the American people, and a division of the world into pro-American allies and anti-American enemies. This is what Smith (2005) would call a "high-mimetic" narrative, which is able to build powerful support for going to war. The challenge for such an argument is not to be deflated by a low-mimetic narrative, which would challenge the case for war by emphasizing the potential unintended consequences of decisive action, the complexity of the situation, and the need for a more realist foreign policy.

During the debate about Bosnia in 1993–1994, we saw precisely this kind of cultural organization of the opinion space, in which high-mimetic narratives about the need for intervention were challenged by low-mimetic ones about the many dangers associated with such a policy choice. In the Bosnia debate, the high-mimetic narrative dominated the op-ed page of the newspapers—particularly in the *New York Times*, where columnists William Safire and Anthony Lewis combined to produce a morally charged narrative about the need to act quickly and decisively. In the television space—particularly on *Crossfire*—the moral narrative was more frequently balanced against a more realist argument about the depth of the historical enmity in the region, the inability to find trustworthy European allies, and the dangers of fanning the flames of a wider regional war in the Balkans.[17]

In the debates about the War on Terror, we saw this kind of low-mimetic narrative on *Face the Nation*, with the shift toward a realist consideration of military strategies and risks. We also saw it on *Crossfire*, with more of a comedic reversion to the standard politicizing hyperbole that increasingly characterized much of the show. On *Hannity & Colmes*, however, the low mimetic was avoided through the articulation of a second high-mimetic narrative about the need to recognize that everything was different in a post-9/11 world. Here, the primary sources of danger were politicians and commentators who failed to recognize that they needed a new analytical lens to understand the world. Actions that once seemed reasonable were now unreasonable. For example, actions like diplomacy and coalition building were dangerous because of the way they had emboldened the forces of evil. What was needed was a visionary leader who was willing to ignore the twentieth-century history of international relations and fight evil without reservations. Those who were unwilling to do so were naïve at best, if not outright terrorist sympathizers. This renewed sense of the high mimetic is captured perfectly in the following description of the Nobel Peace Prize—the emblem of the utopian hopes of modern international relations—and its committee members, who are redescribed by the neoconservative intellectual William Bennett as venal, partisan, and anti-American:

HANNITY: All right before I get back to politics, I want to get your take on Jimmy Carter, because I believe he gets the Nobel Prize, then the admission that it's given, you know, to him to send a message to George Bush.

BENNETT: Yes.

HANNITY: I think he ought to return it.

BENNETT: He should give it back. Absolutely, he should give it back. This prize was given so that this Norwegian bureaucrat could make a point. His particular kind of venom against our president, who is engaged in a war against terrorism, and we may be engaged in a second front on this war, and this guy, who disagrees with our president as a way of showing his contempt for President Bush, awards the prize to Carter with this. Carter goes along with this in order to receive the prize. He should say, even though I disagree with President Bush, you cannot use me as a pawn to make this kind of criticism against my president. . . .

HANNITY: Yes, let's not hold our breath. I thought it was disgraceful because it was an admission here that he was being used. And then Carter, you know, lived up to what the expectation was. And he went out and again publicly criticized the president and his policy. And I find it amazing that Democratic presidents— ex-presidents are now doing this. George Herbert Walker Bush had an awful lot that he could have said about Clinton and he didn't say it. (*Hannity & Colmes*, October 15, 2002)

This exchange features all the key elements of the War on Terror narrative as it had developed on *Hannity & Colmes*. First, there is the hero, George Bush, who is bravely and resolutely fighting the war against terrorism. Allied against him are petty and ideological "bureaucrats," who have polluted the legitimacy of the Nobel Prize by using it to criticize Bush and who threaten the security of the globe by failing to line up in support of Bush. Also polluted is ex-President Jimmy Carter, who is described as a "pawn" and whose previous actions of diplomacy are dismissed as "trotting around the world coddling dictators."[18] Clinton and all of his putative failures are also present, in the background, as the one source of historical argument that continues to be a relevant frame of interpretation.

This is a very clever and complicated reframing of the issues in the War on Terror. It is a historical narrative that manages to delegitimate most other historical narratives. It is a high-mimetic, epic tale of good versus evil that manages to map onto existing political divisions without appearing contrived or disingenuous. It is a deeply political narrative that refuses to give the primary framing power to politicians. In fact, it encourages politicians to make arguments that they would never voice in any other part of the opinion space. Finally, organized as it is into a single, morally charged narrative about good against evil, it makes the more "balanced" format on *Crossfire* look completely contrived and inauthentic. Indeed, the more that *Hannity & Colmes* presented a one-sided analysis of the issues, the more ridiculous the characters on *Crossfire* appeared, as if they were just playing games in an environment that demanded more serious commitments. Ultimately, the cultural reorganization of *Hannity & Colmes* led to the decline of the dueling-hosts format that *Crossfire* had created in the 1980s, leading to further innovation and differentiation in the opinion spaces of cable television. We explore these changes further in the next chapter.

The NewsHour

We end with a consideration of the *NewsHour* as a way of bringing into relief the differences between the older and newer opinion formats. Like the Sunday morning talk shows, the *NewsHour* featured a large number of cabinet-level political officials and a very small number of political strategists. Like the *New York Times*, its guest list included relatively few elected politicians and a higher proportion of academics and think tank intellectuals. This was quite a different cast of characters than those on *Crossfire* or *Hannity & Colmes*.

In terms of the specific cultural elements of its commentaries, the *NewsHour* provided two competing formats. The first was more typical of other television commentaries, initially emphasizing unity and moral condemnation before moving to a focus on policy responses. This narrative was carried forward primarily by those who came from the political field, with a heavy emphasis on former cabinet-level officials. The second narrative was more unusual, particularly for television. Articulated primarily by academics and think tank intellectuals, these commentaries emphasized the complex history in the regions where the United States needed to act and the difficulties associated with crafting an effective foreign policy that avoided destabilizing those regions or creating dangerous unintended consequences.

We can see how these two styles of commentary were combined in one of the initial episodes of the *NewsHour* broadcast after the September 11 attacks. In this broadcast from September 20, the commentary begins with an interview of two elected politicians who are asked to provide information about the kinds of foreign policy, economic policy, and airline security policy proposals that are being discussed in Congress. This segment ended with a series of questions about how unified Congress was and how long this unity might last.

After the interviews with elected politicians, the next segment featured expert analysis, with an academic and a think tank intellectual. In this discussion, the two experts offered a history of the Taliban and an analysis of the domestic politics, alliances, and conflicts that complicated their status in Afghanistan and Pakistan. Compared with other commentaries of the same time period—whether on television or in print—these analyses were striking in the way they conveyed complexities faced by any U.S. foreign policy strategy in the region. Consider the following analysis by Barnett Rubin, a political scientist at New York University and a member of the Council on Foreign Relations.

BARNETT RUBIN: I think that—we tend to think of Afghanistan as if it were a state or a government and we want to know who has the power. But the fact is the institutions of statehood and government have been destroyed there over the past 20 years. And what you have now is networks of armed people who receive aid from foreign countries and international networks from smuggling, and these networks of power and violence have various relationships with each other. So Mullah Omar has a network inside the country and that is also linked to networks in Pakistan. He in turn is allied now increasingly with these Arab and internationalist networks that we have kind of personalized in the name of Osama bin Laden. And they have developed a kind of mutual interest in sticking together. But at the same time there are conflicts between them. It's important for to us bear in mind what the conflicts are and in particular the extent to which the presence of those foreign extremists is against the interests of the Afghan people and is not something that most of the Taliban joined that movement in order to defend. So there definitely is the potential for pressure. There is potential for splits and for helping and for perhaps forcing some parts of the Taliban to ally with other Afghans who are opposed to the Taliban, wish that Afghanistan had a different type of government, a more national government. (*NewsHour*, September 20, 2001)

The picture being presented here is not the image of moral clarity and resolute action that we saw in most of the opinion space at the time. Rather, Rubin's narrative presents a complicated, contradictory, and risky scene in which all actors are compromised and all actions have problematic consequences. This is precisely the kind of alternative perspective that outside experts are supposed to provide. Addressing the viewer as a student, Rubin provides a lesson in the political history of the region, suggesting that this history cannot be reduced to simple formulas or political sound bites. It is closest in style to the guest columns found in the *New York Times*, except that it is not attached to the larger civic transformation narrative that we found in that newspaper.

This emphasis on contingency, complexity, and contradiction was a regular and distinctive part of the *NewsHour*'s commentary on the War on Terror. Articulated almost exclusively by academics and think tank intellectuals, other commentaries included the following topics:

- Discussion about how the war in Afghanistan was destabilizing relations between India and Pakistan and the contradictory pressures facing each country (*NewsHour*, December 31, 2001)
- Discussion about the likely difficulties involved in getting a fair trial for those charged with aiding Al Qaeda (*NewsHour*, January 15, 2002)
- Discussion about the difficulties and risks that previous presidents have faced in trying to craft an effective foreign policy toward the Middle East (*NewsHour*, April 17, 2002)

Of course, the *NewsHour* is not a purely intellectual space, because like all television commentary programs, it is closely connected to the political field. It also devotes considerable time to providing a forum for individuals from the political field to publicize and defend their worldviews. This can be seen clearly in the segment that followed the discussion with Barnett Rubin and Daniel Benjamin (from the Center for Strategic and International Studies). This was a discussion with four individuals who had formerly been presidential chiefs of staff, and the narrative that emerged was much more like the rest of the space of opinion at the time: specifically, it expressed American unity and strength, it emphasized the hatred and irrationality of the enemy, it disavowed diplomacy, and it forecast an eventual American victory. The following three examples from former White House chiefs of staff all illustrate this shift back to the narrative of unity, strength, and moral condemnation:

KEN DUBERSTEIN: The President has to stay firm. This is not a time to negotiate. And the Taliban have to realize that the American government is firm, firm, and solid in making sure that our conditions are met, period—end of item.

JOHN SUNUNU: The Taliban has been harboring a criminal for a long, long time. What they looked for was an easy way out that has no meaning. It was a meaningless gesture on their part. The President I suspect is going to reject what they said out of hand and tell them either go back and do what is right or suffer the consequences. This country, I don't think the world understands how serious the mood is in America today. And I think the President is going to try and convey not only to the American public what has to be done, but part of his message tonight I suspect is going to tell the world you should understand how serious we are about getting this thing done and getting it done right.

HAMILTON JORDAN: Well, the Taliban's word means nothing or should mean nothing to our country. And indeed I think it means very little in the Middle East to even the Muslim countries. So I think the President was right to reject it out of hand. There is no middle ground here. You are with us, or you are against us. You are against terrorism, or you are on the other side nurturing and supporting those people responsible for this dastardly deed. (*NewsHour*, September 20, 2001)

Subsequent episodes of the *Newshour* continued to reproduce this foreign policy emphasis, giving political principals and former principals—supplemented by the input of journalists and columnists—the opportunity to describe, suggest, and criticize specific policy suggestions. An interview with Secretary of State Colin Powell, for example, offered the opportunity to describe the U.S. policy approach to the Israeli-Palestinian conflict and to outline how that was connected to the larger antiterrorism policies of the Bush administration (*NewsHour*, January 25, 2002). A discussion with three former policy analysts with the National Security Council offered support for U.S. policy in the Middle East, asserting that the United States was the only effective actor in the region (*NewsHour*, April 17, 2002). A discussion with two former U.S. ambassadors to the United Nations offered suggestions about the kinds of things that would have to happen for France and Russia to agree to a UN resolution that would ultimately lead to a war with Iraq (*NewsHour*, October 15, 2002). Similarly, a discussion with two columnists focused on the kinds of things that would have to happen for Democratic senators to support such a resolution (*NewsHour*, September 27, 2002).

In addition to this, as the discussions on the *NewsHour* turned to questions of diplomacy and political negotiation, a moralizing narrative developed about the motives of various actors involved in the War on Terror. This was based on a distinction between honest, principled positions and cynical, strategic ones—with the latter, obviously, being the polluted term. Structurally, this distinction bore a resemblance to the kinds of moral arguments we saw on the cable television programs, with one important difference. On the *NewsHour*, the distinction between principle and cynicism was not mapped onto a polarizing narrative of Democrats and Republicans. Consider the following description of American politicians:

DAVID BROOKS: There's something disturbing going on, which is if you are supporting the President, that's a patriotic stance if you're doing it out of principle. If you are opposing him on principle, that's a patriotic stance. There are a lot of people in Congress who are going to vote one way and their conscience tells them to vote the other.

MARGARET WARNER: On both sides.

DAVID BROOKS: On both sides. Absolutely true. If you are voting against your conscience on a matter of war and peace, that really is dishonorable, that is putting party above country. If you are trying to close down debate, to me that's dishonorable. There are villains, something really dishonorable going on. (*NewsHour*, September 27, 2002)

In this exchange, Brooks criticizes self-interested and political calculations, ultimately arguing that "dishonorable" politicians are weak and impotent.

The developing moral discourse at the *NewsHour* came to shape a narrative that the more resolute position of the Bush administration would prevail and that the self-interested actions of morally compromised politicians would fail. Thus, Brooks predicted, "They [the Bush Administration] are going to get a resolution passed by a huge majority out of the Congress" (*NewsHour*, February 27, 2002), and in a different discussion, Richard Holbrooke—former ambassador to the United Nations and a member of the Council of Foreign Relations—suggested that since France and Russia did not really care about the substance of the issues facing the UN, "within a week or so, Secretary Powell and John Negroponte . . . will produce an acceptable resolution that the French and Russians sign into, and then we'll be on the way" (*NewsHour*, October 15, 2002).

In the final analysis, then, we find that the *NewsHour* presented a hybrid narrative that attempted to straddle the very different rhetorical strategies and cultural forms of the political and academic fields. When the discussion included elected politicians or cabinet members, it tended to reflect interests that emerged from the political field, with an emphasis on policy proposals and domestic political considerations. When the discussion included academics, columnists, and think tank intellectuals, however, the narratives that emerged were wider ranging, they were more likely to emphasize complexity and contingency, and they were more likely to include political-cultural considerations that originated outside the United States. By preserving a relatively autonomous space for academics and think tank intellectuals, then, the *NewsHour* managed to produce a wider, deeper discourse about the War on Terror than the other television formats, but this complexity was limited by the presence of powerful speakers who came from the center of the political field.

Conclusion

In the end, there are several things we can say about how a particular cast of characters combines with a specific opinion format to produce a collective narrative about the War on Terror. First, if the chief concern is the autonomy of the opinion space, it seems pretty clear that cabinet-level appointees and other presidential representatives are the most problematic guests, since they are the most effective at commandeering the space of opinion to publicize their policies. These guests tend to concentrate most heavily in the older and more prestigious parts of the television opinion space, namely, the Sunday morning talk shows and PBS's *NewsHour*. On these types of programs, the host's performative style of detached objectivity is virtually powerless to mount any critique of the political principals.

At the same time, certain features of the older television formats have prevented them from becoming completely dependent on state narratives. Each show uses different types of segments to contextualize the discussions with political principals and to inject more analytical and critical elements into their narratives. In these kinds of more critical segments, we find that interpretations become more wide-ranging and complex and that critical argument and complexity are far more likely to occur the further away the guests are from the political field. And both of our case studies suggest that the *NewsHour* has been more successful in this than *Face the Nation*. *Face the Nation* generally highlights a discussion with elected politicians, and thus its overall discursive environment maps closely onto existing political divisions, even in those instances when its discussions are evaluative and critical. The *NewsHour*, by contrast, makes much more effective use of columnists, academics, think tank intellectuals, and other experts to frame and evaluate the narratives offered by political principals.

The second lesson we take from our analysis of the narratives in the War on Terror is that a focus on historical complexity and cultural sensitivity is much more likely in those spaces where academics have higher representation and greater cultural influence, namely, the *New York Times* and the *NewsHour*. By no means are we suggesting that academics are the only speakers capable of expressing complexity in the space of opinion. In fact, we have found many instances where columnists, think tank intellectuals, expert analysts, and even former politicians are able to weave multidimensional narratives. What we are suggesting, however, is that those types of narratives are much more likely to occur when academics and academic styles are a visible part of the discussion. These types of narratives tend toward the low mimetic, generally avoiding moral inflation and suggesting caution as a mode of action. As such, they tend to engage the audience in their roles as citizens or students, explaining all the potential complications and unintended consequences that may emerge from particular actions or policies. These narratives are closest to the ideal-type of "columnist as teacher" that we discussed in chapter 2, and they provide a particular type of critical discourse, probably closest to the self-understandings and public justifications that most media intellectuals would give for the importance of their work.

To be sure, the low-mimetic genre is not one that all viewers and readers enjoy. Nor is it likely to reflect the sharp social divisions and political struggles that organize a great deal of political mobilization in civil society. This insight might help to explain the rise of more morally charged discussions like those often found in the newer opinion formats on cable television. These newer opinion formats are based on a different understanding of critical autonomy, which includes a critique of precisely those low-mimetic narratives and formats that have historically attracted academics and other experts.

Thus, as an alternative to the kind of academic, complex, critical discourse that one can find in the older opinion formats, the newer formats have developed a different kind of critical discourse that is based on highly charged moral critique and political partisanship. On these newer programs, all guests are challenged to develop accounts that can fit into binary moral distinctions, and they are asked to link those moral distinctions to existing political divisions. Guests who come from the political field are not exempted from this demand, a fact that makes the newer formats more able to resist the existing strategies and frames of the political field. Ironically, by replacing the stance of detached objectivity with one of moral argument and political partisanship, the hosts of the newer formats manage to achieve a certain kind of autonomy from the political field that the hosts from the older television formats often find elusive.

The point is that the newer formats present a space of mediated deliberation that is complicated and contradictory. On the one hand, it is obvious that the newer programs are deeply politicized, polarizing, and cynical in their worldview. But on the other hand, the newer shows cover many different kinds of topics, and when they have an extended focus on a single topic, they cover it from a number of different angles—albeit in an overall narrative of polarization. Moreover, the newer shows boast a wider variety of guests than the older shows, and so long as they are sufficiently skilled, these guests can effectively make their own arguments despite repeated demands for moral and political reduction. Most important, hosts on the newer shows almost never allow their guests to simply state their position without critical challenge—and this includes politicians, who are as subject to the critical demands of the newer formats as any other guest. Clearly, this is not perfect deliberation, but it does offer some deliberative advantages over other parts of the opinion space, particularly as it is organized on television.

Of course, the history of these new formats is relatively short, and innovations will no doubt continue to proliferate in a way that continues to refine this alternative style of critical opinion and analysis. Indeed, one of the things we saw in the debate about the War on Terror was a movement away from the "dueling hosts" format that had characterized the newer shows from the early days of CNN. The problem with such a format—where two hosts and two guests engage in serial symbolic confrontation—is that it is too symmetrical and tends to work against narrative complexity. The result is that it easily collapses into hyperbole and caricature, producing performances by the guests that seem deeply inauthentic. The modifications that *Hannity & Colmes* made to the format in 2001 and 2002 created a stronger sense of identification between the show and its viewers, in a way that benefited Fox News at the great expense of CNN. More recently, cable news networks have begun abandoning the dueling hosts format altogether, with Alan Colmes leaving Fox News and with MSNBC establishing successful prime-time programs around single hosts These developments will continue to shape the kinds of narratives that emerge from the opinion space, the kinds of character positions that are available for media intellectuals, and the effects that all of this has on political communication.

9 The Future of Opinion

OUR AIM IN this book has been to explore the organization of media opinion in contemporary civil society. What we found was a highly complex and multifaceted space of opinion. There are many different types of media intellectuals, with different levels of access to the opinion space. There are a variety of different opinion formats, and each combines voices, narratives, and performance styles in its own specific way. Each opinion format has also developed its own distinctive relationship to the political field, its own relationship to the wider journalistic field, and its own understanding of (and commitment to) the general values of critique, autonomy, and complexity. Finally, it seems clear that all of these differences have become more pronounced in recent years, driven in large part by the rapid proliferation of opinion formats that has been occurring on television.

The proliferation of formats has led to innovation in the space of opinion, but it has also resulted in an intensified commitment (by some) to the traditional values of detached commentary. In fact, the traditional project of detached commentary is alive and well in the opinion space, thriving on the newspaper op-ed page, the Sunday morning political talk shows, and public television programs such as the *NewsHour*. Because the different formats offer competing logics of distinction and professional justification, changes in one area of the opinion space have consequences in others.

A more complicated issue concerns the extent to which the proliferation and diversification of opinion formats have encouraged a fragmentation of public communication. To be sure, there is a relationship between the fragmentation of the media audience and the proliferation of more particularistic, morally charged, and polarizing opinion formats. We discussed this in chapter 2 in our examination of the rise of Fox News, and recent work by Jamieson and Cappella (2008), Morris (2005), and Kull (2003) confirms this. Jamieson and Cappella argue that the growth of opinion formats on cable television has created a more fragmented and polarized public sphere because viewers of cable news are more likely to shield themselves from alternative perspectives. Morris's (2005) interesting study of television audiences finds further that the audience for network news is growing older and that audiences for Fox News and CNN are becoming increasingly polarized. Morris argues that this polarization had real consequences during the Iraq War, particularly for the viewers of Fox News. Specifically, when compared with CNN viewers, the Fox News audience was less likely to follow stories that were critical of the Bush administration and more likely to underestimate the number of casualties in Iraq.

More concerning, perhaps, is a 2003 study by the Program on International Policy Attitudes (PIPA), which examined public perceptions about Iraq and explored the extent to which misperceptions about Iraq were connected to the specific types of news that people consumed (Kull 2003). This study found that significant portions of the American public held mistaken views about Iraq in 2003 (Kull 2003: 2). Furthermore, those who held mistaken beliefs were more supportive of the decision to go to war with Iraq (Kull 2003: 8). The specific findings about the Fox News audience probably received the most public attention. Among all the audience types in the study, Fox News viewers were the most likely to believe that Saddam Hussein had close connections with al Qaeda, to believe that inspectors had found weapons of mass destruction in Iraq, and to believe that the United States had broad international support for going to war with Iraq (Kull 2003: 13–15).

A similar type of concern about online news sites is suggested in recent work by Baum and Groeling (2008), which compared traditional news wires with more partisan news Web sites (both left-leaning and right-leaning). They find that more partisan sites operate according to different criteria of newsworthiness; that is, a story is more likely to be covered by the partisan news sites when it fits a clear ideological orientation, which can be easily linked to preference for one political party or antipathy for the other (Baum and Groeling 2008: 359). This kind of news selection makes it easier for readers to surround themselves with "self-reinforcing" news, which has the effect of increasing the strength of the partisan beliefs that they already hold (Baum and Groeling 2008: 360; also see Sunstein 2002).

While none of these studies distinguishes between traditional news and the space of opinion, they still present disturbing challenges to a normative view of mediated deliberation, which insists that viewers and readers need to be exposed to a range of different arguments and perspectives. Our analyses provide partial confirmation for such a concern. Comparing different opinion formats, we found that the more partisan styles found on cable television were much more likely than the others to organize their commentaries around a morally charged narrative about political polarization. Debates about Enron were largely reduced to arguments about whether the Clinton administration or the Bush administration was more corrupt. This was true in the debates about the War on Terror, too, where after the initial displays of national unity subsided, narratives were typically presented as a comparative referendum on the performance of the Republican and Democratic parties. To the extent that these kinds of narratives reinforce the partisan political identification of viewers, and to the extent that they encourage those viewers to see the opposing party as morally weak or even evil, then it becomes more difficult to organize a public dialogue built around mutual respect, trust, or openness.

While these patterns are certainly problematic and justify much of the public concern that has been expressed about the growing influence of the cable news networks, we think it would be a mistake to simply condemn the newer formats. The audience for cable television's opinion shows has different levels of knowledge and media engagement than its general news audience, as a 2007 study by the Pew Research Center for the People and the Press confirms. Looking at the total news audience for each news channel, the Pew study found that viewers of Fox News and CNN had some of the lowest levels of current affairs knowledge in the survey. But the picture grew more complicated when specific news formats were considered. In fact, the highest levels of current affairs knowledge in the Pew study were found among the following four audience groups:

- Comedy Central, *The Daily Show with Jon Stewart*, *The Colbert Report*
- Major newspaper Web sites
- PBS, *NewsHour*
- Fox News, *The O'Reilly Factor*

The Pew study demonstrates that highly knowledgeable audiences can be found in new formats, as well as traditional ones. This does not necessarily mean that the quality of deliberation is better in the newer formats. As we have argued throughout the book, deliberation is more than the private opinions and factual knowledge of a group of individuals. But it does suggest that it is risky to make generalizations about Fox News's opinion offerings based on a study of the total Fox News audience. The same cautionary advice would seem to be equally valid for other cable television channels, whether they be Comedy Central, CNN, or MSNBC. On these channels, even more than in the traditional sectors of print and broadcast media, the space of opinion has its own distinctive and intelligible structure, which must be studied on its own terms.

We suggest that the new opinion formats are best understood in relationship to the larger opinion environment in which they interact. Indeed, one of the more interesting findings of the Pew study is that high-knowledge audiences are much more omnivorous than other audiences, with a daily average consumption of more than seven different media sources. In other words, viewers of *The Daily Show* or *The O'Reilly Factor* or *Hannity & Colmes* do not seem to be isolating themselves from alternative viewpoints or competing media; instead, they are exposing themselves to a variety of different media. And this makes sense, given the deeply intertextual nature of the new opinion formats.

In other words, the proliferation of formats has been accompanied by an ever-expanding network of dense intertextual references, including overlapping personnel, cross-media citation, and metacritique. The result is the circulation of arguments and rhetorics across an increasingly wider variety of different media and institutional domains. This produces a thicker (though probably a more polarized) intersubjective environment within the space of opinion. For the most part, this circulation of opinion still works from the center, where authoritative opinions are produced, and then moves outward. Thus, the traditional formats (the newspaper op-ed page, the Sunday morning political talk show) reference one another frequently but maintain a general unease about the continual encroachment of the newer formats into the space of opinion. The newer formats (e.g., *Hannity & Colmes*, *The O'Reilly Factor*) also reference the traditional formats and the "mainstream media," but they tend to do so in a critical way, with the suggestion that those formats are biased, elitist, or limited. And as these newer formats have themselves become institutionalized, they have been met with critical attention from still newer formats (e.g., *The Daily Show with Jon Stewart*, *Countdown with Keith Olbermann*). Each moment of format diversification has produced a more complex environment of nested cross-commentary between media formats, even as all of these different shows compete to "narrate the social" in the most compelling, authoritative, and influential manner. The end result may still be a fragmented public sphere, but it is one in which audiences are likely to be aware of what is being said in other parts of the space of opinion.

Looking Forward: The Fall of *Crossfire* and the Rise of MSNBC

In the most recent round of innovations, we see the decline of the dueling-hosts format made infamous by *Crossfire* and the corresponding rise of the single-host format with a more explicit point of view. On *Crossfire*, at least one of the hosts was typically a political insider—either a former politician, a cabinet member, or a political consultant of some kind. The other host was usually a political journalist who took a partisan position. Each host was branded as either a liberal or conservative critic, and together they subjected guests to the "crossfire" of competing questions from the "left" and the "right." In its earlier years, with hosts such as Michael Kinsley and Patrick Buchanan, *Crossfire* had been innovative because it challenged political actors with critical (though rarely impartial) questions and because it often placed political actors into uncomfortable dialogues where they had to debate their critics face to face. By the beginning of the new century, however, the dueling-hosts format on *Crossfire* had become increasingly reductive, with hosts and guests cynically rehearsing their polarizing arguments in such hyperbolic terms that it was hard to imagine that they even believed what they were saying. The final version of the program was particularly egregious, with Paul Begala and Tucker Carlson engaging in such a shallow and partisan form of bickering that they drove most serious guests away from the show. In this context, Jon Stewart's well-known 2004 appearance on *Crossfire* sounded the death knell for a program that had been struggling for some years and whose cultural organization had long since crossed any credible boundary of seriousness or authenticity.

Of course, by the time *Crossfire* was canceled, it had been struggling for some time against competition from newer shows like *Hannity & Colmes* and *The O'Reilly Factor*. *The O'Reilly Factor* demonstrated that a more partisan style of opinion program did not need to be "balanced" through dueling hosts. As for *Hannity & Colmes*, it refined the dueling-hosts format by basically "fixing" the outcome. Because Sean Hannity so clearly dominated Alan Colmes, the show came to represent Hannity's fundamentally conservative point of view (notwithstanding the robust opinion Colmes sometimes managed to produce). While Hannity had always enjoyed certain privileges in the cultural organization of the show—for example, the ability to launch into extended political commentaries or the persistent attention to the perceived failures of the mainstream media—his cultural imprint on the show increased dramatically after September 11, 2001. It was downhill from there, and in 2008 Colmes announced that he would leave the show. In 2009, Hannity began hosting his own program on Fox News. Colmes has become a regular guest on *The O'Reilly Factor,* where he plays the same role of "liberal foil", but now mixed with an unmistakable note of comic deflation.

Fox News is not the only cable channel to abandon the dueling-host format. After nearly a decade of struggling to attract a prime-time audience, MSNBC has had great success in recent years by adopting the format of the partisan, single-host program. *Hardball with Chris Matthews*, which has aired on MSNBC since 1999, has increased its audience considerably since 2004 through a series of highly publicized confrontations with conservative politicians and pundits and also through its increasingly pointed criticism of the Bush administration. Airing since 2003, *Countdown with Keith Olbermann* relied on blistering criticisms of conservative politicians and media pundits to become the most popular program on MSNBC. MSNBC completed the transformation of its prime-time lineup in 2008 with *The Rachel Maddow Show*, in effect announcing that it was the liberal-progressive alternative to Fox News. This strategy has so far worked to great effect, with MSNBC moving ahead of CNN in 2009 to become the second most-watched cable news network. Olbermann ended his program in January 2011, after a period of growing conflict with NBC executives, and amidst swirling rumors that his departure was provoked by the merger between NBC and Comcast. But this public saga did not significantly alter MSNBC's new lineup. MSNBC introduced two new programs, and both used single hosts who were generally associated with liberal politics.[1]

Because balance has always been one of the primary ways that traditional journalism performed objectivity, the end of the dueling-hosts format has pushed the cable talk shows even further away from the dominant practices of the journalistic field. This has had important consequences for how these newer formats define and orient to the value of autonomy, leading to a growing competition to define what counts as real or effective autonomy within the space of opinion. Indeed, the attention to multiple forms of autonomy is an advantage of our cultural model of mediated deliberation, and it allows us to assess deliberative possibilities and limitations of different opinion formats.

In the traditional television formats, objectivity is defined as a lack of bias by the politically detached program hosts. Their goal is to remain autonomous *from* politics—to develop a position outside or beyond the rough-and-tumble of partisan politics. The best examples of this are found on shows such as the *NewsHour* or *Face the Nation*, where the hosts of the program studiously avoid taking positions and instead limit themselves to asking questions of political principals and other media intellectuals. As we have seen, the outcomes of these practices are deeply dependent on the particular ensemble of guests on the show. When there is a good mix of different guests, the result is often a narrative that displays great nuance and complexity. When the guests are political principals, however, the resulting narrative differs little from an official state press release. This version of autonomy, in other words, has uneven results.

In the newer formats, the partisan stance of the host reveals a commitment to a different kind of autonomy; rather than autonomy from politics, the goal of the newer formats is to assert and maintain autonomy *in* politics. In this sense, media critics are correct to assert that this part of the journalistic field has moved closer to the political field in recent years. Figures like Sean Hannity, Chris Matthews, and Keith Olbermann are deeply political. At the same time, by abandoning the traditional stances of detachment and neutrality, they have become intellectual and political forces in their own right in a way that gives them a different kind of autonomy than a previous generation of media intellectuals was able to achieve. In the older formats, the autonomy of the hosts came from remaining apart from any particular party and trying to avoid generating political influence of their own. For Olbermann and Hannity, the goal seems to be the identification of a "pure" partisan position, in which they are able to publicize political positions to enormous mass audiences while remaining relatively insulated from the vagaries of electoral politics and political compromise. This has important consequences for the kinds of guests they bring onto their programs, as well as the kinds of narratives they aim to develop. In general, we suspect that the political purity of the newer single-host formats produces much more successful and authentic performances than what was generally found in the dueling-host format, a fact that makes the hosts of these programs even more influential in the space of opinion. This is clearly a different kind of autonomy than what is envisioned by most theories of deliberation.

In this sense, the rise of the new single-host format on cable television continues the trend we saw with the earlier cable format, which involves redefining what autonomy means in the political and journalistic fields. As we saw in chapters 7 and 8, the cable programs were much more likely than the traditional formats to subject politicians to critical questions and critical scrutiny. This continues with the single-host format of the newer cable programs. In addition, with the single-host format, there seems to be less interest in interviewing politicians and more interest in hearing from a diverse range of media intellectuals, such as columnists, academics, think tank intellectuals, and even some political bloggers. Given the new understanding of these shows, which want to maintain autonomy *in* politics, this makes sense. To be sure, the programs need enough politicians to maintain a connection to official political publics, but their real interest lies in developing an autonomous space of political influence and engaged commentary. Thus, while the new programs are deeply political and polarizing in their cultural organization, they often manage to achieve more autonomy (or at the very least, a different kind of autonomy) from the narrative constraints of the political field than other parts of the television opinion space. In this format, then, the trade-off between autonomy and influence is not as sharply drawn as it is in the project of objective professional journalism.

In addition, because these formats can use their explicit point of view as a vantage point for teasing out the nuances of their arguments in great detail, they also have the potential to introduce narrative complexity into the space of opinion as a whole. First, by parsing the details of an explicit political point of view, these formats open a space for exploring subtle differences between different versions of the same narrative, be it conservative or liberal. That is, once the mechanically polarizing logic of the dueling-hosts format is removed, complexity can be reintroduced as part of a dialogue internal to this more specific political opinion format. Second, however, these formats connect themselves to the wider opinion space by positioning themselves as media critics with a particular political position. Where once a liberal argument might have been expressed by Alan Colmes or a liberal guest in the dueling-hosts format of *Hannity & Colmes*, in the single-host format of *Hannity*, the liberal position can be defined in terms of the entire nonconservative opinion space with which Sean Hannity is now in dialogue. In this context, Hannity's interpretation and criticism of nonconservative opinion is aided by an ever-expanding cast of characters who offer expertise, experience, and moral support for Hannity's point of view, thereby giving it depth and lending it authority. Third, as we suggested before, as a structural feature of the opinion space, the success of Bill O'Reilly and Sean Hannity has resulted in the replication of the single-host format to other cable channels. This represents an overall expansion of the opinion space, as the newer liberal cable talk shows define themselves against shows like *Hannity* and *The O'Reilly Factor* and also engage a wide range of other opinion formats by inviting guests to speak from the traditional print and television opinion spaces, as well as bloggers, writers, long-form journalists, guests from radio, and media outsiders like academics and think tank intellectuals. These changes also underline the increasing diversity of personnel and narrative elements in the opinion space overall.

Our refusal to equate the newer formats with the collapse of civil society does not mean that these newer formats are somehow superior to the more traditional ones. These newer shows are clearly committed to the politicization of the public conversation, in a way that is much less obvious on the newspaper op-ed page or the Sunday morning talk shows. This commitment to partisanship and politicization clearly violates any presumption of objectivity that depends on a lack of bias—a presumption that underpins not only professional journalism but also related intellectual fields, like science and the academy. It is also the case that the newer formats, by emphasizing political disagreements and moral certainties, have a tendency toward reductive interpretations of public issues, as compared with complex, contradictory, or ambivalent narratives about social life. And it seems unlikely that these newer programs are encouraging anyone to change an opinion about an issue as a result of the force of the better argument. In short, there is no deliberation on these programs, except among speakers and viewers who already share a common political identification and who are already in full agreement on the issues. In other words, while there may be more narrative diversity, it is a form of diversity that is encased within already established social and political divisions. To the extent that mediated deliberation is occurring in these new formats then, it is a deliberation among allies, rather than a deliberation across points of difference.

But we cannot understand the current state of mediated deliberation by considering the new opinion formats on their own, as if they are isolated from the rest of the opinion space. As we argued in chapter 3, deliberation does not occur in any single mediated space, but rather takes place within the entire ensemble of mediated discussions, arguments, and commentaries that occur across the many spaces of media opinion. Indeed, if we examine any particular media outlet, we inevitably discover that it is restricted in several ways—in terms of who gets to participate, in terms of what kinds of performances are preferred, and in terms of what types of narratives circulate. This does not necessarily foreclose the possibility of deliberation, however. What matters is not the limits of any particular format but rather the totality of views that are represented in the space of opinion as a whole (Jacobs 2000; Page 1996). To what extent does this totality reflect a diverse set of interests and narratives? To what degree do the different mediated publics monitor one another and provide a critical commentary about the gaps and omissions in other parts of the space of opinion? And to what extent are meaningful connections regularly being made between the many partial publics of our complex postmodern societies?

In certain important respects, the newer formats appear to be reducing the deliberative capacity of the space of opinion. For example, while the new formats have certainly increased the presence of certain voices and perspectives (e.g., partisan hosts, think tank intellectuals, binary moral narratives), they have discouraged others (academics, narratives emphasizing historical complexity or unintended consequences). This creates problems for the space of opinion, if one believes (as we do) that complexity improves the quality of deliberation. As our research has demonstrated quite clearly, the presence of academics has a clear and positive role in adding depth and complexity to the discussions that take place in the space of opinion. There are other problems as well. As we have already suggested, the new formats have increased an awareness of other public conversations, but they have often done so through narratives of political partisanship and moral vilification that make trust-based dialogue and hermeneutic sensitivity more difficult to achieve. Because most theories of deliberation prefer trust and openness over partisanship and moral pollution, these trends are cause for concern.

Ultimately, the depth of this concern depends on the impact that the newer formats are having on the entire space of opinion. As our empirical analyses have shown, the traditional opinion formats contribute a distinctive set of voices and cultural styles that are not found in the newer formats. While these traditional formats have not yet shown signs of weakening, it is possible in the future that the cultural styles preferred in the newer formats will begin to achieve hegemony over the larger space of opinion, as the regular voices and preferred styles of the new formats begin to assert themselves in other parts of the space of opinion. It is also possible that the increasing strength of the newer formats could crowd out other "alternative" formats that have been important sources of innovation in the past. Indeed, as we demonstrated in chapter 2, the small opinion magazines, the alternative weeklies, and the programs originating from public broadcast media have all contributed important innovations to the space of opinion. Format innovation should not be left to the owners and programmers of cable television networks, who are motivated by a specific type of market position and who are interested in meeting a very specific (and limited) audience demand.

A second issue of concern stems from the current practices in newer formats of cross-media monitoring and media metacriticism. On the one hand, we think these practices represent a potential expansion in the deliberative capacity of the space of opinion because they produce more intertextual connections, more critique, and more reflexivity about the *mediated* nature of public communication. The problem is that these practices have remained largely one-sided, with the newer formats monitoring the older ones. We think it would be preferable if the older formats provided the same kind of critical commentary about the gaps, mistakes, and biases of the newer formats. At the moment, this seems to be the specialty of media watchdogs, like FAIR, AIM, and MMA, although this kind of critical commentary has sometimes appeared on the newspaper op-ed page—for example, in the Sunday *New York Times* columns of Frank Rich. But there is little of this type of commentary on the Sunday morning talk shows, and the traditional formats in print and on television still have a long way to go to achieve the same level of media metacommentary that one finds in the newer television formats. This speaks to the need for continued innovation within the traditional formats. But it is a change that we think is likely, given the increasingly intertextual processes of monitoring and criticism that occur *across and between formats* in the circulation of personnel, rhetorics, and opinions. Ultimately, if these practices are extended to the entire space of opinion, they will require us to rethink how critical rationality operates in mediated deliberation.

Rethinking Critical Rationality: The Variety of Media Intellectuals and a New Role for the Columnist

There is a mutually reinforcing relationship between classical theories of democratic deliberation and professional projects for objective journalism, as we argued in chapter 3. On one side, normative theories of deliberation have long emphasized the centrality of rational critical debate based on good information, through which citizens can come to a consensus about matters of common concern. On the other side, the traditional project of professional objective journalism has asserted its role as the irreplaceable purveyor of good factual information to such rational, information-processing citizens. The professional newspaper columnist, perhaps best exemplified by Walter Lippmann, was, in some sense, the product of this lucky union between the democratic principles of theorists and the professional aspirations of journalists. As we outlined in chapter 2, when columnists like Walter Lippmann offered opinions, they anchored them firmly in a commitment to the value of facts and the idea that the thoughtful, detached, nonpartisan analysis of major alternative policy choices was required for complex democracies to function. In their critical analyses of competing policy arguments and in their broad historical and social framing of current events, columnists have acted as media intellectuals who triaged issues for wider voting publics. This vision of the media intellectual is shared by many others who aspire to participate in the opinion space, particularly those who come from academia, literature and other relatively autonomous cultural fields.

As we have seen throughout this book, this vision of the columnist as a media intellectual remains central to professional journalism in the contemporary United States. Columnists like David Brooks, Thomas Friedman, E. J. Dionne, and Paul Krugman continue to offer opinions in the best intellectual tradition of Walter Lippmann, James Reston, Dorothy Thompson, and the rest. But as we have also documented, individuals like Krugman and Brooks now offer opinions in a much larger and more complex media landscape than their predecessors did. Columns written by figures like Brooks and Krugman are not just syndicated to many other newspapers; both columnists appear regularly on television opinion shows on public, network, and cable television, and they enjoy significant online presences. In this connection, their opinions are not only widely read but also widely commented on and criticized by a raft of other journalists, pundits, and citizens. In this way, their texts become the jumping-off points for new opinions and arguments in wider and wider circles of discussion and debate, all of which are built on a foundation of this dense intertextual discourse that is circulating rapidly on the Internet, as well as on more traditional media platforms.

What is different today, as we have suggested, is that the columnists' vision of their civic role has been challenged by competing visions of what a media intellectual should be doing. It is not just that the competing vision is more partisan, more politicized, and less committed to the professional project of detached commentary. Central to the performances in the newer formats are blistering critiques of the supposed sloppiness and bias of mainstream media and the traditional opinion formats. As the newer formats have become institutionalized, they have become the object of critical attention by still newer formats, which chart the mistakes and biases of the newer formats that had preceded them. Nowhere in this nested dialogue is there a defense by columnists or traditional talk show hosts of the professional project of objective journalism or of the Lippmann model of detached columnists who should be opinionated without being partisan and disinterested without being disengaged. Rather, the picture that emerges is of a media field where all arguments are partial and partisan and where there is a need for a careful deconstruction of media punditry.

Because of the nature of media metacommentary and the polarization that increasingly defines the opinion space, we believe that "critical rationality" is likely to emerge only in the identification of better and worse opinion. Traditional opinion columnists ignore the metacommentary of the newcomers at their own risk. As in any intellectual field, a central goal must be to identify what is sacred and profane, who are the heroes and who are the villains, who speaks in an authentic voice and who is insincere and inauthentic. The newer formats have been involved in this exercise for some time now, and if anything, we expect that their efforts to symbolically pollute their opponent-interlocutors will only intensify, as the recent feud between Keith Olbermann and Bill O'Reilly demonstrated. The more traditional formats have so far tried to stay above the fray, paying attention only to each other and hoping that somehow the newer formats will just disappear. This is a risky strategy.

For the elite columnists and those who work in the traditional opinion formats, it is probably time to fully enter the arena of media metacommentary through critical monitoring and commentary on the newer formats. In the current environment, it is not enough to write Lippmannesque columns and hope that the public recognizes their value. Nor is it enough to hope that the third-generation formats will effectively deconstruct the second-generation ones, with the result somehow being that the traditional formats will be the only ones left standing. After all, these third-generation formats are based on a deeply politicized or a deeply cynical and ironic worldview, neither of which leads automatically to the vision of public deliberation that the traditional formats have tended to offer. Rather, for the traditional formats to remain relevant, they need to produce their own media metacritique. They need to identify their own enemies in the world of punditry, and produce their own symbolic pollution of what they view as inauthentic or dangerous opinion formats. And they need to connect this symbolic pollution to a clear justification of their own vision of what media intellectuals should be offering to the public and its citizens. They might also engage in some self-reflection, considering when they are in fact providing their readers an autonomous analysis of a complex world, and when they are simply providing a visible forum for representatives of the state to publicize their policies in a display of representative publicity.

In the end, the degree of critical rationality in the opinion space depends not on the arguments that are made within a single format, but rather on the ensemble of spaces and on the nature of critical dialogue that takes place between them. Within this restless, dynamic, and increasingly intertextual set of public discussions, media intellectuals will succeed, we suggest, not simply by offering compelling narratives about matters of common concern. They also need to present themselves as more or less heroic characters in the struggle for civil society, through a defense of their own intellectual projects and through an explicit critique of the projects of their adversaries. It is this binary and agonistic process that defines deliberation in the space of opinion and is a fundamental part of the quest for a more just and rational civil society.

Samples and Data

THE SAMPLE DESIGN has several connected goals. First, we wanted good representative samples that were large enough to compare the first years of Republican and Democratic presidential administrations, since prior research had led us to suspect a relationship between party of administration and the occupational composition of the field of media intellectuals (Townsley 2000). Second, we chose two-year periods during each presidency to capture the second year of a new administration, by which time most cabinet appointments have been made and arguably the honeymoon period with the media has ended (although see Clayman et al. 2007). Finally, choosing twenty-four-month periods helps us to avoid event specificity, for example, our sample being dominated by a single episode, like the events of September 11.

Along with quantitative variables describing regular features of the opinion space, there are approximately 10,000 pages of text data in the newspaper sample and 10,000 pages in the television sample, about 20,000 pages overall. Our goal is to draw connections between the social space of opinion described by the quantitative measures on the one hand—thus, the analysis of authors' occupations, the range of content, length of speech, number of turns, and other characteristics of format—with an in-depth cultural analysis of the narrative features in particular cases, on the other. We supplement the content analyses throughout the chapters with close readings of strategically selected textual material. Indeed, it is our aim throughout the book to enhance both dimensions of our analysis by marrying both.

The Newspaper and Television Samples: Op-Eds, Speaker-Shows, Speaker-Segments

We drew a 12.5 percent sample of days from two twenty-four-month periods—1993–1994 and 2001–2002—and collected all the op-eds published in the *New York Times* and *USA Today* for those days from the full-text database provided by Nexis. The choice of the *New York Times* is

TABLE A.1

SAMPLE DETAILS	
Days sampled print	200
Days sampled television	100
NUMBER OF OBJECTS IN NEXIS	
# Op-eds	910
# Television shows	157
# Show-segments	374
NUMBER OF INDIVIDUAL AUTHORS	
Number of individual print authors	446
Number of individual TV authors	511
Total number of individual opinion authors	923*
UNITS OF ANALYSIS	
Author-op-ed units *(print)*	910
Speaker-show units *(TV)*	909
Author-opinion level *(print and TV)*	1,819
Number of op-eds	910
Number of speaker-segments *(TV)*	1,241
Segment level *(print and TV)*	2,152

*These do not add to 923 because there is overlap of authors between print and television.

obvious, since it is widely regarded as the national paper of record. *USA Today* is the most widely circulated newspaper in the United States, and the flagship brand of the Gannett group, the largest newspaper conglomerate in the country during our sample periods. The unit of analysis in the newspaper sample is the op-ed ($n = 910$).

Television transcripts were sampled using the same logic we followed for newspapers: we took a random sample of days from the same two time periods, 1993–1994 and 2001–2002, and collected transcripts from *Face the Nation*, *Crossfire*, *The NewsHour with Jim Lehrer*, and *Hannity & Colmes* as representatives of the range of political talk shows on Sunday morning and daily television that are aired on network, public, and cable channels. *Hannity & Colmes* appears in the 2001–2002 sample only, reflecting an overall expansion in the number of television talk shows aired over the period. Television transcripts are much longer than individual newspaper op-eds, so we sampled fewer transcripts than op-eds—selecting fifty days from each period—with the goal of producing a sample size roughly comparable with the newspaper sample, which was evenly balanced between Sunday morning and weekday political talk shows. The basic unit of analysis in the television sample is the speaker-show ($n = 909$), that is, the speech of an individual speaker on a particular episode of a television show (table A.1). At this level, we can compare characteristics like occupation and sex of the speaker and overall length of speech between opinion authors in print and on television.

Television transcripts are more complex than newspaper op-eds, however, because they have multiple opinion authors in conversation speaking on a range of different topics. For this reason, we also coded the television transcripts at a second level, where the unit of analysis is the speaker-segment. There were 374 distinct topical segments from 157 shows, yielding 1,241 speaker-segments. At this level of analysis, we compare differences in rhetoric, styles of argument, claims to authority, language use, and topic choice.

Clustering

A conspicuous feature of our samples is that a small number of individuals appear multiple times, notably professional opinion columnists and talk show hosts. In the newspaper sample, 446 unique authors produce 910 op-eds, and in the television sample, 511 unique speakers produced 909 units of opinion (where the unit of analysis is the speaker-show). We discuss this as a substantive finding in chapter 4, and it is a marked feature of the contemporary space of U.S. opinion.

Repeated measures on the same experimental subject are not a structural feature of our sample design, such as it is for time series data, where, for example, medical information is collected from a single experimental subject over time, or for much linguistic data, which typically take multiple measurements on each experimental subject. By contrast, we sample pieces of opinion in the space of opinion and not individual authors; in other words, the unit of analysis is the piece of opinion and not the person, and any opinion text has an equal probability of being selected, given our random sample of weekdays and Sundays.

Nonetheless, we are concerned that the repeated appearance of particular authors could mean there is less within-group variation for units of opinion with the same author. If this is true, the technical effect would be to artificially inflate our findings of significance. We have investigated this possibility by running significance tests that use much more stringent assumptions for the covariance structure than standard tests, and we have also experimented with down-weighting frequent authors to produce more conservative tests of significance. Our initial exploration confirms our sense that clustering is not driving our findings.

TABLE B.1

ACADEMICS APPEARING MORE THAN ONCE

5 appearances

COLE, David
New York Times (2)
The NewsHour (2)
Face the Nation (1)

3 appearances

ESTRICH, Susan
Hannity & Colmes (3)

GERBER, Robin
The NewsHour (1)
USA Today (2)

WILKINS, Roger
New York Times (1)
The NewsHour (2)

2 appearances

BOND, Julian
New York Times (1)
Crossfire (1)

DIBACCO, Thomas V.
USA Today (2)

FRANK, Robert H.
New York Times (2)

FREEDMAN, Samuel G.
USA Today (2)

FREEMAN, Richard
New York Times (2)

KAPLAN, Martin
USA Today (2)

KENNEDY, Donald
New York Times (2)

REICH, Robert B.
New York Times (2)

SCHUCK, Peter H.
New York Times (2)

SONNENFELD, Jeffrey A.
New York Times (2)

TELHAMI, Shibley
New York Times (2)

TYSON, Laura
New York Times (1)
The NewsHour (1)

WOLFE, Alan
New York Times (2)

ACADEMICS WITH SINGLE APPEARANCE

New York Times

ACKERMAN, Bruce
AMAR, Akhil Reed
ANGELL, Marcia

continued

TABLE B.1. (Continued)

BABCOCK, Barbara A.
BERRY, Mary Frances
BRINKLEY, Alan
CAPLAN, Lincoln
CHA, Victor D.
CHAIT, Richard
CLOUD, Morgan
COHEN, Lizabeth
COHEN, Steven
DELANEY, Paul
DER DERIAN, James
DUNN, Robert M.
EISNER, Robert
ELHAUGE, Einer
ERNSTER, Virginia L.
EWALD, Paul W.
FISH, Stanley
GARTEN, Jeffrey A.
GERGES, Fawaz A.
GILLER, Stephen
GITLIN, Todd
GOLDMAN, Merle
GONZALEZ ECHEVARRIA, Roberto
GOODSON, Larry P.
GOULD, Stephen Jay
GRAETZ, Michael
GRANOF, Michael H.
GREENBERG, Paul E.
HARDING, Courtenay M.
HERKEN, Gregg, and James DAVID
HILL, Anita F.
KASSIN, Saul
KENNEDY, William
LAKE, Anthony
LAYCOCK, Douglas
MCFAUL, Michael
MUSKE-DUKES, Carol
OGLETREE Jr., Charles J.
RAKOVE, Jack
REICH, Walter
ROBERTS, Diane
RYBCZYNSKI, Witold
SCHECK, Barry
SEGAL, Jerome M.
SHAHRANI, Nazif

SIEGEL, Fred
SPIEGEL, David
STARR, Paul
STAUDT, Nancy
TURKLE, Sherry
TYACK, Peter
WALD, Richard C.
WALZER, Michael
WEIL, Patrick
WILSON, James Q.
WOLFF, Larry
YELLEN, Janet
YOSHINO, Kenji

USA Today
BRANSON, Douglas M.
BRYJAK, George J.
ETZIONI, Amitai
GRAY, George
HILLIARD, Constance
HOOKER-HARING, Christopher
INGERSOLL, Richard M.
KUPERMAN, Alan J.
MADSEN, Richard
MCNAMARA, Joseph D.
MEYER, Philip
MITCHELL, Lawrence E.
MYERS, Robert
NATHAN, Richard P.
SCOTT, David F.
THUROW, Lester C.

The NewsHour
AJAMI, Fouad
BAHBAH, Bishara
BERRILL, N. G.
CLARKSON, Stephen
CLEAVER, Kathleen
DJEREJIAN, Edward
DUNKELBERG, William
FRIDAY, Bill
JENIFER, Franklyn
LEGVOLD, Robert
PROTHROW-STITH, Deborah
RUBIN, Barnett
SMITH, Richard Norton
SUDARKASA, Niara

continued

TANNEN, Deborah
WHITE, Ronald
YOW, Deborah
Face the Nation
  BLACK, Merle
  GEARHART, John
  KASS, Leon
  KING, Patricia
  LICHTMAN, Allan

POUSSAINT, Alvin
Crossfire
  HUME, Ellen
  MANDELBAUM, Michael
Hannity & Colmes
  FALK, Richard
  TURLEY, Jonathan
  ZUNES, Stephen

TABLE C.1.

ADVOCATES, LOBBY GROUPS, AND SOCIAL MOVEMENTS

Agent Orange Co-ordinating Council, Veteran's Organization	1
Al Sharpton, civil rights advocate	1
American Atheists	1
American Benefits Council	1
American Civil Liberties Union	3
American Conservative Union	1
American Petroleum Institute	1
American Values	1
Americans for Tax Reform	1
Americans United	1
Amnesty International	1
Anti-Defamation League	1
Arab American Institute	1
Aviation Consumer Action Project	1
Brotherhood Organization of New Destiny	1
Business Council for Sustainable Energy	2
Call to Action	1
Catholic Family and Human Rights Institute	1
Catholics for a Free Choice	1
Center for Consumer Freedom	1
Christian Coalition	1
Coalition for a Democratic Majority	1
Coalition on Urban Renewal and Education (CURE)	1

continued

TABLE C.1. (Continued)

ADVOCATES, LOBBY GROUPS, AND SOCIAL MOVEMENTS

Concerned Women for America	1
Concord Coalition	1
Council for Responsible Nutrition (CRN)	1
Council of 100 A.A. Republicans	1
CROSSROADS	1
Director of Gun Owners of America	1
Eagle Forum	1
Empower America	4
Family Research Council	8
Forum for International Policy	1
Gay & Lesbian Alliance Against Defamation	2
Global Justice Center	1
Healthcare Leadership Council	1
Human Rights Campaign	1
Independent Women's Forum	1
Institute for Science and International Security	1
International Campaign to Ban Land Mines	1
Internews	1
Leadership Conference on Civil Rights	1
N.O.W	1
NAACP	2
National Albanian American Council	1
National Association of Manufacturers	1
National Headstart Association	1
National Nutritional Foods Association (NNFA)	1
National Rifle Association	2
National Right to Life Committee	2
Natural Resources Defense Council	1
Operation Rescue and Missionaries to the Preborn	1
Partners for Peace	1
People for the Ethical Treatment of Animals (PETA)	1
Public Citizen, Inc.	1
Ralph Nader, consumer advocate	2
Regulation	1
Rocky Mountain Institute	1
Simon Wiesenthal Center	1
Survivors Network of Priest Abuse	1
The American Cause	1
The Cuba Policy Foundation	1
Tobacco Institute	1
Traditional Family Values Coalition	3
Utah Gun Violence Prevention Center	1
Wilderness Society	1
World Resources Institute	1

continued

THINK TANKS AND POLICY INSTITUTES

American Enterprise Institute for Public Policy Research	11
Brookings Institution	9
Campaign for Fiscal Equity, Columbia University	1
Carnegie Endowment for International Peace	1
Cato Institute	4
Center for International Policy	1
Center for Strategic and International Studies	5
Center for the Advancement of Public Policy, chair of National Council of Women's Organizations	1
Century Foundation	1
Competitive Enterprise Institute	6
Council on Foreign Relations	4
Economic Policy Institute	1
Economic Strategy Institute	1
Environment Working Group	1
Ethics and Public Policy Center	1
European Institute	1
Federation of American Scientists' Strategic Security Project.	1
Forum for International Policy	1
Freedom House	1
Henry Stimson Center	1
Heritage Foundation	3
Hoover Institution, Stanford University	2
Institute for International Economics	1
International Crisis Group	1
Middle East Forum	2
Middle East Institute	1
National Academy of Social Insurance	1
National Center for Policy Analysis	2
National Council on U.S./Arab Relations.	1
National Women's Law Center	1
New America Foundation	3
Objectivist Center	1
Political Economy Research Center, Montana	1
Privacy Foundation	1
RAND	1
Wisconsin Project on Nuclear Arms Control, University of Wisconsin	1
Woodrow Wilson International Center	1

FOUNDATIONS, PROFESSIONAL, TRADE AND SERVICE ORGANIZATIONS

Aircraft Owners and Pilots Association (AOPA) President	1
American Automobile Association	1
American Federation of Teachers	1

continued

TABLE C.1. (Continued)

FOUNDATIONS, PROFESSIONAL, TRADE AND SERVICE ORGANIZATIONS

American Institute of Certified Public Accountants	1
American Society of Travel Agents	1
Association of International Automobile Manufacturers	1
City Year, private-public community service partnership	1
Corporation for National and Community Service	1
Documentation Center of Cambodia	1
Electric Power Supply Association	1
Greater Park Hill Community Association	1
Health Insurance Association of America	2
Hispanic Scholarship Fund	1
International Brotherhood of Teamsters	2
National Air Transportation Association	1
National Association of Manufacturers	1
National Council on Public Polls, PEW Research Center	2
National Education Association	1
National Wrestling Coaches Association	1
Order Saint Francis HealthCare Board	1
Red Cross	2
Regional Airline Association	1
United Mine Workers	1
Women's Sports Foundation	1
Total	192

CONDITIONS OF SPEECH BY OCCUPATION BY FORMAT

		Median # turns/ speaker/ show	Median turn length	Median total length	*N*
	JOURNALISTIC FIELD				
Talk show hosts	*The NewsHour*	17	29	481.5	84
	Face the Nation	23	30	759	67
	Crossfire	33	36	1,060	89
	Hannity & Colmes	81	24	1,961	38
	Total	**26**	**30**	**826**	**278**
Columnists	*The News Hour*	10	95	930	27
	Face the Nation	6	104	482	11
	Crossfire	44.5	22	1,102	8
	Hannity & Colmes	15	29	632	5
	Total	**10**	**79**	**790**	**51**
Journalists	*The NewsHour*	7	105	827.5	20
	Face the Nation	6	82	485	29
	Crossfire	15	53	827	4
	Hannity & Colmes	11	70	670	9
	Total	**8**	**84**	**612**	**62**

continued

TABLE D.1. (Continued)

		Median # turns/ speaker/ show	Median turn length	Median total length	N
Media Strategists	*The NewsHour*	4.5	134	574	4
	Face the Nation	5.5	81	429	2
	Crossfire	16	33	540	14
	Hannity & Colmes	43	14	625	18
	Total	23	24	578	38
	POLITICAL FIELD				
Elected politicians	*The NewsHour*	7	124	799	35
	Face the Nation	10	82	848.5	76
	Crossfire	21	42	861	39
	Hannity & Colmes	17.5	49	653	24
	Total	10.5	75	807.5	174
Executive branch	*The NewsHour*	7	98	658	30
	Face the Nation	9	94	752	31
	Crossfire	16.5	39	759	12
	Hannity & Colmes	20	35	743	13
	Total	9	80	720	86
Civil Society Orgs	*The NewsHour*	6	112	527	47
	Face the Nation	5	108	527	10
	Crossfire	14	35	652	25
	Hannity & Colmes	21	27	502	20
	Total	8	68	527	102
	ACADEMIC FIELD				
Academics	*The NewsHour*	4.5	113	520.5	22
	Face the Nation	4	118	507	7
	Crossfire	20.5	34	706	2
	Hannity & Colmes	20	23	401	6
	Total	5	102	517	37
Lawyers	*The NewsHour*	10	54	540	3
	Face the Nation	13	49	630	2
	Crossfire	12	52	715	10
	Hannity & Colmes	20	25	650	6
	Total	12	46	641	21
Writers	*The NewsHour*	8	99	697.5	10
	Face the Nation	8	70	727	7
	Crossfire	9	56	607	3
	Hannity & Colmes	24.5	23	592.5	4
	Total	9.5	70	659	24

continued

	OTHERS				
Others	*The NewsHour*	5	86	559	18
	Face the Nation	5	84	474	6
	Crossfire	15	33	529	7
	Hannity & Colmes	15	54	818	7
	Total	6	77	550.5	38
Total	*The NewsHour*	8.5	84	606	300
	Face the Nation	10	68	673	248
	Crossfire	25	38	863	213
	Hannity & Colmes	27	27	704	148
	Total	14	50	706	909

Note: Small cell sizes in some categories make some estimates unstable.

TABLE D.2

FORMAT AND CONDITIONS OF SPEECH, TELEVISION OPINION ON THE BUSH ENERGY PLAN, 2001

		# Turns	Median turn length	Total length[*]
	THE NEWSHOUR			
May 17, 2001	CAVANEY	4	113 words	452 words
	CHURCH	4	108 words	431 words
	HOULIHAN	3	133 words	399 words
	MARVIN	3	168 words	504 words
	RABAGO	3	167 words	501 words
	SUAREZ	21	22 words	472 words
	VERLEGER	3	207 words	622 words
All episodes[**]	MEDIAN	8.5	84 words	606 words
	FACE THE NATION			
May 17, 2001	BORGER	13	26 words	952 words
	BOXER	9	106 words	340 words
	CHENEY	24	95 words	2,276 words
	SCHIEFFER	22	25 words	787 words
All episodes	MEDIAN	10	68 words	673 words
	CROSSFIRE			
May 17, 2001	NOVAK	28	41 words	1,155 words
	PRESS	17	49 words	826 words
	TAUZIN	17	50 words	848 words
	WEXLER	25	38 words	949 words
All episodes	MEDIAN	25	38 words	863 words

continued

TABLE D.1. (Continued)

		# Turns	Median turn length	Total length[*]
			HANNITY & COLMES	
May 17, 2001				
(segment 1)	COLMES	21	34 words	724 words
	HANNITY	28	25 words	693 words
	NOONAN	62	16 words	1,003 words
All episodes	MEDIAN	27	27 words	704 words

[*]Totals for each day are actual totals, not the products of number of turns and median length.
[**] This captures differences between formats that are significant at the .001 level ($n = 909$).

Notes

1. A notable exception is Page (1996, esp. pp. 17–37).

2. Among political scientists and political communication scholars, there is a well-established tradition of research documenting the ways that politicians largely ignore the views and correspondence of "the people," substituting instead their own understanding of public opinion or the public interest, which is based largely on their involvement with journalists, politicians, experts, interest group lobbyists, and other professional communicators (see, for example, Jacobs and Shapiro 2000, Herbst 1998, Jamieson 2001, Entman 2003a).

3. On the agenda-setting power of news media, see Iyengar and Kinder (1987), McCombs and Shaw (1972), and Weaver (2007). More sociological approaches to the question of media and opinion formation tend to stress the mediating role of social networks and social relationships, for example, Katz and Lazarsfeld (1955), Park (1941), and Gamson (1992). For a more recent argument, stressing the continuing importance that public recorded communication (in the form of print and broadcast media) has for democracy, see Schudson (2008, esp. pp. 103–104).

4. As their statement of epistemological position in the 2004 report states: "Our aim is for this to be a research report, not an argument. It is not our intention to try to persuade anyone to a particular point of view. Where the facts are clear, we hope we have not shied from explaining what they reveal, making clear what is proven versus what is only suggested. We hope, however, that we are not seen as simply taking sides in any journalistic debates. . . . We have tried to be as transparent as possible about sources and methods, and to make it clear when we are laying out data versus when we have moved into analysis of that data." The Project for Excellence in Journalism makes a similar statement on their webpage: "The Pew Research Center's Project for Excellence in Journalism is dedicated to trying to understand the information revolution. We

specialize in using empirical methods to evaluate and study the performance of the press, particularly content analysis. We are non partisan, non ideological and non political."

5. The earlier reports, 2004–2006, provide more data in the content sections about the extent and transparency of sources, as well as the proportions of fact versus interpretation or opinion in different formats, than the later reports. The 2007–2010 reports rely on earlier findings about audience fragmentation, speedup, and shallowness of content to make similar claims about changes in news culture, but they focus more on an overall empirical snapshot of news content than the earlier reports. This difference appears to correspond with the movement of the Project for Excellence in Journalism from Columbia University's School of Journalism to the Pew Research Center in Washington, DC, where several other Pew projects are housed.

6. On the competing cultural logics that workers in the cultural industries must navigate—between creative autonomy, organizational hierarchy, and market conditions—see Hesmondhalgh (2007) and Miege (1987).

CHAPTER 2

1. "Times-Discovery Deal," *New York Times*, April 22, 2002, p. C7.

2. The best known example of this is probably Markos Moulitsas, who created the Daily Kos blog in May 2002. As the Daily Kos came to be seen as one of the most influential voices in liberal and Democratic Party politics in the United States, Moulitsas became an increasingly regular presence in other parts of the media, appearing on television and writing op-ed columns for newspapers. In November 2007, Moulitsas began writing a regular column for *Newsweek* magazine.

3. As Starr (2004: 79–80) notes, imprisoning the editors of the Republican newspapers only served to make heroes of them. By the 1800 presidential campaign, there were actually more Republican papers than there had been when the Sedition Act was passed; moreover, the papers had become even more partisan than they had been before.

4. The shift to a one-sided partisan editorial stance was a gradual one. In the first half of the nineteenth century, many newspapers went out of their way to represent both sides of a controversial issue, and contributions to the newspaper were often published anonymously or using pseudonyms (Nerone 1993: 144). It was not until the end of the Jacksonian period and the development of the "second party system" that political party organization and journalistic practices become more closely intertwined (Schudson 1998: 112–116).

5. According to Schudson (1998: 121–122), this began with the Jackson administration, in which fifty-nine journalists received political appointments. Other administrations of the mid-nineteenth century appointed editors as postmasters, Treasury agents, governors of territories, and foreign ambassadors.

6. According to Alterman (1999: 24–25), syndication began in 1846, when the *New York Tribune* and *New York Herald* began using the telegraph to run identical political news stories from Washington. In this, the syndicated political columns differed from most of the other syndicated columns that would soon spring up, the majority of which were devoted to the circulation of fiction and humor (see also Riley 1998).

7. On page 1 of the inaugural issue of the *New York Times*, Raymond announced: "We do not mean to write as if we were in a passion unless that should be the case; and we shall make a point to get into a passion as rarely as possible" (quoted in Alterman 1999: 26).

8. Riley (1998: 79–80) identifies Benjamin Perley Poore as the first political columnist. From 1854 to 1883, Poore wrote a column for the *Boston Journal*, under the heading "Waifs from Washington." Poore wrote this column about three times per week, in addition to regular contributions to *Harper's* and *Atlantic Monthly*. What was different about Poore's status, as compared with the modern columnist, was that (a) he was not syndicated and (b) he was paid by the column instead of drawing a regular salary from the paper.

9. The *New York World* was one of the papers most criticized for sensationalism during the 1890s, when the paper was controlled by Joseph Pulitzer. Indeed, the paper's cartoon "Hogan's Alley" (featuring Mickey Dugan, more popularly known as "The Yellow Kid"), which was the first use of color in the newspaper, was the source of the pejorative label "yellow journalism." Under the editorship of Frank Cobb (1904–1923), however, the paper became one of the most respected and literate newspapers of its time (Emery, Emery, and Roberts 2000: 214–215).

10. As we argue in the next chapter, this is a specifically intellectual strategy of inserting a specialized cadre of experts within an already existing social relationship—in this case, between citizens and government (see, for example, Shenhav 1999; Eyal, Szelenyi, and Townsley 2003).

11. These columns are reprinted in Nevins (1932: 78–91).

12. The first plan, proposed by Senator Robinson, was that $2 billion of tax-exempt bonds would be issued to allow the government to support self-liquidating or profitable activities, such as tunnels, bridges, and the destruction of slums. The second proposal, offered by President Hoover, was similar to Robinson's with the exception that it allowed government loans to be made to private corporations, as well as public entities (such as municipal bodies). The third plan, offered by Senators Wagner and La Follette, proposed that the public works financed by the government should not be limited to self-liquidating projects.

13. Despite the common perception that Lippmann advocated an elite-centered theory of democracy guided by experts, in fact Lippmann had a much subtler and more complex theory about the relationship between expertise and democracy. See Schudson (2008).

14. All were published in the *New York Herald-Tribune* as part of Lippmann's "Today and Tomorrow" columns. They have been reprinted in Rossiter and Lare (1963).

15. In a 1932 speech he gave at Columbia University, published later in the *Atlantic Monthly*, Lippmann expressed great skepticism about the scholar's ability to intervene effectively in the public sphere, arguing that academics would be better served by avoiding any active intervention in public affairs and committing themselves instead to the "invisible empire of reason" (Lippmann, in Rossiter and Lare 1963: 514).

16. The influence of *McClure's* declined rapidly in 1906, when most of the magazine's staff left to join the newly established *American Magazine*, which was also the same year that President Roosevelt—a former supporter of the movement—gave a speech criticizing the muckrakers (Wilson 1970: 168–169). The magazine piled up a large amount of debt and lost readers from that point forward.

17. This is not to suggest that *McClure's* rejected advertising altogether. Between 1895 and 1900, *McClure's* carried more advertising than any other magazine in the world (Wilson 1970: 101). But many corporate leaders advertised in *McClure's* grudgingly and disliked its anticorporate tone. In fact, Walter Lippmann recounted numerous confidential conversations he had with financiers who claimed to have a national effort to suppress the muckraking publications during the first decade of the twentieth century (Wilson 1970: 320).

18. Indeed, while the access to Roosevelt and Wilson secured the *New Republic*'s reputation as the insider's source for liberal political commentary, this access came with strong political pressures to align the magazine's editorial policy according to personal loyalties rather than according to principled positions. Croly vowed never again to fall under the spell of "party politicians" in power, and the *New Republic* became increasingly skeptical of politicians, while emphasizing its commitment to the analysis of public policy (see Seideman 1986: 44–67).

19. David Shaw, "Newspapers Offer Forum to Outsiders," *Los Angeles Times*, October 13, 1975, p. B1.

20. Like many of the early television programs, *See It Now* was an adaptation of a successful radio program. Murrow and Fred Friendly had created *Hear It Now* for CBS Radio in 1950 and began broadcasting the television version of the show in November 1951 (Barnouw 1990: 145; McNeil 1996: 740–741).

21. *Meet the Press* began as a radio program in 1945; originally called *American Mercury Presents: Meet the Press*, the radio program was designed to promote *American Mercury* magazine. The show was first broadcast on television in 1947.

22. *Meet the Boss*, a half-hour interview show profiling American business executives, was broadcast on Dumont from June 1952 until May 1953. *Meet the Champions* was a fifteen-minute program broadcast by NBC on Saturday evenings, which consisted of interviews with athletes. It had a very short run, from July 1956 until January 1957. Slightly more successful was ABC's *Meet the Professor*, which was broadcast intermittently on Sunday afternoons between 1961 and 1969. Most guests were professors of history, the social sciences, and the humanities.

23. Howard Smith was ABC's only regular news commentator, from 1969 to 1978. CBS ended its regular commentaries in 1986, while NBC waited until 1995.

24. The following discussion draws on Alterman 1999, esp. pp. 87–105.

25. Initially, *Nightline* was hosted by Frank Reynolds, one of the anchors for ABC's network news broadcast. Koppel was a substitute for Reynolds during the third week of the broadcast and became the regular host of the show shortly thereafter (McNeil 1996: 8).

26. For a brief period, between 1983 and 1984, *Nightline* was expanded to a sixty-minute program, but it returned to its thirty-minute format in February 1984 (McNeil 1996: 8).

27. For a more extended discussion of the cultural strategies of the most influential news magazine program, *60 Minutes*, as well as a consideration of the influence this program had on the practices of television journalism, see Campbell (1991).

28. John Sununu became a cohost of the show in 1992, after leaving the Bush administration. Mary Matalin became a cohost of the program in 1999, leaving in 2001 to join the new White House staff of George W. Bush. Political consultants James Carville and Paul Begala, who were best known for their work directing the Clinton presidential campaign, became hosts of *Crossfire* in 2002.

29. MSNBC was also launched in 1996, as a joint venture between NBC and Microsoft. Primarily opinion shows and rebroadcasts of NBC News programs, MSNBC struggled to attract viewers. It has been much more successful in recent years, in large part as a result of a conscious decision to increase the number and the prominence of shows that emphasize partisan political commentary.

30. *Crossfire* responded by changing its format, increasing the length of the show to an hour in 2002, and adding a live-audience component to the show. But these changes proved

unsuccessful, and CNN canceled *Crossfire* in 2005. Since then, CNN has continued to lose audience to Fox News and has responded by trying to introduce new shows that were less centered on opinion and commentary, but these format changes have been met with limited success, at best.

31. Lewis Grossberger, "The Rush Hours," *New York Times Sunday Magazine*, December 16, 1990.

32. Of course, television news outlets also established the same type of online presence that newspapers were creating.

33. The following discussion draws from Boczkowski (2005, esp. pp. 60–72).

34. Interestingly, this particular use of the Internet allows American newspapers to more closely resemble the "issue of the day" format that Benson (2012) finds so attractive in the French press, in which a variety of article types (straight reporting, analysis, editorial) are combined to present an in-depth and composite view on a particular issue.

CHAPTER 3

1. Gore also writes of the U.S. Constitution as "the software guiding the operations of a massively parallel system for processing political decisions" (2007: 102).

2. Gore is particularly critical of television since, he argued, it reduces the reflective work of apprehension required by reading texts.

3. These criteria are drawn from Young (2000: 24–26). Other key texts that try to identify the communicative requirements for deliberative democracy include Habermas (1996), Gutmann and Thompson (1996), Fishkin (1995), Bohman (1996), and Benhabib (2002).

4. The most well-established confirmation of the media's power of visibility and influence is the research literature on agenda setting. See Iyengar and Kinder (1987), McCombs (2005), McCombs and Shaw (1972), Weaver (1991), and Scheufele and Tewksbury (2007).

5. The media critics who reference processes most closely connected to those described here are Fallows (1997) and Alterman (1999). Other criticisms are related but refer to slightly different aspects of media practice. For example, Cappella and Jamieson (1997) emphasize the problem of strategic news frames for covering politics, and Patterson (2008) emphasizes the increasingly negative tone of political news.

6. Arguments about competing interest groups and the need for autonomous spaces of deliberation among the different groups emerged as a response and critique to Habermas's (1987, 1989) early theory of the public sphere, most notably in the critique made by Fraser (1992). Habermas (1996) incorporated many of these criticisms in more recent statements of his theory, which we can see most clearly with the publication of *Between Facts and Norms*.

7. This argument is dramatically different from (and implies a critique of) much work in political communication, which has adopted Iyengar's (1994) distinction of episodic versus thematic news frames and a strong normative preference for the thematic over the episodic.

8. By the 1970s, the Chicago/Columbia model of media and society had largely disappeared, presaging the end of a vibrant media sociology. See Jacobs 2009 and Katz 2009.

9. Habermas (1996: 374) describes the contemporary public sphere as differentiated by substantive foci as well as "communicative density, level of organizational complexity and range—from the *episodic* publics found in taverns, coffeehouses or on the streets; through the *occasional* publics or "arranged" publics of particular presentations and events, such as theater performances,

rock concerts, party assemblies, or church congresses; up to the *abstract* public sphere of isolated readers, listeners, and viewers scattered across large geographic areas, or even round the globe, and brought together only through the mass media." Habermas argues that despite its differentiation, various parts of the public sphere are always able to be connected together. Various partial publics are always "porous" to each other, he argues, because one "can always build hermeneutical bridges from one text to the next."

10. See Habermas 1996: 307–308. Importantly, Habermas recognizes that the existence and the advantages of informal publics rely on the existence of constitutional guarantees.

11. See Sobieraj 2011 for an excellent empirical account of how this continual activation of informal publics operates in the world of politics, social movements, and nonprofit organizations. For a discussion of the heightened academic orientation toward the world of media and public intellectuals, see Posner (2001: 61–68), Diamond (1993: 278–279), and Townsley (2006).

12. A more general reason that the abstract individual citizen finds such resonance in popular understandings of media and the public sphere, of course, is that Western intellectual traditions typically elevate the idea of the individual rather than relationships as a way to explain social life (see Walzer 1995). In economics, the individual is a producer or consumer in the market. In politics, the individual is conceptualized as a voter, a soldier, a pensioner, or a taxpayer. In religion and culture, the individual is understood as an embodied soul with unique personhood or distinguishing emblems of identity (Taylor 1992). In intellectual life more specifically, the individual is exemplified in the person of the objective scientist or the artist who hews to truth before all other things. What all these ideas have in common is the sacred quality of the individual, understood both as the fundamental unit of society and the symbol of the social whole (Durkheim 1973; see also Cladis 1992). It is unsurprising, then, that most intellectual traditions draw on the tradition of individualism to inform the conduct of their work and to justify it in broad social terms.

13. In fact, empirically, intellectual projects tend to involve intellectuals as mediators of relationships between individuals and groups. Managers, for example, interpose themselves between capital and labor in the process of rationalizing production and profit (Shenhav 1999; Eyal et al. 2003). Social movement leaders position themselves between the rank and file and powerful state or economic actors in the pursuit of social movement goals (Eyerman 1994). Religious intellectuals, scientists, and experts avow their expertise to solve problems or allay uncertainty, and their audiences are understood as individuals—congregants, patients, clients, customers, patrons (Abbott 1988). Journalists are no exception to this pattern.

14. For a recent statement of this position, see Jones (2009).

15. This is well expressed in professional journalistic ethics from the period. For example: "public enlightenment is the forerunner of justice and the foundation of democracy. The duty of the journalist is to further those ends by seeking truth and providing a fair and comprehensive account of events and issues. Conscientious journalists from all media and specialties strive to serve the public with thoroughness and honesty. Professional integrity is the cornerstone of a journalist's credibility" (Society of Professional Journalists Preamble to the Code of Ethics). The full version of the current code was adopted by the 1996 SPJ National Convention, after months of study and debate among the society's members. Sigma Delta Chi's first Code of Ethics was borrowed from the American Society of Newspaper Editors in 1926. In 1973, Sigma Delta Chi wrote its own code, which was revised in 1984, 1987 and 1996.

CHAPTER 4

1. As Benson (2009, 2012) has argued, Bourdieu tends to focus on market principles as the primary source of heteronomous principles of classification; for a more useful theory of the journalistic field, Benson suggests that attention needs to be paid to how a wider range of political and cultural forces can act as "external" classification principles available to actors within the journalistic field.

2. One of Bourdieu's primary interests is to try to connect the range of cultural distinctions that are deployed in a cultural field to the social-structural resources and backgrounds of the different participants. This is not necessary to leverage the analytical usefulness of the theory of cultural fields however. Indeed, if one is interested in cultural actions that take place at the intersection of multiple fields, the focus on class habitus becomes increasingly difficult to sustain, as evidenced by its relative absence in Bourdieu's work on television (Bourdieu 1998) and journalism (Bourdieu 2005).

3. We can see this in the preference for official sources drawn from the state and political parties (Cook 1998; Gans 1979; Schudson 2003), as well as in the way politicians tend to dominate the guest list of many of the political talk shows on television (Darras 2005).

4. Lexis-Nexis reserves the right to alter or withdraw content in their full-text database at any time, and good historical information on collection strategies for Nexis is not readily available. So although Nexis is a commonly used database for media researchers, it is important to emphasize that Nexis is a business and not accountable to scholarly standards. Our own tests against other archives for the *New York Times*, for example, find that Nexis records are subject to some fluctuation in quality associated with changing archiving conventions over time. Moreover, over the years, some newspapers have withdrawn depositing their content to Nexis, although here, too, norms are changing quickly. In the end, we believe that the Nexis database is comprehensive for the large elite sources we study and that we have effectively sampled opinion for these sources and times.

5. There were 132 newspaper groups listed for the United States by the *Editor and Publisher International Yearbook* (2000), which is the authoritative encyclopedia of the newspaper industry. That number, however, is somewhat misleading, since there are five or six newspaper groups that control a substantial proportion of the newspaper industry, including the flagship papers. These are the Gannett Company Inc., Hearst newspapers, Knight Ridder, the New York Times Co., and the Tribune Company, which together account for 14 percent of national circulation figures. The highest circulation newspaper was *USA Today*, with a daily circulation of 1,671,539, followed by the *New York Times* at 1,078,186. These groups are multimedia conglomerates, with TV, film, radio, and associated media holdings, and they all have at least one but sometimes two or three flagship newspapers. Most of the other groups listed in the yearbook are small regional groups with only two or three newspapers and comparatively tiny circulation figures.

6. This trajectory is also described in Quart (2008: 33), which describes bloggers who "cash in their maverick chits for establishment checks."

7. Media watchdogs like FAIR also collect data on the social characteristics of media intellectuals. See, for example, "Taking the Public Out of Public TV" in *Extra!* November 2010.

8. An opinion author's primary occupation is not always immediately apparent, since many elite figures transit positions across several institutional orders over time. Our occupational coding policy was to (1) choose first authors in the rare case where there was more than

one author, (2) code the primary occupation cited in the byline, or failing that (3) to identify the exact institutional location of the opinion author at the time they wrote the column or appeared on a television show.

9.   While professional columnists clearly dominate, notice that reportorial journalists are also particularly well represented in the opinion pages (12 percent of all newspaper op-eds and 6.6 percent of sampled television opinion). These authors tend to claim their authority to speak on the basis of their experience reporting on domestic affairs or working as foreign correspondents. Indeed, the correspondent's role has always implied the work of interpreting the context of remote places for domestic or local publics. And all this, too, is unsurprising; journalists are an attractive talent pool internal to the field of journalistic production, disciplined by the professional norms of journalism and familiar with the working operations of media institutions.

10.   William Safire single-handedly produced more than 6 percent of all the op-eds in our newspaper sample! (57/910) = 6.3 percent.

11.   *Crossfire* aired for sixty minutes for a brief time (from Spring 2002 to February 2003) but was basically a thirty-minute show for most of its run.

12.   The average number of speakers per show increased from between 5 and 6 to 7 per show between 1993–1994 and 2001–2002, the median number of turns per show decreased from around 14 to 13.5, and median turn length dropped overall from about from 53 to 46 words per turn on average. So while there was an expansion of people speaking opinion in the television opinion space, the conditions in which that opinion was spoken had changed somewhat. We return to this point in the following chapter.

13.   There are twenty-eight foreign politicians in our sample, most of whom appear once in our sample. Four appear twice: Nasser Al-Kidwa, Palestinian observer at the United Nations; Kofi Annan, secretary-general of the United Nations; Shimon Peres, Israeli foreign minister; and Nabil Shaath, Palestinian cabinet minister.

CHAPTER 5

1.   For a more extended analysis of the evolution of the fake news genre and its relationship to more traditional news formats, see Baym (2005, 2009).

2.   Unless otherwise indicated, all averages are medians, which discount the impact of outliers.

3.   These were, specifically, a brief discussion with Governor Gray Davis of California asking for some kind of temporary price relief in the California energy crisis, and a segment from a prerecorded interview between Sean Hannity and Robert Kennedy Jr. on the environment, especially drilling in the Alaska National Wildlife Refuge, that was not directly connected to the discussion of the Bush energy plan for that day.

4.   *Crossfire* hosts in our sample are Bob Beckel, Paul Begala, Patrick Buchanan, Tucker Carlson, James Carville, Michael Kinsley, Dee Dee Myers, Robert Novak, Bill Press, John Sununu, Jake Tapper, and Juan Williams.

CHAPTER 6

1.   As the opinion space as a whole expanded between our sample periods, 1993–1994 and 2001–2002, so did the number of distinct segments on each show (appendix A). Only 30 percent (47/157) of the shows in our sample were single segment shows, and most of them were

concentrated in the first sample period. Figure 6.9 depicts the proportion of all opinion spoken by segment number and period. It documents very clearly that in the 1993–1994 sample period, two thirds of all opinion (63.3 percent) was spoken in the first segment of a show, with the remaining third spread over the second and third segments of shows. By the early 2000s, in contrast, only a third of all opinion (36.6 percent) was spoken on the first segment of a show, almost another third was spoken on a second segment (29.9 percent), and the remaining third was spread over third, fourth, fifth, and even sixth segments of shows. This trend was associated with speedup on shows, with more speakers in fewer conversational turns attempting to attract an increasingly scarce share of the attention on each show. A high number of segments characterized *Face the Nation, Crossfire,* and *Hannity & Colmes* but did not occur to the same extent on *The NewsHour*, where more than half the shows were single-segment shows. *The NewsHour* is not a pure opinion show, of course: it offers news before it offers commentary. On the other shows, however, there was a proliferation of segments over time. Many of the new segments were filled by extended banter between the hosts, who emerged increasingly as the main characters of the show.

2. Concurrence (intercoder reliability) was acceptably high. We ran no formal tests but kept a rough tally as we read and found we agreed approximately three quarters of the time.

3. Initially, we tried to develop complex overlapping categories for opinion style. We stopped when we realized that all of our opinion texts at some level contained elements of all of the opinion styles. Coding texts is challenging because they are polysemous and endlessly open to interpretation. In the end, we made the pragmatic choice to develop a variable to capture *primary* opinion style.

4. While most authors write for the "ideal reader" they have imagined, Eco (1998) argues that effective writers also have strategies for directing the empirical reader in the direction of the ideal reader. Authors can cue empirical readers to adopt particular points of view in the text and to place themselves in particular subject positions in the story.

5. The use of providing information styles also increased slightly over time, but this was largely the result of the influx of outsiders in the opinion space, particularly academics, who are more likely than other speakers to use a self-consciously neutral rhetorical form. Changes in the distribution of opinion styles across time were not statistically significant for any style in any format.

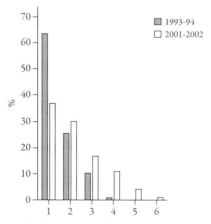

Figure 6.9 Percent of opinion spoken, by segment and period.

6. Note, however, that there were some changes at *The NewsHour* and *Face the Nation* between sample periods. While there was no significant difference in the likelihood that opinion texts would address political insiders or general citizens at the newspapers or on the newer television shows, at *The NewsHour*, there was a decline in the likelihood of addressing general citizens between 1993–1994 and 2001–2002, from 67 to 56 percent, while at *Face the Nation*, there was an increase in the likelihood that opinion speakers would address general citizens, from 48.3 to 66.7 percent. This shift at *Face the Nation* is associated with the addition of Gloria Borger as a host and the consequent increase in the incidence of the asking questions style of opinion, which is heavily associated with speaking to general publics rather than political insiders. See the later discussion.

7. Clayman and Heritage describe the collaborative performance of journalistic neutralism: "A shadowy presence often inhabits the exchanges between interviewers and interviewees. This presence—a third party conjured up by interviewers and oriented to by interviewees—plays an important role in the process by which questions are rendered defensible and a semblance of journalistic professionalism is maintained. Because this third party is cast as primarily responsible for interviewers' more contentious remarks, interviewers are able to express such views while preserving a posture of formal neutrality" (Clayman and Heritage 2002: 187).

8. One exception here is the high incidence of reframing styles among media strategists—who are generally less autonomous speakers in the space of opinion—a finding that suggests that reframing may also serve strategic interests as they attempt to change the terms of the discussion.

9. These differences are also probably associated with the higher proportion of media strategists at the newer television shows. See note 8. The important point is that the differences between television and print are much more substantial than the small differences among the television shows.

10. To be sure, when the most autonomous speakers from the print spaces appear in the television formats and use reframing styles to convey their opinions, then this largely print-based opinion style does find expression on television. And it is true that columnists, journalists, and academics are more likely to appear on *The NewsHour* and *Face the Nation* than on *Crossfire* and *Hannity & Colmes*. But the number of these more autonomous speakers appearing on television remains low.

11. Note, too, that in addition to a decline in the use of scientific discourse in the television formats, there was an associated change in the relationship between the use of scientific discourse and the type of audience addressed in an opinion text. In 1993–1994, there was no significant difference in the use of scientific language associated with the audience addressed by an opinion text; that is, in our first sample period, 53 percent of opinion that addressed political insiders compared with 56 percent of opinion that addressed general citizens used scientific discourse. By our second sample period, however, this relationship had changed considerably. Opinion addressed to the general citizenry was much less likely to contain scientific claims to authority (42.2 percent) than opinion addressed to political insiders (57 percent).

12. There is no significant association between any other direct or indirect authority claim and the likelihood of reframing.

13. Even in the *New York Times*, where the use of historical forms of discourse is the highest, opinion texts that are presented rhetorically as occurring entirely in the present still constitute 34 percent of all columns, and they are 45 percent of all columns at *USA Today*.

14. Overall, 40 percent of our sample made some reference to other media sources as a way to contextualize or support an opinion. This includes 27.7 percent of segments in our sample where authors referred in a *general* way to other media by using words like *media* (8.6 percent), *television* (7.8 percent), *tv* (6 percent), *newspaper* (4.8 percent), *magazine* (4.3 percent), *movie* (3.3 percent), *radio* (3.8 percent), *film* (2 percent), *Internet* (1.5 percent), and *Web* (1.8 percent).

15. The top papers mentioned were the *New York Times* 10.4 percent (92 references), the *Washington Post* 5.8 percent (51 references), the *Wall Street Journal* 2.8 percent (26 references), the *Los Angeles Times* 1.4 percent (12 references), and *USA Today* 1.1 percent (10 references). These print publications are central to the political public sphere. The top television news shows were *CBS News* 4.3 percent (38 references), *Fox News* 4.1 percent (36 references), *CNN* 3.8 percent (34 references), and *Inside Edition* 1.1 percent (10 references). The top print news-magazines referenced were *Time* 2.3 percent (20 references) and *Newsweek* 2.1 percent (19 references).

16. Newspapers tend to rely on scientific and historical discourse, with the use of extended historical discourse tending to be concentrated in the *New York Times*. Both television and print formats exhibit the frequent use of direct authority claims, though we see these more frequently in newspapers. Television discussion programs operate in a more intertextual environment, where the use of indirect authority claims is much more likely to draw on specific media references, especially print references. This again underlines the connections between formats in different parts of the journalistic field, and to the degree that the incidence of intertextual referencing has been growing over time—and there is evidence that it has—then this suggests that the space of opinion is becoming increasingly self-referential, claiming authority on its own account without relying on academic or other sources of authority.

17. In broad terms, the most autonomous speakers and formats in the space of opinion are also the most likely to be associated with scientific and historical claims of authority, which invoke universal criteria of validity for their arguments, address broad publics of general citizens, and are associated with either the potential innovation of reframing or the providing information styles of traditional objective professional journalism. Importantly, too, at the level of opinion styles, we find the older television formats at *The NewsHour* and *Face the Nation* play an important role in anchoring television opinion in the traditions of professional journalism.

18. An analysis of characters is beyond the present scope of our study but is clearly an important, and probably an increasingly important, narrative feature of the space of opinion.

CHAPTER 7

1. See, for example, Hart (2003), Amann and Breuer (2007), and Alterman (2003).

2. Robinson (2002) makes much the same point about media coverage of the 1999 air campaign in Kosovo.

3. Crowley, who has a PhD in international affairs from Columbia University, worked as a foreign policy assistant to former President Richard Nixon between 1990 and 1994 and wrote two popular books about Nixon. She joined Fox News as a political analyst in 1996 and is a regular newspaper columnist and television pundit.

4. On the prevalence of horse race coverage and political strategy frames in political journalism, see Ansolabehere, Behr, and Iyengar (1993: 57–65); Hallin (1994: 144–152); and Cappella and Jamieson (1997: 29–37).

CHAPTER 8

1. See, for example, two columns written by Samuel Freedman, a Columbia University journalism professor, on September 13, 2001, p. A13, and October 8, 2001, p. A17.

2. See, for example, columnist Dewayne Wickham's warnings about overreacting to the anthrax scare (*USA Today*, November 7, 2001, p. A15).

3. There was, however, one column written by Martin Kaplan, a media scholar at the University of Southern California, that used a form of cultural irony to tell a story about the "end of normalcy" that September 11 represented for a postmodern America. Kaplan's column ends with the following juxtaposition between fundamentalism and postmodern secularism:

> Fundamentalist cultures hold durable notions about the Evil One. Their grand narratives include cataclysmic conflict, followed by eternal bliss. But our postmodern condition, it is said, deprives us of grand narratives.
>
> All we have is Harry Potter, whose ultimate victory over Lord Voldemort is the bet that parents place when they buy J. K. Rowling's books for their kids. Even without knowing the ending of the seventh volume of the Harry series, we are prepared to bet that it will be happy; its control lies not in the fates, but in its author's hands, and in her readers' confident assumption that Harry's story will not turn out to be tragic.
>
> Who today is as confident about the epic we call real life? (*USA Today*, November 29, 2001, p. A17)

4. See, for example, the column written by Alan Kuperman (a political scientist at the University of Southern California) that identifies Stinger missiles as the most dangerous threat to commercial airplanes and traces the diffusion of these missiles to U.S. policy toward Afghanistan during the 1980s (*USA Today*, November 14, 2001, p. A17).

5. *USA Today*, October 8, 2001, p. A17.

6. Etzioni has also worked as a guest scholar at the Brookings Institution and held the position of senior advisor to the White House on domestic affairs from 1979 to 1980.

7. See, for example, columns by Tony Mauro (*USA Today*, October 2, 2001, p. A13) and DeWayne Wickham (*USA Today*, November 27, 2001, p. A15).

8. A similar formula was used by columnist Anthony Lewis, replacing the legal interpretation and the legal experts with political ones. See *New York Times*, January 26, 2002, p. A15.

9. Similar arguments were made in Friedman's *New York Times* columns from September 13, 2001, p. A27; December 2, 2001, section 4, p. 15; January 23, 2002, p. A19; March 10, 2002, section 4, p. 19.

10. Similar arguments were made in Friedman's *New York Times* columns from September 13, 2001, p. A27; March 31, 2002, section 4, p. 9.

11. Similar arguments were made in Friedman's *New York Times* columns from September 13, 2001, p. A27; September 21, 2001, p. A35; October 2, 2001, p. A25; November 27, 2001, p. A19; February 20, 2002, p. A21. Also see the column by Nicholas Kristof, November 1, 2002, A31.

12. *New York Times*, October 14, 2001, p. D13.

13. This argument was also made pointedly by columnist Nicholas Kristof, who criticized the Bush administration in the aftermath of the Afghanistan invasion for its failure to send

American diplomats and for its unwillingness to send financial assistance or personnel to help rebuild Afghanistan. See *New York Times*, December 7, 2001, p. A31.

14. We thank one of our anonymous reviewers for contributing this valuable insight.

15. The invocation of a "sacred evil," of which Hitler is perhaps the most frequently and highly charged example, has the effect of heightening the symbolic division of the world into the binary polarization between pure and impure and charging the distinction with an extra measure of emotional and moral intensity. As such, it is never presented as part of a "rational argument" but is always part of a moral discourse; it relies on the power of a past cultural trauma to limit the range of effective symbolic action on the part of the different participants in a representational space. See Alexander (2006, esp. pp. 503–523). Still, the invocation of a sacred evil does not always produce its desired effect; there is always an element of contingency and liminality, as Smith's (2008) work on punishment shows so convincingly.

16. See, for example, the discussion about the Department of Homeland Security, *Hannity & Colmes*, June 6, 2002.

17. It is interesting that the high-mimetic narrative was more dominant in the *New York Times* than it was on *Crossfire*, where there were many more arguments made against intervention. This finding contradicts the "CNN effect," which posited that the rise of cable news was having the effect of encouraging hasty and ill-conceived military intervention in cases of humanitarian crisis. For a defense of the CNN effect, see Minear, Scott, and Weiss (1996). For an empirical and theoretical critique of the CNN effect, see Robinson (2002).

18. William Bennett, on *Hannity & Colmes*, October 15, 2002.

CHAPTER 9

1. Olbermann was replaced by Lawrence O'Donnell, a former aide to Senator Daniel Patrick Moynihan, a producer and writer for the critically acclaimed television show *The West Wing*, and a frequent visitor and guest host for Olbermann's show. O'Donnell, who had held the 10 PM slot for MSNBC since September 2010, was replaced by Ed Schultz, a well-known liberal talk radio host who had been hired by MSNBC in 2009 to fill its 6 PM time slot.

References

Abbott, Andrew. 1988. *The System of Professions: An Essay on the Division of Expert Labor.* Chicago: University of Chicago Press.

Aday, Sean, Steven Livingston, and Maeve Hebert. 2005. "Embedding the Truth: A Cross-Cultural Analysis of Objectivity and Television Coverage of the Iraq War." *Harvard International Journal of Press/Politics* 10(1): 3–21.

Alexander, Jeffrey C. 1988. *Action and Its Environments.* New York: Columbia University Press.

Alexander, Jeffrey C. 2006. *The Civil Sphere.* Oxford: Oxford University Press.

Alexander, Jeffrey C. 2010. *The Performance of Politics: Obama's Victory and the Democratic Struggle for Power.* New York: Oxford University Press.

Allen, Frederick L. 1922. "Newspapers and the Truth." *Atlantic* 29: 44–55.

Alterman, Eric. 1999. *Sound and Fury: The Making of the American Punditocracy.* Ithaca, NY: Cornell University Press.

Alterman, Eric. 2003. *What Liberal Media? The Truth about Bias and the News.* New York: Basic Books.

Amann, Joseph, and Tom Breuer. 2007. *Fair and Balanced, My Ass! An Unbridled Look at the Bizarre Reality of Fox News.* New York: Nation.

Ansolabehere, Stephen, Roy Behr, and Shanto Iyengar. 1993. *The Media Game: American Politics in the Television Age.* New York: Macmillan.

Apter, David. 2006. "Politics as Theater: An Alternative View of the Rationalities of Power." Pp. 218–256 in *Social Performance: Symbolic Action, Cultural Pragmatics, and Ritual.* Edited by J. Alexander, B. Giesen, and J. Mast. Cambridge: Cambridge University Press.

Arendt, Hannah. 1967. "Truth and Politics." Pp. 104–113 in *Philosophy, Politics and Society.* Edited by Peter Laslett and W. C. Runciman. Oxford: Oxford University Press.

Aron, Raymond. 1959. "The Columnist as Teacher and Historian." Pp. 111–125 in *Walter Lippmann and His Times*. Edited by M. Childs and J. Reston. New York: Harcourt, Brace.

Baker, C. Edwin. 2002. *Media, Markets, and Democracy*. Cambridge: Cambridge University Press.

Barber, Benjamin. 1984. *Strong Democracy*. Berkeley: University of California Press.

Barnouw, Erik. 1990. *Tube of Plenty: The Evolution of American Television*. 2nd ed. New York: Oxford University Press.

Baum, Matthew. 2003. *Soft News Goes to War: Public Opinion and American Foreign Policy in the New Media Age*. Princeton, NJ: Princeton University Press.

Baum, Matthew, and Tim Groeling. 2008. "New Media and the Polarization of American Political Discourse." *Political Communication* 25(4): 345–365.

Bauman, Zygmunt. 2003. *Liquid Love: On the Frailty of Human Bonds*. Cambridge: Polity.

Baym, Geoffrey. 2005. "The Daily Show: Discursive Integration and the Reinvention of Political Journalism." *Political Communication* 22: 259–276.

Baym, Geoffrey. 2009. *From Cronkite to Colbert: The Evolution of Broadcast News*. Boulder, CO: Paradigm.

Bender, Thomas. 1997. *Intellect and Public Life: Essays on the Social History of Academic Intellectuals in the United States*. Baltimore: Johns Hopkins University Press.

Bendix, Reinhard. 1980. *Kings or People: Power and the Mandate to Rule*. Berkeley: University of California Press.

Benhabib, Seyla. 2002. *The Claims of Culture*. Princeton, NJ: Princeton University Press.

Bennett, W. Lance, Regina Lawrence, and Steven Livingston. 2007. *When the Press Fails: Political Power and the News Media from Iraq to Katrina*. Chicago: University of Chicago Press.

Bennett, W. Lance, 1990. "Toward a Theory of Press-State Relations in the U.S.", *Journal of Communication* 40(2): 103–125.

Benson, Rodney. 2005. "Mapping Field Variation: Journalism in France and the United States." Pp. 85–112 in *Bourdieu and the Journalistic Field*. Edited by Rodney Benson and Erik Neveu. Cambridge: Polity.

Benson, Rodney. 2007. "Bringing the Sociology of Media Back In." *Political Communication* 21(3): 275–292.

Benson, Rodney. 2009. "Shaping the Public Sphere: Habermas and Beyond." *American Sociologist* 40(3): 175–197.

Benson, Rodney. 2012. *Framing Immigration: How the French and American Media Shape Public Debate*. Cambridge: Cambridge University Press.

Benson, Rodney, and Erik Neveu. Eds. 2005. *Bourdieu and the Journalistic Field*. Cambridge: Polity.

Bernhard, Nancy E. 1999. *U.S. Television News and Cold War Propaganda, 1947–1960*. Cambridge: Cambridge University Press.

Bielby, Denise, and C. Lee Harrington. 2008. *Global TV: Exporting Television and Culture in the World Market*. New York: New York University Press.

Blumer, Herbert. 1948. "Public Opinion and Public Opinion Polling." *American Sociological Review* 13(5): 542–549.

Boczkowski, Pablo B. 2005. *Digitizing the News*. Cambridge, MA: MIT Press.

Boddy, William. 1990. *Fifties Television: The Industry and Its Critics*. Urbana: University of Illinois Press.

Bogart, Leo. 1955. "Adult Talk about Newspaper Comics." *American Journal of Sociology* 61(1): 26–30.

Bohman, James. 1996. *Public Deliberation: Pluralism, Complexity, and Democracy*. Cambridge, MA: MIT Press.

Bourdieu, Pierre. 1990. *In Other Words: Essays towards a Reflexive Sociology*. Stanford, CA: Stanford University Press.

Bourdieu, Pierre, 1991. "Universal Corporatism: The Role of Intellectuals in the Modern World." *Poetics Today* 12, 14: 655–669.

Bourdieu, Pierre. 1993. *The Field of Cultural Production*. New York: Columbia University Press.

Bourdieu, Pierre. [1994] 2005. "Political, Social Science, and Journalistic Fields." Pp. 29–47 in *Bourdieu and the Journalistic Field*. Edited by Rodney Benson and Erik Neveu. Cambridge: Polity.

Bourdieu, Pierre. 1998. *On Television*. New York: New Press.

Bowden, Mark. 2008. "Mr. Murdoch Goes to War." *Atlantic* 301(1): 106–114.

Burawoy, Michael. 2005. "2004 Presidential Address: For Public Sociology." *American Sociological Review* 70(1): 4–28.

Burroughs, Benjamin. 2007. "Kissing Macaca: Blogs, Narrative and Political Discourse." *Journal for Cultural Research* 11(4): 319–335.

Campbell, Richard. 1991. *60 Minutes and the News: A Mythology for Middle America*. Urbana: University of Illinois Press.

Campbell, W. Joseph. 2006. *The Year That Defined American Journalism*. New York. Routledge.

Cappella, Joseph, and Kathleen Hall Jamieson. 1997. *Spiral of Cynicism: The Press and the Public Good*. New York: Oxford University Press.

Chalaby, Jean. 1998. *The Invention of Journalism*. New York: St. Martin's Press.

Cladis, Mark S. 1992. *A Communitarian Defense of Liberalism*. Stanford, CA: Stanford University Press.

Clayman, Steven E., and John Heritage. 2002. *The News Interview: Journalists and Public Figures on the Air*. Cambridge: Cambridge University Press.

Clayman, Steven E., John Heritage, Marc N. Elliott, and Laurie L. McDonald. 2007. "When Does the Watchdog Bark: Conditions of Aggressive Questioning in Presidential News Conferences." *American Sociological Review* 72(1): 23–41

Cohen, Jean, and Andrew Arato. 1992. *Civil Society and Political Theory*. Cambridge, MA: MIT Press.

Cook, Timothy. 1998. *Governing with the News: The News Media as a Political Institution*. Chicago: University of Chicago Press.

Cottle, Simon. 2003. *Media Organization and Production*. Thousand Oaks, CA: Sage.

Cottle, Simon. 2006. *Mediatized Conflict*. New York: Open University Press.

Dahl, Robert. 2000. *On Democracy*. New Haven, CT: Yale University Press.

Dahlgren, Peter. 2005. "The Internet, Public Spheres, and Political Communication: Dispersion and Deliberation." *Political Communication* 22(2): 147–162.

Darras, Eric. 2005. "Media Consecration of the Political Order." Pp. 156–173 in *Bourdieu and the Journalistic Field*. Edited by Rodeny Benson and Erik Neveu. Cambridge: Polity.

Davis, Richard. 2009. *Typing Politics: The Role of Blogs in American Politics*. Oxford: Oxford University Press.

Dayan, Daniel, and Elihu Katz. 1992. *Media Events: The Live Broadcasting of History*. Cambridge, MA: Harvard University Press.

Delli Carpini, Michael, and Bruce Williams. 2001. "Let Us Infotain You: Politics in the New Media Environment." Pp. 160–181 in *Mediated Politics*. Edited by W. Lance Bennett and Robert Entman. Cambridge: Cambridge University Press.

Dewey, John. [1927] 1991. *The Public and Its Problems*. Athens, OH: Swallow.

Diamond, Edwin. 1993. *Behind the Times: Inside the New New York Times*. New York: Villard.

Doherty, Thomas. 2003. *Cold War, Cool Medium: Television, McCarthyism, and American Culture*. New York: Columbia University Press.

Douglas, Paul. 1964. "Remarks on the Occasion of This Journal's 50th Year." *New Republic* 150: 16–17.

Durkheim. Emile. 1973. *Emile Durkheim on Morality and Society*. Edited by Robert N. Bellah. Chicago: University of Chicago Press.

Eco, Umberto. 1998. *Six Walks in the Fictional Woods*. Cambridge, MA: Harvard University Press.

Eliasoph, Nina. 2007. "Beyond the Politics of Denunciation: Cultural Sociology as the 'Sociology of the Meantime.'" Pp. 55–100 in *Culture, Society, and Democracy*. Edited by Isaac Reed and Jeffrey Alexander. Boulder, CO: Paradigm.

Emery, Michael, Edwin Emery, and Nancy Roberts. 2000. *The Press and America: An Interpretive History of the Mass Media*. Boston: Allyn and Bacon.

Entman, Robert. 2003a. *Projections of Power: Framing News, Public Opinion, and U.S. Foreign Policy*. Chicago: University of Chicago Press.

Entman, Robert. 2003b. "Cascading Activation: Contesting the White House's Frame after 9/11." *Political Communication* 20(4): 415–432.

Ericson, Richard, Patricia Baranek, and Janet Chan. 1989. *Negotiating Control: A Study of News Sources*. Toronto, ON: University of Toronto Press.

Ettema, James. 2007. "Journalism as Reason-Giving: Deliberative Democracy, Institutional Accountability, and the News Media's Mission." *Political Communication* 24(2): 143–160.

Eyal, Gil, Ivan Szelenyi, and Eleanor Townsley. 2003. "On Irony: An Invitation to Neoclassical Sociology." *Thesis Eleven* 73(May): 5–41.

Eyerman, Ron. 1994. *Between Culture and Politics: Intellectuals in Modern Society*. Cambridge: Polity.

Eyerman, Ron. 2006. "Performing Opposition or, How Social Movements Move." Pp. 193–217 in *Social Performance: Symbolic Action, Cultural Pragmatics, and Ritual*. Edited by Jeffrey Alexander, Bernhard Giesen, and Jason Mast. Cambridge: Cambridge University Press.

Eyerman, Ron. 2008. *The Assassination of Theo van Gogh: From Social Drama to Cultural Trauma*. Durham, NC: Duke University Press.

Fallows, James. 1997. *Breaking the News: How the Media Undermine American Democracy*. New York: Vintage.

Ferber, Reginald. 1995. "Is Speakers' Gender Discernible in Transcribed Speech?" *Sex Roles* 32(3–4): 209–223.

Ferree, Myra Marx, William A. Gamson, Jurgen Gerhards, and Dieter Rucht. 2002. "Four Models of the Public Sphere in Modern Democracies." *Theory and Society* 31(3): 289–324.

Fishkin, James. 1995. *The Voice of the People*. New Haven, CT: Yale University Press.

Fishman, Mark. 1980. *Manufacturing the News*. Austin: University of Texas Press.

Fiske, John. 1987. *Television Culture*. New York: Routledge.

Foucault, Michel. 1980. *Power/Knowledge: Selected Interviews and Other Writings 1972–1977*. Edited by Colin Gordon. New York: Pantheon.

Fraser, Nancy. 1992. "Rethinking the Public Sphere: A Contribution to the Critique of Actually Existing Democracy." Pp. 109–142 in *Habermas and the Public Sphere*. Edited by Craig Calhoun. Cambridge, MA: MIT Press.

Freidson, Eliot. 1953. "Communications Research and the Concept of the Mass." *American Sociological Review* 18(3): 313–317.

Friel, Howard, and Richard Falk. 2004. *The Record of the Paper: How the New York Times Misreports U.S. Foreign Policy*. London: Verso.

Gamson, William. 1992. *Talking Politics*. Cambridge: Cambridge University Press.

Gans, Herbert. 1979. *Deciding What's News*. New York: Vintage.

Glasser, Theodore, and Stephanie Craft. 1998. "Public Journalism and the Search for Democratic Ideals." Pp. 203–218 in *Media, Ritual and Identity*. Edited by James Curran and Tamar Liebes. New York: Routledge.

Glynn, Kevin. 2000. *Tabloid Culture*. Durham, NC: Duke University Press.

Goldfarb, Jeffrey. 2005. "The Autonomy of Culture and the Invention of the Politics of Small Things: 1968 Revisited." Pp. 428–443 in *The Blackwell Companion to the Sociology of Culture*. Edited by Mark Jacobs and Nancy Hanrahan. Malden, MA: Blackwell.

Gordon, Lynn D. 1994. "Why Dorothy Thompson Lost Her Job: Political Columnists and the Press Wars of the 1930s and 1940s." *History of Education Quarterly* 34(3): 280–303.

Gore, Al. 2007. *The Assault on Reason*. New York: Penguin.

Gould, Lewis. Ed. 2002. *Watching Television Come of Age: New York Times Reviews, by Jack Gould*. Austin: University of Texas Press.

Gouldner, Alvin. 1979. *The Future of Intellectuals and the Rise of the New Class*. New York: Continuum.

Gurevitch, M., and J. Blumler. 1990. "Political Communication Systems and Democratic Values." Pp. 269–280 in *Democracy and the Mass Media*. Edited by Judith Lichtenberg. Cambridge: Cambridge University Press.

Gutmann, Amy, and Dennis Thompson. 1996. *Democracy and Disagreement*. Cambridge, MA: Harvard University Press.

Habermas, Jurgen. [1962] 1989. *The Structural Transformation of the Public Sphere*. Translated by Thomas Burger. Cambridge MA: MIT Press.

Habermas, Jurgen. 1985. *The Theory of Communicative Action, Volume 1: Reason and the Rationalization of Society*. Translated by Thomas McCarthy. Boston: Beacon.

Habermas, Jurgen, 1987. *The Theory of Communicative Action, Volume 2: Lifeworld and System: A Critique of Functionalist Reason. Translated by Thomas McCarthy*. Boston: Beacon.

Habermas, Jurgen. 1996. *Between Facts and Norms: Contributions to a Discourse Theory of Law and Democracy*. Cambridge, MA: MIT Press.

Hallin, Daniel. 1992. "The Passing of the 'High Modernism' of American Journalism." *Journal of Communication* 42(3): 14–25.

Hallin, Daniel. 1994. *We Keep America on Top of the World: Television, Journalism and the Public Sphere*. New York: Routledge.

Hart, Peter. 2003. *The Oh Really? Factor: Unspinning Fox News Channel's Bill O'Reilly*. New York: Seven Stories.

Hartley, John. 2001. "The Infotainment Debate." Pp. 118–122 in *The Television Genre Book*. Edited by G. Creeber. London: BFI.

Hayes, Arthur S. 2008. *Press Critics Are the Fifth Estate*. Westport, CT: Praeger.

Held, David. 2005. *Models of Democracy*. 3rd ed. Malden, MA: Blackwell.

Herbst, Susan. 1998. *Reading Public Opinion: How Political Actors View the Democratic Process*. Chicago: University of Chicago Press.

Hesmondhalgh, David. 2007. *The Cultural Industries*. 2nd ed. Thousand Oaks, CA: Sage.

Iyengar, Shanto. 1994. *Is Anyone Responsible? How Television Frames Political Issues*. Chicago: University of Chicago Press.

Iyengar, Shanto, and Donald Kinder. 1987. *News That Matters: Agenda-Setting and Priming in a Television Age*. Chicago: University of Chicago Press.

Jacobs, Lawrence, and Robert Shapiro. 2000. *Politicians Don't Pander: Political Manipulation and the Loss of Democratic Responsiveness*. Chicago: University of Chicago Press.

Jacobs, Ronald N. 1996. "Civil Society and Crisis: Culture, Discourse and the Rodney King Beating." *American Journal of Sociology* 101(5): 1238–1272.

Jacobs, Ronald N. 2000. *Race, Media, and the Crisis of Civil Society: From Watts to Rodney King*. New York: Cambridge University Press.

Jacobs, Ronald N. 2003. "Toward a Political Sociology of Civil Society." *Research in Political Sociology* 12: 19–47.

Jacobs, Ronald N. 2004. "Bauman's New World Order." *Thesis Eleven* 79: 128–137.

Jacobs, Ronald N. 2005. "Media Culture(s) and Public Life." Pp. 80–96 in *The Blackwell Companion to the Sociology of Culture*. Edited by M. Jacobs and N. Hanrahan. Cambridge, MA: Blackwell.

Jacobs, Ronald N. 2007. "From Mass to Public: Rethinking the Value of the Culture Industry." Pp. 101–128 in *Culture in the World, Volume 1: Cultural Sociology and the Democratic Imperative*. Edited by Jeffrey Alexander and Isaac Reed. Boulder, CO: Paradigm.

Jacobs, Ronald N. 2009. "Culture, the Public Sphere, and Media Sociology: A Search for a Classical Founder in the Work of Robert Park." *American Sociologist* 40(3): 149–166.

Jacobs, Ronald N. 2011. "Entertainment Media and the Aesthetic Public Sphere." in *Oxford Handbook of Cultural Sociology*. Edited by Jeffrey Alexander, Ronald Jacobs, and Philip Smith. New York: Oxford University Press.

Jacobs, Ronald N., and Sarah Sobieraj. 2007. "Narrative and Legitimacy: U.S. Congressional Debates about the Nonprofit Sector." *Sociological Theory* 25(1): 1–25.

Jacoby, Russell. 1987. *The Last Intellectuals: American Culture in an Age of Academe*. New York: Basic Books.

Jamieson, Kathleen H. 2001. "Issue Advocacy in a Changing Discourse Environment." Pp. 323–341 in *Mediated Politics*. Edited by W. Lance Bennett and Robert Entman. Cambridge: Cambridge University Press.

Jamieson, Kathleen, and Joseph Cappella. 2008. *Echo Chamber: Rush Limbaugh and the Conservative Media Establishment*. New York: Oxford University Press.

Johnson, Thomas. J., and Barbara Kaye. 2004. "Wag the Blog: How Reliance on Traditional Media and the Internet Influence Credibility Perceptions of Weblogs among Blog Users." *Journalism and Mass Communication Quarterly* 81(3): 622–642.

Jones, Alex, 2002. "CNN and September 11th: An Interview with Judy Woodruff", *Harvard International Journal of Press/Politics* 7, 2: 6–16

Jones, Alex S. 2009. *Losing the News: The Future of the News That Feeds Democracy*. New York: Oxford University Press.

Jones, Jeffrey. 2004. *Entertaining Politics: New Political Television and Civic Culture*. New York: Rowman and Littlefield.

Katz, Elihu. 1960. "Communication Research and the Image of Society: Convergence of Two Traditions." *American Journal of Sociology* 65(5): 435–440.

Katz, Elihu. 2009. "Why Sociology Abandoned Communication." *American Sociologist* 40(3): 167–174.

Katz, Elihu, and Daniel Dayan. 2006. *Media Events*. Cambridge, MA: Harvard University Press.

Katz, Elihu, and Paul F. Lazarsfeld. 1955. *Personal Influence: The Part Played by People in the Flow of Mass Communications*. Glencoe, IL: Free Press.

Keane, John. 1991. *The Media and Democracy*. Cambridge: Polity.

Klinenberg, Eric. 2005. "Convergence: News Production in a Digital Age." *Annals of the American Academy of Political and Social Science* 597(1): 48–64.

Kovach, Bill, and Tom Rosenstiel. 1999. *Warp Speed: America in the Age of the Mixed Media Culture*. New York: Century Foundation.

Kull, Stephen. 2003. "Misperceptions, the Media, and the Iraq War." *PIPA/Knowledge Networks Poll*. Available at www.pipa.org/OnlineReports/Iraq/IraqMedia_Oct03/IraqMedia_Oct03_rpt.pdf.

Kurasawa, Fuyuki. 2007. "The Healing of Wounds: Forgiveness as a Cultural Practice." Pp. 129–162 in *Culture, Society, and Democracy*. Edited by Isaac Reed and Jeffrey Alexander. Boulder, CO: Paradigm.

Larsen, Otto N., and Richard J. Hill. 1954. "Mass Media and Interpersonal Communication in the Diffusion of a News Event." *American Sociological Review* 19(4): 426–433.

Lewis, Justin. 1991. *The Ideological Octopus: An Exploration of Television and Its Audience*. New York: Routledge.

Lichtenberg, Judith. Ed. 1990. *Democracy and the Mass Media*. Cambridge: Cambridge University Press.

Lippmann, Walter. 1913. *A Preface to Politics*. New York: Mitchell Kennerley.

Lippmann, Walter, [1922] 2007. *Public Opinion*. Sioux Falls, SD: NuVision.

Lippmann, Walter. [1925] 2000. *The Phantom Public*. New Brunswick, NJ: Transaction.

Lippmann, Walter. 1929. *A Preface to Morals*. New York: Macmillan.

Lippmann, Walter. 1947. *The Cold War*. New York: Harper and Brothers.

Lippmann, Walter. 1955. *The Public Philosophy*. New Brunswick, NJ: Transaction.

Lippmann, Walter. 1964. "Remarks on the Occasion of This Journal's 50th Year." *New Republic* 150: 13–14.

Lippmann, Walter, and Charles Merz. 1920. "A Test of the News." *New Republic* 23, 2:Pp. Pp. 1–42.

Mast, Jason. 2006. "The Cultural Pragmatics of Event-ness: The Clinton/Lewinsky Affair." Pp. 115–145 in *Social Performance: Symbolic Action, Cultural Pragmatics, and Ritual*. Edited by Jeffrey Alexander, Bernhard Giesen, and Jason Mast. Cambridge: Cambridge University Press.

Mayhew, Leon. 1997. *The New Public: Professional Communication and the Means of Social Influence*. Cambridge: Cambridge University Press.

McAdam, Doug. 1996. "The Framing Function of Movement Tactics: Strategic Dramaturgy in the American Civil Rights Movement." Pp. 338–355 in *Comparative Perspectives on Social Movements: Political Opportunities, Mobilizing Structures, and Cultural Framings.* Edited by Doug McAdam, John McCarthy, and Mayer Zald. Cambridge: Cambridge University Press.

McAdam, Doug, John McCarthy, and Mayer Zald. 1996. "Introduction: Opportunities, Mobilizing Structures, and Framing Processes—Toward a Synthetic, Comparative Perspective on Social Movements." Pp. 1–20 in *Comparative Perspectives on Social Movements: Political Opportunities, Mobilizing Structures, and Cultural Framings.* Edited by Doug McAdam, John McCarthy, and Mayer Zald. Cambridge: Cambridge University Press.

McCombs, Maxwell. 2004. *Setting the Agenda: The Mass Media and Public Opinion.* Cambridge: Polity.

McCombs, Maxwell. 2005. "A Look at Agenda-Setting: Past, Present and Future." *Journalism Studies* 6: 543–557.

McCombs, Maxwell, and Donald Shaw. 1972. "The Agenda-Setting Function of the Press." *Public Opinion Quarterly* 36(2): 176–187.

McNeil, Alex. 1996. *Total Television.* New York: Penguin.

Medvetz, Thomas. 2006. "The Strength of Weekly Ties: Relations of Material and Symbolic Exchange in the Conservative Movement." *Politics & Society* 34(3): 343–368.

Medvetz, Thomas. 2007. "Think Tanks and Production of Policy-Knowledge in America." Dissertation. University of California, Berkeley.

Miege, Bernard. 1987. "The Logics at Work in the New Cultural Industries." *Media, Culture and Society* 9(3): 273–289.

Minear, Larry, Colin Scott, and Thomas Weiss. 1996. *The News Media, Civil War, and Humanitarian Action.* Boulder, CO: Lynne Rienner.

Mittel, Jason. 2004. "A Cultural Approach to Television Genre Theory." Pp. 171–181 in *The Television Studies Reader.* Edited by Robert C. Allen and Annette Hill. London: Routledge.

Morris, Jonathan. 2005. "The Fox News Factor." *Harvard International Journal of Press/Politics* 10(3): 56–79.

Morse, Margaret. 2004. "News as Performance: The Image as Event." Pp. 209–225 in *The Television Studies Reader.* Edited by Robert C. Allen and Annette Hill. London: Routledge.

Navasky, Victor. 1990. "The Merger That Wasn't." *Nation* 250(1): 22–25

Navasky, Victor. 2005. *A Matter of Opinion.* New York: Farrar, Strauss and Giroux.

Nerone, John C. 1993. "A Local History of the Early U.S. Press: Cincinnati. 1793–1848." Pp. 38–65 in *Ruthless Criticism: New Perspectives in U.S. Communication History.* Edited by William S. Solomon and Robert W. McChesney. Minneapolis: University of Minnesota Press.

Nevins, Allan. Ed. 1932. *Interpretations. 1931–1932, by Walter Lippman.* New York: Macmillan.

Nimmo, Dan, and James E. Combs. 1992. *The Political Pundits.* New York: Praeger.

Page, Benjamin. 1996. *Who Deliberates? Mass Media in Modern Democracy.* Chicago: University of Chicago Press.

Park, Robert. 1940. "News as a Form of Knowledge: A Chapter in the Sociology of Knowledge." *American Journal of Sociology* 45(5): 669–686.

Park, Robert. 1941. "News and the Power of the Press." *American Journal of Sociology* 47(1): 1–11.

Patterson, Thomas E. 2008. "The Negative Effect: News, Politics, and the Public." *Hedgehog Review* 10(2): 46–57.

Pew Research Center for People and the Press. 2004–2010. State of the News Media Reports. Washington, DC: Project for Excellence in Journalism. Available at www.journalism.org/; www.stateofthemedia.org/2010/.

Polletta, Francesca. 2006. *It Was Like a Fever: Storytelling in Protest and Politics*. Chicago: University of Chicago Press.

Posner, Richard A. 2001. *Public Intellectuals: A Study in Decline*. Cambridge, MA: Harvard University Press.

Preble, Christopher. 2003. "Whoever Believed in the Missile Gap? John F. Kennedy and the Politics of National Security." *Presidential Studies Quarterly* 33(4): 801–826.

Price, Vincent, Joseph N. Cappella, and Lilach Nir. 2002. "Does Disagreement Contribute to More Deliberative Opinion?" *Political Communication* 19(1): 95–112.

Quart, Alissa. 2008. "Lost Media, Found Media: Snapshots from the Future of Writing." *Columbia Journalism Review* (May–June): 30–34.

Riley, Sam G. 1998. *The American Newspaper Columnist*. Westport, CT: Praeger.

Robinson, Piers. 2002. *The CNN Effect: The Myth of News Media, Foreign Policy and Intervention*. New York: Routledge.

Rosen, Jay. 2001. *What Are Journalists For?* New Haven, CT: Yale University Press.

Rosenfeld, Stephen S. 2000. "The Op-Ed Page: A Step to a Better Democracy." *Harvard International Journal of Press/Politics* 5(3): 7–11.

Rossiter, Clinton, and James Lare. Eds. 1963. *The Essential Lippmann*. New York: Random House.

Said, Edward. 1994. *Representations of the Intellectual*. New York: Pantheon.

Scheufele, Dietram A., and David Tewksbury. 2007. "Framing, Agenda Setting, and Priming: The Evolution of Three Media Effects Models." *Journal of Communication* 57(1): 9–20.

Schiller, Dan. 1981. *Objectivity and the News. The Public and the Rise of Commercial Journalism*. Philadelphia: University of Pennsylvania Press.

Schlesinger, Arthur M., Jr. 1959. "Walter Lippmann: The Intellectual v. Politics." Pp. 189–225 in *Walter Lippmann and His Times*. Edited by Marquis Childs and James Reston. New York: Harcourt, Brace.

Schudson, Michael. 1978. *Discovering the News*. New York: Basic Books.

Schudson, Michael. 1998. *The Good Citizen: A History of American Civic Life*. New York: Free Press.

Schudson, Michael. 2003. *The Sociology of News*. New York: W. W. Norton.

Schudson, Michael. 2005. "Autonomy from What?" Pp. 214–223 in *Bourdieu and the Journalistic Field*. Edited by Rodney Benson and Erik Neveu. Cambridge: Polity.

Schudson, Michael. 2008. *Why Democracies Need an Unlovable Press*. Cambridge: Polity.

Seideman, David. 1986. *The New Republic: A Voice of Modern Liberalism*. New York: Praeger.

Seligman, Adam. 1992. *The Idea of Civil Society*. New York: Free Press.

Serrin, Judith, and William Serrin. 2002. *Muckraking: The Journalism That Changed America*. New York: New Press.

Shenhav, Yehouda. 1999. *Manufacturing Rationality: The Engineering Foundations of the Managerial Revolution*. Oxford: Oxford University Press.

Sherwood, Steve. 1994. "Narrating the Social." *Journal of Narratives and Life Histories* 4(1–2): 69–88.

Smith, Philip. 2005. *Why War? The Cultural Logic of Iraq, the Gulf War, and Suez*. Chicago: Chicago University Press.

Smith, Philip. 2008. *Punishment and Culture.* Chicago: University of Chicago Press.

Sobieraj, Sarah. 2011. *Soundbitten: The Perils of Media-Centered Political Activism.* New York: New York University Press.

Society of Professional Journalists. "Preamble to the Code of Ethics." Available at www.spj.org/ethicscode.asp.

Sreberny, Annabelle. 2002. "Trauma Talk: Reconfiguring the Inside and Outside." Pp. 220–234 in *Journalism after September 11.* Edited by Barbie Zelizer and Stuart Allan. London: Routledge.

Starr, Paul. 2004. *The Creation of the Media: The Political Origins of Mass Comunications.* New York: Basic Books.

Steel, Richard. 1999. *Walter Lippmann and the American Century.* New Brunswick, NJ: Transaction.

Sunstein, Cass. 2002. *Republic.com.* Princeton, NJ: Princeton University Press.

Taylor, Charles. 1992. *Sources of the Self: The Making of Modern Identity.* Cambridge, MA: Harvard University Press.

Thompson, John. 1995. *The Media and Modernity.* Stanford, CA: Stanford University Press.

Townsley, Eleanor. 2000. "A History of Intellectuals and the Demise of the New Class: Academics and the U.S. Government in the 1960s." *Theory and Society* 29(6): 739–784.

Townsley, Eleanor. 2006. "The Public Intellectual Trope in the United States." *American Sociologist* 37(3): 39–66.

Tuchman, Gaye. 1972. "Objectivity as Strategic Ritual: An Examination of Newsmen's Notions of Objectivity." *American Journal of Sociology* 77(4): 660–679.

Tuchman, Gaye. 1973. "Making News by Doing Work: Routinizing the Unexpected." *American Journal of Sociology* 79(1): 110–131.

Turner, Graeme. 1993. *Film as Social Practice.* New York: Routledge.

Turner, Victor. 1974. *Dramas, Fields, and Metaphors: Symbolic Action in Human Society.* Ithaca, NY: Cornell University Press.

Turow, Joseph. 1997. *Breaking Up America: Advertisers and the New Media World.* Chicago: University of Chicago Press.

Wagner-Pacifici, Robin. 2000. *Theorizing the Standoff: Contingency in Action.* Cambridge: Cambridge University Press.

Waisbord, Silvio. 2002. "Journalism, Risk, and Patriotism." Pp. 201–219 in *Journalism after September 11.* Edited by Barbie Zelizer and Stuart Allan. London: Routledge.

Walker, Martin. 1982. *Powers of the Press: The World's Great Newspapers.* London: Quartet.

Wallstein, Kevin. 2007. "Agenda Setting and the Blogosphere: An Analysis of the Relationship between Mainstream Media and Political Blogs." *Review of Policy Research* 24(6): 567–587.

Walzer, Michael. 1995. "The Communitarian Critique of Liberalism." Pp. 52–70 in *New Communitarian Thinking: Persons, Virtues, Institutions, and Communities.* Edited by Amitai Etzioni. Charlottesville: University Press of Virginia.

Warner, Michael. 1992. *The Letters of the Republic: Publication and the Public Sphere in Eighteenth-Century America.* Cambridge, MA: Harvard University Press.

Weaver, David. 1991. "Issue Salience and Public Opinion: Are There Consequences of Agenda-Setting?" *International Journal of Public Opinion Research* 3(1): 53–68.

Weaver, David H. 2007. "Theories on Agenda Setting, Framing, and Priming." *Journal of Communication* 57(1): 142–147.

Weber, Max. [1917] 1946. "Politics as a Vocation" and "Science as a Vocation." Pp. 77–156 in *From Max Weber.* Edited by Hans Gerth and C. Wright Mills. New York: Oxford University Press.

Webster, James G. 2005. "Beneath the Veneer of Fragmentation: Television Audience Polarization in a Multichannel World." *Journal of Communication* 55(2): 366–382.

Weeks, Edward. Ed. 1965. *Conversations with Walter Lippmann.* Boston: Little, Brown.

Whipple, Mark. 2005. "The Dewey-Lippmann Debate Today: Communication Distortions, Reflective Agency and Participatory Democracy." *Sociological Theory* 23(2): 156–178.

Wilson, Harold S. 1970. *McClure's Magazine and the Muckrakers.* Princeton, NJ: Princeton University Press.

Young, Iris Marion. 2000. *Inclusion and Democracy.* Oxford: Oxford University Press.

Zaret, David. 1992. "Religion, Science, and Printing in the Publics Spheres in Seventeenth-Century England." Pp. 212–235 in *Habermas and the Public Sphere.* Edited by Craig Calhoun. Cambridge, MA: MIT Press.

Zaret, David, 1998. "Neither Faith nor Commerce: Printing and the Unintended Origins of English Public Opinon." Pp. 210–236 in *Real Civil Societies: The Dilemmas of Institutionalization.* Edited by Jeffrey C. Alexander. London: Sage Publications.

Zelizer, Barbie. 2004. *Taking Journalism Seriously: News and the Academy.* Thousand Oaks, CA: Sage.

Index